CONFESSIONS
OF A
PERFORMANCE NINJA

Foreword

Contrary to popular belief, executives must rely on something other than Training solutions to deliver optimized performance. A recent eLearning Industry article, "How To Overcome L&D Challenges By Creating Learning Strategies That Drive Performance," by Looop Marketing, postures that we have reached a point of inflection. I would call it a tipping point and time for a

Strategic Re-Think:

> *"Learning and Development (L&D) is at a point of inflection. It's being forced to reevaluate what it does and what it delivers, not because of fads and not for the sake of change. The desired outcomes for L&D and its stakeholders' expectations have changed. Regarding programs and content, L&D was about delivery and provision and measured by attendance, completion, and satisfaction, and it didn't speak at all to business results. Now, L&D is being charged with affecting performance, productivity, and capability."*

Exacerbating this *tipping point* are sea-change digital initiatives, not the least of which is **Digital Transformation** and the exploding cloud-based technologies options. The implied changes represent disruptions impacting every corner of the enterprise and every workforce member. Status quo Training strategies are falling short, held hostage by the long-held *Myth* that **TRAINING DRIVES PERFORMANCE**. This *Myth* perpetuates a false narrative that limits effectiveness when we depend on training as our default solution.

Is the *Myth* truly a myth? Yes, because there is an assumption commonly made that if Training is completed, competencies are met that enable improved performance. However, a measurable performance change has yet to occur, and the deliverable is only POTENTIAL.

- That means **TRAINING CONTRIBUTES TO POTENTIAL.** *Measurable Performance Outcomes* do NOT manifest until the *Learner* transitions to a *Performer.*
- The transition to *Performer* happens only AFTER Training is complete, and they have returned to their respective Workflows at multiple **Points-of-Work** to complete task-level work that generates measurable results.

This book positions that Workflows at the *Point-of-Work* represent our new **Ground Zero,** where we break from the status quo and apply holistic assessment scrutiny...

Assessing POINT-OF-WORK is mission-critical because it is our best source of what works, what doesn't, and most importantly, WHY!

The current rage in our L&D industry is the CONVERGENCE of Learning with Work. Concepts like *Learning in the Workflow* and *Workflow Learning* promote long overdue traction to drive this sea-change to better equip L&D to become a trusted business partner instead of a drive-thru Training-on-Demand operation.

L&D is our logical go-to business discipline to navigate this new *ground zero*; however, many Training teams still need the requisite discovery skills to assess multiple *Points-of-Work.* Those discovery skills are a mission-critical requirement for L&D, often handled by Performance Consulting Specialists, Performance Strategists, or [*Enter job title*], having similar discovery skills and business savvy.

This book is about my journey to overcome the *Myth* by adopting the thinking that we must go to *Point-of-Work* and apply evolved discovery skills through a proven process called **Point-of-Work Assessment (PWA).** *"Confessions of a Performance Ninja"* is one man's adoption, warts and all, of a new paradigm where P*oint-of-Work* becomes an evolved status quo. This book is divided into five parts:

- Part 1 – *Point-of-Work & Why Give a Rip*
- Part 2 – *Anatomy of a Point-of-Work Assessment (PWA)*
- Part 3 – *Performance Restrainer Discovery Attributes*
- Part 4 – *Point-of-Work Readiness Assessment for Learning & Development*
- Part 5 – *Worksheets & Job Aids*

What changes? It starts with our need for a **Different Conversation** with Stakeholders who make Training requests. This *conversation* needs to ensure three things happen *differently*:

- **Shift thinking** *from default learning solutions to focusing on* **optimizing and sustaining measurable performance** *in Workflows.*
- **Assess Points-of-Work** *within Workflows to deliver prioritized Solution Design Road Maps to the L&D design/development/delivery functions.*
- **Deliver Measurable Proof of Impact** *that confirms our Performance Solutions overcome challenges, enable growth, and maintain business sustainability at Points-of-Work.*

In this book, I will share confessions on things that worked well, some things that never occurred to me, and things that could have worked better on my journey to embrace a **strategic re-think** and adopt **tactical methods** to assess *Points-of-Work* effectively.

Gary G. Wise

Performance Ninja – Writer of Things – Business Advisor/Coach

gdogwise@gmail.com (317) 437-2555

Web: Living In Learning – LinkedIn

Twitter: @gdogwise

Cover Art by Lobostudiohamburg from Pixaby

TABLE OF CONTENTS

PART 1 Point-of-Work & Why Give a Rip? 1

CHAPTER 1 WHAT IS POINT-OF-WORK? 2

CHAPTER 2 POINT-OF-WORK ASSESSMENT (PWA) 5

CHAPTER 3 PWA SUPPORT OF DIGITAL TRANSFORMATION 9

CHAPTER 4 ALIGNMENT & DISCOVERY CASCADE 16

CHAPTER 5 CHANGING THE CONVERSATION 23

CASE STUDY #5A TECHNICAL SUPPORT HOT LINE 24

CASE STUDY #5B 29

CASE STUDY #5C 34

PART 2 Anatomy of PWA Workflow 40

CHAPTER 6 PWA ALIGNMENT 41

CHAPTER 7 PWA DISCOVERY 44

CHAPTER 8 PWA SYSTEMS/TECHNOLOGY FOOTPRINT 47

CHAPTER 9 PWA ANALYTICS/IMPACT 49

CHAPTER 10 PWA DRIVER METHODOLOGY 51

CHAPTER 11 PWA INTENTIONAL DESIGN 57

PART 3 PERFORMANCE RESTRAINER ATTRIBUTES 65

CHAPTER 12 POINT-OF-WORK ASSESSMENT: ENVIRONMENT & CULTURE 66

CHAPTER 13 POINT-OF-WORK ASSESSMENT: PEOPLE & CAPABILITY 74

CHAPTER 14 POINT-OF-WORK ASSESSMENT: WORKFLOWS & PROCESSES 79

CHAPTER 15 POINT-OF-WORK ASSESSMENT: CONTENT & RESOURCES 90

CHAPTER 16 POINT-OF-WORK ASSESSMENT: SYSTEMS & TECHNOLOGY 96

CHAPTER 17 POINT-OF-WORK ASSESSMENT: ANALYTICS & IMPACT 102

PART 4 POINT-OF-WORK READINESS ASSESSMENT (PWRA) FOR LEARNING & DEVELOPMENT 107

CHAPTER 18 WHAT IS A READINESS ASSESSMENT? 108

CHAPTER 19 POINT-OF-WORK READINESS ASSESSMENT FOR L&D – ENVIRONMENT & CULTURE –.. 113

CHAPTER 20 POINT-OF-WORK READINESS ASSESSMENT FOR L&D – PEOPLE & CAPABILITY – 115

CHAPTER 22 POINT-OF-WORK READINESS ASSESSMENT FOR L&D – CONTENT & RESOURCES – 118

CHAPTER 23 POINT-OF-WORK READINESS ASSESSMENT FOR L&D – SYSTEMS & TECHNOLOGY – 120

CHAPTER 24 POINT-OF-WORK READINESS ASSESSMENT FOR L&D – ANALYTICS & IMPACT – 121

CHAPTER 25 FINAL THOUGHTS & NEXT STEPS 123

PART 5 PWA WORKSHEETS (W/ INSTRUCTIONS) & JOB AIDS 125

MASTER PWA WORKSHEET TEMPLATE 126

ALIGN TAB 129

ATTRIBUTE TAB 133

DISCOVERY TAB 135

WORKSHEET TAB 137

DISTRIBUTION TAB 139

PRIORITIES TAB 141

MEASUREMENT TAB 142

MEASUREMENT TAB 143

DRIVERS TAB 145

PART 1

Point-of-Work
&
Why Give a Rip?

CHAPTER 1

WHAT IS POINT-OF-WORK?

Over the last fifteen years and numerous speaking engagements, I must confess that the premise upon which my passion has concentrated – *Point-of-Work* – has never changed in importance regardless of industry or work discipline. *Point-of-Work* represents a common denominator across all elements of our Learning Performance Ecosystems.

<u>**Working Definition:**</u> *Point-of-Work is any point in a workflow where actions are executed or decisions made to effectively and efficiently complete task-level work regardless of business discipline or industry.*

Success at *Point-of-Work* is supported by sustained delivery of measurable Performance and business value rather than by completing Learning programs. Therein lies the *Myth*.

Learning programs are still mostly provided off-task in classrooms or online, and both are NOT in the Workflow. That's where the *Myth* that *Training Drives Performance* gets underfoot and derails or limits our efforts to optimize Performance at *Points-of-Work*. Whether you are a senior leader, a line manager over a department, or an individual performer with defined tasks, the mindset *Myth* gets in the way and limits your effectiveness at all levels. The truth is that Training only contributes to POTENTIAL, and *Point-of-Work* is the only place where measurable PERFORMANCE evidence manifests.

The lowest common denominator is *Point-of-Work*. Why is *Point-of-Work* not a routine part of our thinking? Because *Point-of-Work* needs more mindshare. Mindshare is held hostage by the premise of the *Myth...if we do not train them, they will not perform.* This book is about shifting that mindset and prioritizing discoverable knowledge to frame solution designs for application in Workflows, at moments of need, and within task-centric, role-specific *Points-of-Work*.

The application of this shift in mindset is a *Pre-Design Discovery Methodology called **POINT-OF-WORK ASSESSMENT (PWA).***

More emphasis in L&D is moving toward Workflow Learning, which is excellent news that a shift is finally starting to gain traction. However, the skill set to optimize workflow learning design, development, and delivery must fight through the limits of the *Myth* that focuses on Learning instead of Performance. Our solution designs must **Converge Learning & Support with Work**, which means solution accessibility in live Workflows, at moments of need, and at multiple *Points-of-Work*.

CONFESSION: Jargon Alert — *Speaking of things like Ecosystems to an operational stakeholder is a mistake. The last thing they need to hear from L&D is more of our jargon, no matter how progressive it showcases our thinking. Your time would be better spent teaching a pig to sing…and causing much less annoyance. Speak their language, not ours.*

Still, the interdependencies within a **Dynamic Learning Performance Ecosystem** are at the core of what may be influencing the restrained performance, so we need to redirect our enthusiasm and mastery of jargon into actionable behavior. More importantly, the restraining factors may have nothing to do with poor knowledge and skills. Can you see how the *Myth* can get underfoot if it serves as our default solution consideration?

Confession: *Yeah, I sold the Myth. Sold it for twenty out of thirty-five years. Sold it like a champ! It was job security. My compensation did not depend upon my stakeholders' performance at their Points-of-Work. My objectives were tied to how many butts-in-seats, course completions, good evaluation scores, and hours of training were pumped into the ether.*

To make matters worse, our stakeholders know about the *Myth* too. We sold it to them years ago. If stakeholders have a performance issue, they reach out to Training in a knee-jerk reaction we have been promoting. This is important to understand because the "issue" they experience may have nothing to do with Training, but we get the call. That action puts a challenge we cannot resolve in our laps because of the Myth and not necessarily in the appropriate entity who can fix it. As such, we own a *liaison* role because we completed the PWA discovery that points to other business partners who did NOT get the call. L&D must step up and connect the dots for them.

If a process improvement team like Six Sigma exists, they may ultimately own part of the solution, but who connects the dots required to bring Six Sigma into the pursuit of a solution? L&D should because L&D got the initial call to fix the problem with Training, not Six Sigma. The PWA showed the solution was partially process improvement oriented, so L&D plays an essential liaison role because nobody else got the call.

To preserve limited resources and optimize design, development, and delivery resources, an initial, holistic, *pre-design discovery methodology* that focuses on the root causes behind breakdown(s) in the workflow(s) and the measurable impacts at *Point(s)-of-Work* becomes essential. Why build a course when a Job Aid will do?

This methodology is called **Point-of-Work Assessment (PWA)**, which is this book's primary focus. The next chapters will address the PWA in detail, along with how to:

- Change the Conversation with PWA findings *without mentioning PWA methodology*
- Leverage Change Leadership principles to gain sponsorship to access the workforce
- Define and validate root cause(s) within workflows to avoid chasing symptoms
- Validate and dispel assumptions and hypotheses related to initial Training Requests
- Gain stakeholder(s) buy-in and assign business impact priorities to Solution Road Maps

CONFESSION: *Do not make the mistake of sharing your immense knowledge and expertise by positioning Point-of-Work Assessment jargon as part of your next steps...instead say,* **"I need to ask some questions to ensure the "Training" we build will meet or exceed your expectations."** *You may not build any training, but you need to be prepared to explain what is occurring at Point-of-Work and why Training may not be the solution AFTER completing your PWA discovery.*

You may initially sound like you are on a mission to build Training when ultimately, you are on a mission to optimize performance at one or more *Points-of-Work*. Suppose Training is involved, that's okay. If not, think about how much time you saved on building a performance job aid in a fraction of the time that would have been spent developing training in Articulate. Don't waste time or cause concerns by discussing the new paradigm; hide *the pill in the cheese...*slip into the black pajamas, slide on the cheap sunglasses, and go Ninja.

CHAPTER 2

POINT-OF-WORK ASSESSMENT (PWA)

Working Definition: PWA is a PRE-DESIGN Discovery methodology that frames structured **Solution Design Roadmaps** based on validated sources that restrain performance outcomes at *Points-of-Work*.

The PWA does NOT deliver solutions; instead, it describes what solutions should accomplish when applied successfully in the workflow. In the hands of a performance consultant, the PWA provides clarity and direction regarding the learning performance assets required to effectively resolve and sustain measurable performance specific to the perceived problem(s). Instructional Designers, Developers, and other Business Partners collaborate with the Performance Consultant to fashion the appropriate solution asset(s).

The PWA organizes the attributes of what restrains performance in the workflow into six clusters in a brief graphic: (*See Figure 3-1*). We will spend more time with these attributes later in the book.

ECOSYSTEM Performance Attributes

DISCOVERY	ECOSYSTEM CATEGORYXP	ASSESSMENT DESCRIPTION	PERFORMANCE ATTRIBUTES
	ENVIRONMENT/CULTURE	What internal/external work conditions exist that impact performance? What is the level of workforce engagement and support?	Culture - Change Management - Organizational Design - Regulatory & Legal Compliance - Upstream/Downstream Dependencies - Competition Frustration/Stress - Empathy - Inclusion - Urgency/Risk - Etc.
	PEOPLE/CAPABILITY	Who is engaged in the work? Who supports the work? What required L&D skills are missing or deficient? What is Training's contribution to performance readiness? End-User Readiness?	Leadership - Role Clarity - Accountability - Job Expectations - Communications Collaboration - Workflow Acumen Savvy - Coaching/Mentoring - Career Pathing & Development - Talent Development: *TRAINING (Knowledge & Skills, Competencies*), Wisdom & Insight Sharing, Etc.
	WORKFLOWS/PROCESSES	What is task-level work? Where is it failing? Why? Business criticality? Current design & development frameworks/methods? To what extent is learning & support embedded with workflows?	Task-level Workflows/Processes — Moment of Need Definition - Root Causes Requirements for task-level access to embedded learning & support (*Policies - SOPs - Methods & Procedures - Technical References*) — Insight Curation Protocols - Learning Design/Development Protocols - Performance assessment methods -Etc.
	CONTENT/RESOURCES	What assets are consumed/required to execute in workflows? Are assets accessible? Are assets agile & current? How is content managed & maintained? Are assets "pushed or pulled" or both?	Accessibility at Moments of Need - Search - Relevance to Work/Process Application & Effectiveness @ Point-of-Work - Availability by Role -Current use of *EMBEDDED TRAINING & SUPPORT CONTENT* - Volume/Format - Content Management Protocols - Currency Updatability - Portability/Reusability - Etc.
	TECHNOLOGY/SYSTEMS	What technologies and systems are/should be used to execute work? What systems are capable and necessary to connect learning and support assets to the workforce in their workflows? How does technology avoidance impact performance?	Access to ERP/CMS & Other Business Systems - *LMS/LES & DAP* - Mobility Enablement - Collaboration Platforms - Knowledge Bases - Effective Application of Technology - Migration Map Growth Implications -Technology interconnectivity/ Compatibility - Bandwidth - xAPI/Learning Record Store Content Repository Footprint - Legacy Authoring Platforms - Etc.
	ANALYTICS/IMPACT	How is success measured? Are performance data accessible & actionable? Impact measurement at Levels 3&4? Are KPIs correct/missing/misaligned? How is end-user asset utilization tracked?	Utilization Data Capture - Data sources - Data Analysis - Data Application - Creating Reports - Requesting Reports - KPI/competency Alignment- Missing/Misaligned KPIs - Benchmarking - Level 3 Eval - Level 4 Eval for ROI - Etc.

Copyright 2022 – Living In Learning

See Figure 3-1

An important note is that the PWA does NOT deliver solutions per se. The PWA provides **Solution Design Roadmaps** essential for L&D resources to design, develop, and deliver the final learning performance assets. Some solutions may be Training-related, and some may target *Performance Support*. At the same time, some may require engagement with other business partners like Marketing Communications, IT Methods & Procedure owners, HR Organizational Design resources, etc. If your PWA findings point in directions away from, or in addition to, Training, it is our (*L&D's*) job to serve as liaison to connect those dots from our PWA findings for the affected business partner(s).

Great, another process that adds time that few of us have, right?

The PWA can be as simple as a thirty-minute conversation with a stakeholder or more involved via interviews or surveys with managers and individual contributors. While it may add time on the front end, consider the time saved when the PWA findings render a *Solution Design Roadmap* that eliminates time-consuming training design and development drills. Remember, PWA is *Pre-Design Discovery* that maps where we go next with our solutions' actual design and development.

A frequent mistake we typically make is to accept a request for Training as the *"best-fit solution"* and dive straight into a Training Needs Assessment (TNA) to identify:

- Knowledge objectives
- Who are the training targets
- What competencies need to be addressed
- Delivery method...that influences design and development
- Timeline for project completion
- Determine what development tool should be utilized

Some of us may do more, others less. Honestly, there is nothing wrong with completing a TNA, BUT if a PWA is done first, it *informs* the TNA and streamlines design decisions AND, more importantly, validates whether or not the requested training objectives are the right ones to impact and sustain the desired performance outcomes.

Too many TNAs are pursued due to the assumption that Training is the optimal solution. We are left with which authoring tool to use instead of knowing the root cause(s) triggering restrained performance. What if the solution is a ten-second video or a hot-linked resource with no training required?

My point is to avoid defaulting to a Training solution before examining the *workflow attributes* contributing to the performance challenge(s) with a PWA discovery. Again, the PWA is not an automatic injection of extra time and may be accomplished with a few questions to confirm...or not...whether a deeper discovery effort is warranted. We will dig deeper into Discovery tactics later in this book. Still, the following are examples of a single routine statement and several common questions I lead with to gauge how interdependent the hidden complexities are:

- **Statement**: Yes! We can help with your Training request and need to ask a few questions upfront to ensure the Training Solution we design and deliver to your workforce achieves the results you seek. (*Always use this as the routine response to a Training request*)
- Describe the primary audience for this Training solution.
- Describe the performance you have observed that indicates Training is required.
- What measures are acceptable targets to confirm our Training was successful?
- Describe how you will reinforce the Training concepts after completing the program.

Indeed, there may be more questions to follow up on and clarify, but those shown above are what I consider essential regardless of the nature of the training request.

The next chapter will focus on questioning and several best practices to consider as you follow a cascade down through the organization after fielding the initial Training request. Before the first question is asked, something more essential must happen – ALIGNMENT.

Alignment happens twice, with the second iteration being a RE-alignment:

- **First alignment** – When you meet with the Requestor to gain insights as to why they are requesting Training.
- **Second Re-alignment** – When you meet again with the Requestor to debrief and validate the actual Findings provided by the PWA discovery cascade.

That second *alignment conversation* is likely *changed* and puts you and the Requestor on the same page, not just in the same book.

CHAPTER 3

PWA SUPPORT OF DIGITAL TRANSFORMATION

What could be more disruptive than the pursuit of enterprise-wide **Digital Transformation?** Sadly, history shows most *Digital Transformation* efforts fall short or fail outright because of the many disruptions to workflows, processes, and new demands of using unfamiliar technology on end-user populations. Implications are clear – our status quo Training paradigm falls short.

So why not disrupt the status quo with a new strategy? Why not a **Disruptive Strategic Transformation** called **Point-of-Work** (*also applied enterprise-wide*)? All transformation efforts are destined to fail if we don't move aggressively enough, and likely for the same core reason:

We fall short because we stop short!

CONFESSION: *Despite popular beliefs, reaching* **GoLive** *and successfully launching Training for new technology into the Workforce is not the end. GoLive marks* **Deployment** *and the beginning of two more important things –* **Implementation & Adoption***. Before adopting the PWA mindset, our team's routine objective was to get all end-users trained before the system went live. When training was completed, we were finished...time to breathe out. Wrong! YES, we* **Deployed** *Training, but we did not* **Implement** *anything. We did nothing to optimize* **Adoption***, nor did we ensure post-training* **Sustainability***. We stopped short...and transformational success suffered for it!*

What we should have done started well before building Training. We never fully accomplished holistic **Discovery** within the Workflows we were about to disrupt. The focus instead was on adding new technology training rather than the impact it would have on the Workforce in their Workflow. How would their widely diverse Workflow be disrupted? How would follow-up support and Training happen? How would we map solutions for a follow-up? How could we better prepare new hires to utilize the new technology before transitioning them ill-equipped into their *Points-of-Work*?

GoLive is only **Deployment**, and for that matter, so was our initial system training. **Implementation** happens after GoLive and after training when the application(s) are in the hands of the workforce...in their Workflows...and at their respective *Points-of-Work*. We would never reach full **Adoption** if we stopped at **Deployment** and defaulted to allowing the Help Desk to fight fires erupting in Workflows. That approach has proven over and over again to be unsustainable despite being a routine best practice for many.

We should have planned how to **Sustain** the transformation once everything was up and running for ongoing disruptions due to upgrades, patches, and routine fine-tuning. The whole point of successful **Adoption** flows from supporting Workflow **Implementation** to **OPTIMIZE** end-user utilization in their Workflow at *Points-of-Work*.

The Case for Disruption

Digital transformation is expected to add $100 trillion to the world economy by 2025. Platform-driven interactions are expected to enable approximately two-thirds of the $100 trillion value at stake from digitalization by 2025. (World Economic Forum). The digital transformation market is expected to grow at a CAGR (compound annual growth rate) of 23% from 2019 to $3.3 trillion by 2025. (Research and Markets) These numbers are staggering. Even more staggering is that successfully sustained transformations represent only a fraction of those attempted.

Please feel the urgency regarding what is happening to stress and restrain optimum performance in the Workflow in which our end-user population must operate efficiently and effectively.

Here are a few more nuggets to consider from several different sources:

1. *More than 50% of digital transformation efforts fizzled completely in 2018. (Forrester)*
2. In a *Forbes Interview*, Michael Gale said, "*Virtually every Forbes Global 2000 company is on some digital transformation journey. Some are getting it right, and others struggle. Basically, **one in eight got it right,** and then there were ranges of failure to really where more than 50 percent did not go right. In fact, their expectations were neither met nor exceeded, and the gap between expectations and meeting them was so enormous it was considered a failure.*"

3. *70% of digital transformations fail, most often due to **resistance from employees**. (Mckinsey)*
4. *Only 16% of employees said their company's digital transformations improved performance and were sustainable in the long term. (Mckinsey)*
5. *At least 90% of new enterprise apps will insert AI technology into their processes and products by 2025. (IDC)*
6. *Internet of Things (IoT) had the largest share of the overall digital transformation market in 2019, but AR/VR technology is predicted to have the fastest growth until 2025. (Research and Markets)*
7. *87% of companies think digital will disrupt their industry, but only 44% are prepared for potential digital disruption. (Deloitte)*
8. *From Gartner's perspective, "the transformation journey is taking large enterprises especially at least twice as long and costing twice as much as they originally anticipated." This is largely due to **cultural readiness** — "53% of the organizations surveyed remain untested in the face of digital challenge and their digital transformation readiness therefore uncertain."*

So why share all of these *Digital Transformation* facts, and what do they have to do with *Point-of-Work*? Quite simply – Everything. Every single Workflow that the Workforce encounters will Change. Regardless of how well Training was completed, we are confronted with one common restrainer – How much usable knowledge will be retained long enough to use in a new workflow on new technology? How sustainable is the strategy to position the Help Desk to meet the demands for assistance after Training is complete? How much trial and error in workflows is acceptable? What will the learning curve duration to full adoption cost the business?

Converging support in the Workflow using **Digital Adoption Platform (DAP)** technology is a best-in-class approach. In all honesty, DAP technology is a Workflow Performance tool that enhances Training by integrating Learning into actual Workflow using the same technology that will be utilized to optimize post-training workflow performance. DAP, in every respect, *Converges Learning with Work* by using performance assets *designed intentionally* for consumption in Training AND on the job.

What Is Digital Adoption Platform (DAP) Technology?

DAP is a software tool that gives users of applications the guidance they need to execute application tasks at the Point-of-Work in their Moments of Need. DAP provides this guidance concurrently inside the target application and guides the user through each step of their task.

Common DAP CHALLENGES:

- Premises-based DAP technologies often require embedded code insertion into the enterprise applications that will be supported. This is invasive to any IT owner, and the potential for live application disruption is a showstopper in many cases. The better DAP offerings now are cloud-based, require no embedded code to track with any application, and are application agnostic.

- The most demanded form of digital adoption is the Walk-Through which highlights each step in the live application, instructs the user what to do, allows the user to interact with the live application, then proceeds through each subsequent step until completion. A new cloud-based product that came out late in 2022 uses a FOLLOW ME capability far superior to other platform Walk-Through offerings.

- For most DAP providers creating a Walk-Through is very time-consuming and requires skill in the digital adoption tool. The better offerings enable User Acceptance Test Script development, which is the bane of IT's job, especially in meeting compliance validation testing requirements.

- Since any digital Transformation applications rarely remain static, maintaining Walk-throughs over time as processes change is difficult, and if not maintained, the Walk-Through will break. Compounding those fluid changes due to updates, patches, and fine-tuning to include Training updates for new hires and incumbent users in their workflows and maintenance becomes a huge drag on resources to keep the workforce optimized.

Formerly known as Electronic Performance Support Systems (EPSS) or simply EPS, the concept of DAP is not new; however, the integration into Workflows is radically different, non-invasive to IT infrastructure, cloud-based, and multi-functional at a fraction of the cost of earlier premises-based systems. There are several vendors in this space, and every one of them has a different sweet spot. The question becomes what sweet spot delivers the best operational advantage to your transformation journey.

Key DAP features to shop for are shown in *Figure 3-1* below:

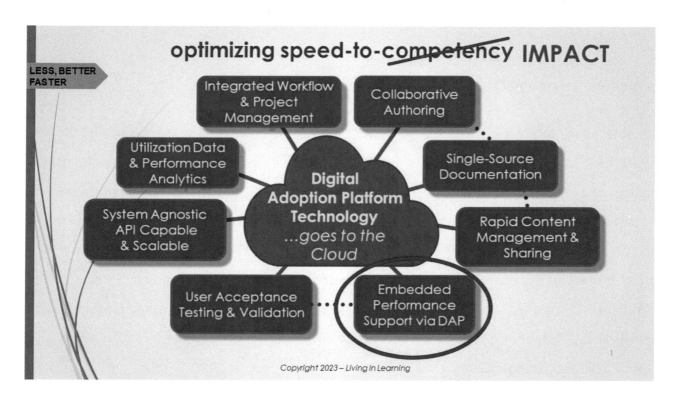

Figure 3-1

CONFESSION: *Content creation, reusability, maintenance, and portability drew me into this technology as an early adopter of EPSS technology (before DAP technology transitioned to the cloud.) The choices were all premises-based, and all had code that needed to be embedded in the host application. That was a mistake because embedded code was required for each application supported. I learned firsthand that IT did NOT want any foreign code inserted into a primary enterprise application, especially the ERP, Medical Records (EMR), or any other enterprise-wide deployment. After a very ugly experience, I learned that being an early adopter can lead to an early exit strategy. I did not get fired, but our vendor did. Despite the embedded code issue, their sweet spot was centered around the three upper right elements* *in the graphic above. Those capabilities were best-in-class at the time and still are after the transition to a cloud-based solution. Despite early version challenges, this vendor should be a regular consideration for any cloud-based DAP integrations.*

Figure 3-1 emphasizes *Embedded Performance Support* as the main event, which is often the most newsworthy feature; however, my experience points to several other considerations that drove vendor selection more so than the main event.

Integrated Workflow and Project Management

Rarely will a single person work in IT and Training Development; however, there is a considerable overlap where IT and Training default to the redundant effort that an Integrated Workflow Management capability can avoid. IT is not a fan of User Acceptance Testing (UAT) due to the tedious workflow process documentation, especially in System Validation efforts. Why not enable IT to run a simple recording capability to build the process flow for UAT that can then be REUSED by Training with added annotations for more information, resources, links, videos, etc., for both Embedded Performance Support AND End-user Training? This unified Workflow and Project Management capability assigns and tracks tasks across disciplines like IT, Training, SMEs, and others under a single project timeline. All handoffs are completed in the cloud without shipping cumbersome files.

Collaborative Authoring & Single-Source Documentation & Rapid Content Management

Integrated Workflow capability this platform enables multiple cross-discipline author assignments to work in the same workflow and hand off content and documentation to serve multiple purposes. Recall the "R" in DRIVER for Replicate: *Create Once – Use Multiple Times*. Keeping content current when things change is a monumental task. Single-Source Documentation tames that beast by everyone working off a single document in the cloud. Not only a single master document but the applications of that content can span Training Content in PPT, user documentation books for Workflows, simulations, and FOLLOW ME Walk-Throughs. A single update to a single document then flows to multiple output types.

System Agnostic

This feature is important because a Digital Transformation project will contain multiple platforms from multiple vendors. Whichever DAP platform you choose, ensure you are not on the hook for buying more licensed capability each time a new technology is added to your transformation project. In other words, buy into *system-agnostic* DAP technology that does not care what systems it supports or Windows applications like Word, Excel, etc. Scalability that does not break the bank is essential for a long-term transformation initiative.

Utilization Data & Performance Analytics

Knowing which end-users are using performance support content is vital information to track the volume of support and which specific support assets are accessed. This data is a flag for further assessment to determine why the asset was used. Was it a Training issue? Was the support asset no longer current? Did the system workflow change? Were end-users not notified?

CHAPTER 4

ALIGNMENT & DISCOVERY CASCADE

I always start at the TOP of the requesting organization to frame *beliefs, perceptions, assumptions, and hypotheses* held by the leadership role making the request. To protect the integrity of discovery, we should ask the same questions in multiple iterations downward through the cascade toward *Individual Contributors*. (*See Figure 4-1*) It is important to note that the questions are the same, although the wording is *localized* for each level interviewed. We need to identify perspectives and beliefs at the top (**Top-Down Discovery**) and make accurate comparisons based on actual Individual Contributor experiences vital to refining and validating what may be a very different reality (**Bottom-Up Validation**).

 A *Re-Alignment Conversation* opportunity will result in fine-tuning the original request if/when cascade findings do not match the original *beliefs, perceptions, assumptions, and hypotheses.* Actual Discovery findings and related validations flow in the opposite direction – **Bottom Up**. The Ultimate Solution Design Flow is also sourced by the realities at the Bottom versus the *beliefs, perceptions, assumptions, and hypotheses* given to us at the Top.

In other words, a Discovery Cascade will minimize, if not eliminate, the problem centered on the *Myth*. We dispel the *Myth* by validating reality at *Points-of-Work*…at the Bottom…by re-aligning expectations before making the first move to design a solution. In addition, if the PWA discovery cascade identifies multiple solutions, we have the opportunity for the stakeholder requestor to prioritize what part(s) of the solution or parts of their target audiences are to be addressed first.

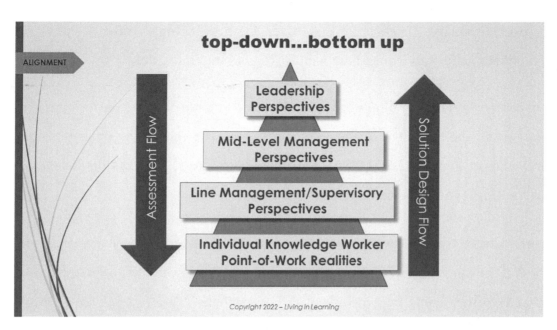

Figure 4-1

Discovery Cascade Categories

What follows are sample statements made during a PWA discovery accomplished by a survey that targets each level of role from Top to Bottom. The hierarchy could be as simple as two levels (*Manager to Contributor*) or consist of multiple levels of senior management aligned with multiple line-level supervisory roles to multiple Individual Contributor roles. Initial discussions with the Requestor will determine how many levels should be targeted.

Confession: Individual Contributors should be grouped as peers in forums or one-on-one when using face-to-face interviews. *Do NOT mix Individual Contributors with supervisory/leadership roles. Mixing levels will promote answer bias or, worse...limited truths. The same situation remains if a survey instrument is utilized. In the example above, there were three management levels. While the same survey is offered to each management level, extracting results specific to each level is essential. Why? If perceptions differ between top-level leadership and line-level managers, we need to know about it and direct more specific questioning to define the disparities uncovered. You may miss significant dysfunction among leadership ranks if you do not separate the levels.*

Typically, a survey approach takes the pulse of an organization versus extracting specific performance issues. The survey approach is a fast and convenient way to identify wh*ich rocks to look under* in advance

17

of more focused discovery. Surveys work well for large or complex ecosystem scenarios where anonymous feedback is desired from a broad audience with multiple roles.

Six ecosystem categories frame multiple attributes that can impede or dilute performance results. There are two groupings on the table; the left-hand column shows the TOP of the cascade (*Leadership*), and the right-hand column shows the BOTTOM (*Individual Contributor*). The example below (*See Table 4A*) was used in a multi-level management scenario.

It is important to note that discovery questions may directly address topics or could use a ranking methodology like the survey shown below. Even if ranking is used, follow-up discovery utilizing active listening and active questioning become essential. For example, *"The survey rated that as a six. Why? What would you change to make it a ten?* Active open-ended questioning promotes expanded answers and better background information.

Below are several discovery statements from a cascade survey organized by the six ecosystem performance restrainer attributes categories. In the case where I used these statements, two are identical, whereas others are *localized* to reflect specific Individual Contributor *Points-of-Work*.

Keywords differing between the perspectives are highlighted. The most important aspect of these statements is their consistency. Consistency throughout the entire cascade across multiple roles and job functions ensure reliable comparisons that shine the light on *assumptions at the Top* with *validations at the Bottom*. This consistency is only accomplished if the questions or statements to each level are localized to their scope and role.

LEADERSHIP CASCADE	INDIVIDUAL CONTRIBUTOR CASCADE
Environment & Culture	
Our organization has a clearly defined culture	My work group has a clearly defined culture
Someone new joining the organization will have a positive first impression.	Someone new coming into my work group will have a positive first impression.
Collaboration within and among all work areas is encouraged, active, and enabled with the means to be effective and efficient.	Collaboration within my work group and with others is encouraged, active, and enabled with the means to be effective and efficient.
People & Capability	
The training received during onboarding fully equips all Performers to be successful in their current roles and workflows.	The training received during onboarding fully equipped me to be successful in my current role and assigned workflows.
As work volumes increase, our training team has been able to keep pace	As work volumes increase, our training team has been able to keep pace
Performance expectations for all current roles are clearly defined and supported across all areas.	My managers clearly define and support performance expectations related to my current role.
Workflows & Processes	
When workflows or processes change, all affected performers are informed and equipped to adjust/adapt quickly & efficiently at their task-level work.	When workflows or processes change, I am informed and equipped to adjust/adapt quickly & efficiently in applying changes to my task-level work.
All current job roles can easily and quickly access information and resources needed to complete their work.	In my current job role, I can easily and quickly access information and resources needed to complete my work.

Accessible information and resources utilized by all performers are designed for immediate & effective application within all workflows.	The accessible information and resources I utilize are designed for immediate & effective application within my workflows.
Content & Resources	
Searching for information and resources is accessible for all to navigate & find the correct content at a moment of need.	Searching for information and resources is accessible for me to navigate & find the correct content during a moment of need.
When critical resources & information change, notification to all affected Performers in their workflow is timely & accurate.	When critical resources & information change impacting one or more of my workflows, notification is timely & accurate.
When resource information needs to be corrected/out-of-date, all affected job roles have a clear path to reach content owners.	When resource information needs to be corrected/out-of-date, I have a clear path to reach appropriate content owners.

Systems & Technology	
Technology systems & business applications utilized in all current roles are easy to use and effectively and efficiently utilized.	Technology systems & business applications utilized in my current role are easy to use and effectively and efficiently utilized.
The correct personal technology and software for all performers to be effective in workflows are currently deployed to all appropriate roles.	The correct personal technology and software for me to be effective in my current role and workflows are currently deployed.
The Learning System (LMS) currently deployed provides adequate opportunities to learn & grow for all performers and roles.	The current Learning System (LMS) deployed provides adequate opportunity for me to learn new skills & grow my capability in my current role.
Impact & Analytics	
All performers are fully aware of the metrics and measures tracked that define their performance contribution.	I am fully aware of the metrics and measures tracked to define my performance contribution.
All performers can see the business value produced by the results of their performance contribution.	I can see the business value produced by the results of my performance contribution.
The best (*most accurate*) measures of workflow performance are currently being tracked.	The best (*most accurate*) measures of workflow performance are currently being tracked.

Table 4-A

Once again, you will notice that some of the statements are identical while others are *localized* to a narrower audience while retaining an equivalent theme. This format example was offered via a survey. The same study could be managed with face-to-face interviews; however, the volume of interviews may become a detractor, plus you would lose the anonymity factor. Survey Monkey (*or some other survey platform*) is advisable if anonymity is an encouraging factor for honest participation in the survey.

Now what?

Does the *Discovery Cascade* render a design solution? Nope! This *pre-design discovery* is used to reconnoiter the situation on the ground compared to the intent behind those issuing the requests/orders at the top. Disparities will exist, and those disparities are source data points to engage in a *Changed Conversation* discussion that recommends a more comprehensive solution design. An effective **Alignment Conversation** can save you a lot of time and resources with a small, focused time investment to reconnoiter *Point-of-Work* up front. Nothing dispels an assumption quite like actual data from the *Point-of-Work.*

- Our ultimate goal is to enable workflow solutions that converge support and learning assets to drive sustainable and measurable performance results. I highly recommend discovering what is driving and restraining performance at each *Point-of-Work* before taking an order to develop training at face value. This posturing will give you the look and feel of an *engaged business partner* to your stakeholder instead of a *training-order-taking-drive-thru* operation.

CHAPTER 5

CHANGING THE CONVERSATION

Over the years, L&D has done a stellar job convincing our operational stakeholders that **Training Drives Performance**. I must confess to perpetuating that *Myth* for many of my 35+ years. Roughly fifteen years ago, I had an epiphany that performance only manifested when workers did something effectively; therefore, **Training ONLY Drives Potential**. Looking back on it, that was not much of an epiphany, but our modus operandi was to take training requests from stakeholders and develop training. Period. That was our job. Our stakeholders expected it, and sadly, so did L&D. What breaks the *Myth* is the recognition that performance results only manifest once the workforce is back in their workflows and effectively addressing role-specific, task-centric *Points-of-Work*.

We must address *Points-of-Work* in the context of workflows and define the work environment attributes that impede performance outcomes. Our charge is to set expectations with our stakeholders that our solutions will be designed to improve and sustain performance outcomes…not just training. That stakeholder guidance can be a tough sell given we are TRAINING…and what do we do? We TRAIN. The tricky part is trying to dispel the myth directly, so my advice is to keep that nugget of knowledge to yourself…for now.

Bottom line? You must gently provide proof that a Different Conversation from their initial request for Training comes from the discovery you wish to accomplish to ensure the new Training is both relevant and effective on the job. Don't try to dispel the myth; change the conversation.

Following are three case studies where *conversations changed* by the outcomes of PWA findings. Names have been changed to protect the innocent, delusional, misinformed, and guilty. The case studies referenced came from real clients with what they thought were genuine training issues. These examples contain paraphrased dialogue and how the PWA outcome **Changed the Conversation**…and blew up the *Myth*.

CASE STUDY #5A

TECHNICAL SUPPORT HOT LINE

Here's a perfect example where the *restrained productivity source fell outside the requested training solution's scope*. In a recent **Point-of-Work Assessment (PWA) Workshop**, the Performance Support Specialist I worked with received a request to *improve training* for the inbound call center technical support function. The stated issues were as follows:

- Decreasing customer satisfaction scores and customer attrition
- Degraded response times with client resolutions
- Technical Support Rep frustration and high employee turnover

While some knowledge deficiencies were discovered, these three factors listed above were priority influencers promoting the simple request - *Fix Training!*

The Requestor's paradigm was wrapped around the Myth...Training will fix my performance issues.

The PWA discovery revealed a *Solution Road Map* that recommended several training-related solutions, and some training would never resolve. One of the biggest non-training obstacles that restrained productivity and caused turnover had nothing to do with insufficient knowledge or skills. Still, it was an *organizational design* (OD) issue that compromised workflows with unnecessary delays, missed performance goals, and job frustration.

Tier One Support Techs had a 24-hour response window, and tier Two (*who accepted escalations for Tier One*) had a separate 48-hour response window to respond to Tier One. For every escalation made, the potential to miss Tier One's response window to the customer was at risk. The organizational design was mismatched because of how performance was measured across two work functions.

The result was a domino effect that extended deeply into the ecosystem, causing the following:

- Tech solution hand-off delays increased client response time
- Which in turn led to degraded customer satisfaction scores
- Mis-matched performance goals between tier-one and tier-two support functions
- This led to job frustration of competent technical specialists by missing call goals
- This led to excessive employee turnover, some were fired for non-performance, and some bailed out of a perceived hopeless situation
- This led to a recruiting backlog and delays in refilling highly talented and skilled roles
- This caused steep learning curves for newbies who lacked access to critical IP knowledge from, guess who...those who had just walked out the door.

Talk about an extreme domino effect...interdependencies do that all day long and are too often perpetuated and overlooked by well-intended requests for more training. This request was NOT exclusively Training related. If Training had been upgraded, how many performance restrainers would have been missed and Training impact diluted to the extent that Training was blamed for a poor course? Hey, been there and done that. That's why I use the PWA as a CYA tactic.

Following is the visual **Conversation Changer** from the PWA Discovery Findings
(*See Figure 5-1*)

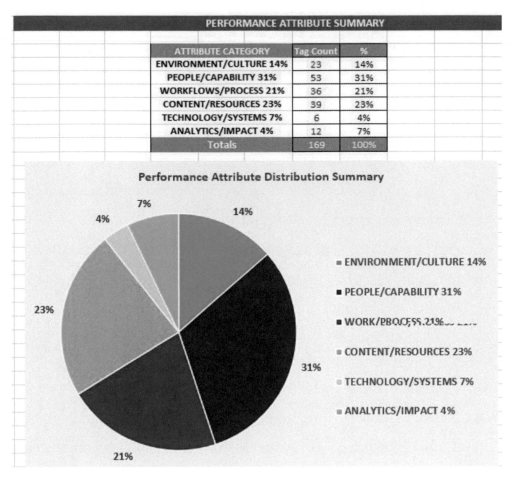

PERFORMANCE ATTRIBUTE SUMMARY		
ATTRIBUTE CATEGORY	Tag Count	%
ENVIRONMENT/CULTURE 14%	23	14%
PEOPLE/CAPABILITY 31%	53	31%
WORKFLOWS/PROCESS 21%	36	21%
CONTENT/RESOURCES 23%	39	23%
TECHNOLOGY/SYSTEMS 7%	6	4%
ANALYTICS/IMPACT 4%	12	7%
Totals	169	100%

Figure 5-1

Did the PWA assessment reveal the need for additional learning? Yes, it did, and those needs were embedded within the 31% People/Capability pie slice above, but...and this is important...they were not courses; they were performance support tools (*targeted Job Aids*) that needed to be accessible in the workflow.

Following are several more *Conversation Changer* topics the graphic highlights:

- **Environment/Culture** – 14% reflected the job frustration stemming from unreachable performance expectations due to goal misalignment between the Tiers. An overlap surfaced in *Analytics/Impact* (*7%*) specific to unfair performance metrics. High employee turnover impacted those left behind with job volume overload, not to mention constant interruptions from peers asking for help because the other experienced tech support staff had quit.

- **People/Capability** – reflected several things beyond Learning and Support, and one major item was the OD misalignment. In the final analysis, no course(s) would fix the OD mismatched hierarchy goal alignment.

- **Content/Resources** – 23% were exclusively related to accessing methods and procedure documents in the workflow and technical specs. If they were hard to gain access to and were out-of-date/not current, they caused severe problems with accurate and timely customer responses.

- **Workflows/Processes** – 21% reflected consistent frustration specific to process and workflow hand-offs between Tier One and Tier Two support teams. While Analytic/Impact addressed metrics directly, many responded that this was a broken workflow or a compromised process. It is important to address both perspectives in a PWA because they are both correct, and overlap is common. Just record and Tag what you hear. Remember, the PWA is not a solution tool but a *Conversation Changer* to promote expanded thinking and informed prioritization.

What **Changed the Conversation** was the expanded scope of this Specialist's new role; she used the PWA to prevent L&D's eventual failure to deliver requested learning solutions whose success would be based upon the expectation that *only training* would fix poor performance in the target group.

Yes, there would likely have been some incremental improvements accomplished, and the Training Box would get a checkmark…BUT…the Performance Box would probably not fare so well…certainly not be optimized…the more significant bottom line Business Value negative impacts would continue.

Based on this case study, we have to ask ourselves, *"What are the chances of optimization being overlooked if strategy and tactics focus only on the learning part of the solution?"*

That eventuality would ensure a negative impact on this client. The same would happen to us and would limit our ultimate effectiveness if we do not enable a holistic *Point-of-Work Assessment* of the ecosystem's performance attributes at *Point(s)-of-Work*.

This example clearly shows how the *interdependencies* in a dynamic ecosystem set up a potential trap when a Training mindset fails to engage in assessment to learn WHY performance was restrained. Would the OD intervention in the example above even have been uncovered? Possibly not, because the requestor was locked onto Training as the solution. Call it a blind spot on the stakeholder's watch, but worse yet, it would have been a blind spot for L&D if a PWA did not reveal the OD-related restrainer.

Here is an essential point – Does L&D own OD redesign? Nope, but the **Point-of-Work Assessment (PWA)** revealed a need to act as a *liaison* to bring OD specialists into the solution mix, and very likely IT systems tracking response times, compensation, and, and, and. This points to another facet of *interdependency*; our need to include other business partners, resources, and specialties to collaborate with us to optimize an ecosystem performance solution, not just a learning solution.

CASE STUDY #5B

Initial Request: Update Sales Training to Align with the Selling Process

Stated Problem: Field Sales Teams need to follow the formal selling process to prevent an increase in time-to-close that degrades overall sales effectiveness and profitability.

Requestor Paradigm: Training will drive my sales team's performance to improve.

VP of Sales Perspectives: *We have some challenges with our field reps needing to follow the formal selling process and are slowing down time-to-close. We need some training to get them back on track. We may require new training; the Miller Heiman course must pay back a return.*

Note: Since my job title was Director of Sales Training, it made sense that I got the call as an undeclared performance Ninja; I remained covert (*no black pajamas*). I responded nonthreateningly, preserving the *Myth* that Training would solve his sales performance issues—no sense pushing back by telling him that Training may not be the issue...or any issue.

My Response: *Sure thing, John; I can help you with training updates. First, I'd like to ask you some questions and, with your blessing, interview some of your Sales Managers and Account Executives in the district sales offices. I want to ensure that any new training we develop meets or exceeds the performance outcomes you seek.*

Note: Several things were accomplished in this single exchange:

- First, I accepted his challenge to update training.
- Second, I aligned (*initially*) with his assumption that new training was the solution.
- Third, I got permission to ask him (*the requestor*) some qualifying questions.
- Fourth, I asked for his permission/sponsorship to speak with his sales team members.

My Response: *John, I have a few key questions to ask you and would like access to you for follow-ups as I begin field interviews. Here are a few initial questions:*

- *Why do you think time-to-close is extending?*
- *What evidence tells you the selling process is not being followed?*
- *How have you confirmed that the current selling process is correct?*
- *What tells you that Miller Heiman Strategic Selling is not effective?*
- *When we update training, what would "better" look like? What needs to change?*

Note: More clarifying questions were asked, but John consistently felt that ineffective Training was at the core of his problems. I found it hard to believe that deviating from a sales process was something to fix with training, but with no validation, I agreed to investigate further at that point. He did agree, however, that confirming the validity of the selling process was worth examining if/when findings revealed a change was necessary. I considered that a small win.

The point worth noting in the Requestor's responses: Accept what you are being told as those facts frame the Requestor's story based on their *beliefs* based on *perspectives, assumptions, biases, and hypotheses.* Your job is to validate or dispel those beliefs with facts from your PWA discovery findings. Always attempt to get a Requestor-approved map of what they believe are the most critical contributors to their performance challenges, *even if it is their best guess.*

Important Note: When interviewing many people and roles, it is best practice to author a draft courtesy message of **sponsorship** for the organization's senior leader (*Requestor*) that they can address to those who will be interviewed to encourage cooperation and facilitation for accessing the appropriate team members for interviews. Never discount the power of establishing senior leader endorsement or sponsorship. Write it for them, and make it easy for them to *sign and send* it on your behalf.

PWA Process: What follows is an abbreviated PWA description with emphasis on what *changed the conversation*. This PWA attempts to find proof that either validates or dispels the Requestor's belief that training is a single solution. Honestly, it may be precisely that, or until it is proven by the PWA to be a false assumption.

PWA Logistics of Discovery:

- Four sales districts with ten to twelve District Sales Managers (DSMs).

- Interviewed eight DSMs – four ranked highly, and four ranked at the low end of the scale.

- Interviewed four Account Executives form each DSM team for a total of 32 AEs, half were considered top guns, and the other half...not so much.

Note: The objective of the interviews is to get a cross-section of high performers who possess the attitudes and work ethics of high performers and also from performers in the inverse population who are challenged with issues that yield poor performance for whatever reason.

PWA Discovery Questions: What follows are questions designed to track the Requestor's perspectives on the source of performance challenges. I have not included follow-up or clarifying questions, but their answers were reflected in the Field Findings. We will spend more time on questions in later chapters.

- The current selling process has 23 steps. On a scale of 1 to 10, how effective is the current process?

- If you could modify anything about the process, what would you change, add, or delete?

- Why would you make those changes, and what benefit would be gained?

- The current sales training is based on Miller Heiman Strategic Selling (MHSS). Is that the right course? Why or why not?

- How is MHSS supported in the field after training?

PWA Discovery Findings:

- A majority determined that the current selling process had too many steps that caused delays in closing sales. (*Ultimately reduced steps to 18*)

- The teams, on average, agreed on eighteen steps as optimum, with three of the eighteen treated as optional.

- The DSMs were split on applying the principles of Miller Heiman post-training. Oddly enough, the top-performing districts followed the practices outlined in the worksheets when pre-planning sales opportunities. Those that did not consistently perform lower.

- The AEs were split as well. If they were in a high-performing sales office, it was because the DSM supported the process. Those without the benefit of DSM support did not perform as well.
- A couple of significant AE quotes spoke volumes about the consistency of applying Miller Heiman principles. *"When we got back from training, my DSM said, 'Okay, now I will show you how selling really gets done here.'"*

Changed Conversation at the Top:

The PWA discovery findings confirmed several things conflicted with the VP of Sales perspectives.

- Training was not a solution for deviations from the selling process.
- The selling process was not optimized, and the teams abandoned it to circumvent the unnecessary steps and made modifications accordingly. Those modifications were inconsistent across all the districts, so a Six Sigma team was assigned to optimize the process. (Not Training; however, a new approach would likely impact future curriculum for all new hires.)
- The jury was out on the use of Miller Heiman. Some loved it, and some did not and chose to do their own thing. Once again, not a training issue per se, but potentially a shift in training would come about.

Note: In the readout of findings, I postured what Training would do in the future and stated the following:

"You are paying us (Training) big dollars to use Miller Heiman. I do not care if we continue with Miller Heiman or shift to Holden Power Base, Application Selling, or whatever we choose to do that's home-grown. Just pick one! The bottom line is to get everybody on the same page and do two things; 1) Commit to consistent training. 2) Consistently commit to support and reinforce Training in the post-training application of the principles we teach."

The *conversation changed* because of the PWA findings. The PWA did not complete a solution but a Solution Road Map detailed a couple of milestones:

- Six Sigma would assign process improvement resources to optimize the selling process.
- Decide what sales training curriculum to pursue.

- Training resources would be applied if and when Training became part of the solution.
  - Training may become engaged after Six Sigma optimizes the selling process
  - Training may become engaged after a sales training discipline is defined

Note: While it's true that Training would likely play a role, the PWA redirected if and when Training would get engaged and acted as a liaison with Six Sigma to optimize the selling process. Another way of looking at the PWA is that it was a ***pre-solution design tool*** to ensure that precious design resources were tasked accordingly and not defaulted to building Training.

The primary Performance Restraint categories were:

- *Environment/Culture* due to inconsistent leadership
- *People/Capability* due to inconsistent Training reinforcement
- *Workflows/Processes* due to inconsistent Workflow adherence.

CASE STUDY #5C

This case is positioned differently by showing the accompanying output of a visual **PWA Conversation Changer**. Later chapters will show you how to use PWA worksheets to create a *Conversation Changer* visual.

The Request: Update the Marketing Curriculum

The Stated Problem: We want our Marketing team to be world-class, and we need a world-class curriculum to get us there. Currently, we have neither.

Requestor Paradigm: Training will drive my Marketing team's performance to equal world-class stature.

Sr. VP of Sales & Marketing Perspectives: *I'm convinced that the recently departed VP of Marketing built the equivalent of an MBA program and loaded it onto the LMS. That Marketing curriculum is not working well enough to take us to world-class status. The solution, therefore, requires that you upgrade the course mix on the LMS to support our journey to world-class.*

By the way, I appreciate what you did for John and his sales team, and I expect similar results on this Marketing training upgrade. However, I don't have time for you to do a deep dive assessment...I want a new curriculum.

Note: Once again, I did not reveal my Ninja tendencies because this Requestor was wrapped a little tighter than his VP of Sales and pushed a marked sense of urgency that is not uncommon for more senior stakeholders. This stakeholder had drunk the *Myth* Kool-Aid, and it was clear that a different conversation would soon be forthcoming.

My Response:

Steve, I can help modify the Marketing curriculum, but I have a few key questions to ask you and would like access to you for follow-ups as I begin department interviews. Here are a few initial questions:

- *Besides Training, what do you think is preventing your team from being world-class?*
- *What workgroup(s) do you see most at risk of reaching world-class status?*
- *What do you think...he cut me off abruptly*

Sr.VP of Sales & Marketing Abrupt Response:

This is a Training issue. Period. None of my workgroups operate at world-class levels; you must concentrate on fixing the curriculum.

Note: It was made crystal clear that the Requestor did not have time for me to take a *deep dive,* and apparently, he did not have time for alignment questions either. So I needed the black pajamas and had to go Ninja...and do a covert *PWA lite*. I closed our meeting with a request to meet with some of his staff. *I did not specify precisely who or how many...I was going Ninja, after all...and what he did not know would not hurt him.* I needed discovery and could not allow a problematic client/Requestor to stop me.

Logistics of Discovery:

- Interviewed were six Directors, eight Group Managers and Supervisors, and a dozen Marketing Specialists from different functional areas.

What follows are **Core Questions** designed to track the Requestor's single perspective that substandard Training was keeping his Marketing team from operating at a world-class level. Notice that the questions focused on world-class performance and not world-class Training. I have not included follow-up or clarifying questions, but their answers were reflected in the Visual *Conversation Changer*. These questions are specific to this Case and represent the entire list of pre-interview questions. Each project will typically result in a unique *Core Question Set*, and more time will be spent on questioning in later chapters.

- Talk to me about what it's like working here. If anything, what would you change?
  - *Seeking Environment/Culture attributes*
- Do teams collaborate well on projects like new product launches? What challenges?
  - *Seeking People/Capability attributes*
- On a scale of 1 to 10, how would you rate the course selection at Marketing University?
  - *Seeking People/Capability attributes*

- Are workflows optimized? If not, what would you change?
  - *Seeking Workflow/Processes attributes*
- Do you/your team members have easy access to the right resources? If not, what's missing?
  - *Seeking Content/Resources attributes*
- Do you have access to the right technology to get the job done in your area? If not, what else do you need?
  - *Seeking Systems/Technology attributes*
- Do the performance metrics for your work/workgroup accurately reflect your contribution? If not, what would be a better measure of your performance?
  - *Seeking Analytics/Impacts attributes*

Note: *Lead core questions are shown above. Some open-ended to encourage broad answers. Some close-ended for specifics. Notice that each closed-ended question had open-ended qualifiers.*

PWA Discovery Findings:

The PWA findings confirmed that the existing curriculum was not optimized and aligned with the Requestor's assessment. What did NOT align with his expectations was that swapping out courses and inserting new ones would improve the curriculum. Those improvements would not pave the road to world-class performance because he had more significant issues that dwarfed what Training could ever hope to resolve...but because of the *Myth*...he had a huge blind spot.

Delivering the news to the Requestor that disputed his *"this is a training issue"* mindset would involve a significantly *different conversation* and could potentially include being tossed out of his office. When dealing with a tightly wrapped client, the best way to describe what will likely be received as contradictory news compared to their preconceived expectations, default to *less is more* but be prepared for more if required. The PWA visual *Conversation Changer* did the job perfectly, and no injuries or tossing events occurred. (*See Figure 5-2*) Surprisingly, only a few words were needed to hit the high spots, and the rest of the discussion fell into the Requestor's lap to set priorities of his choosing. Our debrief session only lasted about a half hour.

Below is the actual *Conversation Changer* placed in front of the Requestor. Using this visual, Findings were summarized on a single sheet of paper...and the only document he reviewed during our debrief, despite having a stack of verbatim interviews and curriculum reviews piled on the corner of his desk; I never touched a single sheet of the fluff.

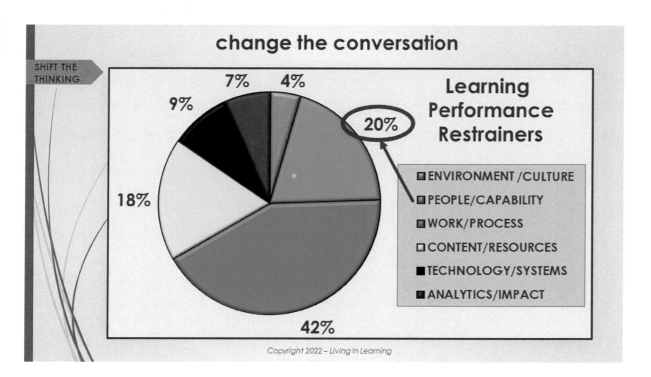

Figure 5-2

PWA Conversation Changer Shared at Debrief:

ME: *You were correct about the existing Marketing curriculum. I leaned over his desk, drew a circle around the 20% figure, and said, "Your Marketing curriculum resides here at the online Marketing University. As you can see, 80% of additional restrainers in the categories impact world-class performance. I only represent the "Training" segment of your solution. **Is being 100% effective on 20% of your challenges enough?"***

Note: I paused after making that last statement and waited for a reaction. He picked up the graphic, sat back in his chair, and did not speak...then I continued:

- *You can easily see that the most significant area of performance restraint is centered around workflows and processes at 42%. Interviews revealed dysfunction and low collaboration among related work functions under your watch. This is a perfect Process Improvement initiative for Six Sigma to optimize.*

- *There were considerable challenges under Content & Resources at 18%. For example, some Specialists in Market Segmentation do not have access to various pricing database details necessary to do their jobs well. That is a Resource Access issue.*

- *Going back to the 20% that I circled are additional attributes that rise above and beyond Training, including Leadership, Role Clarity, Clear Expectations, and Collaboration. That means the Training Curriculum impact is well under 20%, possibly closer to 5%. Honestly, Steve, you have bigger fish to fry than tweaking the Marketing curriculum.*

Note: Again, I paused and waited for his reaction. This time he looked at me with a slow nod, still saying nothing. I wondered if I'd crossed the line with my first Sr. VP adventure. So, I took the opening before he could throw me out and asked, *"So…where do you want to start?"*

His response shocked me, *"I want it all! I'll have an appointment set up for next week for two hours, and let's discuss this in more detail. I'll also invite Nolan (his Six Sigma Black Belt) to get his input. This is good information. Thank you once again!"*

By having *Changed the Conversation*, my stakeholder went from not having the time to invest in a deep dive to suddenly having the motivation to MAKE time to do a much deeper dive. The entire project wound up taking nearly six months to complete. The Solutions were as follows:

- Engaged Six Sigma to pursue a Process Improvement initiative
  - Training partnered in building limited training and performance support solutions based on the recommended changes by Six Sigma.
  - Ten weeks were shaved off product development from ideation to product release timelines.
- A 3rd party vendor was engaged to measure Marketing Attitudes and Values using a survey tool.
  - The results targeted significant dysfunction that was impacting interdepartmental behaviors and collaboration.

- A different 3rd party vendor I knew from a previous life was engaged to use the Attitudes and Values survey results to construct a modified Marketing Curriculum.
  - The vendor delivered structured workshops across different disciplines based on survey results. This curriculum was not one-size-fits-all.
- A Leadership Academy was formed with a curriculum built in collaboration with HR/OD resources that rolled out a standardized Change Leadership discipline for Marketing and, ultimately, the rest of the enterprise.

All of these resolutions came from *Changing the Conversation* using a PWA. The requestor only had the time for a deep dive AFTER the *conversation changed* due to a two-week investment in discovery, which validated a broader need for pursuing world-class capabilities.

Top-Down Discovery started with a modified curriculum request as the assumed solution influenced by the belief that Training would deliver results at a world-class level.

Bottom-Up Validation painted a different picture based on validated facts revealed at *Points-of-Work* that supported a different conversation and holistic interventions that impacted not only Marketing but leadership roles across the entire enterprise.

PART 2

Anatomy of PWA Workflow

CHAPTER 6

PWA ALIGNMENT

In Part 2, I will break down the Workflow of a *Point-of-Work Assessment* (*PWA*) into functional components. The graphics come directly from the PWA Workshop and serve as Job Aids. The first function we will cover is associated with initial Requestor ***Alignment***. (*See Figure 6-1*)

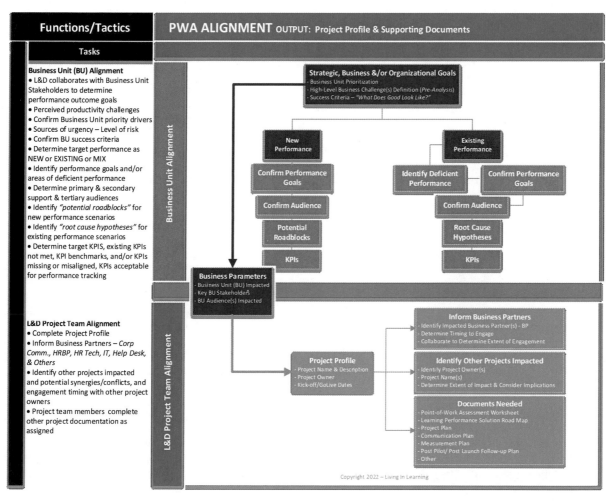

Figure 6-1

Each graphic has a Functions/Tactics section on the left with activities suitable for Project Plan milestones. The visuals on the right align with the tactical activities. The header on each graphic displays the Output of the described activity. In *Figure 6-1*, the Activity is *Alignment* – the Output supports a *Project Profile & Supporting Documents.*

Notice there are two sections on the graphic:

- **Business Unit Alignment** – Details specific to the Requestor's organization to accomplish Business Unit prioritization of challenges, high-level descriptions of perceived challenges, and success metrics for two types of performance:
  - *New Performance* – This indicates you have no history and must confirm performance goals, target audience, potential roadblocks anticipated, and Key Performance Indicators (KPIs) (*Requestor defined Metrics for success*)
  - *Existing Performance* – This indicates you have a history and must benchmark current performance challenges against existing performance goals. With existing performance, we must re-confirm the audience and identify Requestor beliefs, assumptions, and hypotheses related to the root cause(s) contributing to the challenges and the Requestor's success metrics.

- **L&D Project Team Alignment** – The *Business Unit Alignment* establishes the parameters under which a PWA is scoped, including the breadth of the PWA in terms of the Business Unit(s) impacted, who are the key stakeholders of each, and the targeted audience(s). The BU Alignment clarifies how the L&D Project Team should come together in the form of a Project Profile.
  - *Identify Business Partners* – Who should be included or, at a minimum, be notified of the PWA efforts that have implications for their engagement and timing?
  - *Overlap with Other Projects* – Are there projects currently underway that may conflict with or benefit from the PWA discovery? Check-in with the project owners to ensure there are no redundant efforts in either camp and identify synergies if there are any.

o *Set Document Expectations* – Some documents, like the PWA Worksheet, will be a work-in-progress and serve as a central repository for capturing data gathered during the PWA. Other documents may include:

- *Project Plan – Created and maintained by the Project Manager*
- *Communication Plan – What will be communicated, to whom, how often, and when*
- *Measurement Plan – Stakeholder identified metrics for success and the logistics of capturing, start/stop, duration, frequency, formatting, and results sharing*
- *Post Pilot/Launch Follow-up Plans –* Defined feedback loops and methods for extracting and evaluating adoption and utilization data

- These documents typically apply when the PWA scope is complex within the ecosystem. PWAs that are accomplished with a 30-minute phone conversation may not require formal documentation, although the subject matter of each document should not be overlooked.

CHAPTER 7

PWA DISCOVERY

In *Figure 7-1*, the Activity is *Discovery* – and the Output yields a Learning Performance Solution Road Map intended for collaboration with L&D Design/Development/Delivery resources and/or other Business Partners. More details on the PWA Workflow are provided in later chapters.

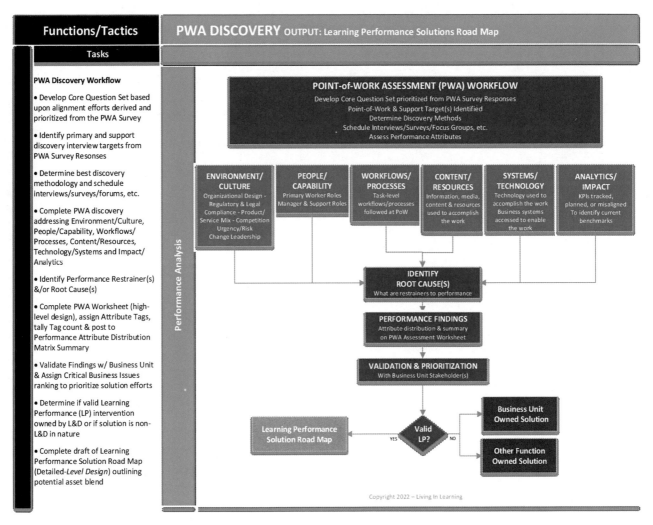

Figure 7-1

Stakeholder alignment shown in Figure 6-1 provides the source context for establishing a Core Question Set that any one or all of the six Attribute Categories with the intent of drilling down to root cause(s). The PWA Discovery Worksheet will enable the creation of a visual Conversation Changer pie chart that supports the Bottom-Up validation conversation with the Requestor for prioritization.

The *Changed Conversation* determines if this is a valid Learning Performance scenario, and if so, proceed to interface with the L&D Design team. If not, the solution could be a combination of an in-house-owned solution within the Business Unit itself or the intervention should be owned by another Business Partner entity.

What Is a Core Question Set?

Rather than go into a Discovery interview with a long list of questions, I suggest a *Core Question Set* of several key questions open up a dialogue with the interviewee. Below are seven (7) *Core Questions* I asked supporting the Marketing Curriculum Upgrade in Case 5B.

- Talk to me about what it's like working here. If anything, what would you change?
  - *Seeking Environment/Culture attributes*
- Do teams collaborate well on projects like new product launches? Challenges?
  - *Seeking People/Capability attributes*
- On a scale of 1 to 10, how would you rate the course selection at Marketing University? What should change?
  - *Seeking People/Capability attributes*
- Are current workflows and processes optimized? If not, what should change?
  - *Seeking Workflow/Processes attributes*
- Do you/your team members have easy access to the right resources? If not, what's missing?
  - *Seeking Content/Resources attributes*
- Do you/your team have access to the right technology to get the job done in your area? If not, what else is needed?
  - *Seeking Systems/Technology attributes*
- Do the performance metrics for your work and workgroup accurately reflect your/their contributions? If not, what would be better measures of performance?
  - *Seeking Analytics/Impacts attributes*

Figure 7-2 provides another sample listing of potential Core Questions.

PWA Core Question Set – Sample

DISCOVERY

ECOSYSTEM CATEGORY	CORE QUESTIONS
ENVIRONMENT/CULTURE	What is it like to work in this area? How does the work culture in this area match with corporate culture? What would you change? What internal/external work conditions impact performance in your area of responsibility? On a scale of 1-to-10, how would you rate workforce engagement? How balanced are workload assignments & volumes? How well do current corporate communications inform you and your team? What would you change?
PEOPLE/CAPABILITY	On a scale of 1-to-10, how equipped is your team with the skills necessary to complete their jobs? What would you change? How well-informed are your workers regarding clear performance expectations and goals? What required skills are missing or deficient? What is missing? How well-equipped are new hires after onboarding? How effective is ongoing training? What is needed? Unnecessary?
WORKFLOWS/PROCESSES	What workflows need optimization? Specifically, which processes are most essential and not optimized? What is at risk? How accessible are performance support resources in the Workflow? Are those resources embedded in workflows? How quickly are workers informed and equipped to adjust to changes in workflows or processes? What would you change? On a scale of 1-to-10, how prevalent is Active Supervision for your workers in their workflows? Who coaches? Mentors? What would you change?
CONTENT/RESOURCES	How accessible are resources & information needed to execute workflows? Are assets kept current? What would you change? How are resources managed & maintained? How are changes to resources communicated to your workers? How often are curated information resources distributed to your team? How effective is that process? What would you change? How often are resources *"pushed"* to your team? How do team members *"pull"* or download resources needed in their workflows?
TECHNOLOGY/SYSTEMS	What technologies and systems are/should be used routinely to execute work? Which systems are underutilized? Why? Which systems or technologies represent your workforce's greatest challenge or are most difficult to use? Why? What systems are capable and necessary to connect learning and support assets to the workforce in their workflows? How effective is the current Learning Management System in providing your team opportunities to learn and grow?
ANALYTICS/IMPACT	How is success measured? Are your workers aware of and can see the metrics used to track their performance? If not, why? Are KPIs correct/missing/misaligned? Are performance data accessible & actionable? How are performance data shared? How often are Impact measurements accomplished at Levels 3&4? Which systems provide access to utilization data? How is end-user asset utilization tracked? If not, why?

Figure 7-2

CHAPTER 8

PWA SYSTEMS/TECHNOLOGY FOOTPRINT

In *Figure 8-1*, PWA activity continues with a Technology Footprint (*Inventory of Current Systems*) and technologies used at *Point-of-Work*. The Output informs the Performance Solution Road Map specific to systems and technology. The sample below came from a PWA completed for a retail company.

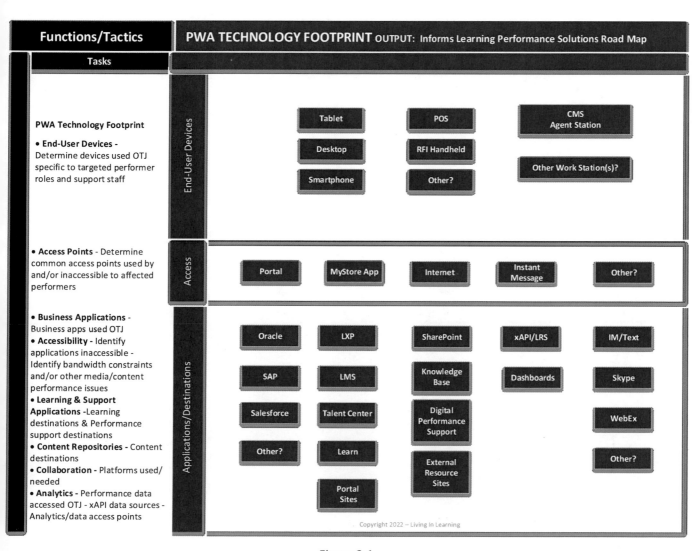

Figure 8-1

There are three primary sections to this discovery focus:

- *End-User Devices* – What technology is either in the hands of individual users or shared systems accessed as part of routine work? It is essential to know what the inventory consists of and if there are performance gaps associated with end-user proficiency.
- *Access* – How are the technologies and systems accessed from the Workflow? From what End-User device is access achieved, and are access rights correctly assigned to ensure End-User connectivity?
- *Applications/Destinations* – This category is crucial because we are dealing with End-User utilization and proficiency across the inventory of systems used and technology accessed.

CHAPTER 9

PWA ANALYTICS/IMPACT

In *Figure 9-1*, PWA activity continues with *Analytics and Impact Mapping,* and the Output informs the Measurement Plan Worksheet specific to analytics and impact. The Measurement Plan Worksheet is a unique Tab under the PWA Master Worksheet that will be covered later in this book.

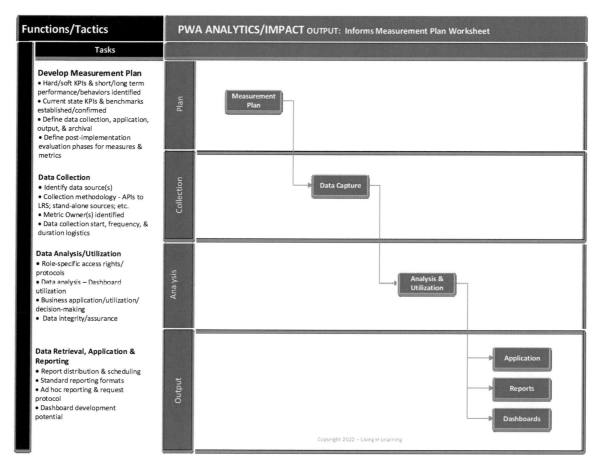

Figure 9-1

There are four sections to this graphic:

- *The Measurement Plan* – where current state benchmarks are established where existing performance exists and new performance KPIs where a new performance is planned. The actual definition of what will be tracked throughout and find post-project metrics and measures to confirm success and sustainability.

- *Collection* – Where is the data? Who owns it? Can we access it? How long do we track it, and what is the frequency for sampling the data?

- *Analysis* – Who has access to the data for analysis? Is analysis manual or dashboard-centric? How is the data utilized to support decision-making?

- *Output* – What is the format for reports? Who requests? Who delivers? What format is best?

CHAPTER 10

PWA DRIVER METHODOLOGY

In *Figure 10-1*, PWA activity continues with the collaborative DRIVER methodology, and the Output informs Intentional Design Documents to Enable Production, Incremental Test/Pilot Releases, & ultimately, GoLive.

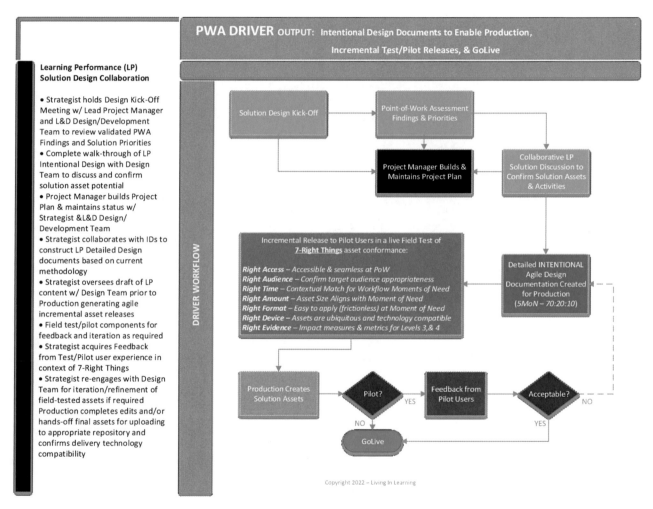

Figure 10-1

You may find a longtime survivor in the L&D profession that has yet to be a fan of one or more design methodologies, ADDIE being the oldest and likely foundational to everything else. My issues with design methodologies are defined by the limits of scope centering on *"design,"* with the assumption that learning/training *design* is the primary solution. I am convinced the *best-fit* solution set is often more significant and easily overlooked when *Point-of-Work* is ignored. The **DRIVER** methodology (*See Figure 10-1*) is a cradle-to-grave methodology encompassing whatever design method has already been adopted. My favorite is the <u>*Five Moments of Need*</u>, developed by Bob Mosher and Conrad Gottfredson of <u>Apply Synergies.com</u>.

A more detailed discussion of the DRIVER Workflow follows as shown in *Figure 10-2* below:

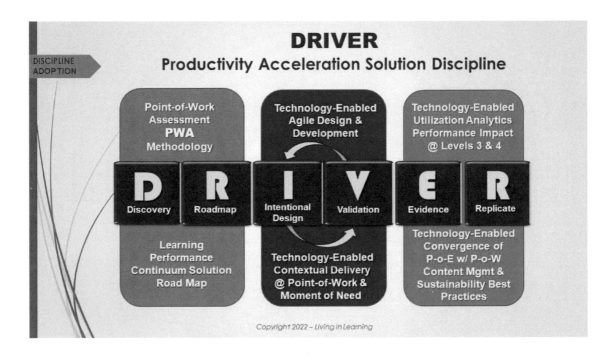

Figure 10-2

DRIVER was designed to include a more holistic approach to Discovery using *Point-of-Work Assessment (PWA)* methodology. As I mentioned earlier, PWA is NOT a design tool; instead, it is a PRE-DESIGN Road Mapping tool whose output enables collaboration and targets deeper dive discovery by core L&D resources like Five Moments of Need before engaging in Design and Development functions. PWA Pre-Design Discovery starts the entire process.

DRIVER's components require refined discovery skills (**Performance Consulting**) and agile design/development tactics (**Intentional Design**). More importantly, we find cultural mindsets locked and cocked to fire training at every performance challenge that also requires a strategic, if not a tactical, shift in thinking. Refer back to the concept of *Changing the Conversation*. PWA is the tool to accomplish that shift. The beauty of DRIVER is its compatibility with existing agile design methodologies. DRIVER provides a greater granularity for designing workflow-based performance and learning assets.

Additionally, foundational technologies that include **Digital Adoption Platforms (DAPs)**, formerly known as Electronic Performance Support Systems (EPS/EPSS), synchronize and converge performance assets within actual workflows.

Let us take a closer look at DRIVER:

- **"D" Discovery** – *Holistic Point-of-Work Assessment (PWA)*
    - Investigate All Six Performance Restrainer Categories of the PWA
    - Strategy & Business Goal Alignment (*Stakeholder Leadership-Defined*)
    - Define PWA Performance Restrainers (*Task-centric, Role-specific*)
    - Identify Root Cause(s) (*Contributing to Sub-optimal Performance Outcomes*)
    - Consider Ecosystem Interdependencies (*Ripple Effect*)
    - Business Issue Prioritization (*Requestor-Defined at Debrief*)
    - Complete Evidence-of-Impact Criteria/Target Planning (*Level 3 & 4 Analytics*)
- **"R" Roadmap** – *Ecosystem-wide Learning Performance Solution RoadMap*
    - Competency Alignment if/when Appropriate
    - Holistic Performance Continuum Mapping from *Point-of-Entry* to *Point-of-Work*
    - Align High-Level Pre-Design with Identified Performance Challenges
    - Design Change Management and Communications Plans
    - Leverage PWA Discovery to Support Agile Design/Development/Delivery
    - Ensure the presence of all characteristics of **7-Right Things** Critical for Agile Design
- **"I³" Intentional Design** – *Evolved Scope for Holistic Learning Performance Continuum*
    - Utilize Agile Design & Pilots for Incremental Solution Testing
    - Address the **7 Right Things** Addressed in the Performance Road Map

- o Integrate Solution Assets into Workflow(s) Utilizing Digital Adoption Platform (DAP) Technology
- o Include User/SME/BME Feedback Loop for Iteration Refinement Best Practices
- o Iterate Based Upon Pilot Feedback from End-Users, SMEs, and BMEs

- **"V" <u>Validate</u>** – *Confirm "7 Right Things" Are Addressed at Point-of-Work*
  - o **Right Access** to Effective, Efficient, and Relevant Solution Assets
  - o By the **Right End-User Population** (*Role-Specific& Task-Centric*)
  - o At the **Right Time** (*Accessible @ Moments of Need*)
  - o In the **Right Amount** (*Designed for Efficient Workflow Consumption @PoW*)
  - o In the **Right Format** (*Designed for Effective Workflow Application @ PoW*)
  - o Utilizing the **Right Technology** (*Optimize Access Within Workflows @ PoW*)
  - o Yielding the **Right Evidence of Measurable Impact** (*@ Levels 3 & 4 @ PoW*)
  - o Validate all **7-Right Things** Through End-user/SME Feedback
  - o Utilize Feedback as Source Data to Support Asset Refinement Iterations
  - o Deploy/Implement Validated Solutions to Appropriate Target Users

- **"E" <u>Evidence</u>** – *Performance Impact Analytics Acquisition*
  - o Execution of Business Impact Evaluation Plan Defined in *"Discovery."*
  - o Acquisition of Data Targeted for Levels 3 & 4 Impact Evidence
  - o Identify Potential Integration with xAPI Performance Dashboards (*if any*)
  - o Extract Analytics to Confirm Business Impact for Leadership Reporting
  - o Leverage Impact Evidence for Potential Future Asset Refinement

- **"R" <u>Replicate</u>** – *Support "Create Once – Use Many Times" Development Tactics*
  - o Define Content Management & Maintenance Protocols
  - o Leverage Agile Content Assets for Rapid Re-Use/Re-Deployment
  - o Seamlessly Re-Deploy Assets Across Ecosystem
  - o Embed Solution Assets in Formal Learning as well as Workflows to ensure consistency along the **Learning Performance Continuum** from *Point-of-Entry to Point-of-Work* (*See Figure 10-3*)
  - o Enable Asset Scalability That Is Seamless, Frictionless, and Ubiquitous

What is the Learning Performance Continuum?

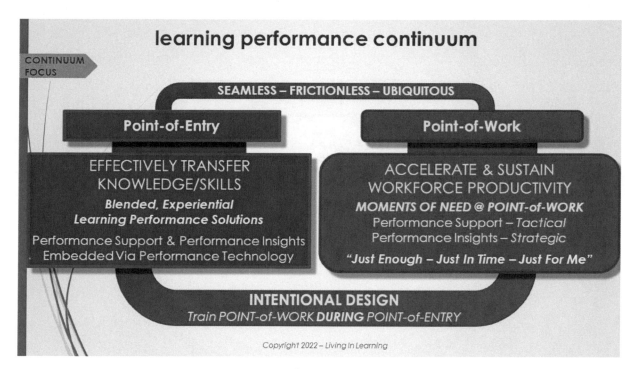

Figure 10-3

Here are a couple of thoughts related to the *Learning Performance Continuum*. Why continuum? Think about the journey to competency in any job role. It happens over time, beginning with **Point-of-Entry** **(PoE),** where initial knowledge and skills are acquired. *PoE* could be new hire onboarding or related to an incumbent moving internally to a new role or function. Here is where *Moment of Need 1* (NEW) & *Moment of Need 2* (MORE) is encountered. Training content is consumed in these Moments in some form like the classroom, eLearning, virtual, etc.

The continuum concept requires that performance assets designed ***intentionally*** for **Point-of-Work** should also be embedded in *Point-of-Entry* learning moments. This refers to the "R" in DRIVER – Replicate – (*Build Once – Use Many Times*).

If a new hire is confronted with the same assets during *Point-of-Entry* training that will be utilized in their actual Workflows, there is a sense of continuity that protects learning retention to *Point-of-Work*. Learning becomes *"sticky."* Additionally, Training should include the use of the DAP technology so that there is continuity of learning that aligns with actual workflows. In every respect, we are bringing *Point-of-Work* into the *Point-of-Entry*.

Confession: *My gap for the first 20 years of my L&D career, I never considered there was a need to engage at Point-of-Work. The Help Desk had that covered. Training WAS the standard solution, so why look beyond the obvious? Our L&D teams were order-takers and more focused on efficiently and effectively transferring knowledge which is/was what we were scoped and compensated for doing. The blind spot of never considering the Point-of-Work prevented us from taking our status quo methodology and solution design downstream to include sustaining workforce capability at Point-of-Work. Can you say "Cultural Blindspot?"*

CHAPTER 11

PWA INTENTIONAL DESIGN

Intentional Design supports "I" in DRIVER – Intentional Agile Design, and it also refers to the "R" in DRIVER – Replicate – (*Build Once – Use Many Times*). But there is more to intentionality than simple repurposing and re-using content. *(See Figure 11-1)*

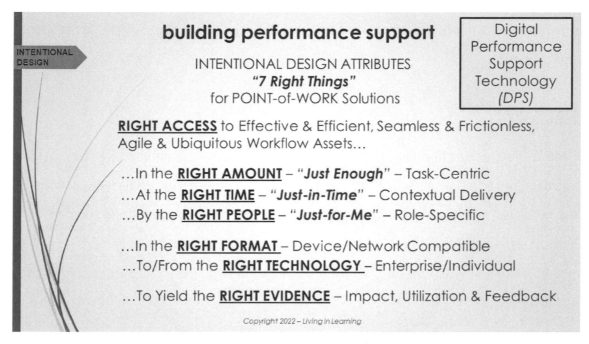

Figure 11-1

Intentional Design - ID does not replace *Instructional Systems Design - ISD*; rather, it enhances and expands ISD by looking through a longer lens (*greater magnification like a telephoto lens*) to gain clarity of what lies beyond the scope of Training solutions at *Point-of-Entry*.

What we must be able to see downstream and post-training is the *Point-of-Work*, a dynamic work environment where moments of need are as dynamic and diverse as the Workflows and the Workforce facing them. The need for both *performance agility* and *responsiveness* to the dynamics and urgency of workflow challenges is essential. Our design, development, and delivery of the required assets must be *intentionally* aligned with the dynamics of those Workflows.

This longer lens shapes a new perspective that requires an evolved approach to several key areas where disruption to the status quo will be felt:

- **Solution Pre-Design Discovery** – <u>Point-of-Work Assessment</u>
- **Solution Design** – Intentional design to inform ISD
- **Solution Delivery** – Integration of Digital Adoption Platform (DAP) Technology
- **Solution Impact** – Utilization of solution assets & Measurable outcomes at levels 3&4

Indeed, some disruptions are implied in the list above, but placing all our eggs in the Training discipline basket limits our impact downstream at *Point-of-Work,* where measurable business outcomes are won, compromised, or lost.

Solution Pre-Design Discovery

ISD roles are largely maintained with minimal disruption, and Storyboards remain a steady diet; however, both may target smaller and more concise assets. The actual challenge surfaces when we consider the reasons for being *"smaller and more concise."* Our primary ground zero being *Point-of-Work* implies we must assess the attributes restraining consistent performance. As history shows, not every performance challenge begets a training content solution when a small, targeted Job Aid, video clip, or live chat will do.

While content assets will be part of any solution, the greater need for ISD pre-design clarity rests upon the context of the workflow and ALL attributes causing impeded performance. The *Point-of-Work Assessment - PWA* is *"intentionally designed"* to do precisely that – *precede* ISD routines and *inform* how *context-sensitive assets* are to be applied in the workflow. Context-sensitivity impacts design, and design impacts how those assets are delivered, which impacts how the assets are measured to show evidence of business impact and value generation.

Solution Design

The solution product is designed *"intentionally"* to enable sustained performance at moments of need and most often at *Points-of-Work.* Those solution assets are not training assets; they are characterized by **"Just enough - Just in time - Just for me"** and are accessible in the workflow using *Digital Adoption Platform (DAP) Technology*. If designed appropriately, those assets are re-used during formal training in experiential, scenario-based exercises that mirror *Point-of-Work* and are applied using the same DAP technology. There is no other way to say it...We *"intentionally"* bring *Point-of-Work (Performance)* into *Point-of-Entry (Training)*.

The assets designed *intentionally* enable immediate access with *"Just enough"* information to overcome a moment of need that is usually *task-centric & role-specific*. Under these conditions, it's easy to see how small and targeted these assets may become. Being that small and diverse and numerous based on the universe of tasks and discreet roles, another disruption surfaces:

- How in the world do we author these assets?
- How can we deliver this flood of assets into the workflow?
- How do we keep these assets current?
- How do we integrate these assets into Training and *Point-of-Work* simultaneously?
- How do we ensure that access to them is seamless, frictionless, and ubiquitous?

Answers to these questions are addressed by the DAP technology depending on the vendor selected.

CONFESSION: *There are several leading DAP vendors; however, each has its sweet spot. Evaluation and selection of a DAP vendor require a comprehensive assessment of your unique business requirements before pursuing bright shiny objects or being seduced by a compelling sales pitch. It would be best if you had Current State requirements AND future migration projections because DAP implementations start small and scale. What is needed today must also serve tomorrow in both increased application volumes and covering additional business systems.*

Solution Delivery

Legacy learning technology, like the LMS, has a role and continues to have a role, though becoming more secondary as a Workflow delivery tool. The LMS is great for launching compliance eLearning like *Fire Safety* courses but does not have the agility for *Point-of-Work* moments of need urgency like *"hair on fire."*

There are no business risks or urgency to perform during formal training; it is a safe environment. We are very good at this and can prove our activity levels and successes, but only at evaluation levels 1 & 2. We will always need the LMS for this tracking and maintaining training history. Still, **Digital Adoption Platform (DAP) Technology** offers the best *Just enough – Just in time – Just for me* solutions that are agile and responsive enough to address the immediacy of workflow challenges…AND…contextually in the active Workflows.

Intentionally Designed Solution assets vary based upon moments of need; hence the essential nature of the PWA. Some moments of need are **tactical** in nature, and the solutions are called Performance Support. Cloud-based **Digital Adoption Platform (DAP) Technology** enables seamless, frictionless, and ubiquitous accessibility at the moment of need AND contextually inside the application workflow. Bob Mosher describes contextual delivery as successful if accomplished within *"2-clicks or 10-seconds"*.

Digital Insight Curation Engines (ICE)

What about **strategic** asset solution delivery where moments of need require optimized *speed-to-insight* essential for supporting *critical thinking* and *informed decision-making*? Cloud-based **Digital Insight Curation Engines - ICE** have become the technology of choice. Curation is popular today but is also a source of bulk knowledge gluttony that overwhelms our workforce.

Here is some context around *curation gluttony* that needs to be considered, not to mention that it is happening right under our noses.

Does curated content ever reach the point (*or the right person*) to deliver knowledge, wisdom, and insights essential for *critical thinking* and *informed decision-making* to drive productivity forward? How much productivity is diverted to non-productive activities (*like extensive reading*) despite curated content intended to accelerate productivity? Curated content that arrives as bulk information can blow up productivity upon delivery by pulling a worker off-task to re-read what has been curated to extract the useful information needed. Content curation is a necessary evil that can quickly deliver a tsunami of non-productive time if it is not optimized early. Starting a file *"to read later"* is not sustainable, no matter how well intended, and at the expense of missing important information buried in the bulk.

When you consider that roughly 2% (*according to Pandexio*) of bulk knowledge embedded within curated content is extractable as wisdom and supportive of critical thinking, and essential for establishing *actionable insights*, we can see that the act of content curation alone is only part of the cost to get to the 2%. What if the curated content is *limited* to the embedded relevant insights...the *embedded actionable 2%* of knowledge and wisdom BEFORE the original curated content is forwarded?

How much productive time would be protected by everyone no longer being tasked to reread the original curations to extract the *"right insights?"*

Do the math...take two documents...read by 8-team members... require a 20-minute read each...and only on the project-relevant curated content. To me, that looks like 5-hours of productive time spent reading what had *already* been curated as bulk information. Plus...what guarantee do we have that the eight readers will extract the same 2%...or the *"right insights?"* What if they find *"other relevant insights"* that might be missed by the original curators or their team members? How are those new insights shared?

How do they capture their *"new insights"* and share them with the rest of the team without prompting another reading? They don't! Who has that kind of time? How many times will those same curated content documents get re-forwarded to perpetuate a *"rinse & repeat"* cycle of distracting the productive time of another worker? Sure, they're gaining positive knowledge and wisdom and forming their insights, but at what cost?

This scenario is one I've lived over and over in previous corporate gigs. Remember that this fictitious example is not unlike our day-to-day workflows as knowledge workers. If *accelerating productivity* is something we seek, I'm convinced part of the solution includes eliminating or minimizing the non-productive cycles we spend in pursuit of generating actual productivity.

One such solution is increasing **Speed-To-Insight** using a cloud-based *Insight Curation Engine (ICE)* technology like Pandexio to accomplish something I've referred to as **Curation 2.0.** *(See Figure 11-2)* Following is a sample workflow:

1. Curator extracts the relevant 2% from bulk knowledge from multiple sources

2. Highlight *actionable insight(s)* using 140-characters

3. Clarify the 140-character *insight* with a free-text abstract note

4. Tag the *actionable insight* with multiple relevant keywords

5. Group the *insights* by Topic (*multiple keywords also are tagged*)

6. Save the *insight* in a searchable Digital Brain accessible by a specific recipient, group distribution list, or the whole enterprise

7. Attach the source document to the *insight* as an *optional* read versus making the primary task to reread the entire document

8. Enable recipients to capture their *insights* and share by repeating 1 through 7

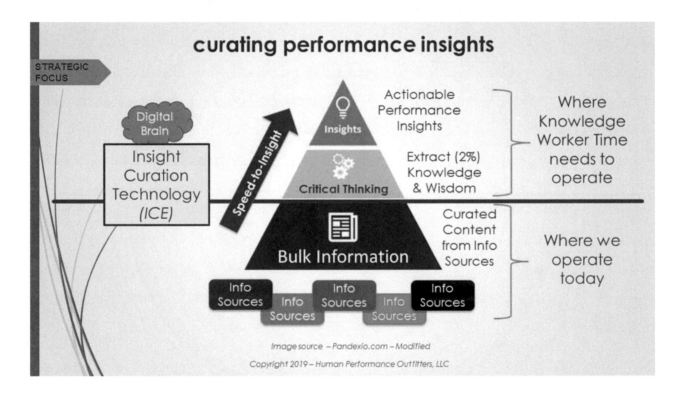

Figure 11-2

The graphic shows that our current state processes are operating below the red line. If we operate above the red line, we can accelerate **Speed-to-Insight** by curating those Insights from the 2% of knowledge and wisdom buried in the curated bulk information to highlight **Actionable Performance Insights** BEFORE distributing the content. Why burden knowledge workers to grind through and extract (*curate*) already curated content to extract their *Actionable Insights* in hopes that they are the *right insights*? That performance restrainer falls under the PWA discovery category of *workflow/process* and *content/resource* improvements that directly **protect the productive time** of each worker in their workflow on the receiving end of curated Bulk Information distributions. Is there a solution that enables this productive time saver?

The answer is "YES!" A new cloud-based technology – **Insight Curation Engines (ICE)** – enables a scalable solution suited to any role where *"Curation"* takes place. L&D would be a great example where curation plays a role in sourcing relevant learning materials for development and sharing with the workforce. Here's another example that may not be so obvious; capturing Insights from soon-to-retire Boomers with heads full of IP…extracting those Insights, and plugging them into a searchable **Digital Brain** by Topic.

There's little doubt that enabling *user-generated knowledge* is a rapidly growing necessity in sustaining a dynamic Learning Performance Ecosystem. I'm not suggesting that ICE technology is exclusive to the L&D function. However, I wish our teams had access to these capabilities while researching bulk knowledge sources that supported learning content and performance support solution design, development, and delivery in previous lives.

But there's more…there may be a more extensive audience scattered across the ecosystem. Consider boomers with hard drives, heads, and hearts full of knowledge, hard-earned wisdom, shortcuts, undocumented best practices, and countless *actionable insights* who are poised to abandon ship in retirement. Yes, those same souls are about to retire and walk right out the door with all that knowledge, wisdom, and insight to go fishing forever. Would it be more cost-effective to curate that walking knowledge, archive, and capture their wisdom and insights now rather than attempt to reacquire what was once in-house?

Hmmm…so maybe it's not all about curating new content…maybe it's also about capturing embedded knowledge as brain-based *intellectual property* while still in-house property.

Whether DAP or ICE assets are integrated as Workflow support, it remains foundational that they are all *intentionally designed* based upon accurately defined attributes at *Point-of-Work* that represent the source(s) of root cause(s) behind performance deficiency.

Solution Impact

Collecting data is the rage these days, and as is often the case, more is collected than is of value. Why do we collect it? Because we can. Virtually every enterprise system produces utilization data. Virtually all are API-capable and can pass data to digital warehouses and business intelligence technology. Tracking performance data is enabled through xAPI and Learning Record Stores – (*LRSs*), and all can populate performance dashboards. DAP and ICE have onboard analytics that track asset utilization and user engagement. In its infancy is the next wave of performance analytics supported by Artificial Intelligence (AI) beginning in manufacturing where complex process elements are of primary focus.

All this tracking capability is reasonable, provided a plan is in place to confirm that the correct data is captured and for the right reasons. Again, the PWA addresses Impact/Analytics as part of the discovery assessment to ensure our analytics addiction is controlled and...*intentional.*

So, is *intentional design* disruptive or non-disruptive? The simple answer is "YES!" I hope you see that *intentional design* is much broader than *instructional design* in scope and application.

- The PWA is *intentionally designed* for the L&D Performance Strategists to assess their respective *Points-of-Work* before collaborating on design requirements with ISD.
- ISD uses *intentional design* informed by PWA assessment findings to build asset solutions for both *Point-of-Work* Workflow applications and formal Training.
- Integration of Productivity Acceleration Technologies are *intentionally designed* to scale with Digital Transformation initiatives and ongoing performance challenge priorities in keeping with *start small - then scale* best practices.
- Impact and Analytics data are captured and analyzed based on *intentionally designed* evaluation plans.

PART 3

PERFORMANCE RESTRAINER ATTRIBUTES

CHAPTER 12

POINT-OF-WORK ASSESSMENT: ENVIRONMENT & CULTURE

In the following chapters, we will take a closer look at each of the six-performance restrainer attribute clusters found in every Ecosystem and covered in PWA discovery. We will examine performance-restraining attributes with accompanying specific discovery questions. We will begin with **Environment & Culture**. (*See Figure 12-1*)

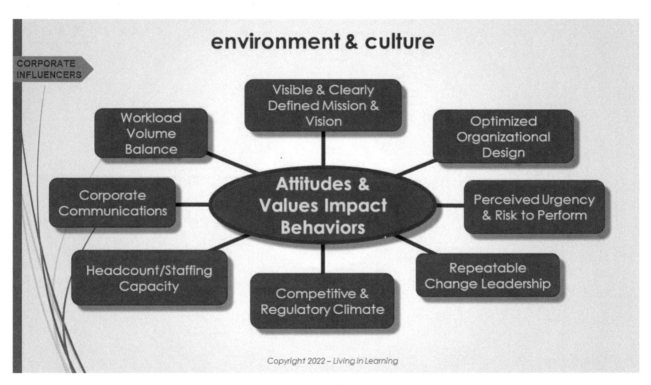

Figure 12-1

Ask ten people to define Culture and expect ten different definitions. I typically begin interviews with an innocent question like, *"What's it like to work here?"* So much of what shapes the culture in any environment is in the heads and hearts of the workers who live in the environment daily, and their *Attitudes* and *Values* shape their *Thinking,* and how they think shapes their *Behavior*. This is rich ground from which to harvest cultural thinking even without the interviewee's ability to define culture.

The rest of what you see influencing the Environment in *Figure 12-1* above can be internal and/or external. As shown in the graphic, we seek behavioral agility to respond to the potential influencers... or the inability to do so.

When Training is requested, our (L&D's) first inclination is to deliver a solution responsively and effectively. It's what we do and what is expected of us and part of a *learning culture*. It's also part of the perspective that perpetuates our existing paradigm (*Myth*) that limits, if not prevents, a deliverable of measurable solution outcomes our stakeholders seek. There's nothing wrong with building a *learning culture*...but at the expense of a *performance culture*? Training advocates think my position is just *word-smithing*, but I would call it something more accurate – *mind-smithing*. Learning opportunities for our workforce are essential for personal and career growth...but at the expense of neglecting enablement of measurable performance and workforce job satisfaction at the *Point-of-Work*? If performance does not happen, who cares about learning? Our Learners don't care how many courses they take; they care about how productive they are in their job roles.

Do we excel at learning and then fall short of creating an environment where the workforce can perform effectively by applying that learning to deliver productivity and business value at their *Points-of-Work*? I am happy to call *Learning a desirable by-product* while performing in the Workflow, but not what is the primary objective. Yes, it is the objective for L&D, but is that the same objective for the operational stakeholder? Methinks not, and I would prefer to be on the same page as my stakeholder with expectations framed as performance outcomes not completed training.

The underlying reality and motivation for operational stakeholders making training requests are likely prompted by productivity or performance deficiencies at one or more *Points-of-Work*. Those requests are based upon a *learning culture* and a belief (Myth) that *training drives performance* and that perception frames the limits of the existing paradigm and perpetuates the *Myth*. If leadership believes this to be true, how do we take top-down perspectives and successfully assess what bottom-up realities dictate as effective and sustainable solutions that will accelerate productivity at *Point-of-Work*?

Though *accelerated productivity* is often not clearly articulated in the original request, no stakeholder turns away from that as a measurable outcome. *Figure 12-2* is another snippet from the *Point-of-Work Assessment (PWA) Workshop.* It illustrates the assessment flow that begins at the top, or as close to the top as accessible, to understand the *perspectives, assumptions, hypotheses, and objectives* of the Requestor(s). This early effort is essential to establish an ALIGNMENT of expectations, urgency, and priorities prompting the request, the target work group, and desired tangible productivity/performance outcomes.

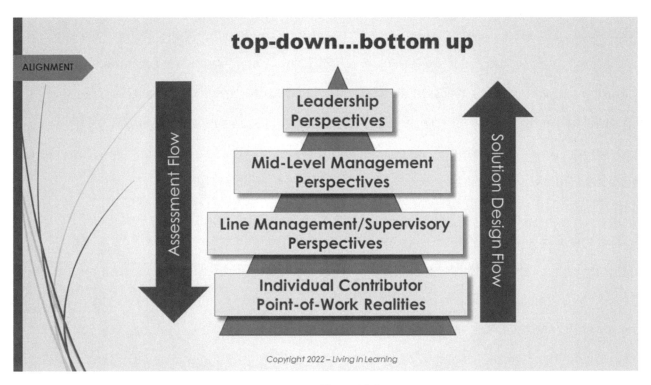

Figure 12-2

Those top-down perspectives often differ from the REALITIES revealed at the *Point-of-Work*. Assessment at targeted *Points-of-Work* will render the *realities* of actual root cause(s) that combine to restrain productivity and sub-par performance known most intimately by the Individual Contributor workforce tasked to execute; that degree of intimacy is not part of the reality known by most layers of leadership above and far removed from the reality of work.

That's not leadership's fault; it's just not in the scope of their day-to-day reality. It is, however, part of the ENVIRONMENT we must assess. Earlier, I mentioned leadership *assumptions* and *hypotheses* behind training requests…those are the things we must *assess, test, validate or invalidate* based on the attributes we confirm as realities found at *Point-of-Work*.

Task-centric and *role-specific* attributes that limit or restrain productivity at *Point-of-Work* become the basis for road mapping a blend of solution deliverables from the *bottom-up*. These attributes are defined by ground zero, where we find poor productivity and performance outcomes that serve as source information to inform and launch **intentional, blended-solution design** projects.

ORDER-takers formulate solutions based on requests that often are flavored by top-down perspectives of what's causing the problems. PERFORMANCE Consultants absorb the top-down perspectives to do a better job with *Point-of-Work* assessment to enable validated bottom-up solution recommendations.

No muss, no fuss, right? If only changing traditions were that simple…First things first…

Change Management – Preparing the ENVIRONMENT & Refocusing the CULTURE

Using the PWA and building holistic learning performance solutions represents our end game. The end game assumes a Learning Performance Paradigm has been adopted as part of what shapes the organization's culture. Indeed, L&D represents a significant adoptee and plays the primary role in execution in this culture, BUT…L&D and a PWA cannot be sprung upon unsuspecting operational stakeholders as a new secret weapon. Remember, we've sold them (*for years*) on the old paradigm (*the Myth*) that *training drives performance*. We have some conversations that need to change in this refocused culture before unleashing a new approach as our response when fielding training requests.

CONFESSION: *I mention unsuspecting stakeholders in the preceding paragraph, but what's even more important is unsuspecting leadership in L&D. If your leadership is not sponsoring the Point-of-Work discipline, you will be pushing a very large stone uphill. My first DAP deployment was evidence of this when a risk-averse boss denied our request for funding. The eventual deployment and implementation were successful, but getting there was complicated and delayed by politics and failure to gain sponsorship from L&D leadership first. Honestly, that scenario is why I built the PWA because it could change the conversation with stakeholders AND within my L&D leadership.*

Adoption of a Learning Performance Paradigm (LPP) is not limited to L&D – adoption must include the business's operational side, top-down acceptance, and *visible, accessible, and engaged sponsorship* to be sustainable. LPP must become a refocusing force to evolve beyond a limited *learning culture* and adopt a *performance culture*.

"Visible and Accessible Sponsorship" is essential to establish comprehensive communications because all levels of management need to be on the same page. Alignment and buy-in are essential because *"how far from the top"* our top-down assessments begin will vary depending upon the complexity of the request. From senior leadership to mid-level to line-level supervisory management roles, all need to know and understand the new face of engagement to expect from L&D. As I mentioned earlier, *PWAs* are not Training Needs Assessments.

I cannot stress enough that a thorough understanding of the workforce's ENVIRONMENT at their respective *Points-of-Work* and the underlying influences of CULTURE impact productivity and performance. Here are three perspectives that a PWA considers:

- **Corporate:** Culture/Mission/Vision; Corp Communications; Repeatable Change Leadership Model; Reward & Recognition; Empathy; Diversity & Inclusion; etc.
- **Internal:** Organizational Design; Degree of Work Difficulty; Cross Team/Departmental Dependencies/Accountability; Budget Restrictions; Urgency/Risk; etc.
- **External:** Competition; Product/Service Mix; Company Consolidation; Reduction-n-Force; M&A Implications; Regulatory & Legal Compliance; etc.

These are not exhaustive lists by any means; instead, they are only examples of numerous attributes that can play a role in restraining productivity/performance. Some of what you see above have tactical implications, and others fall into more personal motivating...or demotivating impacts.

PWA interview questions like those that follow often provide dynamic and revealing answers across multiple work groups. Capturing diverse perspectives and opinions is precisely what we are seeking to discover because our solution mix may be equally as diverse across roles.

The questions in the following matrix are considered core questions and do not represent an exhaustive list. Additional follow-up questions (*Active Listening*) to expand upon responses are to be expected and encouraged. The most potent follow-up questions you can ask for clarification of root causes include:

- *"Why?" "Tell me more." "What do you think causes...?"*
- *"What happens when that happens...?"*

When responses indicate the potential for repetitive errors or multiple occurrences, always attempt to quantify. We need *measurable impacts* on time, resources, output volumes, and money if we have a prayer of showing evidence of impact at Levels 3 & 4:

- *"How often does that happen...?" "How much time does it take to resolve...?"*
- *"How much delay is introduced to work time...?"*
- *"When that happens, how much does it cost us...?"*

Following in *Matrix 12-3* is a partial list of sample questions from the PWA Workshop. It is important to note that only some questions on this matrix would be asked during an interview, and targets for building a <u>Core Question Set</u> would be framed during the Alignment Conversation with the Requestor. Also, it is typical for the direction of the interview to change by making different questions a better fit.

Confession: *One of the worst habits to fall into is creating a list of questions you can read verbatim in an interview. A list is not bad, just don't read down the list as you ask questions. It is way too easy to focus on your next question and not actively listen to the answers you are given.*

#	ATTRIBUTE CATEGORY	DISCOVERY QUESTIONS
		How does the organization describe company culture? - How does that culture description differ from what you experience in your work area? - What's different in your area of responsibility? - How could it be improved?
		For someone coming into this role brand new, would this work environment leave positive or negative first impressions? Why? What were your first impressions? If negative, what do you feel would prevent or improve that impression?
		In your role what do you see as your most valuable contributions to the mission of this organization?
		Of the areas under your scope of work which would you tag as highest priority &/or most URGENT to perform effectively? - What makes them highest priority? What's at risk?
		What do you feel are the greatest RISKS (resulting consequences) associated with issues that prevent/impede successful completion of work in your job responsibility? - Define the sources of those risks - What are the potential impacts to the business?
	ENVIRONMENT/CULTURE	On a scale of 1 to 10 how balanced is your workload compared to you and your team's capacity? What contributes to the imbalance?
		What are the top three sources of challenge or difficulty that interfere or limit your productive time?
		On a scale of 1-to-10, how effective do you feel current L&D solutions are in producing your requested performance outcomes?
		On a scale of 1 to 10 how cohesive & engaged is your group/team? What would improve it?
		What other work teams/groups/functions do you depend upon to accomplish your work tasks accurately and on time? Challenges?
		What other work teams/groups/functions depend upon your work output for their subsequent task-level work? Challenges?
		Are corporate-level communications effective to the extent you feel well-informed on top priorities? - If not, how could they be improved?
		As Changes to the business take place, do you feel communications are handled effectively and consistently? - If not, how could communications be improved? As Changes take place, do you feel you receive clear expectations specific to your contributions to the business? - If not, how could it be improved?

Matrix 12-3

At the top of my bucket list, I'd like to facilitate a discussion in the deep carpet of the board room addressing an organization's senior leadership and request, *"Individually describe your culture in two or three words"* on a sheet of paper, collect, and then read them aloud. What do you think would happen? How closely would their two or three-word descriptions match? Would any Leadership Team even agree to the exercise? Or would we receive an invitation to leave?

Not sure if I'll ever get to check this adventure off my bucket list, but methinks it would reveal an interesting dynamic at the top. Why do this?

If the definition of *culture* varies at the top, what definitions and realities would you expect to consistently, if any, exist downstream? Those variances could validate findings taken back to the top for debrief, especially if *Workforce Engagement* is on the radar to address.

Here's a sobering thought – ***The absence of a cohesive culture…IS a culture!***

"So...what's it like to work here?" I'm certainly not an expert on culture, but I am pretty sure asking a simple question like this could reveal a great deal of insight at multiple levels and paint an interesting abstract.

CHAPTER 13

POINT-OF-WORK ASSESSMENT: PEOPLE & CAPABILITY

Next, we will examine the restraining attributes specific to People & Capability, followed by more specific discovery questions (*See Figure 13-1*)

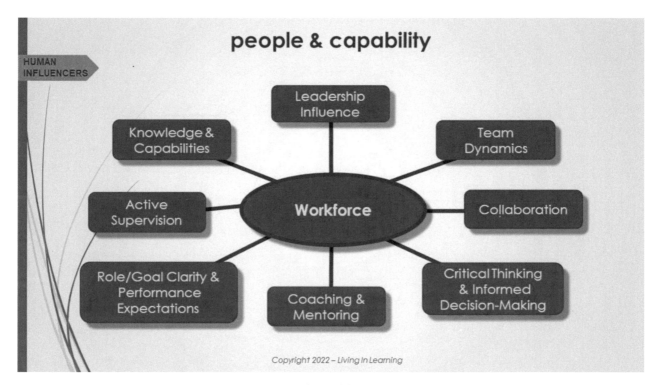

Figure 13-1

This graphic is from the Point-of-Work Assessment (PWA) Workshop and focuses on the Workforce (*Human*) attributes that influence roles and capabilities at *Point-of-Work*. Typically, when we (*L&D*) consider the *"People"* variable in our training solutions, the key focus is on the Learner and essential job-related knowledge transfer requirements.

That's not wrong; it's just not enough...

Suppose sustained and measurable workforce performance at *Point-of-Work* is the end game. In that case, we cannot take this narrow focus, or we risk missing multiple influencers that drive or restrain productivity/performance, as shown above. (*See Figure 13-1*)

It is safe to say that raising workforce competency takes a village. That leaves us with pivotal questions, *"Who is the village? Where is the village? How will the village help? Is assistance from the village accessible in the workflow?"*

As you see in *Figure 13-1*, there are eight clusters of attributes specific to human influences on the performance of the Workforce. The degree of influence varies, some more direct than others, but suffice it to say none should be discounted or overlooked; therefore, it should be included in every PWA effort.

Leadership Influence

It's funny how Leadership is often the Requestor and turns out to be a guilty party contributing to restraining influence on productivity and performance. Sound like a minefield? It can be if findings are flavored with blame. *Clarity of Performance Expectations* surface in the PWA:

- Do workers expect what they are to do in their assigned roles?
- Do workers clearly understand *"What good looks like?"*
- Do Primary Workers receive enough active supervision to ensure clear direction, and are reinforcement resources accessible?
- Is feedback immediate and relevant to performance outcomes?

Team Dynamics

In some ways, Team Dynamics overlap with Environment & Culture when considering things like *Engagement and Motivation*. And it's important to note that I'm not talking about engagement in the process of taking Training classes but engagement in the collaborative process to achieve success at the *Point-of-Work*. Team Dynamics extends beyond the concept of roles when you consider the impact on the Primary Worker on a personal level, like *Career Development and Performance Management* interactions. Are these interactions built on consistency, integrity, and freedom from fear?

Collaboration, Coaching & Mentoring

Do Primary Workers work in an environment with *Trusting Relationships* with managers and peers? Do the Primary Workers have the opportunity to *Collaborate* and build relationships through *Peer-to-Peer Networking*? Does the organization facilitate the ability for *Collaboration* and *Knowledge Sharing*?

Role/Goal Clarity & Performance Expectations

We must clearly understand who the Primary Workers are:

- Who does the work?
- Is the role clearly understood?
- Are performance expectations clear and concise?

Not to be overlooked are those individuals (*likely with different roles and responsibilities*) who are

Secondary Workers

- Who supervises the Primary Worker?
- Who coaches? Who mentors?
- Who provides *Active Supervision*?
- Who supports moments of need during the workflow?

Further downstream (*or even upstream*), there may be **Tertiary Workers** who have interdependencies that should be considered:

- Who are the end-consumers of the Primary Worker's output?
- Do vendors play a role? Affiliates? Re-Sellers?
- Are there other entities that could benefit from the Primary Worker's solution?

Workforce Knowledge Capabilities

Workforce Capabilities deal directly with *"readiness to perform"* instead of *"completed training."* L&D (*Training*) is part of competency development; however, it is not the silver bullet. Competency is reached over time and through hands-on experience at the *Point-of-Work,* along with knowledge gained through mistakes and failures in the workflow. Is *"in the workflow"* support available? Mentors? Coaching? How much attention is paid to ensuring the ability to *Think Critically*? Are those support resources aligned with the right competencies? Have we identified the most impactful mistakes?

The PWA is designed to discover those mistakes and their impact on business value and then refine learning and performance support assets to eliminate/minimize their occurrence. Status quo strategies are not sustainable when Performance outcomes form our primary focus, especially when we consider other Truth(s) that Training alone cannot handle effectively:

- Every organization owns a Dynamic Learning **Performance** Ecosystem
- Training drives Potential – not Performance – dispelling the *Myth*
- Performance manifests ONLY at the *Point-of-Work* in Workflows
- Knowledge retention degrades before Workers can APPLY it at *Point-of-Work*
- Competency cannot be *"trained in."* It is reached over time and with practice on the job – How much time and cost are incurred due to errors and mistakes?
- There are 5-Moments of Need – Training ONLY addresses 2 of them (*New & More*) – the other three manifest in workflows at *Points-of-Work* (*Apply, Solve & Change*)
- Workforce sustainability & value generation happens at *Point-of-Work.* Is that where L&D shows up ill-equipped or, worse, MIA altogether?

Confession: *If you have not figured it out by now, I can unleash more passion than may be necessary to drive home a point, but hey, that's what thirty-five years in this profession can do to a person. I respect the disciplines of L&D but have little tolerance for maintaining the status quo when the survival of our at-large organization is at stake. I've been downsized from Training organizations three times in seven years, and none of them addressed Performance as a priority. None of those Reductions in Force would have been necessary if L&D functions had a positive, measurable business impact. Being busy does not spell impact...it spells cost center. Don't be a cost center...be a Performance Ninja.*

Following in *Matrix 13-2* is a partial list of sample questions from the PWA Workshop:

#	ATTRIBUTE CATEGORY	DISCOVERY QUESTIONS
		On a scale of 1 to 10 how collaborative is your group/team with knowledge-sharing? How could that be improved?
		How do you collaborate with SMEs/peers/partners to share knowledge and best practices?
		What, if anything, would you like to see change to better facilitate sharing and collaboration within your team and across other teams?
		Of your current job responsibilities which of them would you tag most difficult or time-consuming? Why?
		Considering whom you depend upon for success, and who depends upon you – What obstacles do you encounter? - Why do you think these obstacles exist and what would improve or overcome them?
		Did your onboarding experience enable you and/or your team to be effective at your job? - If not, what would you add/change/delete to improve it?
		Prior to starting your current job role, what about your training would you add more of...prefer less of...or simply delete altogether to be better prepared?
	PEOPLE/CAPABILITY	How has the training you receive changed in the recent past? - What additional changes do you feel would improve training efficiency & effectiveness?
		As you grow in your current role do you feel existing training opportunities are sufficient to help you develop? - If not, what would you like to see added as options to increase your skills and capabilities?
		How are training concepts supported/reinforced after you are back on the job? - How could support or reinforcement be improved?
		In your role do you feel performance goals and/or performance expectations were clearly defined? - How could additional clarity of your role/performance expectations be improved?
		Who provides coaching/mentoring to you/your team? - Is it sufficient? If not, what would you change to improve those opportunities?
		If your role requires that you coach or mentor others, do you feel you have been adequately prepared and equipped to be effective? - If not, what do you feel would improve your coaching/mentoring capabilities?
		If your role requires leading your team's day-to-day activities - encouraging their engagement - driving productivity, what are your toughest challenges?

Matrix 13-2

Regarding this list of questions, should you ask all of them? Not likely. During your pre-interview preparations and in the Alignment phase with your Requestor, you should have a general idea of which questions are most relevant and should receive priority.

Confession: *As a new Performance Consultant, I had a tendency, also known as a bad habit, of heading toward a solution before the problem was thoroughly revealed. This is especially hard for an L&D pro who knows beyond a shadow of a doubt that this solution will be built in Articulate. Articulate may get the call, but eight of the fifteen objects built into Articulate could be stand-alone Performance Support Objects available in Workflows at Moments of Need. That design decision is part of the Intentional Design discussed in Chapter 11. Best advice... sit on your hands and listen with no preconceived solution judgments.*

CHAPTER 14

POINT-OF-WORK ASSESSMENT: WORKFLOWS & PROCESSES

Workflow & Process performance attributes help us understand relevant *task-centric, role-specific* work situations that either drive or restrain productivity and performance at multiple *Points-of-Work*. Typically, every PWA will have elements that restrain performance within this segment. What is most critical is defining the nature of restraint from broken or non-optimized processes from knowledge and skill gaps associated with Workforce competencies.

(*See Figure 14-1*)

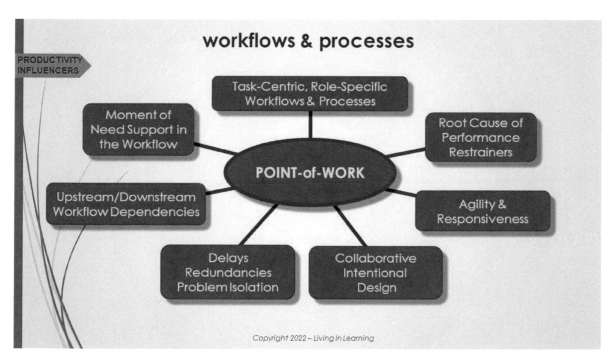

Figure 14-1

Both Workforce and L&D *Point-of-Work* perspectives are influenced in *Figure 14-1*. Every element in the graphic applies to both; Workforce, specific to job execution, and L&D, from a solution design perspective. Each aligns with their discreet *Points-of-Work*. There are seven influencers shown above that are related to Workflows & Processes that impact the Workforce and, equally as necessary, are specific to L&D functions:

- Identify restrained workflows and processes by roles and tasks
- Assess root causes restraining productivity and performance at *Points-of-Work*
- Develop road maps for learning performance solutions to inform subsequent design that supports workflow agility and responsiveness to change
- Collaborative support of *Intentional Design* and development of *Moment of Need/Point-of-Work* asset solutions (*Discussed in Chapter 11*)
- Isolating workflow delays and redundancies that restrict optimized operations
- Identifying ripple effects upstream and downstream that influence performance
- Define access, recommend, and manage Moment of Need access to and delivery of *Point-of-Work* solution assets in the Workflow

1 – Task-Centric & Role-Specific Workflows & Processes – Individual Contributor Focus

Workflows & Processes that directly generate [*or compromise*] tangible business value by our workforce are characterized by assorted **TASKS** and assigned by different **ROLES**. Cat herding comes to mind almost immediately because of the diversity of moving parts. The implied solution design by L&D requires us to compartmentalize by *priority* where we discover the most significant business risk, determine where the greatest reward is to be found…and then build learning performance solutions to overcome or achieve them. That *prioritization* happens during our Bottom-Up debrief with the Requestor. The Requestor defines priorities based on our PWA Findings.

Then? Rinse & Repeat on each subsequent priority until the effort to overcome or achieve becomes more expensive than the return on the solution results. Don't recommend a $5,000 solution to a $300 problem.

Primarily, we are focused on how work gets done:

- What is/are the root cause(s) contributing to workflow challenges?
- Knowledge gaps cause how much restraint?
- How much restraint is related to broken processes?
- How prepared is the workforce to be effective in their task-level work?
- How much support to function effectively is accessible within workflows?
- How much of the perceived performance challenge is caused elsewhere?

2 – Root Cause of Performance Restrainers

This segment is a primary L&D discovery skill set that requires a degree of business acumen/savvy and business awareness to handle discussions and interviews with operational stakeholders at multiple levels. Typically, this role requires skills found in Performance Consultants or Performance Strategists, and I have seen capable Instructional Designers fill the role with some guidance.

The objectives in this phase target where to begin based on the most significant impact. *"Greatest impact"* is stakeholder-defined in terms of exposure to business loss, liability, delay, creation of material waste, or other anomalies affecting bottom-line results.

3 – Agility and Responsiveness

Discovery details from identified root causes revealed in the PWA serve as source input that informs subsequent collaborative *intentional design* discussions. When performance manifests in the workflow, our solution design must be as *agile* as the workflow in which it is applied, and our workforce is as *responsive* to the constant dynamics of day-to-day Change. The Solution Design Road Map supports a *different conversation* critical to a shift in thinking that *Training* is the only answer…to integrating Learning Performance solutions at Moments of Need and within workflows found at the *Point-of-Work.*

4 – Collaborative Intentional Design

Chapter 11 introduced the **7-Right Things**. We will look at them again in the context of the Solution Design Road Map responsibility belonging to the L&D Performance Consultant/Strategist. This role summarizes the sources of restraining attributes impacting productivity and performance. The objective is to produce the source document from which the Consultant/Strategist collaborates with Instructional Design and Development resources to apply whatever agile design methodologies they have adopted.

Whatever design methodology is used, *intentionality is* aligned with workflow performance and should frame the design criteria. PWA discovery findings should clearly define the complexity of deficient performance and the reasons behind it. Sometimes, a deeper dive into Workflows & Processes requires a more robust agile design methodology like the <u>Five Moments of Need (5MoN)</u>.

Once again, the PWA is not a design methodology like 5MoN; instead, PWA serves as a *front-end pre-design diagnostic* intended to identify where a methodology like 5MoN should be utilized for deeper Task Analysis for detailed solution design. In short, PWA informs 5MoN design decisions where the *intentions* are focused on specific assets for accelerating productivity and performance by closing gaps at affected *Points-of-Work*.

The primary drivers for *intentionally designed* assets include:

- **Accessibility** at the Moment of Need
- **Relevance** to identified roles tasked within the Workflow
- **Effectiveness** at the Moment of Need when APPLIED at the *Point-of-Work*
- **Sustainability** of post-development currency after insertion into the ecosystem

PWA informs the **Intentional Design** of learning performance assets (*often Performance Support*) characterized by encompassing **7-Right Things:** *(See Figure 14-2)*

Figure 14-2

These *7-Right Things* are foundational to Learning Performance Solution assets regardless of the agile design methodology utilized.

- **RIGHT ACCESS** is most critical of all
  - For solution assets to be most *effective* and *efficient* in the application, the Workforce must have access from within their Workflow.
  - *Seamless* and *Frictionless* describe streamlined access where the Workforce does not need to waste time searching, remembering where to find them, or exiting their workflow to gain access to the asset.
  - The asset design should be as *Agile* in the application as the Moment of Need dictates for a successful problem resolution.
  - *Ubiquitous* access from an active Workflow that enables immediate access to assets at any time, from anywhere, and from any device.

Effective and Efficient application of the content Intentionally Designed for problem resolution follows a phrase picked up at a conference years ago from Aaron Silvers in an xAPI breakout session. xAPI assets were characterized by being small in size and targeted to specific work; hence the phrase – *Just Enough – Just In Time – Just For Me*. The phrase stuck with me and fitted perfectly in the *Intentional Design* conversation.

- **RIGHT AMOUNT –** *Just Enough* describes intentional designs that *"fit"* the need. This is a perfect definition of a job aid or quick reference asset designed for a specific Task.
- **RIGHT TIME –** *Just In Time* speaks to accessing the asset while engaged in the workflow at a specific Moment of Need.
- **RIGHT WORKER –** *Just For Me* speaks to an intentionally designed asset for a specific role.
- **RIGHT FORMAT –** Relates in many ways to the Ubiquitous requirements of the Right Access but from a design perspective. Does the content need to be accessible from several different devices? Can every potential device handle video? Do we need to consider responsive design to enable screen sizes across multiple device platforms?

- **RIGHT TECHNOLOGY** – Technology is a two-way proposition. Are we accessing the right technology to PULL assets in Moments of Need...AND...do we even have access to that technology from our device? On the flip side, do the devices in the hands of the workforce interface with the technology that will PUSH assets to them in Workflows?
- **RIGHT EVIDENCE** – Evidence can mean several things:
  - Can we extract evidence of *Impact* from asset application in workflows?
  - Can we extract *Utilization* metrics providing evidence that systems are being accessed and gauging the frequency and proficiency of usage?
  - Are feedback loops provided to channel communications back to asset owners from the Workforce users? This is critical to maintaining currency and fine-tuning when asset applications are unclear or out-of-date.

5 – Solution Asset Maintenance

Managing and maintaining learning performance assets after development and deployment can quickly become the tail that wags the dog. *Intentionally designed* assets vary from training-specific content, to stand-alone performance support, to performance insights enabling critical thinking...to social interaction and collaboration opportunities. Given that these assets are not always destined for formal training, we must consider several things regarding their application at the Moment of Need and workflows at *Points-of-Work*. Questions that require answers include:

- Where are the assets reposited?
- How are solution assets accessed?
- What taxonomy metadata is attached to enable efficient search and ownership?
- Who owns the assets and the ongoing responsibility to maintain currency?
- How are tracking asset utilization analytics accomplished?
- How are updates and new assets communicated to the Workforce?

Confession: *Do not make the mistake of overlooking the creation of protocols for maintaining ownership of content, maintaining visibility of ownership, and providing easily accessible feedback loops to and from end-users with content owners. This becomes extremely important when the number of learning performance assets increases, and I am serious about the asset tail wagging the dog.*

6 – Upstream & Downstream Dependencies

Where do the ripples go if a stone is thrown onto the still surface of a pond? Everywhere, right? Even the edges of the pond receive ripples dependent upon the proximity to the initial point of impact; such are the dependencies in our ecosystems. A core Six Sigma topic (SIPOC) maps the upstream and downstream dependencies from which we may source improved performance. What do upstream processes have to do with our Primary *Point-of-Work* process target? Does a ripple impact our Point-of-Work from upstream? Likewise, what does a change in our Primary *Point-of-Work* process mean to the processes downstream from our target? We need to know both to account for ripples incoming and outgoing accurately. (*See Figure 14-3*)

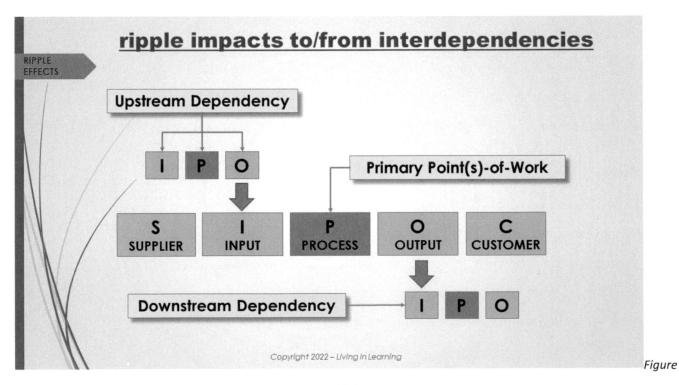

Figure 14-3

In short, *Upstream Processes* create *Output* that becomes *Input* for our *Target Process*. Similarly, our *Target Process* creates *Output* for whomever or whatever *Downstream Process* receives as *Input*. Remember that *ripples* can be significant to others caused by our primary target solution.

7 - Moment of Need Support in the Workflow

Our solution designs need to facilitate the CONVERGENCE of learning performance support opportunities with Workflows. That reduces the viability of Training as a primary solution and escalates smaller targeted Performance Support resources accessible in Moments of Need in Workflows at multiple *Points-of-Work.*

Remember that Performance Support resources may not always be content-based; instead, support may require live collaboration with Business Matter Experts (BMEs), coaches, mentors, or supervisors.

The nature of the *Point-of-Work* challenge and the work context of the Moment of Need will point to the best-fit solution.

Recall the Five Moments of Need:

- **Moment 1 (NEW)** – First-time learning, often during new hire onboarding but may be associated with first-time learning related to a job or function change of an incumbent worker.
- **Moment 2 (MORE)** – Next level of learning, greater complexity, additional advanced learning.
- **Moment 3 (APPLY)** – When the worker must complete a task or decide to take action during a workflow at *Point-of-Work.*
- **Moment 4 (SOLVE)** – When a worker is faced with an anomaly, a broken process, a malfunctioning system, or out-of-date content and needs to revert to Plan B.
- **Moment 5 (CHANGE)** – When routine workflows or processes change due to an update or upgrade in policy, new technology, regulatory demands, etc.

Following in *Matrix 14-4* is a partial list of sample questions from the PWA Workshop:

#	ATTRIBUTE CATEGORY	DISCOVERY QUESTIONS
		What are the most critical tasks you handle in the routine of your job? - What's at risk if these tasks are not effectively and efficiently completed?
		Of the tasks under your current work responsibilities which of them would you tag most difficult?
		What are your greatest pain points or roadblocks associated with those tasks? - What are the obstacles/roadblocks? What causes them to surface? - How often do they occur? - What is the impact to your work productivity when these roadblocks surface? - What do you feel would lessen or remove those pain points?
		After onboarding and new on the job, what key work processes need immediate reinforcement and support in your workflows? - What do you feel would be the most effective way to reinforce or support you in the workflow?
	WORKFLOWS/PROCESSES	When confronted by an issue that stops your workflow, where and/or to whom do you go to for help? - What other options are available to help overcome an issue or challenge during a workflow? - How long does it typically take to find an answer or solution?
		Describe your access to job aids or checklist immediately available the moment they are needed in current work processes or system-based business applications?
		How efficient is the process when searching for help or information resources? - What would improve the search and acquisition of necessary information at your moments of need? - How much time does a typical search require? - How often is search required?
		How are changes to workflows or processes communicated to you? - Are those communications timely and effective? If not, what would improve them?
		How are you trained on changes to workflows or processes? - What kind of follow-up support is provided after training completion?
		If training is not provided, how do you become effective in the new or modified processes or workflows?
		Are there aspects of current workflows you feel are inefficient, redundant, or unnecessary? - If any, what would be the tangible benefit of eliminating or minimizing them?

Matrix 14-4

As you can see, the WORKFLOWS & PROCESSES attributes assessed in the PWA have implications for not only the Workforce environment but the engagement and influencing of L&D decisions regarding solution design and post-deployment support.

Once again, the PWA Methodology is not a design model nor a development tool; instead, PWA is a *front-end pre-design diagnostic discipline* that informs the deeper dive completed during detailed solution design phases where agile design tools and tactics are applied. PWA provides a road map that identifies and prioritizes *what rocks to look under*…not the details of *what's under them.* Please don't consider that wasted motion; rather, the PWA effort *prevents wasted motion*, where we typically build solutions for symptoms and miss root causes altogether.

PWA deliverables facilitate the ***Changed Conversations*** we must have with operational stakeholders to re-examine their training requests to prevent our subsequent training solutions from only partially addressing the productivity and performance challenges they face. Training may or may not be a viable solution, and it's our job to make that distinction, and doing so shifts our role to a true business partner instead of running a drive-through window where orders are quickly filled.

Workflows & Processes represent the most relevant measurable ecosystem attributes contributing to work delays, wasted motion, errors, material waste, business liability, mistakes, rework, redundancies, uninformed decisions, and...and...and...take place. These attributes are essential to quantify if we have a prayer to measure impact at levels 3 & 4.

CONFESSION: *Do not stop questioning when you acquire a good definition of a behavior change. Ask, "SO WHAT?" So what will be the impact in observable performance that we can measure...and by how much. Do not neglect to establish a* **Current State Benchmark,** *so you have something to compare performance changes to after post-solution implementation. It is a mistake to zero in exclusively on training when workflow assets in a dynamic learning performance ecosystem require workflow application, especially when a hard-dollar impact can be attached. Stakeholders want proof...here is where we find the source data to provide it.*

In chapters 18-23, we will examine related considerations for L&D because our Workflows & Processes run parallel with those facing the workforce. New assessments, skills, and technology imply a change to L&D paradigms and solutions. There is an inherent risk in confusing *"ready to change"* with *"readiness to change."* More later...

CHAPTER 15

POINT-OF-WORK ASSESSMENT:

CONTENT & RESOURCES

As we progress through the Point-of-Work Assessment, in previous chapters, we've considered performance attribute clusters specific to *Environment & Culture – People & Capability – Workflows & Processes*. Hopefully, you've seen a degree of overlap and interdependencies among these three clusters. This chapter describes the importance of **Content & Resources** our Workforce relies upon to optimize their performance at task-centric and role-specific levels. As you see in *Figure 15-1,* the potential for performance restrainers has many influencers we need to address in our PWA discovery efforts.

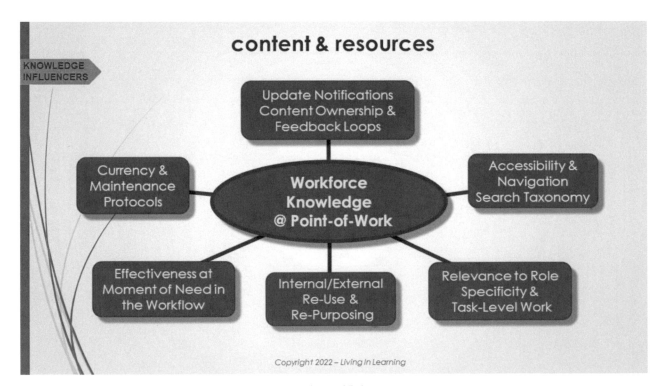

Figure 15-1

POINT-of-WORK ASSESSMENT: Content & Resources

Assessing attributes across critical *Content & Resources* overlaps directly with *Workflows & Processes.* However, it is more specific to efficient accessibility and practical application at the Moment of Need at the *Point-of-Work*. Why? Would you stop assessing the toolbox and not include the tools inside?

The first consideration of significance deals with what form *Content & Resources* take. When considering how our Workforce accomplishes their jobs, we must determine how readily they can get their hands on the *Right* assets (*tools*) at the *Right* time...Recall the *7-Right Things* mentioned earlier in Chapter 11. What that list of tools includes may not always be content based. Consider:

- Job aids and checklists
- Contextually delivered step-by-step instructions – *Pulled at Moment of Need*
- Contextually delivered step-by-step instructions – *Pushed when things have changed, or limits have been exceeded or overlooked*
- Policy documents, Methods & Procedures (M&Ps) or Standard Ops Procedures (SOPs)
- Compliance Guidelines, Rules of Engagement
- Direct contact with Subject-Matter Experts (SMEs) or Business-Matter Experts (BMEs)
- Collaborations with peers, project team members
- Active Supervision in Workflows and Feedback Loops
- Confidence in asset currency and accuracy

You may be able to think of others, but regardless of what may be missing from the list above, there are several commonalities relative to all.

Accessibility & Navigation

Of the 7-Right Things, you may recall that *Accessibility* is at the top of the list. What good are the right assets if they are not readily accessible? What are other factors restraining or wasting productivity specific to accessing the assets?

- By whom should they be accessible?
- What are the work conditions and urgency at the right moment of need?
- How difficult is searching for and finding the right assets?
- How effective is the taxonomy structure and metadata tagging on content?
- How efficient is interfacing/collaborating with the right human assets?
- Does the right technology exist to enable access at the Moment of Need?
- What is the cost to the business when access is restrained or nonexistent?

Relevance to Role Specificity and Task Level Work

Typically, at the Moment of Need, there likely exist degrees of implied urgency to APPLY the asset to resolve the Moment. What are the business implications when that *urgency* is not intentionally factored into the design and delivery of the assets to the Right People (*Just For Me*)? Do we need instructions to build a watch to tell what time it is? Relevance to telling time is one thing, but what about *relevance* to telling time under the workflow's physical, geographic, or network connectivity constraints by functional role? Are there role variances to consider?

Role-specific, individualized designs match roles with tasks and identifiable performance restraints experienced in the workflow at *Point-of-Work*. Remember that *Right People* may include secondary support, coaches, mentors, and vendors/clients/customers.

Task-level centricity is at the core of *Intentional Design,* where *intentionality* is framed by the task(s) to be accomplished and the conditions under which that must happen. The content design of the resource must be formatted and relevant and directly in lockstep with the task, and that can only happen by first determining the nature and complexity of the *task* at the *Point-of-Work*.

Effectiveness at Moment of Need in the Workflow

At first glance, *Effectiveness* sounds much like *Relevance*, and in some respects, they are related; however, *Effectiveness* is borne out by something else - **Results**. Effectiveness is also a function of the Right Time (*Just In Time*) – Moment of Need. Add in the Right Amount (*Just Enough*). Does the worker need to leave the Workflow to access the support asset? This overlaps with Accessibility and Search; the urgency drives both to perform in the Workflow and the business risks associated with performing poorly or with significant delay. DAP technology plays a significant role in addressing accessibility in the moment of need.

Currency & Maintenance Protocols

This is a big one. Retaining the currency of performance assets becomes even more critical when the work environment is fast-moving and susceptible to frequent Change. We do a yeoman's job of creating content and providing resources, but do we have effective *Maintenance* protocols in place? This category overlaps with Update Notifications, Content Ownership, and Feedback

- What is the current process of updating content? How long does that take?
- Who owns the content? Are those owners visible and accessible to End Users?
- How many generations (*versions*) of the original content exist, and where are they?
- How much of the same content is embedded in PDFs, PPTs, Training content, etc.?
- How are changes communicated to the Workforce?
- Are notifications *PUSHed* directly into contextual workflows to protect time on task?
- Do existing resources need to be pulled out of service to perform updates?
- How many approval/review gates do updates have to clear before redeployment?
- What's the cost to the business for delays in performing updates on outdated content?
- Does existing technology enable rapid development and updating of these assets?
- Are we able to measure if our *Maintenance* protocols are even sustainable?
- Do we have visibility to asset utilization co-related with an actual performance at the *Point-of-Work*?
- Is that level of visibility even possible in the current state?

Here we see the interdependency and overlap with attribute clusters *Impact & Analytics* and *Systems & Technology*. Can you see how inaccurate performance support assets that take two weeks to be updated can impact bottom-line performance results? Our client-facing support services are only as well-informed as the *Content & Resources* available to them. It amazes me that updating essential information is not one of the highest response priorities in our ecosystem.

CONFESSION: *Be sure to maintain line-of-sight to content owners with mission-critical support assets and the assets themselves. Jobs change, and content owners transfer or leave the organization. Does a maintenance protocol exist that re-connects content to a new owner? Keep in mind that it is easier to track content by functionality than by owner. That said, set up a "Content Issue Database" and have a role that oversees activity and can serve as a traffic cop to get ownership aligned with an issue as a priority when an issue is reported. Years ago, I suggested that an overseer role like Content Czar was needed to wrangle database issues, but that idea did not fly...maybe I should have been in pajamas with cheap sunglasses at the time....*

Following in *Matrix 15-2* is a partial list of sample questions from the PWA Workshop:

#	ATTRIBUTE CATEGORY	DISCOVERY QUESTIONS
	✚	When you consider the information and resources used in current workflows, which ones are most difficult to access? What contributes to the difficulty?
		Are the resources you utilize effective and easy to apply at the moment of need? - If not, how could they be improved?
		Describe your search process. - How much time would you estimate you spend searching for the right information? - If you could change anything about searching for information or resources, what would it be?
		What information/resources do you need that you currently do not have...or are unable to access quickly?
		How many different content locations do you have to search through to find the information resources you need? - What are they?
		How are the right resources/information accessed when you are engaged in a workflow and encounter a moment of need?
		Once resources have been located, is the content specific enough for immediate application to a task or is additional reading or searching within a document required to find the right information?
		To whom and how do you send notifications to when you find something that is out of date or incorrect? - Do you receive acknowledgement or confirmation concerning receipt of your notification?
	CONTENT/RESOURCES	How are content owners identified, tracked and updated as roles change, promotions, moving job roles, or leaving the company?
		How long does it take for content identified as out of date to be updated? - What is the associated risk/liability in your role if there is any delay?
		How do you access and/or share Knowledge Assets and Best Practices associated with your workflows?
		What home-grown hacks or cheats have you or a colleague developed that have improved work productivity? - Who else in the organization could benefit from these hacks? - How would you accomplish sharing them?
		How is curated content distributed to you/your team? (IE. E-mail attachments, shared drives, forums, etc.) - Do you feel the delivery method and curated content format are optimized? - Do you feel there would be value in having Actionable Insights already extracted from curated content before you had to open and read the entire curated document?
		Are curated content/resources you receive relevant and specific enough to effectively support task-level workflows and processes you handle? - If not, how could they be improved?
		How do you extract insights and actionable knowledge from curated content/resources forwarded to you? (I.E. white papers, articles, blog posts etc.) - How do you share valuable information you discover in your own searches?

Matrix 15-2

As you can see, the CONTENT & RESOURCES attributes assessed in the PWA have implications for not only the Workforce environment but the engagement and influencing of L&D decisions regarding solution design and post-deployment support. Several questions are key on the topic of Insight Curation. You will see additional references in the Systems & Technology (*Chapter 16*) for Insight Curation Engines (ICE).

CONFESSION: *"If only Madeline were still here, we could ask her. She was the resident expert." Or "I sure wish John was still here; he knew where all those documents were stored." Ever heard side conversations like these? Sadly, I had a chance to minimize those mournful conversations by spending quality time picking the brains of the more senior workers who were about to retire and leave...along with their intellectual property knowledge. I would call those workers Business Matter Experts (BMEs) because they knew the business...knew where the bodies were buried...not simply what a process was but how to do it and why it mattered. Always make an effort to include BMEs in your PWA interviews.*

CHAPTER 16

POINT-OF-WORK ASSESSMENT:

SYSTEMS & TECHNOLOGY

In this Chapter, the PWA methodology focuses on Systems (which may include multiple enterprise systems, software apps, and human systems) and Technology utilized by our Workforce to accomplish task-level work. (See Figure 16-1)

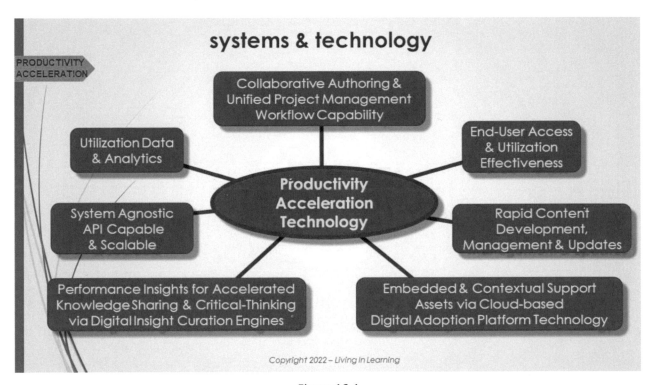

Figure 16-1

End User Access, Utilization, and Effectiveness

Workflows often require accessing any combination of work systems from End-User technology (which may include mobile phones, tablets, desktop computers, and other hand-held devices). Unfortunately, End-Users having access does not ensure effective utilization. We often experience this when a new *system goes live. Training is complete, but utilization is low, tendency to make mistakes is high, and the Help Desk has been overrun. That is not sustainable, yet it remains as status quo more often than not.*

Optimizing usage should happen within the Workflow with contextually accessible performance support. Forcing the worker to leave a workflow for support is inefficient, and the answer is a technology that converges performance support contextually in the Workflow. Formerly known as Electronic Performance Support Systems (EPSS) have evolved into cloud-based Digital Adoption Platforms (DAPs). DAP capability directly impacts L&D and the consistent application of Intentional Design specific to WHAT, WHEN, and HOW to support the Workforce in their Workflows. DAP technology is essential for proficiency development along the Workers' Learning Performance Continuum from Point-of-Entry (During Training) and their ultimate Points-of-Work (Post-Training) destination.

While *Productivity Acceleration* manifests when reaching *Point-of-Work*, applying the new technology should be first experienced during *Point-of-Entry Training*. As such, introducing this new technology has implications for the solutions designed (*intentionally, of course*) to serve as experiential source content for exercises and activities that emulate/simulate actual *Point-of-Work* scenarios. The performance assets designed for *Point-of-Entry* are the same assets recommended in the PWA Road Map for application at *Point-of-Work*. Doing this accomplishes a couple of favorable outcomes:

- The amount of time spent training and the volume of training are reduced dramatically
- Content development time and ongoing maintenance and updates are reduced
- The Workforce experiences actual *Point-of-Work* scenarios DURING *Point-of-Entry*
- Workers have less to remember/recall when back at their *Points-of-Work*
- An *experiential continuity* during the learning experience accelerates *time-to-competency*
- Faster *time-to-competency* accelerates productivity and decreases the cost of mistakes, error isolation, rework delays, material waste, business liabilities...and...and...and...

Compartmentalizing Systems & Technology

The objective of the PWA is to establish a *current state* benchmark of the *Systems & Technology* footprint; this becomes doubly important if the organization is on the path to achieving **Digital Transformation**. Why? Because every phase of the transformation has implications of CHANGE that will impact:

- The Work *Environment* demonstrates a *Cultural* shift toward accelerating productivity as a priority
- The workforce (*People*) and their **readiness** (*Capability*) to adapt to and adopt work activities using new technology interfaces
- Different *Workflows* and *Processes* that are updated or changed, disrupting task-level workflows and familiar routines
- Access to and acquisition of new supporting *Content & Resources*
- Utilization of *"new"* *Systems & Technology* for optimized application of embedded and evolved capabilities at *Point-of-Work*
- *Analytics* essential to gauge adoption and *Utilization Impact* at the *Point-of-Work*

In other words, **Transformational Change**, which often restrains/limits/delays the success and sustainability of our transformation efforts, may need to be revised. Simply put, we are not discussing a GoLive event where the default post-GoLive plan directs calls to the Help Desk, and that's not sustainable.

We have to get closer to, if not within, the workflows and the *systems* utilized at *Point-of-Work*. The LMS will not *"deliver the mail"* in that regard. We've all been through the chaos of these singular events; now multiply those events over a couple of years of new phase iterations of **Digital Transformation** and the fallout dependent upon **training the workforce to the point of readiness** to deliver optimized results and remain productive as learning curves are extended... AND...at what cost?

IT will handle the heavy lifting and leverage their IT version of *Change Management* to ensure successful GoLive events; however, that's only a slice of what defines successful implementation. But what about GoLive events related to *workforce readiness to perform* and full adoption we count on to accelerate their productivity? ***Digital Transformation*** represents a headlong movement to the cloud. Should we also position *Productivity Acceleration Technology* like DAP and ICE there as well? We absolutely should, especially when the load on IT resources and internal disruption falls on them to maintain the infrastructure.

Considering the elements shown in *Figure 16-1*, you may note that the focus largely involves the L&D role and is centered around **Productivity Acceleration Technology**. While there are many tools and apps on the market, and with more surfacing every day, there are two varieties I see as foundational:

- **Strategic** – where the outcomes key to accelerating critical thinking and informed decision-making from ***Performance Insights*** curated from bulk source content before burying recipients with redundant effort. Yes, curating curations...to improve *speed-to-insight* using ***ICE Technology***.
- **Tactical** – where task-level support assets are contextually embedded directly into workflows and the enterprise systems themselves at *Point-of-Work*...AND...embedded within experiential learning opportunities during *Point-of-Entry* using ***DAP Technology***.

The upper right section focuses largely on the *Workflows & Processes* related to:

- Cross-discipline efforts to rapidly collaborate and author learning performance assets
- Unify project management to streamline activities across disparate team responsibilities
- Rapidly develop, update, and maintain assets in multiple formats from a single source

At the bottom of *Figure 16-1,* we see where Productivity Acceleration Technology blows the doors off any LMS and serves as the capability to embed learning performance assets into both the workflows and systems along with actual Training opportunities, whether Performance Insights or Learning Performance Support.

Given that multiple enterprise technologies will be involved in ***Digital Transformation***, minimum selection criteria require choosing ***system-agnostic platforms***. Also, since the transformation will scale over a couple of years in larger installations, the acceleration technology should be ***non-disruptive and scalable***. The newer cloud-based acceleration technologies require little, if any, direct IT hardware/software involvement.

Finally, how do we know we've been successful? As part of the PWA, we determined *"What good looks like"* in terms of Level 3 & 4 impacts, but how will we know if we've arrived at those results without access to **utilization analytics** that tracks Workforce engagement and actual performance results? Again, the choice of platform should include this level of visibility as onboard capabilities.

CONFESSION: *Invest time proactively with IT; Partner with them early in any new enterprise system introduction. The typical approach of waiting for IT to release the final system screens to begin building training does not come close to "final" because of frequent fine-tuning. If collaborating early, L&D can leverage DAP technology to accommodate **single-source authoring** for making quick updates on the fly. Additionally, the most hated job in IT is writing UAT and system validation scripts. Why not leverage the DAP technology to **record/write those scripts** AND serve as intentionally designed sources for learning performance support content? It is inefficient to wait for IT to toss a finished system to L&D to build training. Likewise, L&D shouting "Incoming!" to the IT Help Desk after training is completed and GoLive has launched is not very cool either.*

Quite a lot to think about, right? My advice…step away from bright, shiny *Productivity Acceleration Technology* until you've established a few things:

- A benchmark of *current state* technology. What is the current footprint?
- Where is it headed in conjunction with **Digital Transformation** strategy?
- What new technology is planned, and what is the migration timeline for prioritization?
- When is it going to happen?
- Who is going to be responsible for utilizing it successfully?

This may be oversimplified, but these elements of knowledge will inform a decision regarding *Productivity Acceleration Technology* that will be as brilliantly planned and executed 18 months down the road as it was 30 days after GoLive. You can quickly go from hero to goat in 90 days to six months if the vendor decision prevents scalability.

Following in *Matrix 16-2* is a partial list of sample questions from the PWA Workshop:

#	ATTRIBUTE CATEGORY	DISCOVERY QUESTIONS
		When you consider the different Systems, Applications & Tools you and your team use on the job today, which ones represent the greatest challenge to use effectively? - What is most difficult in the use of these systems/applications/tools and how does that impact your work? - What do you think would help overcome or minimize these challenges?
		Do you feel you are well-prepared at the point of GoLive to effectively use new systems/applications/tools? - What would you add/change/eliminate to improve your success?
		How difficult is it to gain access to or move between systems? (I.E. single sign-on, access rights/privileges)
		If you need to exit a business application to access support information, do you lose your work in progress?
		What systems do you use to complete Training? - What is your biggest complaint in how easy these systems are to use? What would you change?
	SYSTEMS/TECHNOLOGY	What systems do you use to access support information when engaged in a workflow? - What is your biggest complaint in how easy these systems are to use? What would you change?
		How are you trained when a new system comes on-line? - Do you feel the training technology helps prepare you to be effective on the business system? If not, what would you like to change?
		How do you receive training when changes or system updates are made? - How are you notified of changes? - Does that training take you off task? - What would you change about that approach?
		Are you and your team equipped with the right personal technology (including mobile capabilities) to be effective on the job? - If not, what devices, apps, or tools do you need?
		How do bandwidth and/or network connectivity impact your performance? Or to the performance of your apps?

Matrix 16-2

CHAPTER 17

POINT-OF-WORK ASSESSMENT:

ANALYTICS & IMPACT

In this Chapter, we focus on assessing the attributes of *Impact & Analytics*. Traditionally, we (*L&D*) do an excellent job of evaluating at Level 1 (*the training experience was satisfactory*) and often at Level 2 (*knowledge was transferred during training evidenced by a test or activity*) to document successful learning interventions. In reality, those evaluations only represent our activity and *POTENTIAL* since none of our participants have delivered any tangible business value or impact at Levels 3 (*observable changes in behavior in the Workflow*) & Level 4 (*measurable financial benefit to the business*), which only manifest at *Point-of-Work*. Often, Levels 3 & 4 are defined in general, non-specific terms and represent a challenge when the business asks for verifiable evidence from L&D of tangible impact. More proof is needed! (*See Figure 17-1*)

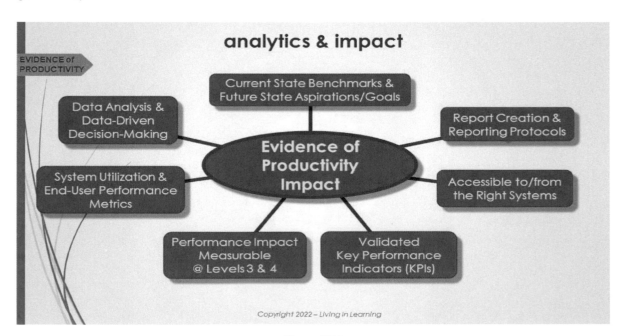

Figure 17-1

To accurately demonstrate impact, we must begin with an accurate *benchmark* to establish the **current state** and a basis for **future state** metrics and measures before building any solution.

CONFESSION: *We must establish the current state of performance and the measures currently used to track that performance. Without **current state benchmarks**, there is no valid basis for future state comparisons. Defining the Current State results must be accomplished at the beginning. Most scenarios where Levels 3 & 4 are not tracked are because no current state benchmarks were defined upfront. Building a successful measurement foundation demands upfront assessment of the analytics available, accuracy, and relevance to tangible impact only visible at Point-of-Work. Don't settle for confirming how busy you are…when how effective your solutions are is most desired by stakeholders.*

Current State Benchmarks

Figure 17-1 illustrates seven key assessment areas, beginning with *"Where are we today?"* to establish *Current State Benchmarks*. As with any journey, even our GPS is useless without identifying the *point of origin*. We know where we need to go…just as our stakeholders have an idea of where they want to go based on our efforts…BUT…we need to establish *current state* performance measures to establish a *"before"* benchmark if we hope to provide evidence of improvement in *future state* outcomes in our *"after"* results at Levels 3 & 4. Neglecting this level of assessment dramatically limits our ability to show evidence that L&D contributed meaningfully to the bottom line…which is typical of a non-contributory cost center.

Reporting & Accessibility

The use of data, or *"big data,"* is rapidly integrating into workflows to drive decisions and actions across the enterprise. I often find there is no shortage of analytical data; the challenges become more demanding of peripheral logistics like:

- Does a measurement plan exist, and is it aligned with the *future state*?
- What data is available, where is it, and should we utilize it?
- Do we have access rights to acquire the data?
- Can we analyze efficiently and effectively enough to enable informed decisions?

- How are results reported...in what format...how and to whom are the results shared?
- Do analytics feed a performance dashboard? Are performance dashboards desirable?
- Does the right technology exist to support multi-platform data capture?

In addition to identifying relevant measures, we must consider several things:

- Where in the ecosystem will these KPIs surface?
- Which systems are sources of data?
- How do we...can we...access them?
- Are there protocols in place related to Who accesses the data?
- When do we measure...How long...How often do we measure?

Validated Key Performance Indicators (KPIs) & Measurable Impact

Part of establishing the *current state* is making sure the existing key performance indicators (*KPIs*) are appropriate measures and relevant to the performance targeted for improvement.

- Do KPIs even exist?
- Are there KPIs that are misaligned?
- Are there KPIs that are missing?
- Are there KPIs that are irrelevant?
- Will new performance requirements create new KPIs for monitoring and tracking?
- How long will it take for measurable impact to manifest? Immediately? 2-Months?

These questions must be answered when we craft *future state* measures to show evidence of our learning performance success.

Utilization & Performance Analysis

We want evidence of positive business outcomes from sustainable performance. Do not overlook the *"sustainable"* aspect of performance in that statement. Measuring impact as a *"snapshot"* quality and easy to call it good when we see improvement; however, *a flash in the pan* does not confirm that we have established a trend or pattern of *sustainability* over time. The Measurement Plan defines a beginning and an end (*or ongoing*) to measuring data, how often, by whom, etc.

Also, from an L&D perspective, it is very helpful to know **"who is using what"** of the resources and performance support solution assets we provide. First, we learn quickly how often a particular asset is being used...but...we do not know *where* in a workflow or *why*. The point for L&D's benefit is *knowing what and who*...and this enables follow-up investigation to find out *where and why*. DAP technology can make this a reality...except for *why*. Secondly, we need to establish a communication loop for knowledge workers to provide *feedback to content owners* to address asset usability, relevance, and accuracy and offer suggestions and ideas for improvement.

Utilization of systems and resource assets also serves to show levels of *engagement*, and engagement is essential in the longer-term goal of reaching full *adoption* and *sustainability*. The IT team has a primary interest in systems utilization, and IT is one of the richest areas for Workforce performance data, and that data resides in the hands of the IT help desk. The call logs are usually categorized by *"reason codes"* or *"tagged"* in some way that points to the need to collaborate with IT during our PWA efforts. What better information could we have upfront than to know the reason behind calls to the help desk? ALWAYS include the Help Desk in a PWA.

A Measurement Plan should include all the components in this chapter, whether the Plan provided is used or not. Hopefully, the message is clear...*we must plan for post-training impact measurement BEFORE training and support solution design and development*. Who knows, the solution may not be training, opening the door for making tangible performance impacts with non-training solutions applied and tracked at *Point-of-Work*. That said, L&D needs to own and be equipped to work effectively in both venues.

On a recent LinkedIn thread, someone lamented how outdated Kirkpatrick's four evaluation levels were. Truthfully, I see L&D only using half (*Levels 1 & 2*) and framing Training, not performance results. *Achieving Potential* is good, but does it pay the rent?

Our business stakeholders ask for improved and accelerated performance and, more importantly, verifiable evidence of outcomes hitting the bottom line. L&D is in the best position to provide this evidence, but only if we prepare through assessing the attributes at *Point-of-Work* that are relevant, accessible, and reportable as stakeholder-accepted evidence of impact. We must have an advanced plan for measuring observable, measurable behavior changes (*Level 3*) and bottom-line business value generation (*Level 4*). The mistake so often made by L&D is NOT defining the metrics for either in advance with accompanying *current state benchmarks* as points of comparison.

Following in *Matrix 17-2* is a partial list of sample questions from the PWA Workshop:

#	ATTRIBUTE CATEGORY	DISCOVERY QUESTIONS
		Specific to work tasks in your area - What key performance measures are currently tracked?
		What other measures of performance are not currently tracked that would better demonstrate results? - How accessible are those data points? - From what system(s) would those data points be extracted?
		How would those measures be meaningful to the business? - What story would they tell that's not being told currently?
		To what extent do you see activity taking advantage of metrics (gaming the system) to inflate or "cook" results positively for measurement sake?
		What challenges exist in capturing the right performance data?
	ANALYTICS/IMPACT	If you request reports in your role, what challenges do you experience when you make requests?
		What challenges do you encounter specific to analyzing and applying business data from reports to make informed decisions?
		What real-time performance data would help you manage your job better and/or enable quicker decisions?
		What challenges do you encounter specific to analyzing and applying business data from existing reports?
		To what extent are performance dashboards used currently? - If dashboards exist, what performance data are tracked? - For what purpose? - What data are not tracked that should be included on the dashboard? - What is preventing tracking that data?

Matrix 17-2

PART 4

POINT-OF-WORK READINESS ASSESSMENT (PWRA)
FOR
LEARNING & DEVELOPMENT

CHAPTER 18

WHAT IS A READINESS ASSESSMENT?

Implementing the PWA discipline within a dynamic learning performance ecosystem requires enhanced discovery skills and evolved roles within the L&D team in collaboration with:

- Operational Leadership & Stakeholders
- Subject Matter Experts (SMEs) and Business Matter Experts (BMEs)
- Individual Contributors functioning in Workflows at multiple *Points-of-Work*
- Potentially external contributors like vendors, affiliates, resellers, or customers

This level of discovery is often out-of-scope and beyond traditional L&D skill sets and prompts the single most critical question that needs an answer...

Is your team "READY" to deploy & implement the PWA methodology?
Or is your team in a state of "READINESS" to adopt the PWA methodology?

A *PWA Readiness Assessment (PWRA)* represents a starting point to establish the *"current state"* of L&D readiness to deploy, fully implement, adopt, and sustain the PWA methodology for in-house application. The PWA version used for *L&D Readiness Assessment* is the same tool used to define the ***current state readiness*** of operational stakeholders seeking to accelerate and sustain operational performance results. What differs are the interview questions asked.

PWRA recommendations for L&D implementation and adoption may suggest the following:

- *Step-change shift in strategy & planning* to re-orient solution emphasis from *training* to enabling sustainable, measurable *performance* outcomes
- *Adoption of agile, intentional design methods* & tactics that utilize methods like the Five Moments of Need

- *Integration of Digital Adoption Platform (DAP) Technology* to optimize contextual workflow delivery and accessibility of performance support resources.
- *Tracking new analytics* that deliver tangible evidence of performance impact & accelerated productivity realized at *Points-of-Work* at Levels 3 & 4

An L&D optimization roadmap essential to implement, adopt, and sustain the PWA discipline requires an accurate, *current state benchmark*. Trying to enable a sea-change L&D strategy evolution without accurately defining the *current state* is like using GPS mapping without the benefit of *point of origin*.

Point-of-Work Readiness Assessment (PWRA) methodology represents a precursor assessment to prioritize where specific optimization should focus. Readiness is assessed top-down, whereas detailed learning performance solution optimization is a bottom-up activity based upon PWRA readiness findings at *Points-of-Work*.

Like the generic PWA, bottom-up design becomes prioritized based on assessment findings to ensure accurate definitions of specific Moments of Need within workflows. It ensures an optimized level of effort when creating solution assets. The design objective is to enable asset accessibility through *Digital Adoption Platform* technology and effective and efficient application in the workflow that accelerates productivity and measurable performance outcomes at *Point-of-Work*.

PWRA Phases

- **Phase 1** – One-on-one or peer-level team engagement at the senior leadership level having scope and authority to accomplish the following:

    o Participation in an Executive level presentation and discussion to establish a *Point-of-Work* strategic vision and operational context to gain commitment and sponsorship to move forward.

    o Discuss *current state* performance outcomes against existing goal expectations.

    o Share the top view of known or suspected *current state* performance challenges and anticipated *future state* challenges related to the execution of the strategic PWA plan.

- Share the vision of anticipated *future state* major initiatives or transformations, technology migrations, etc.

- Identify *current state* Talent Development and Continuous Improvement collaboration initiatives.

- Establish tactical prioritization and confirm points of contact for subsequent downstream *PWRA* discovery interviews, focus groups, or surveys.

- **Phase 2** – One-on-one or group mid-level/line management interview engagements having key functional stakeholder roles to accomplish the following:

  - Participate in discovery to address *current state* performance per functional role across relevant Attribute categories shown in *Figure 18-1*.

  - Provide root cause perceptions, assumptions, or hypotheses regarding *current state* performance challenges; identify current steps taken toward mitigation; and results, if any.

  - Define *current state* training methodologies; needs assessment methods; design methods & roles; authoring platforms; delivery methods & technology; availability & access to business resources & information, performance support integration; information curation methods; utilization of actionable insight curation; asset distribution & archival protocols; taxonomy and metadata application practices; training content ownership & maintenance protocols; update notification protocols; etc.

  - Observations of *current state* training delivery sessions (*if available*) and/or access to relevant legacy training content samples.

  - Identify key Individual Contributor roles and/or functional L&D teams/groups for subsequent discovery interviews, focus groups, and/or surveys.

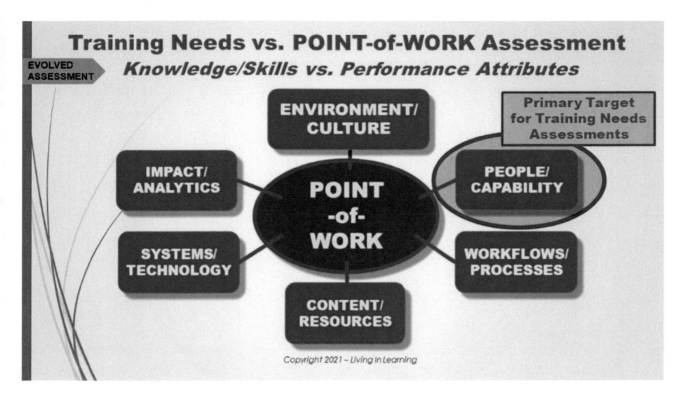

Figure 18-1

- **Phase 3** – One-on-one or peer-level group forum interviews or surveys engaging Individual Contributors having key roles to accomplish the following:
    - Participate in/observe discovery interviews to address the *current state* per functional performance role across relevant Attribute categories described in *Figure 18-1*.
    - Evaluate current assessment/discovery tactics or needs analysis methods.
    - Observe Instructor-led Training (ILT) or Virtual (VILT) sessions if available.
    - Determine the degree of sharing legacy training content across *current state* delivery venues.
    - Degree of integration of performance support assets in formal training content and delivery venues.

Who should administer the PWRA in your organization? Choose the person(s) who will also administer PWA assessments with your operational stakeholder population. Please enable them to become the PWA BME who can spread the skills to others as growth demands.

This role is best suited for a Performance Consultant or Performance Strategist. Those skills enable a conversation with Operational Leadership of any business discipline where business savvy and operational acumen are commonplace. The most important skill sets are active questioning and listening.

The following chapters align with the six categories of *performance restrainer attributes* specific to L&D. The interview questions provided are designed to identify functional areas in L&D where a state of readiness to serve as a business partner with our operational stakeholders effectively needs to be optimized.

CHAPTER 19

POINT-OF-WORK READINESS ASSESSMENT FOR

L&D

– ENVIRONMENT & CULTURE –

The following Matrix 19-1 addresses questions relevant to L&D specific to *Environment & Culture.*

On a scale of 1-to-10, how effective do you feel Operational Stakeholders believe L&D's training outputs produce requested performance outcomes? Why was that rating chosen?
What trends do you experience in the requests you receive from stakeholders for building training solutions?
What shifts in training expectations are you experiencing with Millennials as they become the larger percentage of the workforce?
Who determines that Training is the "*solution of choice*" for improving knowledge, skills, or capabilities for improving performance outcomes? How should that change?
Trends show that more training responsibilities are being pushed outward to supervisory roles for delivery. How does that compare with what you are experiencing in your environment?
On a scale of 1-to-10, how successful have you been in creating a *"culture of continuous learning?"* Explain your ranking.
The L&D Industry is shifting rapidly toward the **Point-of-Work** by adopting approaches like **Workflow Learning** and **Learning in the Workflow**. How readily do you see your organization's leadership embracing this adoption? Explain your answer. What are you doing to influence this shift? What impedes or limits the shift?

Describe the methodology or framework applied to support initiatives where principles of Change Management are essential success factors in implementing a solution.
Is a documented, repeatable Change protocol followed when Change Management is part of a solution application?

Matrix 19-1

CHAPTER 20

POINT-OF-WORK L&D READINESS ASSESSMENT

– PEOPLE & CAPABILITY –

The following Matrix 20-1 addresses questions relevant to L&D specific to *People & Capability.*

How do training requests originate, and what is the standard follow-up practice?   • How could it be improved or more efficient?
Who determines that Training is the "**_solution of choice_**" for improving knowledge, skills, capability, and/or improving performance outcomes? How should that change?
How are training concepts supported and reinforced after the completion of the event?
How has training changed in the recent past?   • What additional changes do you feel would improve training efficiency & effectiveness?   • How has Learner engagement shifted over the recent past?
What steps are underway to address the concepts of either **_"Workflow Learning"_** or **_"Learning in the Workflow?"_**   • What challenges are you facing now? Anticipated in the future?
Who (*what role*) handles Training Needs Assessments (TNA)?   • With whom do they interact when identifying needs?   • To what extent are job role competencies addressed?
What are the expected outcomes of completing a TNA?
How are TNA findings shared with design and production staff?   • How could that be improved?

Matrix 20-1

CHAPTER 21

POINT-OF-WORK L&D READINESS ASSESSMENT

– WORKFLOWS & PROCESSES –

The following Matrix 21-1 addresses questions relevant to L&D specific to *Workflows & Processes.*

How does a work/project request trigger responses from your team to get pre-qualified, screened, and assigned?   • How do you feel this process could be improved?
How often are Training Needs Assessments (TNA) completed on training requests?   • What information is routinely gained from your TNAs?   • How are TNAs assigned, progress reported, and tracked?
How are urgent knowledge and/or skills changes critical to performance at *Point-of-Work* addressed?   • How are they determined to be specific to knowledge or skill deficiencies?   • Who defines the urgency?   • How is business risk defined if the urgency is not addressed?   • How are measurable performance outcomes *(Levels 3 & 4)* aligned with training objectives? If not aligned, why?
What are formal design methodologies followed currently?   • Are they considered agile methodologies?   • Do you feel an agile design methodology should be adopted? Why or why not?
Where do delays typically occur in your design and production workflow?   • What do you feel would alleviate those delays?
What causes the delays?

• How much delay is added? • What is the frequency of these delays?

Describe the workflow associated with training and support content updates.
 	
  • Is there a standard protocol for handling updates?
 	
  • What challenges exist in maintaining content with content owners?

How are update notifications communicated to the user population?
 	
  • Are these notifications efficient and timely? If not, why not?
 	
  • How could they be improved, and what would be the impact?

How much time delay exists between receiving an urgent change request and the coincident update of training and/or support materials? • What causes the delays, and how do you feel they could be minimized?
Describe the communication process to reach content owners by end-users.   • If the path is not efficient, effective, and timely, how would you change it?

CHAPTER 22

POINT-OF-WORK L&D READINESS ASSESSMENT

– CONTENT & RESOURCES –

The following Matrix 22-1 addresses relevant questions to L&D specific to *Content & Resources.*

How long does it take for training and support content identified as out-of-date to be updated?   • How are content owners and their content aligned and tracked?   • What is the associated risk/liability?
How are multiple authors/SMEs assigned tasks and workflows managed within a single project?   • How are task milestones tracked and notifications for timely hand-offs handled with multiple content authors?
How does your review and QA process work?   • Are compliance or legal reviews required, and if so, how are documents shared, annotated, and returned? How many review iterations are typically required?   • Do you feel the review process is optimized? If not, how could it be improved?
Describe the process for updating training and supplemental resource content.   • Do you feel the process is optimized? If not, how could it be improved?
To what extent are performance support assets being used in Workflows currently?   • Give examples
To what extent are performance support assets embedded within formal training content?   • Give examples

To what extent are training content and support assets reused in other training and non-training venues? (I.E., Help Desk, Vendor education, Customer education, etc.)	Matrix 22-1
To what extent are learning and/or performance support technologies used to support formal training content and in-session exercises/activities?	
What options do training participants have for immediately accessing critical information resources at moments of need while active in ***system-based applications*** and ***non-system-based workflow*** exercises? *(I.E., embedded links to Intranet; direct links to SharePoint; activities integrated with knowledge bases, performance support technology, etc.)*	

CHAPTER 23

POINT-OF-WORK L&D READINESS ASSESSMENT

– SYSTEMS & TECHNOLOGY –

The following Matrix 23-1 addresses relevant questions to L&D specific to *Systems & Technology.*

What Learning Technology do you utilize currently?
What plans are in place for upgrades or replacements?
What Digital Adoption Platform Technology (*Performance Support*) do you utilize currently?
What Curation capability is currently in use?
What are your current authoring tools of choice?
How does available bandwidth and/or network connectivity impact the delivery of formal training? • How do you determine if there are issues between training content and end-user technology? (*I.E., audio/video capability, etc.*)
To what extent do you utilize live systems/applications **during** training that users will be expected to use on the job after they complete the training?
How do you deliver training when changes or system updates have been made? • How are you notified of changes that indicate additional training or follow-up? • Do you feel this process is optimized? If not, how could it be improved?
How do you confirm available bandwidth, connectivity, and/or device compatibility that could impact your design/production decisions and your ability to provide training for your stakeholders?
How geographically dispersed are your End-Users? • What connectivity challenges do they face?

CHAPTER 24

POINT-OF-WORK L&D READINESS ASSESSMENT

– ANALYTICS & IMPACT –

The following Matrix 24-1 addresses relevant questions to L&D specific to *Analytics & Impact.*

What Learning-specific data are currently tracked?
How often are Level 1 evaluations administered, and related to which training venues?   • How are Level 1 evaluation data utilized?
How often are Level 2 evaluations administered and related to which training venues?   • How are Level 2 evaluation data utilized?
How often are Level 3 evaluations administered, and related to which training venues? If not tracked, why not?   • How are Level 3 evaluations *(observable behavior changes)* accomplished?   • How are the data utilized?   • With whom are the data shared?
How often are Level 4 evaluations *(financial impact)* administered & related to which training venues? If not tracked, why not?   • How are Level 4 evaluations accomplished?   • How are the data utilized?   • With whom are the data shared?
To what extent are content utilization data tracked/monitored? If not tracked, why?   • Which content utilization data points are tracked?   • Which systems do you have access to for extracting utilization data?   • How are utilization data used?

Describe how you determine measurable business impact with current training if Level 3 & 4 evaluations are not completed.
What challenges do you encounter specific to analyzing Learning results and applying them as evidence that proves measurable Business Impact?
If you capture performance data and/or generate reports, what issues do you encounter in data capture and reporting? Which systems do you have access to for extracting performance data? • If you do not have direct access, do you have a resource who can acquire the data? • How would direct access help you?

CHAPTER 25
FINAL THOUGHTS & NEXT STEPS

I sincerely hope you have found value in reading *"Confessions of a Performance Ninja."* This book has been in progress for many months, and some of the content was captured over several years from actual field experiences. Creating the book was a great deal easier than the journey it details. I say that because the *Point-of-Work* discipline represents a paradigm shift in thinking. As paradigm shifts do, new or evolved thinking is invoked, accompanied by new skills, which spells *Change*. People tend to resist change when there is a comfortable, familiar, and embedded status quo already in place, and that resistance is precisely why I felt Ninja tactics would be called upon. True, the black pajamas and cheap sunglasses were optional equipment, but new thinking is at the core of a Point-of-Work discipline.

Do not misunderstand; the Ninja role is not as covert as you might think. What's *"Ninja"* about it is that you will accomplish holistic discovery at *Points-of-Work* without broadcasting that you are doing holistic discovery at *Points-of-Work*. Our business stakeholders want performance results; therefore, we must discover what is happening...or not...and why...at *Point-of-Work* where results manifest. This discipline is NOT a solution in and of itself; it is a pre-design discovery tool to ensure that what is ultimately developed by L&D ISD/Dev resources will impact performance at *Points-of-Work* and produce measurable results.

In closing, I will make another confession: The *Point-of-Work* discipline is not rocket science. There is nothing involved that a Performance Consultant or any role that has a shred of business savvy and operational acumen will struggle with. This is a shift in thinking and an evolved discovery skill set.

My role in what may be your next steps are primarily advisory in nature and in the form of delivering PWA workshops and coaching for L&D professionals desiring to adopt the *Point-of-Work* discipline all or in part. I say *"All, or in part,"* because there may well be much you already do tactically to support your stakeholders. The <u>Readiness Assessment Chapter</u> will provide a good guideline of what capabilities should be intact and can serve as a decent readiness checklist.

Whatever you choose to do...or not...I offer my thanks to you for reading the book. As always, I welcome deeper discussions and hope to receive any feedback you care to share.

Thanks for reading, and take good care!

G.

Gary G. Wise

Performance Ninja, Coach/Advisor, Writer of Things

gdogwise@gmail.com

(317) 437-2555

Web: Living In Learning

LinkedIn

PART 5

PWA WORKSHEETS (W/ INSTRUCTIONS) & JOB AIDS

MASTER PWA WORKSHEET TEMPLATE

Download Worksheet here – **Master PWA Worksheet Template**

PWA Master Worksheet Template Instructions:

This Excel spreadsheet is not password protected and has nine (9) tabs:

IMPORTANT NOTE: Before using this template, open it in Excel and immediately SAVE AS with a different filename (i.e., PWA Worksheet – WORKING COPY) so the Master version remains a true Master. Any future update downloads will contain an Update Version # and retain this naming convention (**PWA Master Worksheet Template – Version X.0**). Always begin a new PWA discovery from your WORKING COPY file and SAVE AS a new filename. Much of this spreadsheet has embedded links; keeping your Master as a Master will protect those links. The spreadsheet is NOT password protected, so making a master copy is a good plan.

INSTRUCTION FORMAT: The following instructions show illustrations that walk you through the TABS and pages under each. You will notice there are cell-by-cell guidance notes on the spreadsheet pages. You may print these Instruction Tabs listed below unless you have a dual-screen extension arrangement.

- *PROFILE TAB*
- *ALIGN TAB*
- *ATTRIBUTE TAB*
- *DISCOVERY TAB*
- *WORKSHEET TAB*
- *DISTRIBUTION TAB*
- *PRIORITIES TAB*
- *MEASUREMENT TAB*
- *DRIVERS TAB*

CONFESSION: I'm not a fan of filling out forms; hence, these pages in this spreadsheet may never be used more than once, most likely only as an initial guide. Some may never be used. So why provide them? Everything in this spreadsheet should be considered during a PWA, whether the worksheet is used or not. As such, I've defaulted to the lowest common denominator once again and included the minutia that I trust your judgment to include or exclude as your PWA project prowess dictates.

Profile-1 shown below is basic information about the Project and primary contacts.

TOC

PROFILE TAB

PWA - PROJECT PROFILE

PWA for	Enter Client Name		Busness Unit	Enter BU Name	Date	Enter Project Start Date
Project Initiative Name	Enter Project Name		Lead Business Owner(s)	Enter Primary Owner Contact		Enter Secondary Owner Contact
Projected GoLive Date	Enter GoLive Date		Phone	Enter Phone		Enter Phone
			Email	Enter Email		Enter Email

Profile – 1

Profile-2, shown below is a continuation of the Profile Tab

BUSINESS UNITS IMPACTED	Enter BU Name				
BU Stakeholder Name	Enter BU Contact				
Phone					
Email					
Engagement Notification Date	Enter when to notify affected BU contact				
Extent of Engagement	Description of BU Engagement to/from Project				
BU Roles Impacted	Impacted Role(s)				
Other Projects Impacted	Enter Up or Downstream Projects Impacted				

Profile – 2

- **Business Units Impacted** – What OTHER Business Units may this project impact?

- **Engagement Notification Date** – When will the OTHER Bus need to be notified – Used by the Project Manager to build a timeline and milestone targets.

- **Extent of Engagement** – Description of the engagement related to the input or output of this project to/from the OTHER BU.

- **BU Roles Impacted** – What roles (if any) in the OTHER Bus will be impacted? This information serves to identify potential support assets necessary to aid those roles. Recall the SIPOC model where up/downstream RIPPLE effects must be considered. Recall the "R" in DRIVER for *Replicating Content*...(Create Once - Use Many times)

- **OTHER Projects Impacted** – What projects besides yours are underway that may be impacted? Are there elements of those projects that would be redundant efforts? Are there assets from the OTHER projects that make new creations unnecessary and can be repurposed or reused in your project? Etc.

CONFESSION: *If your solution generates positive results, remember to make sure those results do not negatively disrupt another group's workflow. Our team improved productivity in an order-entry function by 70% every week and never considered the downstream RIPPLE effects of 70% more orders landing in the laps of the FULFILLMENT team every week. This impact was positive, BUT there was a period of chaos (backlogs) to adjust to the higher volume of orders. Suppose we had run a limited pilot to gain experience on the productivity impact. In that case, we could have at least minimized the "Holy Backlogs, Batman!" moment and not blown out the Fulfillment team's performance metrics for timely order fulfillment.*

*Recall the "I" in DRIVER for Intentional Design...especially the incremental deployment drill using pilot tests. We failed to **start small and scale**...always a best practice.*

ALIGN TAB

#	Statement of Business Challenge (Current State)	Performance Benchmarks (Current State)	KPIs (Current State)
	Enter a description of the stakeholder's challenge(s)- It may be stated as a missed goal or deficient performance in general terms if specifics are unknown initially.	What performance is currently measured and what are current results or level of performance - May be general or specific	Current KPI units tracked
	Operational/Behavioral Evidence of Impact – Level 3 *(Future State Performance Targets)*	**Financial Evidence of Impact – Level 4** *(Future State Financial Targets)*	**KPIs** *(Future State)*
	Desired level of observable behavioral performance (Level 3) as defined by the stakeholder	Desired targeted level of financial impact (Level 4) as defined by the stakeholder	Define KPIs if different from current

Align – 1

- **Current State Business Challenge** – Enter a description of the stakeholder's challenge(s). It may be stated as a missed goal or deficient performance in general terms if specifics are unknown initially.

- **Current State Benchmarks** – What performance is currently measured, and what are the current results or level of performance?

- **Current State KPIs** – Current KPI units tracked.

- **Future State Behavioral Evidence of Impact at Level 3** – Anticipated observable behavioral performance (Level 3) as defined by the stakeholder. (*If any is known*)

- **Future State Financial Evidence of Impact at Level 4** – Anticipated financial impact (Level 4) as defined by the stakeholder. (*If any is known*)

CONFESSION: *We should have asked for these impact numbers more often than not. Try not to allow disappointment to show on your face when the Requesting stakeholder is not prepared to quantify measures at Level 3 and especially Level 4, but be sure to ask, as these measures are critical to quantifying the business impact of your project. You may find out the best measures from your PWA interviews, and* that's okay, be sure to validate them with the Requestor. These numbers are essential to extract the evidence stakeholders want, so try to get them, even if they are best guesses.

ALIGN TAB (Continued)

#	Description of Driver (Future State)	KPI(s) (Future State)	Restrainers – Root Cause(s) Hypotheses (Current State)	Potential Performance Roadblocks (Future State)
		PWA - ALIGNMENT		
	DRIVERS & RESTRAINERS - Required Performance Outcomes - *[4-6]*			
A	*Enter a description of the stakeholder's challenge(s)- It may be stated as a missed goal or deficient performance in general terms if specifics are unknown initially.*	*What are KPIs used to track performance?*	*Description of Requestor's perceptions, assumptions, or hypotheses related to root causes (if any)*	Anticipated areas that may impact performance. This is typically an unknown and serves as a touch point for follow-up post-implementation to confirm or modify as appropriate.
B				

Align – 2

- **Future State Drivers** – Enter a description of what **Outcomes** must be accomplished to overcome the stakeholder's challenge(s) and contribute to Business Goals.

- **Future State KPIs** – What KPIs will track performance?

- **Current State Restrainers – Root Cause – Hypotheses** – Description of Requestor's perceptions, assumptions, or hypotheses related to root causes (if any). If unknown, try for *"best guess"* from the Requestor and notate accordingly.

- **Future State Potential Roadblocks** – (*Used for New Performance scenarios*) Anticipated areas that may impact performance. This is typically an unknown and serves as a touch point for follow-up re-assessment post-implementation to confirm or modify as appropriate.

PWA Discovery at *Action – Task – Activity* levels contribute to one or more Business Drivers (Outcomes) that contribute to one or more Business Goals. (*See Align – 3*)

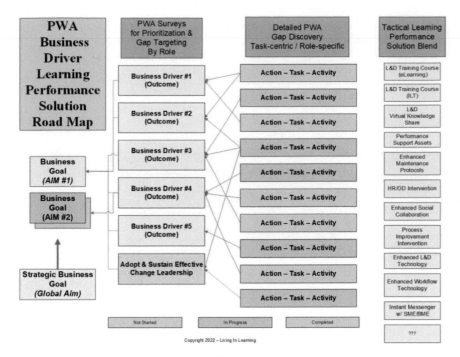

Align – 3

ATTRIBUTE TAB

The graphic *Attribute – 1* is embedded in the PWA Worksheet on the Attribute Tab and can be printed and used as a **Job Aid**.

Note the **ATTRIBUTE TAGS** highlighted in yellow:

- **E** – Environment/Culture
- **P** – People/Capability
- **W** – Workflows/Processes
- **C** – Content/ Resources
- **S** – Systems/Technology
- **A** – Analytics/Impact

These TAGS will be used in the Discovery Tab for categorizing interview responses. The Attributes in each category of restrainer are not an exclusive list. Feel free to add or ignore it based on your environment. I've included what I've experienced most often.

PWA - ATTRIBUTE MATRIX

ATTRIBUTE CATEGORIES - (6)	E	ENVIRONMENT/CULTURE	What internal/external attributes influence environment & culture at PoW?
		Culture – Mission – Vision – Organizational Design – Cross Team/Departmental Dependencies – Change Leadership – Corporate Communications – Inclusiveness Cohesive Teams – Engagement – Regulatory & Legal Compliance – Product/Service Mix – Competition – Pricing – Product Availability – Perceived Urgency/Risk to Perform Pace/Velocity of Demand – Workload/Volume Balance – Headcount/Staffing/Capacity M&A Implications – Budget Restrictions/Pressure Empathy/Value/Caring		
	P	PEOPLE / CAPABILITIES	Who is involved? What human attributes influence roles & capabilities at PoW?
		Leadership – Role/Goal Clarity – Role Accountability – Performance Expectations – Team Communications – Intra-Team/Inter-Team Collaboration – Active Supervision Coaching/Mentoring – Talent Development (*Training - Knowledge - Skills - Competencies*) – Career Development Performance Management – Succession Planning		
	W	WORKFLOW / PROCESSES	What is the work? What attributes influence workflows & processes at PoW?
		Task-Level, Role-Specific Workflows/Processes – Root Cause Performance Restrainers – Productivity – Project Management – Process/Procedural Change Management Decision Support – Critical-Thinking Support – Informed Decision-Making Support – Moment of Need Support – Policy/Methods/Procedures/SOPs – Delays – Redundant Effort – Problem Isolation – Process Improvement Opportunities – Creation of Excess Material Waste – Absent or Slow Feedback/Notification – Inefficient or Compromised Upstream/Downstream Hand-Offs/Contacts – Workflow Dependencies		
	C	CONTENT / RESOURCES	What information, content, media & other resources are used at PoW?
		Accessibility – Navigation – Search – Taxonomy – Relevance to Task-Level Workflows & Processes – Application & Effectiveness @ Point-of-Work Availability at Moments of Need – Distribution of Resources – Content Volume/Format – Content & Resource Ownership & Maintenance Resource Update Notification Protocols – Sustainability Content/Portability – Repurposing/Reusability – Missing Content		
	S	SYSTEMS / TECHNOLOGY	What systems and end-user technology are involved at Point-of-Work?
		Access to Appropriate Business Systems – Mobility & Utilization – Effective End-User Application of Technology & Apps – System Search Functions Content Repositories – Learning Management/Experience Platforms – Collaboration Platforms – Analytics Platforms – xAPI/Learning Record Stores Additional/Missing Technology Required Upgrades/Consolidations – New Technology Deployment – Bandwidth/Connectivity Migration Road Map Implications – Digital Transformation – Systems Transition/Migration		
	A	ANALYTICS / IMPACT	What metrics and measures serve as validated evidence of impact at PoW?
		KPI Alignment (*Current State/Future State*) – Benchmarking – Report Creation – Requesting Reports – Performance Dashboards – Forecasting Planning – Modeling – Data Analysis – Application of Data – Data-based Decision-making – Learning Impact Measurement at Levels 3 & 4		

Criticality Ranking	Optional 1	Nominal 2	Important 3	Mission Critical 4

Attribute - 1

DISCOVERY TAB

The Discovery Tab shows all six categories of *Performance Restrainer Attributes* provided earlier in Chapter 17. These questions may serve as Job Aids or source content for establishing a **Core Question Set** before Discovery interviews. *(See Discovery – 1)*

Discovery – 1

Will you ask every one of these questions? Probably not. For example, the seven **Core Questions** I asked in Case Study 5B are listed below. Many follow-ups were asked, like *"Tell me more about that. Why do you think that happens? What would you do differently?"*

- Talk to me about what it's like working here. If anything, what would you change?
  - *Seeking Environment/Culture attributes*
- Do teams collaborate well on projects like new product launches? Challenges?
  - *Seeking People/Capability attributes*
- On a scale of 1 to 10, how would you rate the course selection at Marketing University? What should change?
  - *Seeking People/Capability attributes*
- Are current workflows and processes optimized? If not, what should change?
  - *Seeking Workflow/Processes attributes*

- Do you/your team members have easy access to the right resources? If not, what's missing?
  - *Seeking Content/Resources attributes*
- Do you/your team have access to the right technology to get the job done in your area? If not, what else is needed?
  - *Seeking Systems/Technology attributes*
- Do the performance metrics for your work and workgroup accurately reflect your/their contributions? If not, what would be better measures of performance?
  - *Seeking Analytics/Impacts attributes*

WORKSHEET TAB

The PWA Discovery Worksheet is used to RECORD, and TAG responses by restrainer Category for each question asked. *(See Worksheet – 1)* The worksheet TAG entries feed the algorithm that populates the **Conversation Changer** Pie Chart in the Distribution Tab.

PWA - SUMMARY WORKSHEET

This worksheet can be used during discovery interviews or as a summary of responses post-interview. If used after the interview, be sure to take good notes, as it is important to include specific details of the responses to attach the appropriate TAGS. Each response TAG is marked with a numeral denoting how many responses fall into each TAG category. For example, if two responses matched with Environment/Culture, then the "E" TAG would be marked with a two (2). If in that same response column there was a reference to Systems/Technology, a one (1) would be marked under the "S." Upon completion of the interview, a **Criticality Ranking (CR)** of 1 to 4 would be added in the CR column where **1 = Optional 2 = Nominal 3 = Important 4 = Critical**. This ranking is accomplished collaboratively with the Requestor during debriefing.

DISCOVERY QUESTION	RESPONSE	E	P	W	C	S	A	CR	GAPS/ROOT CAUSES/RESTRAINERS
What's it like to work in this area?	The workload is very high since people have left - E A lot of frustration exists from not getting support - E The new pricing system is very difficult to use - S	2				1		4	Workloads out of balance Supervisors not providing support in the workflow Users not prepared to use the new pricing system

Worksheet – 1

It would be best if you used this worksheet to generate the visual pie chart Conversation Changer that is automatically built in the following Distribution Tab.

I've found it easiest to use after the interviews and work from my notes or a recording.

CONFESSION: *I am wired half-duplex, meaning I can do two things, but only one at a time; hence, I always try to use a recorder, so my full attention is on the responses given during the interviews. In other words, I cannot take effective notes AND listen actively. I find it easier to listen to the recorded questions and responses given after the fact so I can accurately fill out this worksheet.*

The Workbook is built with only two pages—the second page *(See Worksheet – 2)* has instructions to add rows. Note that this sheet's summary of Restrainer Attributes resides at the bottom of the last page. To protect the algorithm's integrity, you MUST add additional rows above the Gold Line.

Add/Delete rows above this line (*as required*) to preserve formula integrity in Summary Section & the Conversation Changer Distribution Graph on the DISTRIBUTION TAB		
PWA Restrainer Attribute Summary Section		
ENVIRONMENT/CULTURE	2	
PEOPLE/CAPABILITY	0	
WORKFLOW/PROCESSES	0	
CONTENT/RESOURCES	0	
SYSTEMS/TECHNOLOGY	1	
ANALYTICS/IMPACT	0	

Worksheet - 2

DISTRIBUTION TAB

The Distribution Tab is fully protected and populated from the data input on the Worksheet Tab. (See Distribution – 1)

CONFESSION: *I find that I do not need to use this worksheet in its entirety. Despite the size and complexity of this Worksheet, you may quickly find that you can **Change the Conversation** by using only the WORKSHEET TAB and the DISTRIBUTION TAB. So why did I build the rest of this Workbook? It is a field guide, and I believe in the Learning Performance Continuum, which means building competency by supporting Point-of-Entry through to Point-of-Work. That said, you may be more comfortable using fewer tabs; for example, you may already have project management software, so you may not need to bother with the PROFILE TAB.*

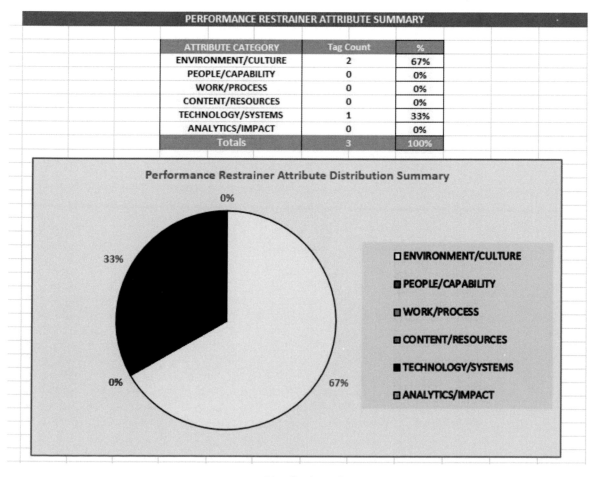

PERFORMANCE RESTRAINER ATTRIBUTE SUMMARY		
ATTRIBUTE CATEGORY	Tag Count	%
ENVIRONMENT/CULTURE	2	67%
PEOPLE/CAPABILITY	0	0%
WORK/PROCESS	0	0%
CONTENT/RESOURCES	0	0%
TECHNOLOGY/SYSTEMS	1	33%
ANALYTICS/IMPACT	0	0%
Totals	3	100%

Distribution - 1

Recall the example from the Worksheet Tab where we had two Environment/Culture responses and a single Systems/Technology response. Those data are carried forward to this Distribution graphic. The pie chart changes dynamically based on changes you may make in the Worksheet Tab.

The pie chart is your **Conversation Changer** visual.

PRIORITIES TAB

The PRIORITIES TAB *(See Priorities – 1)* is used for several reasons:

- **Stakeholder Requestor Debrief** – Where Discovery Findings are shared with the Requestor to validate what is happening at Point-of-Work by Attribute Category and Root Cause.

- **Prioritizing Solution Design** – In support of the "I" of DRIVER – *Intentional Design* and incremental deployment in Test Pilots to validate effectiveness. Prioritization is completed collaboratively with the Requestor.

- **Establishing Success Metrics** – Confirm with the Stakeholder Requestor which measures of success are acceptable to establish Future performance goal targets by projecting impact.

Priorities – 1 is an example screenshot of a Solution/Action Priorities page from an actual PWA.

PWA - SOLUTION/ACTION PRIORITIES

#	ATTRIBUTE CATEGORY	GAPS/ROOT CAUSES/RESTRAINERS	PROJECT/ACTION INITIATIVE/OWNER	PROJECTED IMPACT	CBI
	Restrainer Attribute Category *Sub-Category*	Cause(s) of Performance Gap	Description of Recommended Actions Responsible Owner Contact	Description of impact evidence KPIs if available for Levels 3 & 4 evaluation source data	Critical Rank (1-4)
1	Content/Resources *Application Effectiveness*	* Use and process around KB articles: * No single point of accountability; * No process to confirm currency or updates;	* Continue KB Deep Dive Project * Currently being driven by Ginger with aspects managed by vaious members of Technical Support Managememt Team	Call Hold Times <9 min/call First Call Resolution increase to > 75% Decreased escalation to Tier 2 by >25% Improved Customer Sat scores to >90%	4
2	Content/Resources *Missing*	* Difficulty finding the right information resources for technical problem resolution in timely manner * Search function not returning appropriate information * Some KB resource info may be missing altogther	* Identification of items that are currently available but possibly overlooked by team * Clarify with team on individual aspects for details on what is missing * Collaborate with SEs on creating content confirmed to be missing * Confirm nature of search challenges and develop job aids for workflow and training insertion	Call Hold Times <9 min/call First Call Resolution increase to > 75% Decreased escalation to Tier 2 by >25% Improved Customer Sat scores to >90%	4

Priorities - 1

MEASUREMENT TAB

The MEASUREMENT TAB has links from the PROFILE TAB where entered data is carried forward to this tab except for the *Start Date of Measurement. (See Measurement – 1)* This sheet is protected, so if you did NOT use the PROFILE TAB, break the links and manually fill in the Measurement Plan.

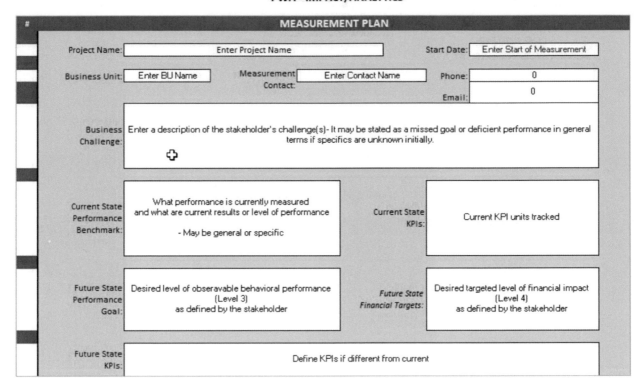

Measurement – 1

CONFESSION: *For years, we NEVER planned for measuring beyond how many butts-in-seats, classes held, eLearning courses completed, participant satisfaction scores, etc.*

We evaluated (L & D) performance on activity, not impact! We consistently had Level 1 for Sat scores and, not quite as consistently, Level 2 when we had a final exam or some pre-test/post-test indicators. Level 3 & 4 evaluations on impact were a pipe dream; we either made it up or cooked the books. We could only prove how busy we were...not how effective.

MEASUREMENT TAB

The second page of the MEASUREMENT TAB is not linked, so all entries must be made manually.

PWA - IMPACT/ANALYTICS

Data Collection Start Date:	Enter when measurement begins	End Date:	Enter when measurement ceases
Collection Source:	Enter what system(s) hold the target data	Collection Units:	Enter units of measure
Collection Frequency:	Enter daily, weekly, real-time, etc	Data Access Point:	Enter where to retrieve data
Data Analysis By:	Enter who analyzes the collected data	Reporting Format:	Enter type - Spreadsheet, graphical, etc.
Analytics Report To:	Enter Contact Name	Reporting Frequency:	Enter reporting cadence
Phone:	0		
Email:	0		

Measurement – 2

All data fields on this second page must be filled in manually except for the *"Analytics Report To:"* field carried forward from the PROFILE TAB.

IMPORTANT NOTE: If you are serious about responding to Stakeholders asking for proof of impact, you will need to build a *Measurement Plan*. Data points on this example plan should be included before the solution is launched. Collecting impact data is a post-training or post-implementation event, as is reporting results to the stakeholders.

Ongoing measurement is a great source for tracking Sustainability, highlighting where performance may be dropping off. Measuring performance in that manner should trigger a follow-up limited scope PWA to find out why performance dropped and then optimize with updated solution(s).

Words to live by: If you have not or cannot measure impact – it never happened!

DRIVERS TAB

The DRIVERS TAB *(See DRIVERS – 1)* is intended to support post-discovery collaboration with Instructional Design, Development, and Delivery resources in L&D.

Working Definition: A DRIVER is any successfully executed *activity/task/decision* that produces measurable results necessary to deliver a desired business OUTCOME. In other words, a DRIVER represents the successful *"finished state"* of a specific activity.

#					DRIVER ASSET INTEGRATION						
Driver #A	Enter a description of the stakeholder's challenge(s)- It may be stated as a missed goal or deficient performance in general terms if specifics are unknown initially.			**Root Cause Hypothesis**	Description of Requestor's perceptions, assumptions, or hypotheses related to root causes (if any)						
Process BME		**Phone**			**Content Owner**					**Phone**	
		Email								**Email**	
			TASKS/STEPS Critical to Business Driver								
#	Description of Task - A1	Deficient Performance?	KPI	PS Object Description	Medium	Source/Link		Access Technology	Direction	Embed?	
#	Description of Root Cause Impact		Source of Root Cause			Potential Ripple Effect					
#	Description of Task - A2	Deficient Performance?	KPI	PS Object Description	Medium	Source/Link		Access Technology	Direction	Embed?	
#	Description of Root Cause Impact		Source of Root Cause			Potential Ripple Effect					

Drivers – 1

The DRIVERS TAB has room to describe six DRIVERS with three TASKS under each.

CONFESSION: *This is another Tab designed to serve as a field guide, not necessarily a form to complete for every task identified.* **A word of caution**; *however, I can recall many times a team member needed to accomplish an update to an existing asset only to have no clue where the original author may (or may not) have stashed it. This is even more critical when a video is involved because it may be stashed in a completely different archive. Recall the "R" – Replicate in the DRIVER model.* **Manage your content, or it will manage you!**

- **Description of Task** – What must be completed successfully?
- **Deficient Performance** – Is this Task a source of the problem?
- **KPI** – What are the units of measure?

- **PS Object Description** – What should the performance support object be? Job Aid? Video clip? Hotlink to a Policy file? Etc.

- **Medium** – What will the delivery medium consist of? Video, links to database, etc.

- **Source/Link** – How do designers/developers get to the asset?

- **Access Technology** – How do end-users access the asset? Digital Adoption Platform (DAP), Link to SharePoint? Etc.

- **Direction** – Is this asset to be Pushed, Pulled, or both by the end user?

- **Embed?** – Will this asset be embedded in formal learning programs or other documents?

This book is due on the last date stamped below.
Failure to return books on the date due may result
in assessment of overdue fees.

FEB 1 1 2014 *RS* FEB 0 6 REC'D		
FINES .50	per day	

Managing Without Walls

Colleen Garton
and
Kevin Wegryn

Managing Without Walls
Colleen Garton and Kevin Wegryn

First Edition

First Printing—October 2006

MC Press offers excellent discounts on this book when ordered in quantity for bulk purchases or special sales, which may include custom covers and content particular to your business, training goals, marketing focus, and branding interest.

For information regarding permissions or special orders, please contact:
    MC Press
    Corporate Offices
    125 N. Woodland Trail
    Lewisville, TX 75077 USA

For information regarding sales and/or customer service, please contact:
    MC Press
    P.O. Box 4300
    Big Sandy, TX 75755-4300 USA

ISBN: 1-58347-062-X

For Charlie and Melanie Swanson, my "local" team.

—Colleen

For my wife Sheila, who gave me
the incentive and encouragement to write this book.

—Kevin

Special Thanks

We would like to thank the following people for their contributions during the creation of this book:

A special "thank you" to Charlie Swanson for his unwavering support and encouragement during the writing of this book. Heartfelt thanks to Sheila Wegryn, for the incentive and encouragement to write this book. Thanks also to Merrikay Lee at MC Press for her invaluable feedback and suggestions and for her continued support and enthusiasm for this project. Very special thanks to Suzanne Crane for her valuable input on the unique challenges of virtual training.

About This Book

This book is designed as a practical guide to virtual, global, and cross-cultural management. This book assumes that you have some basic knowledge and understanding of general management or project management, or have some experience working in a virtual environment. This book is ideal for managers at any level of expertise and for aspiring managers looking to develop the skills necessary to move into a virtual management role. This book clearly explains the differences between traditional, hybrid, and virtual teams, and will equip you with the knowledge required to successfully manage a virtual project or team.

In this book, you will discover not only what the virtual manager needs to know, but also how to apply that knowledge in a virtual environment, no matter what percentage of the virtual team is working remotely. You will learn how to build, manage, and develop a virtual team, including the steps for hiring the team members who will be best suited to the virtual environment. This book defines the skill sets and qualities you should be looking for in prospective team members and gives advice on how to evaluate those qualities.

Once your team is in place, you can look to this book for help on how to coach, train, and develop virtual team members from afar, and how to set performance objectives and evaluate individual performance. This book gives practical advice on building strong and effective teamwork among geographically and culturally diverse team members. You will learn how to design effective and appropriate processes and procedures for managing day-to-day virtual team communication and activities, as well as for managing high-risk situations and catastrophic events. This book teaches you how to recognize, manage, and control virtual politics and virtual conflict. It explains, in detail, how virtual communication differs from traditional communication, and what the virtual manager must do to overcome the unique challenges of working together, apart.

With this book, you have the information and tools needed to build the skills and knowledge for managing virtual teams in the real world. You will be prepared to manage virtual teams in cross-cultural and global environments with a high level of confidence and expertise.

We hope you will find it useful as you travel down your own virtual path.

—Colleen and Kevin

About the Authors

Colleen Garton

Colleen Garton has over 20 years of experience in traditional and virtual management in the financial, technology, analytics, and multimedia industries. She has an educational background in electronic/electrical engineering and business management. She has extensive experience in project management, product management, consulting, development, and engineering in the both the United Kingdom and the United States In addition to working in senior management positions for companies such as Intuit and Fair Isaac Corporation, she has also owned and operated her own management and technical consulting firms.

Ms. Garton possesses strong business and technical management skills, together with excellent cross-cultural and global team-building skills. She is an experienced virtual manager, managing remote team members in the United States and internationally. She has a proven record of accomplishment for successfully managing and deploying large, complex, multi-million dollar projects in very diverse market spaces. She has extensive knowledge and experience in leadership and management styles and philosophies.

Ms. Garton has formal training and project experience in quality management processes such as Six Sigma and CMMI. She has participated in and taught numerous management, leadership, communication, mentoring, and conflict management classes. Ms. Garton is a member of the Project Management Institute (PMI), Toastmasters International, American Mensa, and The Authors Guild. She is the president of the British American Society. Ms. Garton is the product-management program director for global fraud solutions at Fair Isaac Corporation in San Diego, California.

Colleen Garton is the co-author of the books: *The AS/400 & Microsoft Office Integration Handbook* published by MC Press in 1998, and *Fundamentals of Technology Project Management* published by MC Press in 2004.

Kevin R. Wegryn

Kevin R. Wegryn, PMP, CPM, MA is an experienced project manager, consultant, and presenter, leading and working with virtual teams and virtual customers. Over the past 20 years, he has successfully managed teams as large as 220 and annual budgets of over $70 million dollars. His clients have included companies in the financial services, manufacturing, telecommunications, banking, mortgage, health care, pharmaceutical, nonprofit, publishing, and educational industries. Currently, Kevin is a senior project manager at Agilysys, Inc.

Kevin has a master's degree (MA) in economics. He is a PMI-certified Project Management Professional (PMP), member of the PMI National Organization, volunteer for the PMI-PMBOK Guide 2004 Update team, and a member of the panel of judges for the PMI-Educational Foundation 2004–2005 Student Scholarship Awards. He is a Certified Project Manager (CPM) from the International Association of Project and Program Management and is a member of the International Association of Project and Program Management. He also was elected to the PMI-Information Systems Specific Interest Group Board of Directors in 2005.

Kevin has published articles for various publications, including *Project Management Weekly*, the *PM Boulevard* newsletter and the Allpm.com newsletter.

Contents

Introduction . . . . **xxi**

Chapter 1: Virtual Management **1**
The Need for Virtual Management. 1
The Differences between Virtual and Traditional Organizations 3
    The Traditional Organization. 3
    The Virtual Company. 6
Managing the Virtual Team. 11

Chapter 2: The Virtual Manager **17**
Definition of a Virtual Manager 18
    The Traditional Manager 19
    The Virtual or Hybrid Manager 20
Skill Sets Required for the Virtual Manager 28
    General Management 28
    People Management 32
    Communication 36
    Technical Knowledge 38
    Decision Making 40
    Problem Solving 43
    Team Building. 44
    Administration 45
Skill Sets Required for the Remote Worker 46
    General Management 46
    People Skills 47

Communication 48
Technical Knowledge 49
Decision Making 50
Problem Solving 50
Team Orientation 50
Administration 51
What Employees Want from a Virtual Manager 51
How to Find Out What Your Team Members Need from You 58

**Chapter 3: Creating and Managing
the Virtual Team** **61**
Virtual Work Locations 62
Home Office 64
Local Library 65
Local Community Center 66
Caber Café or Coffee House 67
Hotel 67
Onsite at a Client Location 68
Shared Office/Hoteling 69
Bus, Train, or Airplane 70
Airport (or Other Transit Station) 71
Small Local Office or Corporate Office 73
Creating the Virtual Team 73
Choose Team Members 74
Interview Team Members 80
Consider the Team Dynamics 85
Consider the Personalities of the Virtual Team Members 86
Evaluate the Abilities of the Team Members 87
Defining Virtual Team Roles and Responsibilities 88
Understanding Interaction Styles 89
Interaction Styles and the Virtual Team 90
Learning Styles 92
Communication Preferences 95
Managing a Team Split between Two Locations 96
Setting Goals and Objectives for Team Members 98
Managing Performance and Performance Reviews 99
Personal Development Plans 100
Employee One-on-Ones with Manager 103
Virtual Coaching 104

Virtual Training 105

How to Make Virtual Training Successful 108

Online Training Tools 110

Chapter 4: Managing Global Teams. 113

International Business and Global Marketspaces 114

The Global Decision 114

Before You Start 115

Time Differences 119

Managing Language Differences 122

Communicating Effectively with People for Whom English Is a
Second Language 122

Translating 124

Speaking Clearly 125

Listening and Understanding 127

Gestures 128

Asking Questions 129

Managing Cultural Differences 130

The Stages of Cultural Adjustment 133

Honeymoon Stage 133

Conflict Stage 134

Integration Stage 134

Adaptation Stage 135

Building Teamwork in a Global Environment 135

Chapter 5: Outsourcing 139

The Decision to Outsource 140

Offshoring 145

Offshore Outsourcing 146

Offshore Office 148

Domestic Inshoring and Farmshoring 149

Unique Challenges of Outsourcing 151

Managing Outsourced Projects 153

Specific Project Outsourcing 154

Ongoing Business-Function Outsourcing 156

Building Relationships with Outsource Vendor Managers 157

Importance of the Statement of Work and Outsourcing Contract 158

Introduction 160

Objectives 160

Project Scope 160
Period of Contract 161
Specific Tasks 161
Schedule of Deliverables 161
Completion Criteria 162
Fees and Payments 162
Roles and Responsibilities 164
Assumptions and Constraints 165
Staffing 166
General Provisions 167

Chapter 6: Time Management **169**
The Importance of Time Management 169
Time Management for Virtual Managers and Remote Workers 170
Team Time Management 172
Personal Time Management 173
Meeting Time Management 181
Time Management Tools 183
Tips on Speeding Up the Process for Time-Consuming Tasks . . . 183
Prioritizing Tasks 185
Forced-Pair Comparisons 185

Chapter 7: Virtual Teamwork **189**
Discovering Commonalities 190
Creating Trust 191
Understanding the Dynamics of the Team 193
Creating the Virtual Community 193
Team Member Interaction 195
Virtual Communication 197
In-Person Communication 198
Virtual Team Day 199
Sharing Best Practices 200
The Brainstorming Process 202
Making It Fun! 207
Celebrations and Rewards 208

Chapter 8: Team Processes and Procedures **211**
Communication Process 212
Stakeholder Groups 213

      Formal Communication Plan 214

      Informal Communication Plan. 216

      Communication Rules 217

   Change-Control Process 218

      Resources 220

      Schedule 221

      Technical. 222

      Organizational 224

      Business 225

      Scope. 225

      New Projects. 226

      Maintenance 226

      Catastrophic Failures or Events 227

      Change Requests. 228

   Defect-Tracking Process (for Technical Projects) 230

   Organizational Processes 232

   Client and Vendor Processes 233

   Status Reporting Process 233

      Status Report from Team Members to Manager. 234

      Status Report from Manager to Team Members. 234

      Status Report from Project Manager to Client. 236

      Monthly Status Report to Senior Executives 236

   Escalation Procedures 237

   Risk-Management Process 240

      Identifying Risks. 241

   Documentation Processes 243

   Process Management 245

Chapter 9: Virtual Communication **247**

   Communication Complexities 249

      Tone of Voice 249

      Body Language 250

   Which Communication Method to Use in Which Situation? 252

   Effective Use of Email 253

   Effective Use of the Phone 257

   Effective Use of Cell Phones 262

   Face-to-Face Communication 263

   Project Meetings 265

   Team Meetings 266

Weekly Status Reports 268
Presentations and Reporting 269
Communicating Bad News 270

Chapter 10: Virtual Politics **273**
Understanding Company Culture and Politics 273
How Your Team Creates Its Own Politics 275
No Complaining About or Blaming Each Other or Other Teams . . 278
No Superstars or Superstar Behavior 279
No Reprimanding Anyone in Front of Others 279
No Congratulating Individual Results in Team Meetings 280
No Comparing Team Members to Each Other 281
No Derogatory Remarks about Team Members or Stakeholders . . 282
No Thinking or Assuming You Are Better than Someone Else . . . 283
Identifying Potential Troublemakers 284
Nipping Trouble in the Bud 286

Chapter 11: Managing Conflict **289**
Recognizing a Potential Conflict Situation 291
Knowing When and How to Act 292
Mediating a Phone Conference 296
Proactive Conflict Management 297
Change Management 300
Removing a Team Member from the Team 304
Understanding Your Limitations and When to Ask for Help 307

Chapter 12: Virtual Management of High-Risk and Catastrophic Events. **309**
What Is a High-Risk or Catastrophic Event? 310
Planning for High-Risk Events 311
Planning for Catastrophic Events 313
How to Recognize and Respond to a Potential Catastrophe. 316
Natural Disasters. 316
Project or Product Issues. 316
Personnel Issues 317
Public Transport 317
Freak Accidents 317
Acts of War or Terrorism 318
Risk Management 318
Scope Management 318

Contents

How to React to and Manage a Catastrophic Event 320
Evaluating the Catastrophe 322
Minimizing the Damage 323
Keeping Team Members and Stakeholders Informed 324
Communication Methods 327
    Phone Calls: Landline and Mobile 327
    Pager 328
    Text Message via Pager, Phone, or PDA 329
    Instant Messaging via Phone, PDA, or Computer 330
    Online Chat 330
    Email 330
    Conference Calls: Audio or Video 332
    Onsite Meetings 333
Managing the Aftermath 334
Lessons Learned and Best Practices 335

Chapter 13: Virtual Management and Communication Tools 337
Collaborative Tools 339
    Integrated Virtual-Management Tools 340
    Online Meeting Tools 341
    Document-Management Systems 342
    Online Scheduling and Time Tracking 343
PDAs and Smartphones 344
IM and SMS 345
Video Conferencing 346
Phone Conferencing 347

Chapter 14: Virtual Leadership 349
Leading the Virtual Team 350
Maintaining Professional Integrity 351
Controlling Your Emotions 353
Professionalism at All Costs 355
Prejudice in the Workplace—Intentional and Unintentional 356
Inspiring Others 358

Appendix A: Virtual Skill Set Checklists 359
Skill Sets Required for the Virtual Manager 359
    General-Management Skill Set 360
    People-Management Skill Set 361

Communication Skill Set 362
Technical Skill Set 364
Decision-Making Skill Set. 365
Problem-Solving Skill Set 366
Team-Building Skill Set 367
Administrative Skill Set 368
Personal Qualities 369
Required Skill Sets for the Remote Team Member 370
General-Management Skill Set 370
People-Management Skill Set 371
Communication Skill Set 371
Technical Skill Set 372
Decision-Making Skill Set. 374
Problem-Solving Skill Set 374
Team-Orientation Skill Set 375
Administrative Skill Set 376
Personal Qualities 377

Appendix B: Reports and Documentation **379**

Appendix C: Case Study **399**
Company Background 399
The Business Decision. 399
The Virtual Solution 399
The Virtual Team's Operations 400
Communication 401
Personnel Management 403
Outsourced Operations 404
Offshore Outsourcing in India 404
Inshore Outsourcing in Chicago 405
Contracted-Out Work 405
Benefits 405
Challenges 406
Lessons Learned 407

Index **409**

Introduction

Ten years ago, most workers in the United States and Europe were employed outside the home. To go to work, they had to leave their homes and *go* to work. Times have changed. These days, a growing percentage of the work population goes to work by staying at home. These people no longer work in a local environment, but a virtual one. This change has led to an ever-increasing need for *virtual* skills. To be successful in the virtual world, today's employers must equip both managers and workers with the necessary skill Sets, knowledge, and communication technologies to facilitate effective communication and collaboration.

Virtual management in one form or another has existed for centuries. Religious institutions, for example, have maintained networks of globally distributed workers throughout history and continue to do so today. However, virtual management in its modern form started to emerge in the 1990s. Until then, manufacturing accounted for most outsourced and offshored work. In the 1990s, the business landscape started to change considerably. Driven by the need to stay competitive in a market that demanded quicker and cheaper goods and services, companies began outsourcing and offshoring non-manufacturing functions, such as customer service and software development.

Since the 1990s, companies have been forced to adapt to global changes, reshaping their business models in an effort to guarantee higher revenues, better profit margins, and faster time to market. Many organizations around the world have adopted the new business model of geographically diverse, multicultural, multinational, and multilingual teams. The result is a shortage of workers with the desperately needed virtual management skills. If they are to triumph, virtual organizations need workers with an in-depth understanding of culture, diversity, global business, and virtual communication.

Just when companies are starting to feel confident that they have gained traction in the realm of project management training, they are now struggling to figure out how to do the same in the area of virtual management. Some organizations are ahead of the curve, but most are lagging behind. While many companies are busy congratulating themselves on the great project management skills their managers now possess, their outsourced projects are failing due to lack of expertise in global, cultural, and offshore management. Many of these organizations have not yet realized that the project management skill Sets needed for managing local projects are very different from those required for managing in a virtual environment.

In some companies, the transition from a traditional to a virtual company has been a gradual process, without much long-term planning. The realities of being virtual have crept up on these organizations, and their managers are taken by surprise when they suddenly realize that they are failing to meet expectations in some critical areas. Often, the move to a virtual environment starts with a few employees being allowed to work at home once or twice a week. It then moves to one or more employees working from home every day, and increases over time to one or two projects outsourced to India or China. This gradual shift in local to virtual continues, until one day you suddenly realize that you are managing a virtual team!

The changes created by virtual teams are evident even for those employees working in a local office environment. At least one of the local team's members is probably working virtually some or all of the time. In many companies today, not a single meeting takes place without remote workers "dialing in" through an audio-conferencing system. For companies in a 100% virtual environment, all team members interact with little or no daily face-to-face communication. Without adequate training, the managers in these environments can quickly find themselves in over their heads.

Management skill Sets have not kept pace with the growth in virtual projects and teams. Virtual managers need to acquire the key skill Sets that are the trademarks of virtual management: the abilities to manage across functional and geographic areas, and to overcome cultural and linguistic boundaries. In the coming decade, these skill Sets will be required for managers at all levels in most organizations.

Virtual Management

Virtual management is a growing phenomenon in today's business world. It is becoming more and more unusual to find an organization that does not have some "virtual" aspect to it. In fact, sales teams have been virtual for decades. They just didn't have such a fancy title! Traditionally, sales organizations have been scattered around the country or the globe, with salespeople spending a considerable amount of time either driving or flying around their assigned region. With the advent of newer and more mobile technology, virtual management is a growing trend in service as well as sales organizations.

The Need for Virtual Management

The need for virtual management and geographically dispersed teams continues to increase for many reasons, including these:

- Financial considerations
- Geographical diversity
- Faster time to market
- Pressures of the global marketplace and economy

From a financial perspective, it makes sound business sense for many companies to take a decentralized approach to their organizational structures. Outsourcing saves U.S. companies millions of dollars per year. The costs to hire in the United States are much higher than in countries such as India and China. The costs of healthcare and workers' compensation in the United States have also continued to increase, at a time when many companies are under pressure from shareholders to cut costs and increase the bottom line. Outsourcing to reduce short-term workforce costs may affect the U.S. economy in the longer term, but for now, it is a very attractive option for many companies.

Moving to a model where more employees work at home can reduce facility costs significantly. The costs of leasing and maintaining corporate office space can be very high. Additional costs like onsite gyms, cafeterias, kitchens, and parking increase the overhead even more. Removing the need for employee relocation packages can also save many thousands of dollars. A company with a network of employees across the country or the globe can quickly and inexpensively get employees to a particular geographical region, as needed.

A workforce that is geographically diverse can be a huge business benefit in less tangible ways, too. Companies tend to like working with other companies that have local representatives. A U.S.-based company with employees in Brazil, Japan, and Italy who are natives of those countries or speak the local language fluently has a strong competitive edge in those countries over solely U.S.-based competitors. Moving into new and emerging markets is also much easier when a company has someone local who understands the political, financial, and corporate landscape.

Needing everything faster used to be something unique to the United States. With globalization, however, worldwide fast food and drive-throughs have whetted the appetite for faster, cheaper, and better everything, no matter where in the world the customer is located. In today's fast-moving and ever-changing business environment, companies are increasingly demanding more speed without affecting quality or price. This demand requires that highly skilled and effective teams be created quickly without regard to time zones or locations. The ability to work together just as effectively while geographically distant as when local makes this possible. If a company had to relocate an entire team to one location, find accommodations, and pay expenses, it would be very difficult to move quickly, and almost impossible to do so without passing the costs on to the customer.

Globalization has increased the need for virtual management. Working in an international market space is easier than it has ever been before. However, along with this ease of conducting business internationally comes the challenges of working with cross-cultural teams and the need to understand and overcome cultural and language differences.

From a high-level management perspective, global business and virtual management are the answers to many business problems. A company can increase its geographic footprint and more effectively do business in multiple countries. At the mid-management level, however, these business advantages are not as clear. In some instances, they are positively hazy. On a day-to-day basis, for managers dealing with employees or associates in remote locations, who have different cultural backgrounds, work ethics, and languages, the virtual solution can create more problems than it solves.

Even in teams that are located in the same geographic region, at least one team member often works remotely. This person might work remotely because he or she did not want to relocate; because there was no requirement to work locally with the team to be able to do the job; or because the hiring company felt there was some benefit to having the employee located in the specific region in which he or she lives. Relocation packages can be prohibitively expensive, so the ability to hire the best people without having to relocate them is a huge financial benefit. In addition, the ability to hire employees without having to supply office space to them is a great way to decrease overhead costs and improve the bottom line. The cost of office space, electricity, equipment, parking spaces, restrooms, kitchens, cleaning, etc. can add up to a hefty expense.

While the trend toward virtual teams is destined to continue for the foreseeable future, there is currently a distinct lack of virtual management expertise across all industries. Managers who learn virtual management skills will help their companies avoid a rocky road.

The Differences between Virtual and Traditional Organizations

A virtual, or remote, company is any company that has at least one team member working remotely. Team members might be working as close as in the same city, or as distant as across oceans and time zones. A traditional company is one in which all team members work in a single office location.

The Traditional Organization

There are, of course, many different types of traditional companies and teams. They operate in different ways, with different management structures and organizational hierarchies. The traditional company might be a large national organization with thousands of employees, or a small start-up with less than ten employees. The company might consist of team members from one cultural background or from many. Some traditional companies might be comprised of primarily native English speakers, while others might be dominated by foreign nationals who are non-native English speakers.

While recognizing that these are huge differences, and that culturally these organizations might differ greatly in their levels of diversity, for the purpose of this book, they are all categorized as *traditional companies*. The commonality among traditional companies is that employees conduct their work collectively at the same location each day. Team members are working together in the same office, warehouse, or factory. Employees see each other on a daily basis. They can easily communicate using face-to-face conversation. The employees might choose to communicate via phone or email on a regular basis, but the option to "stop by" and talk to someone in person is always there.

A traditional company does not necessarily have all of its employees working in the same building. Many companies have compounds or business parks, where the employees are located in various buildings. There might be up to a mile between buildings, but this does not constitute a virtual or remote company. The buildings are close enough for the employees to work together when necessary, and employees can walk between the buildings to facilitate face-to-face communication. Figure 1.1, for example, shows a traditional company where there are four major buildings: an executive office suite, two administrative office buildings, and a warehouse.

Determining where a traditional company ends and a virtual company begins is not an exact science. Suppose a company has outgrown its office space and leases an additional office building five miles away. This could be considered a virtual company if the employees needed to communicate across locations on a daily basis, requiring team members to communicate and collaborate on projects virtually. However, when companies add buildings in the same local area but not close enough to walk between, they usually locate departments according to function, so that minimal face-to-face interaction is required between the employees at different locations. When this is the case, the company would generally not be considered a virtual company.

It has been a common practice for many years for companies to locate certain groups, such as accounting and other administrative departments, in different locations from the main office. These companies are not considered virtual, since regular participation in interdepartmental meetings is not critical to the success of most projects.

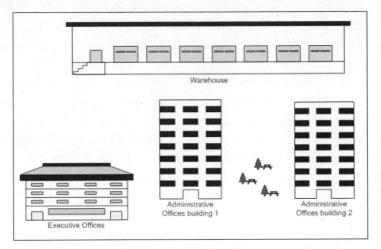

Figure 1.1: The traditional company

A traditional company typically has a hierarchal structure with a middle management layer separating individual contributors from senior management. Each employee works in the same location as his or her manager, as shown in Figure 1.2.

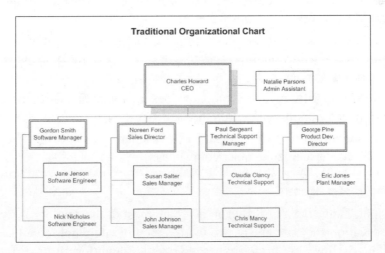

Figure 1.2: Traditional organizational chart

The Virtual Company

A virtual company has at least one worker not in the same physical location each day as coworkers on the same team or project. In many teams today, team members are never physically in the same room or office location. The physical distance between team members creates a team dynamic and personality that is very different from that found on a traditional team. This is why applying a traditional management approach to a virtual team does not work.

Your team will not thrive in a virtual environment if the team's structure and process has been designed as if it were a traditional team. If you want to learn how to salsa dance, you would not ask a ballet dancer to teach you. All that time spent stretching at the bar might be good for your flexibility, but it is not going to be much use to you out on the dance floor!

There are several different types of virtual companies and teams. These range from companies that have just one employee working from home a mile away from the company's office to companies that have entire divisions of workers working 5,000 miles away from the corporate office.

Here are some examples of the different flavors of virtual companies:

- Some Remote Team Members—The company has one or more local employees who consistently work from a remote location.
- Split Team—The company has two or more main office locations, where employees work out of whichever office is closer to them.
- Satellite Team Members—The company has a main corporate office, with numerous satellite employees around the country or the globe who work from home offices.
- 100% Virtual Team—The company does not maintain an office. All employees work remotely from home offices.
- Outsourced Team—The company has a main corporate office, with some functions outsourced to other companies.

Some Remote Team Members

At first sight, managing a virtual team in which most of the employees work at the same location and only one or two work remotely might not seem like much of a challenge. However, this is not necessarily as straightforward as it might appear. If you are used to managing a local team, you might find the task of managing some remote team members a lot more demanding and time consuming than you anticipated.

You and your team might not have many virtual management tools at your disposal. It is unlikely that your local team members will be using virtual management software and tools to communicate with each other when most of them are located on the same floor. This leaves the remote workers in a very isolated working environment. Because these people are not around the office very much, they might be forgotten. As the manager, you need to make sure that all team members know they work on a virtual team, and that they use the tools and processes necessary to make the virtual team successful.

If one member of a family is deaf, the other family members learn how to communicate using sign language. The family would not refuse to learn sign language and allow the deaf family member to feel isolated and ignored. In the same way, a team that includes a remote worker needs to use the necessary tools to ensure that all team members are able to communicate with each other. The local team members might not use those tools very often to communicate with each other, but they should be encouraged to use them to communicate with the remote workers.

Split Team

Some virtual companies have two or more main office locations, where employees work out of the office that is local to them. One distinct advantage here is that most non-management employees will have a local manager. It is much easier to manage and to be managed when the direct-line employees are in the same location. However, supervisors or managers often report to a remote manager.

Figure 1.3 shows an example split-team company with headquarters in the United States and six regional offices in China, Ireland, India, Brazil, Hong Kong, and England. Each location has its own management hierarchy, with only the most senior managers reporting directly to an executive in the U.S. office.

These types of companies might have projects that require cross-location and cross-team communication and participation. Virtual management skills and knowledge are key to the success of those projects. It is very easy for an "us and them" mentality to develop in a setting such as this. Without close attention and a high level of good-quality virtual management, teamwork can soon deteriorate into a negative and competitive environment, with the different teams being reluctant to work together or help each other out. Eventually, finger-pointing and apportioning blame become more important than meeting the objectives of the project. The situation can get so bad that one team intentionally sabotages the other. This situation might sound far-fetched, but it can occur even in traditional companies where the teams are located in adjacent hallways!

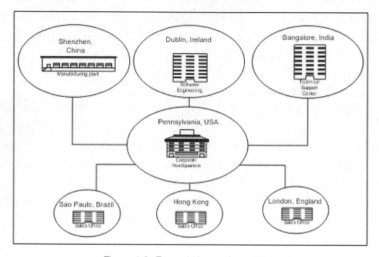

Figure 1.3: Example layout for a split team

If you start bad-mouthing other teams, hinting that they might not be competent or are intentionally unhelpful, the rest of your team will adopt this negative attitude. We have personally heard a manager say these words to her team, "X team will not do what we need them to because they do not like us." What kind of effect do you think this statement has on a team? It hardly inspires confidence in the other team or promotes good teamwork. It also makes the manager look rather helpless and incompetent.

Satellite Team Members

Some virtual companies have a main corporate office with numerous satellite employees around the country or the globe who work from home offices. This is a very typical setup for global sales organizations, and it is fast becoming common in other types of organizations. Some technology companies are moving to this distributed virtual team environment, as are consulting organizations in various industries.

In a satellite-office situation, the manager might be located in the corporate office and might perhaps have an administrative assistant or receptionist working onsite. Alternatively, the manager might work virtually from the rest of the team. In either case, many of the team members will be working remotely from each other and from the manager. In a satellite-team setup, the corporate office maintains some kind of virtual private network (VPN) to enable the team members to communicate securely with each other and to access a centralized server and network system. This requires that each employee must set up and maintain his or her own virtual office. Each team member needs a more in-depth knowledge of computers and networks than would be required for someone working in a local, corporate environment.

If there is a corporate office and centralized network, there is likely to be a technical support or help desk organization for employees, so they should be able to get some technical help with their equipment if there are problems. However, some of the team members might be using nonstandard equipment, so it might not always be possible for a centralized help desl to successfully troubleshoot a problem.

The satellite-team organizational structure has some significant advantages from a business perspective. It reduces facilities overhead, in addition to allowing employees to live wherever they like (though there might be some geographical restrictions, such as limited to North America). In this way, virtual teams can be created based on the skill Sets required and the geographical location of the team members.

The exact geographical location of your team members might not have a huge affect on the effectiveness of your team. From a virtual team perspective, a team member located 1,000 miles away is not much different from a team member located 4,000 miles away. From a corporate perspective, the geographical location of each team member can have a more significant impact on the company's ability to conduct business in different parts of the world. If the team members are located in different geographical regions, the company can maintain global coverage while reducing costs for such things as travel for onsite meetings with customers. Also, salaries are cheaper in some regions than others. These cost efficiencies lead to more competitively priced products and services

100% Virtual Team

The purest form of virtual management is a situation in which a company does not maintain a centralized office at all, and has all employees working remotely from home offices. This 100% virtual company is becoming more popular, especially with smaller companies. It can be difficult to maintain a 100% virtual setup for mid- to large-sized companies due to the complexity that occurs as the virtual system is scaled up. Most large companies prefer to keep centralized business and technical functions such as accounting, legal, human resources, and data centers in-house. Many smaller companies outsource these business functions, as it can be prohibitively expensive to maintain dedicated employees for these functions on a small scale. For this reason, it makes a lot of economic sense for small companies to operate in a 100% virtual environment.

Outsourced Team

Some companies have a main corporate office or offices where the employees are located, while outsourcing certain functions to other companies. The organizational chart in Figure 1.4 gives an example of this structure.

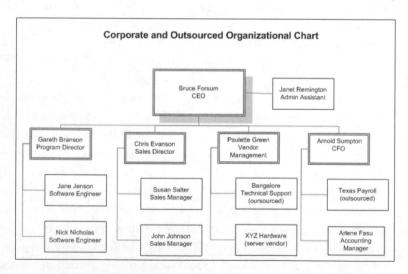

Figure 1.4: Organizational chart for outsourced and vendor projects

This might not seem like a true virtual company, as the employees are all working at local offices. However, if the functions being outsourced are key functions, the employees at those outsource companies become key players in the day-to-day business or projects of the main company. This type of organization requires virtual management processes and techniques to be successful. Another similar situation occurs when a company relies heavily on one or more vendors to implement or manage business functions or projects. Again, this is not strictly a virtual company, but certain departments within the company will be working as part of a virtual team.

When working with outsourcers or vendors, it can be much more difficult getting the high level of attention or escalation of issues that would be expected from internal groups. Careful management is required to ensure that things do not get out of control. An outsource company might be taking care of technical support for your company, but might also have 20 other clients for which it is doing the same. Likewise, an outside vendor will have other clients with their own needs and demands, and will need to balance and manage those. If another client has a problem that is deemed more important than the one you are experiencing, your problems will not get top priority. The issue you are experiencing might be the most serious, but if it does not have the highest revenue potential for the vendor company, they are not necessarily going to drop everything to jump on it. If they have another client with whom they are signing a new contract that is worth a few million dollars, you might find yourself on the back burner until the deal is closed. If you just signed a five-year contract, there might not be much motivation for them to continue to woo you; they will focus their attention on their latest flame instead!

Managing the Virtual Team

Managing remote employees requires a very different approach from managing local employees. However, it is important for you to be as available to your remote employees as to your local ones.

As shown in Figure 1.5, local employees bump into each other at various times throughout the day in all kinds of places:

➤ In the kitchen getting a cup of coffee

➤ At the water cooler

➤ In the elevator

➤ In a meeting

➤ In the restroom

➤ Walking up the stairs

➤ Wandering down the hallway

➤ In the cafeteria or at a local restaurant at lunchtime

➤ In the parking lot or the lobby of the office building

These incidental meetings are great opportunities to share information, communicate status, and generally chat and build rapport.

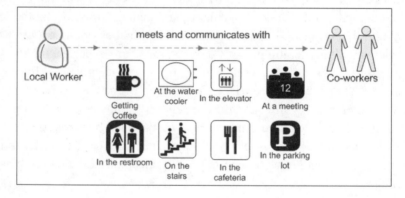

Figure 1.5: Local employee communication opportunities

Such incidental meetings do not occur with remote employees. Virtual management tools can help with virtual simulation of meeting on the stairs or at the coffee machine, but they cannot completely replace this valuable communication method. The virtual manager needs to create opportunities and workspaces that facilitate effective communication.

When remote employees are forgotten, all sorts of problems can be created. If you inadvertently omit these employees from the invite list for meetings, your team and your company loses valuable input from those people. You are also alienating the remote employees from the rest of the team, and they will start to feel that they are less important than the local employees.

Even when you invite remote workers to participate in meetings, there can be problems. If the company uses a phone conference system, as the meeting organizer, you must remember to include the dial-in instructions in the meeting request and must remember to dial into the conference. If the remote team members call in and you do not, they will be left waiting on hold for the entire meeting! Once a phone conference meeting has started, you need to ensure that the attendees speak up and remember to not talk over one another. Otherwise, the remote callers will be unable to understand what is being said. If the local meeting attendees forget that they have remote team members on the phone, they might make decisions without asking for input or opinions from the remote callers. All these issues lead to the remote workers feeling ignored, undervalued, and neglected. After a time, the remote team members will stop calling in for your meetings. They will feel that their involvement is not desired or required.

If a remote worker is located in a different time zone, you need to take this into account when scheduling meetings. If the main office is located on the east coast of the United States, it is not polite to schedule a 9:00 AM meeting that includes attendees from the west coast, where it will be 6:00 AM!

As shown in Figure 1.6, informal communication with virtual employees is possible using various communication mediums, including these:

- ‣ Phone calls and conference calls
- ‣ Virtual meetings
- ‣ Audio conferencing
- ‣ Video conferencing
- ‣ Peer-to-peer instant messaging
- ‣ Peer-to-peer messaging using audio and video (Webcam)
- ‣ Sending emails
- ‣ Sending messages via PDA or mobile phone
- ‣ Using a virtual private network (VPN)
- ‣ Using a virtual management workspace

Some of these communication methods can be used to facilitate the type of spontaneous communication that would occur in the elevator or the lunchroom. If team members leave instant messaging running while logged into the computer, for example, other team members can send informal greetings or ask questions that do not require a more formal method of communication or documentation. The use of a Webcam and microphone for online meetings enables participants to see and hear each other, in addition to seeing the material that is being shared online. Team members being available via mobile phone or PDA at times when it is not possible to be at the computer can help to minimize the geographical distances among the virtual team members.

Instant messaging, in particular, is an ideal way of negating the importance of geography for team members. It doesn't matter if someone is in the next office or on the other side of the world, it is nice to get a "hello" or a "did you have a nice weekend?" greeting when you are sitting at your desk. Instant messaging is a valuable tool for building teamwork and rapport that is not as easy to emulate via email. It allows both work-related and non-work related conversations to take place daily among team members. It's a virtual water cooler!

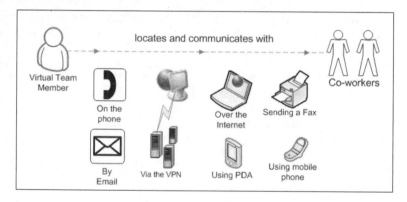

Figure 1.6: Virtual employee communication opportunities

You should make the most of every opportunity to build teamwork. Remember to schedule team events whenever possible. There might be times when your remote workers will be onsite at the corporate office, or when the whole team will be in one offsite location for a meeting or conference. These are ideal times to schedule some team events. Don't leave planning a team event until the day before, or decide on an impromptu dinner a few hours in advance. This will not allow the team members to make the necessary arrangements to be there. Be respectful of team members' time. They might have made other plans or have arranged to be traveling at that time. It is down-heartening to arrive at corporate headquarters for a week of training, only to discover that a team dinner is scheduled for 6:00 PM Friday—one hour after your flight leaves to take you home!

If you, the virtual manager, forget to set up regular one-on-one meetings with remote workers, or do not make yourself available for questions via instant messaging, email, or phone, the relationship between you and your remote team members will deteriorate quickly. The relationship between the local team and the remote team members usually reflects the relationship between the manager and remote employee. It is not healthy for a team to have poor or no relationships among the team members.

It is important that you set the same standard of expectation for remote employees as for local ones. If a remote employee is not reprimanded for submitting a time sheet late while local employees are, or vice versa, there will be tension and a competitive attitude among the team members. The local team should have visibility into the contributions of the remote workers. It doesn't take much for local team members to start thinking that a team member who works from home might not be putting in as many hours or as much effort as the rest of the team. This attitude often comes about due to the corporate tendency for workers to work fewer hours when the boss is out of the office and not able to keep tabs on everyone! People assume that remote workers are doing the same thing, when they are very likely working even more hours than the local employees!

> It is important that you set the same standard of expectation for remote employees as for local ones.

You need a virtual management process for tracking and measuring what virtual employees are working on, just as you need systems in place to do the same for local workers. The same standards and requirements must apply to everyone on your team, regardless of location. Just because a worker is remote does not mean that he or she can skip meetings without a good reason, or not respond to emails in a timely manner. It is vitally important that remote workers have a daily presence on the team. As this is not possible in person, it must be via remote tools. Email, instant messaging, phone calls, and calling in for meetings are all ways for remote employees to make their presence felt.

It is interesting that once teams get into the habit of working virtually, they find it hard to stop. At one particular company, the team was composed of some employees who worked locally and some who worked remotely. Many of the local employees also worked remotely for one or more days per week, so a lot of virtual communication took place. The majority of meetings were conference calls to accommodate the remote workers. On one particular morning, 10 team members dialed in for a weekly phone conference. After being on the call for about 10 minutes, one of the attendees asked, "Who is calling in from the main office?" Each of the 10 people confirmed that they were calling in from the local office. They were all located on the same hallway, and most of them were in offices next door to each other. The team members were so used to communicating virtually that it had become part of their daily routines. It is possible to create a remote working environment even when people work in the same office building. When a team starts to behave in this way, you know that you have been successful in creating a team that thinks and behaves virtually!

> It is vitally important that remote workers have a daily presence on the team.

The global marketplace has made the world a much smaller place. Along with increased business opportunities comes increased competition. For many years, it was incredibly rare for a non-manufacturing company operating in a developed country to feel threatened by a competitor in a developing country. This is not so today. Many companies in developing countries have figured out how to compete in the global marketplace with lower costs and comparable quality. Companies in developed countries are under a lot of pressure to either partner with or compete with these companies. Virtual management has to be part of the solution!

The Virtual Manager

A virtual manager can be defined as someone who has responsibility for at least one team member, vendor, or project at a different location. The manager might be located in the same physical office as all of his or her direct reports, but might be managing a vendor or a client who is located in a different city, state, or country. Managing a relationship or owning a project in a remote location defines the manager as "virtual." As described in chapter 1, there are various levels of virtual or remote management, ranging from having one team member working virtually to having the whole team working virtually.

The virtual manager is responsible for building and maintaining a highly productive and functional team that incorporates all team members, no matter where they are located or which company they work for.

It will never be possible for a virtual team to work in exactly the same way as a traditional team. If it were possible, you would be limited by the same restrictions as a traditional team, and you would lose the benefits of a virtual team. It is important to focus on the benefits of being virtual and not spend unnecessary time and energy trying to align yourself with a traditional model. Otherwise, you will feel like you have failed when you discover that you cannot do everything as well virtually as you could traditionally. It doesn't matter. What matters is that you can do different things well and that you can be effective and successful.

Fast-food restaurants will never be able to offer the quality of food and service that a traditional restaurant offers. What fast-food restaurants are selling is speed, efficiency, convenience, and low cost. The traditional restaurant is selling quality, service, and relaxed and comfortable surroundings to kick back and savor the experience. Both types of restaurants offer the same basic product—food—but in very different ways. They cater to different needs, and they both have strengths and weaknesses.

Virtual management and traditional management offer the same basic service —management—but in different ways. Both types of management fulfill important needs, but not in the same way. Each one has its own strengths and weaknesses. A fast-food restaurant cannot try fulfill all the needs of a traditional restaurant customer. The fast-food company must focus on what it does well and not try to compete in areas where it cannot possibly succeed. Likewise, the virtual company or team needs to focus on what it does best and not try to compete with the traditional organization in areas where it is not as strong.

Definition of a Virtual Manager

To understand what a virtual manager is, you must understand how the virtual manager differs from other types of managers. There are hundreds of different types of managers and management structures, all with their own idiosyncrasies. However, most of them fit into one of the following three broad categories:

- ‣ Traditional–The non-virtual manager
- ‣ Virtual–The virtual manager
- ‣ Virtual hybrid–A combination of the traditional and the virtual manager

Traditional management is still the primary form of management across all industries. However, within certain industries, a very different picture emerges. In technology and consulting organizations and, most particularly, in global organizations, the traditional management role has declined considerably, to be replaced by the virtual or hybrid manager.

The current trend in these industries is the transformation of the traditional manager into a virtual or hybrid manager. This trend looks likely to continue into the foreseeable future. Companies that are 100% virtual are still quite rare, although such companies do exist, and many of them are highly successful. The totally virtual model is not an easy one to apply to mid- and large-sized companies, due to the infrastructure needed to keep those companies running. However, managers who work 100% virtually are becoming much more common. Most of these managers work for hybrid companies, where specific functional units are virtual and others are traditional.

The Traditional Manager

Over the past few years, the role of the traditional manager has evolved into something very different from what it was 20 years ago. The manager might still work in a traditional, local environment, but the similarities often end there. Despite the differences in day-to-day tasks and duties, traditional management remains an appropriate and successful form of management in many industries. The traditional manager has had to learn new skill Sets and tools in order to continue to manage successfully, but the hierarchy and geography of his or her team has not changed much.

The traditional manager can be defined as someone who works locally with all of his or her employees, as shown in Figure 2.1. Traditional managers can be found working in many different industries, ranging from retail to health care. Traditional managers might use virtual tools such as email, instant messaging, and the Internet in the course of daily work, but the use of these tools does not change the fact that they are traditional managers. It is the location of the employees that defines whether a company is virtual or traditional, not the technology or communication tools used.

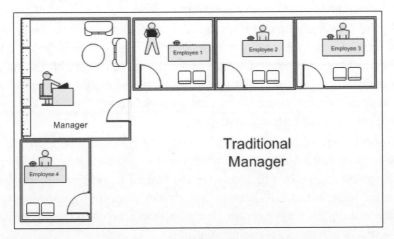

Figure 2.1: The traditional manager's office

> It is the location of the employees that defines whether a company is virtual or traditional, not the technology or communication tools used.

Using the word *traditional* to describe this type of management does not imply that it is old-fashioned or "wrong." A traditional style of management is a necessity in many industries. Manufacturing companies, for example, need to have local managers for the employees on the shop floor. The health care industry is another great example. Doctors and nurses cannot care for patients virtually. Hospital managers need to be onsite to respond to the needs of the health care providers quickly and effectively. A hospital in the United States being run by a virtual manager in India would find it hard to successfully treat patients.

The Virtual or Hybrid Manager

A decade ago, the term *virtual manager* would have meant nothing to most people. It would very likely have been interpreted as meaning "almost a manager" or "only just a manager," similar in meaning to the statement "the company was virtually bankrupt." In contrast, in some industries today, it is almost impossible to find a manager who is not functionally virtual at least part of the time. The transition from traditional to virtual management is not an easy one. The virtual manager must learn new skill Sets, new management strategies and styles, new communication techniques, and cross-cultural skills.

The virtual hybrid manager is someone who manages a team or a project that is a combination of a traditional (local) team and a virtual (remote) team. This is by far the most common type of virtual team. Hybrid teams are becoming the norm in many industries today. This business model works exceptionally well in mid- to large-sized companies, where some business functions need to be centralized while others work better decentralized.

Outsourcing creates a lot of hybrid teams. For example, a core project team might be located in the United States with a software development team in India, or a core project team might be located in the United Kingdom with a software development team in Eastern Europe. United States and European companies are constantly looking for ways to reduce costs; offshore outsourcing has proved to be a very successful model for achieving this.

A 100% virtual manager works remotely from all of his or her team members, and all those team members work remotely from each other, as shown in

Figure 2.2. The 100% virtual company can work extremely well in environments in which the team members have a very creative and entrepreneurial spirit. This business model is a great way for small- to mid-sized businesses to minimize overhead and give employees autonomy and flexibility. It is not as well-suited to some large businesses, however. A team comprised of career corporate employees might find it very difficult to adjust to the lack of face-to-face time and to not spending hours in meetings in the boardroom!

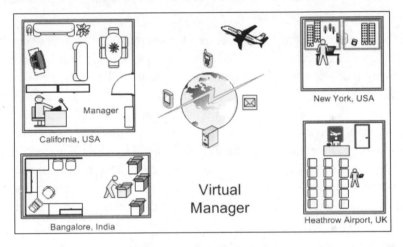

Figure 2.2: The virtual manager

Regardless of the ratio of virtual to local employees, the virtual team members need to be independent and able to take care of their own work environments. They need to be comfortable working alone, isolated from the rest of the team, while at the same time being committed to regular, good-quality communication with each other.

The Virtual Challenge

Virtual management is a challenging role, particularly because it is such a new phenomenon. There are very few tried and tested ways of doing things. Few management training classes are designed to teach the manager how to coach and develop team members remotely or how to build strong teamwork among employees who have never met in person.

A lot of companies are moving to a virtual or hybrid model of management, but many of those companies are not equipping their managers with the tools and knowledge they need to be successful. Just because a manager has strong management and team-building skills does not mean that he or she will be able to step into a virtual role and know exactly what to do. If a manager is used to operating with team members onsite, he or she will have developed processes that work well in that environment. Simply adapting the same processes to enable remote workers to use them will, more often than not, result in a substandard product and frustrated team members.

The biggest mistake you can make as a virtual manager is to do everything the same way as in a local office. This approach does not work. It might seem like everything is going along just fine; you might feel like you get plenty of time to work on your own tasks, and that managing via email is easy. Beneath the surface, however, all sorts of things might be going on that you have absolutely no clue about. By the time you're aware of what is occurring, it will be too late to do anything about it. People need attention. Teams need to be built and maintained. Projects need to be managed. Employees need feedback, coaching, and development. Everyone needs to feel that they are important and appreciated. Sending out a lot of emails and expecting it all to just get done is not going to work as a long-term solution.

If you leave a note in your child's bedroom telling her to please make her bed every day, to put dirty clothes in the hamper, and to do her homework, do you think that she would magically start doing those things everyday? Would you be able to rest easy now that your child has her list of chores? Can you stop reminding her every day (or multiple times per day) to make her bed, pick up her clothes, and do her homework? Not unless she is a very unusual child. She might do those things today because you left the note, but she is unlikely to continue doing them for the next 10 years without some additional coaching.

And what about your relationship with her? If you decide not to speak to her when she gets home from school because you have nothing to say apart from what is in the note, do you think that will make her feel good? Of course not. She will feel neglected and ignored. Telling someone what you would like to get done is not synonymous with having him or her do it. Your team members are adults, not children, but everyone needs personal attention, guidance, and regular communication to function successfully.

Virtual management requires a high level of commitment to good-quality communication with each team member. The virtual style of management needs to be less "command and control," and more "guiding and advising," but with a comparable or greater level of attention than is required for traditional management. Depending on the personal management style of the virtual manager, this might be a relatively easy adjustment or quite a stretch.

What Is Everyone Doing?

One of the biggest challenges with managing a virtual team is knowing who is available and where everyone is. Is someone not answering the phone or responding to email intentionally? If that person were down the hall, you could walk by his or her office and find out. Working virtually, you have to rely on team members to be responsive and responsible. Is that team member visiting her customers, working on a report, out shopping, or at a job interview? How do you know? She might have done no work at all for three weeks apart from responding to a few emails. Is another team member really in his New York home office, or has he gone to the Bahamas for a two-week vacation and taken his BlackBerry with him so he can reply to your emails from time to time?

Our goal isn't to make you paranoid or cause you to continually question your team members about their whereabouts. However, we do want to make you aware that you have a responsibility to create an environment of team cooperation and interaction, which is conducive to high productivity and a high level of mutual respect. You can't do that by just letting your employees get on with it and not contacting them unless there is a problem!

Consider for a moment the motivation behind a virtual worker who does not call in for meetings and makes herself "unavailable" to the manager and the rest of the team on a regular basis. There could be one of a number of things going on here. The first is that the team member is not actually working when she should be. She might make herself elusive so that no one knows what she is doing or when she is doing it. That way, she has a lot more freedom to decide how much work she actually does. On the other hand, it might be that she just wants to work independently and feels that too much contact with the main office takes time away from getting her work done; she would rather just get on with it. It is also possible that the team member is unreliable and unmotivated and thinks that as long as she is not too accessible, she will not be assigned too many additional tasks. None of these situations is good. The problem you have is figuring out which one you are in.

When managing a virtual team, you must lay the ground rules regarding communication expectations from team members. Make clear which meetings are compulsory for all team members. If necessary, you can have a team rule that a team member must notify you ahead of time if he or she is unable to attend the meeting, and explain the reason why. This is not an unreasonable request. If you, as the virtual manager, define a meeting as a top priority, then it should be the top priority for each team member.

Team members should be required to return phone calls or emails in a specified time period. Let's assume 24 hours is a reasonable time for a non-urgent issue. If you cannot get a response from one of your remote workers despite numerous attempts at contact, you have a problem with that employee that needs to be addressed immediately. It is time to have a serious talk about expectations, and to let the team member know that his or her behavior and response time is unacceptable. A remote worker must agree to work within the virtual structure and to follow the guidelines. Otherwise, he or she is not going to be successful working on a virtual team. If an employee who worked in a local office refused to attend meetings, return phone calls, or come into the office during work hours, he or she would sooner or later be fired. The expectations for a remote worker should not be any more relaxed than those for a local worker. As the virtual manager, you are responsible for defining the roles and responsibilities of each team member and holding each of them accountable. The team members are responsible for fulfilling their roles and being accountable to you. If your team members are consistently unable to work within the structure of a virtual team, they are not good virtual-team material. You will need to work with them to get them to where they need to be, whether that is remaining on your team or taking their skill Sets elsewhere!

If all else fails, consider giving team members personal, written objectives regarding communication and meeting attendance. If compensation is tied to the successful completion of personal objectives, the team members who fail to meet the requirements will see this reflected in their salary increases and/or bonuses.

Make sure that you have an effective team-status reporting system in place, so each team member is reporting progress weekly, and is committed to meeting specific objectives for the next week. You need to make sure that the objectives are very clear and measurable. If you cannot measure or validate an objective, it is too vague!

All team members need to be aware that you are the manager and that your role is to manage. You are not there just to help them out with roadblocks or to run meetings now and then. As the manager, you have the ultimate responsibility and accountability for the results of everything your team is working on.

The most important commitments needed from every member of a virtual team, not just the manager, are to communication, responsibility, and accountability. Without these, you don't have a functional team.

Virtual Project Teams

Business and technology consulting firms often have some percentage of their team members working virtually. Often, these organizations form virtual teams on a per-project basis. These teams might work together for a few weeks or a couple of years. If the nature of the projects is that the consultants need to travel regularly, it might not be all that important where they are located. Team members might be in different states or countries. Alternatively, the team members might be located in the same city, but all working from their own home offices. No matter what the geographical distance, if the team members are working out of different offices, they are a virtual team.

For many organizations, having a geographically diverse team is considered advantageous and an effective business model. It makes sense to have team members with similar skill Sets located in different regions, so that a virtual team can be created in the region closest to a customer. This minimizes travel expenses and loss of productive time while traveling.

The virtual project team member needs to be able to work independently and with minimal supervision. Having said that, it is also imperative that remote project team members be "team players," or the project team will not be successful. It is vitally important that those members of your team who work remotely are proactively keeping in touch with you and the rest of the team, and that there is visibility and transparency into what the team members are working on and the status of their tasks.

Dual Management Roles

Responsibility for a hybrid team can create a lot of pressure on the manager, who must demonstrate a high level of competency in the dual roles of traditional and virtual manager. The two roles require many of the same skill Sets, but applied in different ways. Also, the manager needs to be highly skilled in situational leadership in order to seamlessly blend the traditional part of the team with the virtual part of team. This is a very challenging role and one that is often not performed particularly well. Figure 2.3 shows a typical setup for a hybrid manager working with both local and remote team members.

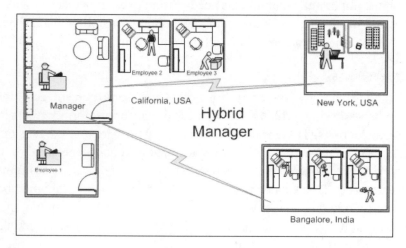

Figure 2.3: The virtual hybrid manager

What often happens in a hybrid team environment is that the team members working locally with the manager get a lot of support from the manager, while those working remotely are neglected. Sometimes this is the fault of the manager, and sometimes it is the virtual workers who create the situation. For example, a virtual worker who is non-locatable or is not responding to communications in a timely manner is preventing the manager from giving any support.

It is the responsibility of the manager to build and maintain a strong and connected team. If the local team members have regular, productive meetings to discuss statuses and resolve issues, but the remote team members are either not invited or do not attend, the team is dysfunctional. By the time this becomes obvious, it will be too late to fix the problem. The manager is the glue that holds a team together. If a manager is only gluing half the team together, it is going to fall apart.

Imagine that you have accidentally dropped a vase given to you by your Auntie Beatrice. She always admires the vase whenever she visits, and you cannot bear the thought of throwing it away and explaining to her that you broke it. You decide to glue it back together. Brilliant idea! However, you find that a few pieces are missing here and there, and you don't have enough glue to stick all the pieces that you do have back together in exactly the right place. Instead of buying more glue, you decide to do your best with what you have. You use the pieces you can find and you stick as much of it as you can back together. How does the vase look when you have finished repairing it? Pretty dreadful. Is the vase functional? Does it still hold water? Unlikely. It looks ugly and it doesn't hold water, which means it is no longer a vase. It just resembles something similar to a vase. This is what happens to your team when you forget to glue half of it together. It somewhat resembles a team, but it does not function as it should, and it cannot be used effectively for its original purpose!

> The manager is the glue that holds a team together. If a manager is only gluing half the team together, it is going to fall apart.

A virtual manager must never forget about the remote team members. Whether it is scheduling a quick meeting or sending birthday cards, everyone must be included. This might seem obvious, but it is amazing how often managers forget about the team members they do not see everyday. The expression "out of sight is out of mind" is often very true!

Spontaneity

In order to accommodate remote team members, meetings need to be planned in advance. Those spontaneous "let's just go to John's office to discuss this" meetings are not going to be as easy to arrange. However, if you keep your team members connected via instant messaging, you will be able to see who is logged on. You might be able to send a quick message asking remote team members to call John's office in five minutes or to call into a conference room in half an hour. As a virtual manager, you don't have to take all the spontaneity out of work life, but you will sometimes need to be more creative and flexible to make it work.

Skill Sets Required for the Virtual Manager

A virtual manager needs to be proficient in the same skills as a traditional manager, in addition to having some new and specialized skills. The level of skill that the manager needs in a given area might be quite different for a virtual manager compared to a traditional manager. A solid foundation in business and/or technical management skills is essential for any manager, no matter what level of virtual management will be required. A checklist of virtual manager and remote team member skill Sets is included in appendix A.

Virtual management skills can be broken down into these key areas:

- General management
- People management
- Communication
- Technical knowledge
- Decision making
- Problem solving
- Team building
- Administration

In the following pages, we will discuss each of these areas in detail.

General Management

A solid foundation in general management is essential for any manager. This is the foundation upon which the virtual management skill Set must be built. General management skills include the following:

- Scheduling
- Organization
- Time management
- Leadership
- Prioritization
- Goal setting
- Tracking and reporting progress
- Managing change
- Budgeting and finance

The specific methods or tools used in general management might differ based on whether the manager is traditional or virtual, but the skills themselves are the same. For example, the ability to track and report progress is the same, whether the progress is tracked on a whiteboard or on a Website.

The general management skill is the ability to stay in control of the project, contract, or team; to keep things on track; and to know the current status. The technical or communication skill is the ability to use tools and methods to physically track and report on progress.

The virtual manager needs to employ some additional knowledge and a deeper level of skill than the traditional manager in some areas. For example, leadership skills manifests itself in different ways when you are working with people in different countries instead of in the same room. Leading a team that never gets to see you in person is not as easy as leading a team who you can personally meet with on a daily or weekly basis.

When working in a local environment with team members, you can lead your team by being a strong personal presence in their everyday lives. It's relatively easy to understand what each person is working on and what each person needs from you, so you can guide team members in the right direction and keep them on track, gauging the mood of the team and adjusting your management style accordingly.

When managing a virtual team, none of these is as easy to accomplish. Being a personal presence and understanding what each person is working on has to be done via virtual tools and not by "walking the halls." The virtual team has no walls and no halls! On a traditional team, you can find out what team members need from you by observing them and by asking them. On the virtual team, you can observe only by paying attention to what you hear in verbal communications and what you see in written communications. If you want to know what someone needs, you have to ask. You might need to ask more than once. Never assume that what someone needs from you this week is the same as what will be needed next week. To guide your team in the right direction, you need a good sense of what direction they are going in now. You also need to know if they are all going in the same direction. This can only be accomplished with a lot of very high-quality communication and a commitment to lead your team by example. You will only know that they are following you if you are in regular contact with each of them and if the communication is open, honest, and appropriate.

Gauging the mood of the virtual team is very different from gauging the mood of a local team. Get a team together in one room, and you will find that the team members feed off each other's energy, whether it be positive or negative. In a few minutes or a few hours, you will have the team's collective mood. This happens with virtual teams, too, but it takes a lot more time to get to the point where enough people are in the same mood for it be reflective of the team.

A groan about something in a meeting room is heard by all immediately, and responded to quickly. The groan might be echoed around the room, or other people might express disagreement with the complaint. Either way, it is not ignored. In contrast, a groan via conference call might not get any response at all. This does not necessarily mean that the mood of your team is good. It might just mean that the other team members have too many of their own problems to want to listen to someone else's! Even worse is a groan via email, which can take days or weeks to reach everyone, depending on how well the team members are managing their time and how quickly they are reading their emails. It might elicit some responses, but it is not as likely to generate a "get it off your chest" or "clear the air" session as in a meeting room. You need to read between the lines and try to figure out if there is a collective mood on the team. If so, what is it? Is it better to have a collective mood or a group of different moods? It can depend on the situation. As a leader, you might want your team to feel inspired about something in particular, which means you need to work to instill that emotion in each team member so that, when they come together virtually, the mood is universal.

If your team members feel confident that they know what you expect from them, and you know what they expect from you, they will be more inclined to follow your lead. Virtual leadership is covered in more detail in chapter 14.

The ability to track and report progress is a lot more challenging virtually than locally. For the virtual manager working remotely from the rest of the team, it is vitally important to have well-defined work hours. When working from home, it is easy to slip into bad behaviors that are not conducive to a good work or home life. For example, getting out of bed in the mornings and starting work wearing your pajamas is not a good work method. It blurs the lines between work time and personal time. Working here and there throughout the day and not really keeping track of how much time you are spending working and how much time you are spending on personal tasks will make it almost impossible to know when you should be finished for the day, or how to track and report on your work time.

You might end up working at all hours of the day and night and feel like you can never plan to do anything during your personal time, as you have no idea when that should be. It is very likely that you have met someone who works this way. You might wonder if such a person ever has any fun and if he or she really needs to work 16 hours every single day! You will feel more motivated by your work, be less stressed, and enjoy your life a lot more if you can clearly define when your work should stop and your personal time should begin.

First, you should have a set start and finish time for your workday. If you start earlier some days, then finish earlier. If you have to work late to attend a meeting, give yourself back the time the next day or finish early on Friday. Try to work regular hours as much as you can. Some weeks, you might need to work more hours than others, but it is important not to work yourself into the ground. If you consistently need an extra 20 hours per week to get your work finished, there is a problem. You are working on too many unimportant tasks, you are not organizing and prioritizing your work appropriately, or you are being assigned too much work for one person! Extra hours to meet a deadline or deal with a crisis is one thing; working all the hours under the sun every single week is another. Managers who consistently work much longer than 40 or 50 hours per week will, over time, become less effective than their counterparts.

After you get up in the morning, make sure that you shower, get dressed, have breakfast, and do anything else that you would before work if you were working in a traditional office. Perhaps you would usually go for run, take the dog for walk, or drop the children off at school. Do all these things just as you would if you had a regular office job. The more structure you have in your work life, the easier it will be to maintain clearly defined lines between it and your home life.

If you have a home office, it is a good idea to use a different computer for work and personal computing. If you only have one computer, set it up with two separate profiles. Use the work profile during work hours and the personal profile during your own time. Take a lunch break each day. Allow yourself some time off to eat, go to the gym, pop out to the shops, or run some other errands. It is your workday, and you are entitled to a break in the middle of it.

Keep track of what tasks you work on and how many hours you work on each one. This will help you with your time management as well as your work/home delineation. When it is time for your workday to end, close down the computer, put your work materials away, and do whatever it is that you do in your personal time.

These are not very difficult guidelines to follow. The positive effect they have on how you feel about your work, and your life in general, is much larger than the effort you put in to achieve them. If you have direct reports who are also working remotely, you should coach them on how to balance their work and personal time. A motivated and energized team will be a successful team. Time management is covered in more detail in chapter 6.

People Management

People management skills are required for managers whether or not they have direct reports. They are also required for both virtual and traditional teams. If a manager is leading a team, he or she needs to be able to manage the individuals on the team and the team as a whole. If a manager is responsible for managing a project instead of team members, that does not mean the manager does not need people skills. Managing by influence rather than authority can be much more challenging!

Skills involved in people management include the following:

- Active listening
- Coordination and scheduling
- Hiring and firing
- Making pay decisions
- Setting goals
- Setting personal objectives
- Evaluating performance
- Facilitating meetings
- Resolving conflict
- Coaching and development

Managing people who work in the same building can be a difficult job. Managing people whom you hardly ever see in person adds a lot more complexity to the role of the manager. Add to that a matrix-management system where you are not the direct line manager, and you could find yourself losing control of the situation and feeling overwhelmed very quickly.

Managing your own time can be difficult enough. Helping others to manage theirs is a lot more tricky. It is harder to measure how well someone is managing his or her time when you cannot stop by and see that person. If someone comes into your office at 11:00 each morning, takes a lunch break from 12:30 to 2:00 in the afternoon, and then spends much of the rest of the day involved in issues that are interesting to that person but not directly related to business tasks or objectives, it will soon be obvious why he or she is unable to keep on track and meet his deliverables. If that person is working remotely, however, it could take quite some time until you discover what is going on. This is why it is of utmost importance that all team members, whether they report to you directly or not, have clearly defined objectives and deliverables on a weekly basis. You, as the virtual manager, need to be able to determine as early as possible if a team member is failing to meet commitments. It is not ideal to communicate virtually with an employee that he or she is underperforming or underdelivering, but it must be done. Team members sometimes take advantage of the fact that they are working virtually and will try to avoid having that conversation if they see it coming.

> Managing people whom you hardly ever see in person adds a lot more complexity to the role of the manager.

It is hard to have a delicate conversation about performance and results without being able to see the effect you are having on an employee. For most people, about 80% of emotions are obvious from looking at the face and observing body language. If you are lucky, you might get some feedback in the voice, but will you be able to decipher its meaning? Silence on the other end of the phone might mean the person is angry, sad, or maybe speechless with shock. How will you know? Here is an obvious answer: You have to ask. You need to share the news, wait for it to sink it, and then ask what the person is thinking or feeling. The point of a conversation like this is to resolve the problem, not to punish someone for it.

Active listening is a key communication skill for any manager. For the virtual manager, it is even more important. You cannot read body language or facial expressions over the phone, so reading between the lines is not going to be easy. People do not always tell you what they really think. Sometimes they tell you what they think you want to hear. Sometimes they tell you what you do *not* want to hear, not because it's what they really think, but because they are having a bad day or because they have a tendency to exaggerate. It is also easy to misinterpret what someone is trying to tell you when they are on the phone, especially if the person is not very articulate. Some people find it hard to finish a sentence, complete a thought, or stay focused long enough to keep from jumping to another issue.

By repeating to your virtual employees what you hear when speaking with them and voicing what you believe to be the highlights of the conversation, you give them a chance to correct you or to add more information. Listening and making notes during virtual meetings with team members is key to ensuring that you are hearing a consistent message. If your virtual team member tells you one thing today and another thing tomorrow about why he or she has not been calling in for meetings, you will have a pretty good idea that maybe that person is trying to pull the wool over your eyes, after all.

Coaching and development can also be difficult to accomplish remotely, but it is possible to achieve good results with some up-front planning and a well-defined process. The use of templates to track progress, and scheduling time to meet and work through any issues that need attention, will add a lot of value to the time you spend interacting with team members virtually. Such a process needs a lot of involvement from both parties. The manager and the virtual worker both need to be honest and open with feedback in order to effectively coach and develop remotely. When hiring remote employees, it is important to ensure that the team members have the core skill Sets required to work remotely. If not, you will be spending way too much time trying to train, coach, and develop team members so that they can effectively do their jobs. Ideally, coaching and development should only be needed to help team members meet their annual objectives and to improve in specific areas so they can move to the next level.

You should schedule personal development meetings with each team member to give feedback on how well he or she is performing, to review the team member's objectives for the next period, and to discuss the team member's personal growth and development plan. There will always be some areas for improvement. It is not possible to improve on lots of things at the same time, so focus on one or two key areas and come up with standard or creative ways of helping the team member improve. Some development areas are very difficult to evaluate virtually. For example, suppose you suspect a team member needs to improve presentation skills. If you are not involved in those presentations person-ally, how can you evaluate how well he is performing? Unless he videos the pre-sentation, you probably will not be able to. There are options, however:

- You could ask the team member to video one of his presentations, either onsite or at home.
- You could ask attendees at the presentations for feedback.
- You could set up a video conference with the team member and ask him to give his presentation to you.
- You could fly to a client site and watch a presentation.
- You could ask the team member for a self-evaluation.

You don't have to be in the room watching a presentation to be able to coach someone on how to be a better presenter. You do, however, have to listen to what is being said and give constructive feedback. You can talk to someone on the phone and tell whether that person would be an effective presenter based on fac-tors such as these:

- Fluency of speech—Does the person use a lot of filler words, pauses, repeats, "ahs" and "ums," or phrases like "you know"?
- Organization of thought—Does the person transition from one point to another in a logical and understandable way?
- Comprehension—Can you understand what the person is trying to communicate to you?
- Interest—Does the person keep you interested, so that you pay attention?

Someone who is confusing and hard to follow on the phone will be just as confusing and hard to follow in person!

Stay positive, and focus attention on accomplishing all that you can virtually, rather than worrying about the things that you have not figured out how to do yet. There will always be some things that will not work as well virtually as locally, and vice versa.

Communication

Effective and well-managed communication is key to virtual management. Communication encompasses many areas and is a vital ingredient in the daily life of a virtual manager. There are lots of tools to help with the various forms of communicating. The most important thing to remember about communicating is that email, phones, instant messaging, etc. are *tools* for communicating. They cannot create or manage the communication for you. The person using the tools must have a clearly defined communication process and must be skilled at using the tools if the results are going to be positive. Here are some examples of different types of communication:

- Email
- Phone calls
- Instant messaging
- Team meetings
- Agendas and minutes
- One-on-one meetings
- Status reporting
- Communicating change
- Issues and disaster-management reporting
- Documentation management
- Presentations

A documented communication plan will be a huge asset to any virtual team. This topic is covered in more detail in chapter 8.

A key thing to remember when communicating virtually is that over 80% of our communication is nonverbal. When we communicate with each other, what we say is not necessarily the most important part of our message that gets communicated. Think about presentations you have attended. What is it that makes someone a good speaker? How does a speaker keep your attention? If someone talks at you for four hours in a slow monotone voice, how much of what they are saying do you retain or understand? Not very much. Body language, gestures, eye contact, clothing, grooming, and tone of voice all contribute to communication. An interesting speaker is one who draws you in. The way a speaker looks adds depth and breadth to what he or she says. A smile, a frown, or hands thrown up in the air all convey important messages aside from what is being communicated verbally.

How you say something can completely change its meaning. In a phone call, you retain the tone of voice, but lose the body language. In an email, you lose both and are left with only text. You can effectively convey facts via written communication, but it is much more challenging to convey the "sense" of a message. Sarcasm, humor, happiness, and frustration can all be easily confused in written communication. Likewise, there can be confusion in an audio conference. Nobody can see the raised eyebrows, the smile, the sigh, the head in the hands—all of the communication that signifies these emotions is lost. In effect, virtual communications are devoid of emotion. Webcams and video conferencing can help to some extent, but they are not always readily available, and if the connection is slow or jumpy, it is still difficult trying to figure out if that was a smile or a grimace!

> A key thing to remember when communicating virtually is that over 80% of our communication is nonverbal.

Being able to see what someone looks like is conducive to feeling like you know that person better. Some companies have intranets with photos of each employee. If your company has one of these sites, use it. You might want to print out photos of your team members and keep them in your office, so you are more aware of who you are talking to when on a phone call.

Many leaders are deemed "good" because of their charismatic nature. They are articulate and use body language to build rapport and trust with others. It is much harder to convey charisma via a phone line. There is a large visual aspect to conveying charisma. Coming across as open, friendly, and approachable *is* possible by phone, however, and a good leader will use every opportunity to build rapport and trust with team members. People start to recognize voices after a time, so even on a call with 20 people, it is possible to know who is speaking without needing that person announced. As the virtual manager, focus your attention on learning the different voices so that you can respond to each person by name rather than constantly asking, "Who is speaking?" Team members will feel more valued if you recognize them. Having said this, not everyone on the call will recognize who is speaking, so rather than asking a person to state his or her name, use it when you respond so that everyone else knows who spoke. Even if all you say is, "Thank you, Francesca, for sharing that information," it informs the other people on the call who just spoke so they do not have to ask.

Language problems can also hamper virtual meetings. Some people for whom English is a second language will understand written English better than spoken English. Colloquialisms and slang might not be understood. If the line is crackly and it is hard to hear, that can further detract from the ability to understand what is being discussed. The meeting facilitator needs to ensure that he or she is summarizing key points and decisions, so that all attendees are sure of what has been discussed and what decisions have been made. This might slow down the meeting a little, but it will make it more effective.

Good documentation and note-taking go a long way toward keeping the team members feeling connected with what is going on. There is nothing worse than feeling "out of the loop," on the outer fringes of the team rather than part of the inner circle. If the same information is available to everyone on the team, it becomes the team members' responsibility to make sure that they are staying connected and informed. Attending meetings is ideal, but time zones and other work commitments mean that not everyone will be able to attend every meeting. If the meeting organizer is sending out an agenda and minutes for every meeting, team members will be able to more effectively prioritize between meetings and will be able to read minutes for those meetings they were not able to attend.

Technical Knowledge

When working in a home office, it is important to have some level of technical knowledge so you can keep equipment and communications up and running. In a traditional office, there is usually a full-time information systems group that can help with setting up computers and tracking down problems. If you are working remotely, you might have access to some technical help via email or phone, or you might be pretty much on your own. Below are some examples of the type of technical knowledge and skills required to work virtually:

- ➤ Setting up a computer
- ➤ Connecting a printer
- ➤ Setting up a home network
- ➤ Installing and configuring software
- ➤ Setting up email accounts

- ► Configuring a connection to a VPN
- ► Creating spreadsheets and presentations
- ► Managing documents
- ► Setting up a mobile phone or PDA
- ► Setting up Internet service (cable, DSL, or dial-up)
- ► Troubleshooting connectivity or technical issues

Working from a home office requires that you be self-sufficient with the equipment and tools you need to do your job. In a traditional office environment, your job will most likely not include configuring software or troubleshooting a printer problem. In a home office, however, you are the system administrator, the printer technician, the network engineer, and the phone technician, as well as a manager! If you do not have these skills and wish to work in a virtual environment, consider taking a few computer classes. Keep the user documentation at hand for all electronic and computer equipment. You can usually solve problems by taking the time to read through them. Learn how to use "help" in computer programs before calling someone. Use online help and message forums to get information on problems you do not know how to solve. Many companies have online FAQs, and more and more companies are making their knowledge bases available via the Internet to help users troubleshoot their own problems. The information is probably there; you just have to learn how to find it.

In addition to general technical troubleshooting skills, you will need a high level of skill with software programs, including those for spreadsheets and presentations. There will not be an admin assistant close at hand to help you figure out how to add a graphic to a presentation, import a table, or add a calculation to a spreadsheet. You will need to be proficient in many software programs, so that you can make use of all the tools at your disposal. Once again, learning how to use the "help" functions in the programs will enable you to solve many problems independently.

Some companies maintain a help desl to support employees working locally or remotely. This is a great resource, if you have access to it. Unless a remote worker is using standard, recommended equipment and tools, however, it might be difficult for the help desl technicians to fully troubleshoot and resolve the problems.

Decision Making

All managers have to make decisions. The virtual manager is no exception. The challenge with virtual decision-making is ensuring that everyone knows that the decision has been made, and that everyone accepts and acts on it. Although the manager has decision-making authority, that authority is worth nothing if team members are not aware that an opinion has become a decision, or if they choose to ignore decisions they don't like. Communication, yet again, is the key to success. It is vital to build a team in which roles and responsibilities are clearly defined, and where there is no confusion about who the decision maker is. Communicating decisions must be done in an unambiguous and assertive manner. Otherwise, the recipients of the communication will be unclear about how to act upon the information.

Consider an example. You are the manager of a team that has been pursuing three major clients, with a view to signing contracts in the next two fiscal quarters. A lot of time and effort has already been spent on building prototypes and putting together presentations to woo these clients. It has now come to light that one of the prospective clients is about to be acquired by a large corporation, which holds a controlling share in your organization's major competitor. Though the prospective client had been very excited by your proposal and was ready to sign a contract, they now want to wait before signing the contract because of the acquisition. The client has asked you to continue building the prototype and to continue holding meetings with them, as they are sure they will be able to close the deal as soon as the acquisition is final. It is obvious to you that this will never happen; the new parent company would not give business to a competitor, no matter how good the product.

> The main problem with conference calls is that attendees are often not giving the meeting their full attention.

You make the decision that your team will discontinue working on this deal. There is no point in spending even more money and time on a deal that will never close. There is also a concern that the client now has a lot of information about your product and, although they have signed nondisclosure agreements, it is very risky sharing any more information with them. You plan to gracefully extricate yourself from the deal by letting the client know that you hope you can still work together in the future, but that you need to put the prototype on hold until there is more clarity around their intentions to sign a contract with your company. So far, so good.

How do you effectively communicate this decision to your team members? In an ideal world, you would call them all into a conference room for a meeting, where you would discuss the issue and communicate the decision. However, your team is virtual, so you cannot do that. Another alternative would be to set up a conference call. The main problem with conference calls is that attendees are often not giving the meeting their full attention. They might mute their phones and read a few emails, while keeping one ear open in case someone mentions their names. If they were not listening well, they will leave the meeting unaware of the gravity of the situation or the importance of the decision. We have experienced this many times.

For critical information or decisions, communicate the same information to your virtual team several times within the same week, because you can assume some of them were not listening attentively. On the fourth time, someone who has been in attendance on every single one of the previous conference calls will invariably remark, "I can't believe this decision was made and I am only just hearing about it. When was the decision made?" You might be able to minimize this, but you will never be able to eradicate it. Virtual management requires more communication than does local management.

When you cannot see your team members, you don't know what they are doing while they are on a conference call with you. If their phones are muted, you have no idea if they are even within earshot of the phone. The best method is to send an email describing the issue and the decision, and identifying the decision maker. Then, reiterate the decision in at least one conference call.

People retain very little of what they hear, even when they are paying attention. If you communicate once, you will be lucky if they remember what you told them. If you communicate the same information twice, you have a much better chance that they will recall it at the appropriate time. If you communicate the same information, clearly and unambiguously, three times and make sure the recipients both heard it and read it, you have a much better chance that they will remember what you said, and there will no confusion about the meaning of your message. A decision is not going to be effective unless everybody understands and accepts it.

Figure 2.4 shows an example of a communication that does not clearly convey the decision or the action that needs to be taken.

From: George
Sent: June 24th
to: My Team
subject: ABC Account

It has come to our attention during the last week that ABC company is in negotiations with XYZ Incorporated who are planning to acquire them. I think that we should probably not spend much more time working on this deal as it is unclear how things will progress with the pending acquisition. Please make the other three prospective client the highest priority. Paul, I trust that you will communicate our decision to put this on the back burner to the client.

Regards

George

Figure 2.4: Unclear decision communication

The communication is ambiguous. George has not clearly communicated all the facts, nor has he specifically asked the team *not* to work on this project. It is not clear that this project is canceled until further notice. Virtual team members who see this will most likely ignore it, as they do not know quite what is expected of them. Virtual communication needs to be concise, to the point, and accurate. Figure 2.5 demonstrates much more clearly the decision that has been made, why the decision was made, what the expectation is of each team member, and who is responsible for communicating with the client.

It is important that all team members understand not only what decision has been made, but also why it was made. Virtual team members on a hybrid team are often out of the loop on some of the everyday things going on in the local office. If you only communicate information to the local employees and forget about the virtual ones, you will have team members going off in all directions with no cohesive plan.

As the manager of the team, you are the decision maker. Make sure your team members know that. You do not just have ideas and suggestions that you share with the team; you are responsible for making the final decisions. You are accountable for making the decisions, taking responsibility for them, communicating them, enforcing them, sometimes justifying them, and from time to time possibly changing or updating them. It is OK to change a decision, as long as everyone on the team is aware of the change. Remote workers need to know what is happening, and if the manager is changing his or her mind from day to day without communicating those decisions, they will be working on the wrong things and taking the wrong action.

From: George
Sent: June 24th
to: My Team
subject: ABC Account

It has come to our attention during the last week that ABC company is in negotiations with XYZ Incorporated who are planning to acquire them. XYZ holds a controlling share of the CCP organization who is our largest competitor. CCP has a competing product which is used as a standard product at all XYZ companies.

I have spoken to ABC about the pending acquisition and they have requested that we continue working on this project as they feel confident that there is an opportunity for us to do business with them. I have told them that we are very interested in doing business with them and that we value our relationship highly but that we cannot continue with the prototyping project until the acquisition is finalized as they will be unable to make contractual decisions until that point.

We have a non disclosure agreement with the company but in light of the fact that they are being acquired by our competitors we should all be highly vigilant in making sure that no further information is discussed or shared in any way with any employees of ABC company. Please cease all communications immediately. If you receive any communications asking for information please refer the requester directly to me.

Thank you for all your hard work on this proposal and project. It is disappointing to have made such good progress and to be thwarted at the 11th hour but it is in the best interests of our company and our team to switch our attention to our other prospects and to focus all our efforts on closing those deals as quickly as possible.

Please let me know if you have any questions.

Regards

George

Figure 2.5: Clear decision communication

Problem Solving

In many respects, virtual problem solving is the same as any other kind of problem solving. What sets it apart from regular problem solving is that you might not recognize that there is a problem until the molehill has already turned into a mountain. At that point, it could take a huge amount of time and effort to understand the complexities of the problem and solve it in a timely manner.

Problem solving might be technical, political, administrative, or managerial. The problem might be something about which you have direct knowledge, or it might be something a team member is experiencing that does not directly affect you. It might be inside your control or outside your control. No matter what type of problem or where it occurs, if it affects your team's ability to meet its goals and objectives, you need to step up and take ownership for driving it to resolution. That ownership might be limited to being aware that a team member is working on an issue and making yourself available, or it might require that you take ownership for the whole problem and actively work on a solution.

It is much easier to ignore a problem when you are working remotely, which means it is much easier to get into trouble!

Meeting regularly with your team members, requesting and reading status reports, and generally building strong, open communication and teamwork will allow you to identify when trouble is brewing. By paying attention to what is being said and how it is being said, you will start to pick up on areas of stress and get a sense of when someone is not telling you the whole story. Learning how to probe to get all the facts will enable you to get to the bottom of what is going on. Trying to solve a problem without full and complete information is a big handicap, which is likely to result in a resolution that is inappropriate and ultimately unsuccessful.

It is much easier to ignore a problem when you are working remotely, which means it is much easier to get into trouble! An issue can sometimes seem a long way away if it is occurring in a different continent—why worry about it right now? Remote team members might be reluctant to communicate problems, and it is much easier to hide them when nobody else can see what you are doing. The denial of the problem will not make it go away, of course, and the longer you ignore it, the worse it is going to get. The problem might be easier to ignore remotely, but it is likely to also be exponentially more difficult to resolve remotely, so beware of leaving it for too long. You might create a monster! Instead, deal with it as quickly as possible. You can then move on and not spend the next three weeks worrying about it!

Team Building

Team building needs a unique approach when being managed virtually. Taking your team out to lunch or the movies is not possible when you are in geographically diverse locations. Building rapport will require a lot more effort and creativity than in a non-virtual environment. Team members who interact daily or weekly will build rapport among themselves without your involvement or knowledge. It is not as straightforward or free-flowing when you speak on the phone or send emails with no personal contact.

One way to enhance the team-building process is to encourage the use of instant messaging. This is a great tool for informal chats. It doesn't have to be limited to strictly business. Saying "hi" when you see someone logged into an instant messenger is like saying "hi" and chatting for a few minutes when you see someone at the coffee machine. It is OK to take a few minutes of your day now and again to talk about non–work-related topics. This collection of non–work-related exchanges builds rapport among team members.

The manager bonds the virtual team together. Without the manager's constant and close attention, the team really will fall apart. A team is not just a collection of people working toward the same goal. It is collection of people who feel connected to each other and who want to work together and help each other meet shared goals. The team is an entity in itself, greater than the sum of its parts. The manager creates and builds the team. He or she must guide the team in the right direction and help the team adapt and embrace change. Each change that affects the team affects the dynamics of the team. The manager must find the positive aspects of the change and use them to enhance the strength of the team. If he or she loses focus on the team, the team loses focus on its goals.

Virtual team days are a great way of building teamwork. This is covered in more detail in chapter 7.

Administration

Most middle managers today take care of a lot of their own administrative work. Admin assistants often support multiple managers, and there is only a limited amount of time available to each. As a virtual manager, you will be taking care of even more of your own administrative tasks. Here are just some of the tasks you will find yourself responsible for:

- Typing correspondence and reports
- Scheduling meetings
- Taking meeting minutes, typing them, and distributing them to meeting attendees
- Filing
- Preparing and submitting expense claims
- Reading and responding to emails
- Replenishing stationery supplies
- Sending and delivering mail
- Making travel arrangements

Many of these skill Sets are comparable to those of the traditional manager. These days, most managers type their own correspondence, schedule their own meetings, write minutes and emails, and prepare expense reports. Not all managers will be used to ordering or purchasing their own stationery and computer supplies, however, or taking mail to the post office every day. It is important to schedule time on your calendar to work on these tasks as they constitute part of the normal working week for the virtual manager. Going to the post office or stationery store are work related tasks so there is no reason they cannot be scheduled during your normal working hours.

The worst thing about working remotely when it comes to administrative tasks is that there is nobody to check your work for you before you finalize it. For example, if you are crafting a delicately worded piece of correspondence to a client, in a traditional office you might ask one of your coworkers to review it for you. As a virtual manager, you are on your own with these things, so you must take extra care.

Skill Sets Required for the Remote Worker

Just as the virtual manager requires both traditional and virtual management skill Sets, so does the remote worker. These skill Sets can be broken down into the following categories:

- General management
- People skills
- Communication
- Technical knowledge
- Decision making
- Problem solving
- Team building
- Administration

General Management

Why, you might ask, would a remote worker need general management skills? A worker located remotely from his or her manager will need to fulfill some functions that would not usually be required of a local worker. The skill Sets that fall within the general management category are:

- ▸ Organization
- ▸ Time management
- ▸ Decision making
- ▸ Prioritization
- ▸ Goal setting
- ▸ Tracking and reporting progress
- ▸ Budgeting and finance

Any remote worker, manager or not, needs to be very organized and have good time-management skills. Someone who is easily distracted and finds it hard to stay on task is going to struggle with accomplishing very much in a virtual environment. The ability to make decisions and to prioritize tasks is essential. Procrastination will lead to nothing getting done. The remote worker needs to track and report on daily or weekly accomplishments, which requires the ability to focus.

The amount of budgeting that needs to be done by the remote worker will differ from company to company. At a minimum, the remote worker needs to manage a supplies budget (for office and computer supplies). He or she might also have a travel budget, and might possibly need to keep track of costs for project budgets.

People Skills

People skills are obviously useful for everyone, no matter what type of team or company he works for. The remote worker needs the ability to persuade and influence others with limited face-to-face time. Any lack of people skills is going to be a huge roadblock to accomplishing this. The following skill Sets are key:

- ▸ Active listening
- ▸ Coordination and scheduling
- ▸ Meeting facilitation
- ▸ Conflict management

As with the virtual manager, the virtual worker must be able to practice active listening. If the majority of communication is via phone, it is important to have good verbal communication skills. Listening and understanding is of vital importance to virtual workers. Coordinating and scheduling their own tasks, and working with other team members and clients to coordinate and schedule joint tasks, is also necessary for remote workers.

Meeting-facilitation skills are desirable skills for everyone on a virtual team, regardless of whether she actually facilitates meetings. Understanding the rules and etiquette for meetings will make virtual team meetings more productive and participative.

Conflict management is another skill that everyone should possess. Virtual team conflict is interesting, as the conflict can brew much more slowly, and the effects of it can last a much longer time. There are not many opportunities to "make up" after virtual team members get into conflict, so sometimes the resentment can hang in there for a very long time. Understanding how to manage and control conflict will lead to a more harmonious and honest team. Nobody will need to tread on eggshells and be afraid of saying the wrong thing if the whole team is skilled in conflict management.

Communication

Most of what the virtual worker does is communicate. Since almost all his or her work is done alone, the virtual worker needs to do a lot of communication to ensure that others know what is going on. There are many essential tools and methods in the remote worker's toolbox:

- ➤ Email
- ➤ Phone calls
- ➤ Instant messaging
- ➤ Team meetings
- ➤ Agendas and minutes
- ➤ One-on-one meetings
- ➤ Status reporting
- ➤ Documentation management
- ➤ Presentations

Pretty much everything in regards to communication for the virtual manager also applies to the remote worker. Good-quality communication, a high level of written and verbal communication and presentation skills, and the ability to communicate clearly and concisely are all key skill Sets for the remote worker. Some people are great at communicating a lot of information about everything they do. The hard part is often learning how to condense all those details in a high-level description that is appropriate for 80% of the audience. The ability to express oneself well within a time limit, while including all the key points, is vital for the remote worker.

Technical Knowledge

As with the virtual manager, the remote worker must have a minimum level of technical knowledge to keep work equipment and communications up and running in a home office. The skill Sets are the same as those needed for the virtual manager:

- ➤ Setting up a computer
- ➤ Setting up a home network
- ➤ Connecting a printer
- ➤ Installing and configuring software
- ➤ Setting up email accounts
- ➤ Configuring and connecting to a VPN
- ➤ Creating spreadsheets and presentations
- ➤ Managing documents
- ➤ Setting up a mobile phone or PDA
- ➤ Setting up Internet service (cable, DSL, or dial-up)
- ➤ Troubleshooting connectivity or technical issues

The ability to troubleshoot and track down issues quickly is essential. You cannot afford three days of downtime for a remote worker because he or she cannot get a network connection functioning. The remote worker needs to know the limits of his or her own expertise, to know when to call in the experts. He or she also needs to have identified some experts ahead of time. You do not want someone going through the Yellow Pages looking for a technician in the middle of a technical crisis!

Decision Making

Remote workers make more of their own decisions than do their counterparts in a local office. As a virtual manager, you should expect your remote workers to be independent and self-motivated, and to know how to get things done and achieve results. A remote worker who cannot make a decision without waiting for management approval is not going to be very effective. Of course, a remote worker needs to understand what kinds of decisions are appropriate for him or her to make, and which ones need to be approved by management first. Good reasoning skills and common sense need to be partnered with effective decision-making skills.

Problem Solving

We all need to be able to solve problems. Remote workers, especially, need to be able to figure things out and "get on with it." There is not a large support network waiting in the wings to jump in and resolve every issue that arises. Problem solving doesn't mean that the remote worker has to know the answers to everything, but he or she does have to be resourceful and organized in solving problems. Being able to work virtually with others and collaborate on problem solving is essential. Virtual team members who refuse to share problems are going to be a hindrance to the team.

Team Orientation

Being team oriented is vitally important for a remote worker. He or she is working in a isolated environment, and yet needs to feel a strong tie to fellow teammates. Without this contradictory combination of independence and team orientation, a remote worker is not going to thrive in a virtual team environment. The remote worker needs to have the ability and the motivation to be an active and contributing part of a team that is working together, apart.

> Virtual team members who refuse to share problems are going to be a hindrance to the team.

Great teamwork is possible in a virtual environment, but it requires commitment from the manager and each team member. Do not hire anyone onto your team who is a "lone ranger." If someone doesn't work well with others, you don't need that person on your team no matter how talented or knowledgeable he or she is in other areas. Such a person is like a brick wall built across the freeway, preventing anyone from moving forward, and preventing those coming in one direction from seeing or communicating with those going in the other.

Administration

Administrative tasks for remote workers are the same as for virtual managers. There is no administrative help to assist with any of it. The remote worker must be prepared to take ownership of these administrative tasks:

- Typing correspondence
- Scheduling meetings
- Taking meeting minutes, typing them, and distributing them to meeting attendees
- Filing
- Preparing and submitting expense claims
- Reading and responding to emails
- Ordering/replenishing stationery supplies
- Mail
- Travel arrangements
- Typing and submitting status reports

The remote worker who is unable to organize and manage these administrative tasks on an ongoing basis quickly becomes ineffective. For example, forgetting to make travel arrangements for a client visit until the day before means paying two to three times as much for an airline ticket, and possibly having a problem finding a hotel room. Forgetting to order stationery supplies means unnecessary problems and delays when the remote worker is unable to print from an empty printer cartridge. Running to the computer store for emergency supplies can be very disruptive to the planned work schedule.

What Employees Want from a Virtual Manager

Employees need a high level of support and guidance from their manager, no matter how often they actually meet in person. Each employee needs to feel that he or she is an important and valuable member of the team. This means that the manager needs to be accessible and available to the employee outside of scheduled meeting times.

If an employee calls you because she has an urgent problem, she needs you to call her back within hours, not in three days. She is not going to feel that you care about what she is doing if you completely ignore her email or phone message. If you answer the phone and tell her you are busy but will call her back in one hour, she expects to receive a call back. If she does not receive a call and decides to contact you again the next day to follow up, she doesn't want to find that you have gone on vacation for a week. If you are unable to help, you must find someone else who can. Ignoring others because you are busy is not acceptable. You need to set standards for the team, and then you need to live up to them. Use your whiteboard to remind you to call people who need to speak to you, or schedule a 30-minute conference call on your calendars so you don't forget. Let your team members know that if they call you about an important issue and cannot track you down, it is OK to schedule a meeting with you using your online calendar (assuming they have access to your calendar), so that they have a high level of confidence of being able to get some time with you. In a local office, employees can swing by your office as soon as they see you are there. Virtually, you need to employ different tactics, but make sure you are just as available as you would be in person.

Regular one-on-one and status meetings with employees should be scheduled in advance. If you are unable to keep a scheduled appointment, it is important to let the team member know in advance that you are unavailable and to reschedule the postponed meeting. Employees will start to feel neglected if you continually use their one-on-one time for other meetings and fail to reschedule them for another time.

Another negative behavior to avoid is attending the one-on-one meeting and telling the employee, "I only have 15 minutes since I have another meeting, and I am also waiting for an important phone call. If it comes while we are talking, I will have to take it." The employee might not feel too bad if this is a one-time occurrence, but if this happens every week, the employee is going to stop preparing for the meeting and start to think of it as unimportant, too. Scheduled, exclusive, one-on-one time with the manager is a necessity, not a luxury! When participating in phone conferences with a team member, give him your undivided attention. Do not read your email (or respond to it) while he is talking. Listen and respond. Take notes during the meeting. Review status reports, objectives, or personal development plans. Use the time that you have with your remote workers to its best advantage. Prepare for the meeting. Don't just make the phone call and ask, "What shall we talk about today?"

Employees want a manager who can build an effective and productive team. The way team members interact with each other is a reflection of how the manager interacts with each of them. If all team members are treated equally, they will treat each other equally. If the manager has "favorites," the team members will form cliques and there will be a lot of distrust, disrespect, and jealousy among the team members and their cliques. Everyone wants a manager who makes him or her feel good. All team members need to feel good about themselves and about the team as a whole. The manager needs to create a team that is its own identity.

Team building starts with fun. If the team members look forward to being on conference calls with each other, they will call in for the meetings. You can add little extras to the meetings to make them more interesting. Perhaps you can have one person on the Webcam each week, and rotate this through the team so that every team member is seen regularly. This way, everyone has a person to look at while the meeting is in progress. You now have two things you are sharing with the team: You are all listening to each other, and you are all looking at the same person. You can all go out and buy your own donut to eat during the meeting. Make it a "coffee and donut" meeting. It might be seem a bit silly, but it is fun, and it creates a bond among the team members as they are sharing experiences. In 10 years, nobody will remember what you talked about in those meetings, but everyone will remember that you ate donuts together, and some will even remember what everyone's favorite was!

Team members need to know what is expected of them. Clearly defined roles and responsibilities are critical for each team member. However, knowing what is expected goes beyond what is in a job description. As the manager, you need to make sure that the team charter, rules, and best practices are known and understood by each member of the team, and that the team feels that it "owns" them. If you feel it is important that the team members work together to solve critical issues, you must communicate this expectation to the team members. If each person on the team knows your expectations, each can figure out what to do to meet those expectations. Create an online presentation about your expectations, and run a Web meeting combined with a conference call to share it with the team. Sending out documents accomplishes a certain amount, but you never know who is reading the documents or if they understood them. Share this information in a meeting with your team members, so you know they have seen it and understood it. (Of course, personal goals, objectives, and job descriptions should be shared one-on-one with each team member, not publicly with the whole team.)

Employees need clear direction from their manager. Goals and objectives should not continually change. If they do change, be sure to communicate to the team members what the change is and why it was made. Team members also need honest and constructive feedback. It does not all have to be positive, but it does all have to be honest and based on facts. Telling a team member that he is doing a great job every time you speak to him and then giving him a list of 100 things that he needs to improve on in his annual review is not very helpful! This does not give the employee any opportunity to grow and learn, or to demonstrate a commitment to improvement. Deal with problems and conflicts quickly and appropriately. Give employees the opportunity to work on areas of weakness. They might surprise you!

Make sure that you review personal goals and objectives regularly in your one-on-one phone conferences with each employee. The team goals and objectives should be reviewed in the virtual team meetings. If you never review goals and objectives, how do you know you are going in the right direction to achieve them? It is very easy to lose sight of the goal when you are working in your own little world, far removed from everyone else. Being virtual can make team members feel isolated not only from each other, but also from the company in general. It is like reading news reports about thousands of people dying in a far-off country. You read it, think how sad it is, and then you go and get your breakfast as though nothing had happened. If the tragedy were 10 miles away, you would be devastated by the news. You would be concerned that someone you knew might have been involved in it, and the chances are that you would know at least one person whose life was personally affected by it. If it happens close to home, it seems real. If it happens far away, it does not take on the same significance. Working in a local office, it's relatively easy to stay in touch and understand the significance of events. Working virtually, team members might read an email, think about it for a couple of minutes, and then get their breakfast and forget about it. Remote workers need the manager to focus and guide them in the right direction by explaining what is significant and what is not. It is not possible for them to figure all that out for themselves. There is too much information, and they are too far removed from what is happening to feel personally touched by it.

Team members need their manager to take an interest in their personal goals and objectives. If you discuss goals and objectives regularly with each person, you will not even have to look them up in a document after a while; you will be familiar with the goals and objectives of each team member. This is a great thing for you and your team. You can identify opportunities for team members, as well as making it much easier for yourself writing annual or biannual performance reviews!

Newer or less experienced team members need more ongoing support and guidance than do the more experienced members of your team. Remember to give these new employees the attention that they need. They will never become experienced, high-quality team members if you do not have time to work with them and help them grow and develop their skills. You should also consider setting up a mentoring system on the team, with the more senior members mentoring the more junior members. The junior members will increase their skills and knowledge much more quickly, and it takes the pressure off you to try to do all the mentoring yourself! Being a virtual mentor is a great growth opportunity for remote workers. It increases virtual communication skills as well as general supervisory skills.

Employees want their manager to be truthful and honest. Do not tell team members that a report is due on Monday morning if you do not need it until Tuesday afternoon. Do not tell them they have to do something because the CEO said so or because your manager made the decision. Tell your employees what you need and why you need it. Do not blame someone else, even if it was someone else's decision. This is regardless of whether you agreed with the decision. Your employees need you to be an assertive decision maker and to share corporate policy and messages in a positive and cooperative way. They look to you to be the person who is decisive and in control, and who does the right thing regardless of your own personal feelings or opinions. Add due dates for tasks, documents, and status reports to the virtual team workspace or Website, so all team members have access to the same information. Trust your team members to get things done on time. They work virtually, which means they have to be adept at managing their own time. Give them the benefit of the doubt, and trust that they will do the right thing just as you are doing the right thing. You are leading by example.

Employees want their manager to listen to them. They are not always asking for a solution or for help in solving the problem. Sometimes they just want to talk about it and let the manager know what is going on in their world. Listening, and understanding the need to talk or to vent frustrations, is an important part of being a manager. If an employee has asked for some last-minute leave due to family issues, listen to what the person is telling you before you make a decision. Even if you are going to say "yes" anyway, listen to the whole story first. If someone is trying to tell you that her child has a serious illness, she is going to feel rejected and embarrassed when you cut her off halfway through her explanation and say, "I have another phone conference in a few minutes. You can just fill in the time-off request form. You don't need to give me all the details." Show compassion and have respect for others. There are times when you just need to be quiet and listen. It is not all about you and your timetable. When you are listening, remember to give your full attention to what is being said. Your team member might be building up to telling you something else, and without being able to see her demeanor, that might not be obvious. Listen and don't interrupt. Don't jump in as soon as there is a pause. The team member might be thinking.

> Listening, and understanding the need to talk or to vent frustrations, is an important part of being a manager.

Employees want to feel that their virtual manager cares about their careers. Employees need management support to achieve their training and career development objectives. Work with each direct report to create a growth and development plan. Give employees opportunities to learn and gain experience in the skills they need to move to the next level in their careers. The manager has expectations from each employee, and each employee has expectations from his or her manager. Just because your team members work remotely does not mean that they have any less career ambition, or that you are any less able to help them achieve their goals.

Employees want and need a virtual manager who has passion for the job. As a virtual manager, you need to love the job, and your employees need to know that you feel this way. Your passion and enthusiasm will filter through the team and create an energized and excited group. If you are all "doom and gloom," complaining constantly about the company, the clients, and the project, your team members are not going to be enthused and energized to be working with you. They will dread having to speak to you, will probably stop returning your phone calls, and will not feel good about their own jobs. It is very difficult to contradict your manager, especially on the phone. An employee will feel belittled if he feels excited about his job and his manager is always telling him what an awful job it is. The manager creates the environment for the team. Make it a positive and fun environment. Remember, even if you cannot see the people you are working with, you still have a huge influence over how they feel about decisions, issues, and situations. In many cases, you are their "eyes." They need you to help them see the truth. If you are not giving what they need, then your whole team will be misguided.

As a virtual manager, you must be comfortable with dealing with unknown and uncomfortable situations and problems that arise. From time to time, your virtual team members will have problems that they have trouble expressing directly to you. You might learn of the problem from someone else, or you might sense it and have to ask probing questions to find its underlying cause. Do not run away or turn a blind eye to these problems. A team member might be embarrassed to tell you about a problem she feels she should have been able to solve herself. Alternatively, she might feel that it is her fault that the problem occurred, and therefore she should solve it herself. It is so much easier to hide a problem from your manager when you are not working in the same office. For this reason, it is even more important that you have trust and honesty on your team. You are going to find it very difficult to "figure it out" on your own! If your team members trust you to help them when they are in trouble, and not to make them feel bad about it, they will be more inclined to let you know about problems before they escalate out of control. A good escalation process can help you recognize and deal with issues early enough to avoid a disaster. Escalation processes are covered in detail in chapter 8.

> Team members want their manager to know them personally and individually.

Team members want their manager to know them personally and individually. A team member does not want to be known solely as the person who has the most knowledge about databases. He wants to be known to his manager as the team member who was on the Olympic ski team five years ago, and who has a wife and two children with whom he loves to spend time. He wants his manager to know him as the person who raises $10,000 each year for the Leukemia Society, and to know that it is something very important to him. He wants his manager to know that he has a good sense of humor that he uses in stressful situations to try to calm the team down and make them more productive. He is not just a good choice for project "X" because he will be able to sort out the problems with the Oracle database and he is in the right geographical location. He is a good choice for project "X" because he is conscientious, hardworking, a great team player, and an excellent database administrator!

Knowing the team members personally is an ongoing part of the virtual manager's job. You must remember to ask your team members questions so that they know how much you know about them. Ask how the fund raising is going, or if the skiing was good last weekend. Just because you are a virtual team does not mean you can't have a little chitchat here and there during your phone conferences.

Most importantly, employees want their manager to know what is important to them. What motivates them and what irritates them. What makes them happy in their jobs, and what they aspire to being or doing in the future. They want to be valued for their individuality and uniqueness, and they want their manager to notice them.

How to Find Out What Your Team Members Need from You

This might sound rather obvious, but the best way to find out what your team members need from you is to ask them!

You can ask your team members individually what is important to them, and you can also meet as a team to discuss it. A virtual team meeting is a great opportunity to talk about expectations. You can talk about your expectations from each team member, and the team members can talk about their expectations from the manager. You can work together to prioritize the expectations, so you all know which are the most important. You can also discuss what to do if you are unable to meet an expectation. For example, let's say the manager is going on vacation and gets a message from a team member late the day before asking for help with a problem. If the team has an expectation of the manager that requests for help are responded to within one day, the manager will be unable to meet this expectation. There should be a contingency plan in place that states the manager might appoint another team member to respond to a request for help if he or she is unable to respond in the designated time frame. Expectations should be documented and posted to the team's virtual workspace or Website so team members can review the documents at any time.

The team as a whole will have expectations from the manager. Individuals on the team will also have expectations of the manager that might be different from one another's. It would be surprising if all team members had the same expectations. This is because people are not motivated by the same things, nor do they all wish to receive the same rewards for a job well done. The growth and development plan can be very helpful to the manager in understanding what each team member needs. Growth and development plans are covered in detail in the next chapter.

Virtual management is creating new and exciting opportunities in management. It requires a unique approach to communication, team building, and time management. The move to virtual and hybrid teams is a growing trend that is destined to continue for the foreseeable future. Geographically diverse teams are becoming increasingly more common, and the need for virtual skill Sets is increasing with it.

There is a plethora of tools available to help facilitate virtual management, such as email, mobile phones, PDAs, VPNs, and IM. There remains, however, a real need for strong virtual management skills in the virtual manager. Virtual management is not the same as just managing a local team using the phone and email in place of face-to-face communication. It is a whole different style of management that requires a new breed of middle managers. Soon, "virtual manager" will become a functional title like "project manager" or "sales manager." It will require the specific tangible and measurable skill Sets that we describe in this book. The world is changing, and the tomorrow's manager—the virtual manager —must change with it!

Creating and Managing the Virtual Team

Creating a successful virtual team requires a number of essential components. You need a virtual manager with the necessary knowledge and skill Sets to manage a virtual team. You also need remote workers with the necessary knowledge and skill Sets to work virtually. You need virtual tools, some virtual processes, and a plan. Put all these components together, and you have the makings of a virtual team.

For more tried and tested methods of management, you would usually also require experience in those methods. It might not be possible to find many workers with virtual experience, however. If you find someone with virtual experience, how do you know it was good experience? Just because someone has worked as part of a virtual team does not necessarily mean he or she is good at it. We know people who have managed virtual teams and failed miserably. They can still claim to be experienced virtual managers and might not necessarily disclose that most of that experience is in how *not* to manage a virtual team!

Evaluate team members' suitability based on the skill Sets defined in chapter 2 and the skill Set checklist in appendix A. Attitude is everything. A desire to make the virtual team work goes a long way toward making your team successful. A commitment to experimenting and trying new methods until you find one that works well is essential. New tools and technologies are becoming available all the time. To leverage these tools, you might have to rethink some of your processes. This is OK, as long as the overall results justify the upheaval of making changes. If your team is comprised of people who do not like change, you are going to be in trouble! Adaptability and versatility are vital.

Virtual workers must be comfortable being isolated from the rest of the team. It is not always easy, but there are huge benefits. Local workers assigned to hybrid teams must be comfortable working in a virtual team environment. If one person is virtual, the whole team is a virtual team, even if some of the members are local. Local workers assigned to virtual teams must have skill Sets similar to remote workers and have the ability to be a team player with and without walls.

Virtual Work Locations

One of the great advantages of working virtually is the flexibility it affords virtual workers in choosing work locations. You are not limited to working in just one or two locations. You can work while traveling or at home. You can work at your in-laws or at the library. As a virtual manager, you need to ensure that you and your virtual workers have an appropriate work environment.

Some of the work environments available to remote workers might be ideal temporarily, such as while traveling, but might not be considered appropriate as a long-term work environment. Other possible remote work environments might not be appropriate in any circumstance. For example, a coffee shop would not be considered an appropriate work environment in some organizations. The environment is not secure; displaying proprietary information on a computer screen in a public place would not be in compliance with privacy and security policies for many companies.

The virtual manager needs to ensure that each remote worker is working in an environment that is conducive to productive and high-quality work. An employee who is working at home and taking care of a two-year-old at the same time is not in an acceptable work environment. Working remotely does not correlate to free child care. In order to enforce company policy, the virtual manager needs to do a certain amount of "policing" to ensure that remote team members are working responsibly and within the rules. The virtual manager must ensure that each remote worker is given adequate training on work environments and the company's policies, to ensure there is no misunderstanding about what is acceptable and what is unacceptable.

Suitable work environments might include these:

- A home office
- A local library
- A local community center
- A caber café or coffee house
- A hotel
- Onsite at a client location
- A shared office/hoteling office
- A bus, train, or airplane
- An airport
- A car
- A small local office (or a corporate office)

There are advantages and disadvantages to each of these locations. You need to consider the positive and negative aspects of each potential work location and judge the suitability of it for the specific task or tasks at hand.

The key is to select the most appropriate virtual work location based on the type of environment that suits you best and that is also most suitable for the type of work being undertaken. If you are new to virtual work, you might not know what the most productive environment will be for you yet. You might have to experiment with various virtual work environments to find the one that allows you to be most productive. It is not a good idea to spend a lot of money, time, and effort building or converting a room in your house for a home office if you are not sure that working at home is going to be the best option. The home environment might be too noisy, or there might be too many interruptions. If you are going to be traveling 70% of the time, a home office could be a huge expense for very little benefit. You might build a new office at your home, and then find that it gets too cold, so you are constantly taking your laptop into the kitchen to work instead! There are many important factors to consider when choosing a work environment. The best solution is to try a few options and see what works well.

It is very common to find that different work environments work well for different tasks, so choosing just one option might not be the best decision. Working onsite with a client for a few weeks could be the best option if the client is about to "go live" with a new product and needs a lot of troubleshooting assistance. The home office might be an ideal work environment for most of the year, apart from the one month in the summer when your in-laws come to visit. At that time, the house might be very busy and noisy, and you find that you are constantly interrupted by your mother-in-law wanting to make you a sandwich, bringing you a cup of coffee, or telling you that you are working too hard! At these times, the local library, a WiFi hotspot, or a coffee shop might be a better alternative.

Home Office

The home office is by far the most popular work location for the virtual worker. The most effective setup for a home office is a separate room that has a separate phone, a separate Internet connection, and a door. The home office would typically have a laptop computer with docking station, computer printer, personal digital assistant (PDA), Internet connection, landline, and cell phone. If there are

> The home office is by far the most popular work location for the virtual worker.

other household occupants who are constantly coming into the home office looking for attention or creating a distraction, you are not going to get much work done. As a home office worker, you need to focus on your work, not on the demands or distractions of the home. If neighbors are in and out of the house constantly, family members are visiting each day, the children are watching television with the volume turned up very high, or the housekeeper is vacuuming outside the office door, the home office is probably not going to be a good work location. If, however, you enjoy the hustle and bustle of all the activity, and the noise does not distract you at all, this might be an ideal workspace for you.

If the home environment is too busy and noisy, it might be possible to locate the home office in the garage, basement, or attic, or in a building separate from the house. The workspace needs to have proper heating and air conditioning, so it does not get too hot or too cold to work in. If a more distant location keeps you away from the mayhem of the household, it could be a great alternative to turning a spare bedroom into an office.

If you live alone or have a family that is out of the house during work hours, it might be possible to use an existing room for work. For example, a desk could be set up in the dining room or family room. As long as a room has all the connectivity and amenities you need, you can work just about anywhere. This kind of dual-purpose setup is not ideal, as it removes any boundaries between work and personal life. However, if you spend a lot of time on the road and only work out of the home occasionally, it might make more sense than devoting a room to a home office full-time.

The virtual workspace should ideally have good lighting, a desk, a phone, an Internet connection, and climate control. The environment should be interesting and relaxing to work in. A desk in the garage, surrounded by lawn mowers, garden chemicals, and drying laundry, is hardly an inspiring work environment! An office needs to be pleasing to the person who will be working there. Nice pictures on the wall, a tidy and organized workspace, photos, and other personal objects that make the space feel comfortable are all very important to setting up a great virtual workspace.

Many home-office workers like working from home because of the quiet environment that gives them the ability to focus on their work without interruption. Other virtual workers prefer working in a noisy environment, and find it hard to be creative or innovative if it is too quiet. If the home environment is quiet and you need lots of noise and activity to be creative and productive, you would be better-suited finding alternative places to work, like a caber café or the local coffee bar.

Local Library

Many virtual workers find they enjoy working at the local library some or all of the time. If your current project involves doing a lot of research, the library is a great place to be. The library workers can help with research and will find you some desk space on which to work. There is no charge for working in the library, but Internet access or printing might have small charges associated with them. Going to the library to work does involve some planning, as you will need to bring your own laptop, PDA, and cell phone. Many libraries have Internet access, but only for the library computers, which means you must sign up and wait your turn. This can make it difficult to work if you need online access to email or if you need to save Internet files to your own computer. Not many libraries will allow users to plug their own laptops into the library's network, and most libraries do not have wireless Internet.

Library visitors have to turn off the ring on cell phones while in the library and are not permitted to sit and talk on the phone inside, as it disturbs other people. You might be wary about going outside the library to talk on the phone if it means leaving your laptop unattended inside. It is not practical to pack every-thing up every time you need to make or take a call. For people who are typically on the phone most of the day, the library might not be the best location. Also, li-braries do not generally permit eating or drinking inside, so if you like a cup of coffee in the morning while you work, you will be out of luck. You will be sent outside to drink it!

Libraries are a great backup workspace when it is not possible to work at home. There can be many reasons why the home office might be temporarily out of service or not an appropriate place to work. Per-haps family members are at home, or you might be having work done at the house, with contractors stomping around making lots of noise. A temporary loss of electricity or water could also render the home office unusable for some period of time.

> Libraries are a great backup workspace when it is not possible to work at home.

The library is a good alternative to the home of-fice for virtual workers who want a quiet environment, but want to be around other people rather than being alone at home. When you are working on a project alone for weeks, without seeing another soul, the home office can become quite an isolated place. A visit to the library to work for a few hours can be a refresh-ing change of scenery.

Local Community Center

In many towns, the local community center has Internet connectivity and rooms or sectioned off places to work. These community centers generally have good lighting, Internet connectivity, heat, and air conditioning, and might not have as many restrictions as the local library. Rules and regulations vary among centers, so it would be wise to contact your local community center in advance to find out what amenities are available, the cost, and the conditions of use.

Community centers are often busier environments than libraries, with more people moving about while attending to their business. This means the workspace might not be as quiet as the library, but it also might mean that you will be per-mitted to use your cell phone without going outside. You might be able to con-nect your laptop directly to the center's Internet network and might have the added bonus of being able to bring food and drinks into the center with you. So, that morning cup of coffee might not need to be forsaken after all!

The community center, like the library, can be a good backup alternative to working in the home office if there is a short-term problem or because you need a change of scenery.

Caber Café or Coffee House

For a more casual and modern working environment, many virtual workers choose a caber café or local coffee house as the preferred place to work. The atmosphere is lively and interesting, with coffee and food on hand continuously. High-speed wireless connectivity is available, so you can use your own laptop just as you would at home. It is OK to speak on a cell phone, although some establishments might not tolerate loud phone conversations that might disturb other patrons. While this type of environment is not suitable for someone who likes to work alone in a quiet and peaceful atmosphere, it is ideal for people who need hustle, bustle, and noise to be productive. Some caber cafés even have live entertainment later in the day to entice the virtual workers to stay in the establishment spending money, outside of work hours!

> For a more casual and modern working environment, many virtual workers choose a caber café or local coffee house as the preferred place to work.

Many coffee chains, as well as many large bookstores, offer wireless Internet connectivity for their patrons. They encourage their customers to read, eat, drink, and buy their products, all while they are working or surfing the Net. Many restaurants are also starting to jump on the wireless Internet bandwagon. An establishment that offers free wireless Internet will usually display a sign letting the public know that it is a WiFi hotspot.

Hotel

When traveling, you will often find yourself working in a hotel. Most large hotel chains now have high-speed Internet connections in all the guest rooms. Some also have Ethernet connections in guest rooms. Unfortunately, wireless Internet is not always 100% reliable; there are sometimes wireless dead spots in the hotel, which means some guests will be unable to connect to the Internet from their rooms. It is usually possible to take a laptop into the lobby or restaurant to work, but it might not be the most convenient work location.

Most large hotels also have business centers for guests. The facilities generally include photocopiers, fax machines, printers, and computers.

When a virtual worker is working from a hotel, that person is usually also working onsite with a client or at a conference or seminar. If the virtual worker is also spending hours working in a hotel room, he or she very likely has had little downtime from work. The employee is working all day on the business assignment, and all night catching up on email and other work-related tasks. It is important that all team members get some downtime, even when traveling. Virtual managers should try not to assign too much other work to team members who are traveling on business, or they will be exhausted by the time they return from the trip.

The nice thing about being able to work from a hotel room is that it is usually quiet, and there are few interruptions. You can order dinner in your room, turn the television on for some background noise if you need it, and check and respond to emails in a comfortable and unhurried environment. Working from a hotel is not usually a long-term arrangement unless you are constantly on the road. Salespeople, business consultants, and trainers often travel 50–80% of the time, which means they regularly work from hotel rooms.

Onsite at a Client Location

Virtual workers often work from a client site. Many companies have cubicles set up for visiting or temporary workers. This gives the virtual worker a private place to make phone calls and connect his or her laptop to the local network. Business consultants, customer relationship managers, project implementation engineers, project management consultants, and salespeople often spend periods of time working onsite with clients. They might spend a morning or a few days onsite. Either way, all they need is a laptop, cell phone, and PDA, and they are ready to work anywhere. The onsite location has the added benefit of making the worker available for face-to-face meetings with the client. If other virtual team members are also onsite, you can arrange face-to-face meetings between them, perhaps with a team lunch or dinner. The close proximity of virtual team members is beneficial to both the team and the client. Mixing a few social activities into the work calendar can add a very significant and positive enhancement to teamwork and collaboration.

This type of work environment is ideal for any virtual worker who spends a lot of time on the road visiting clients. Spending more time onsite rather than going back to a hotel room to work helps to build familiarity with the client's employees and makes the virtual worker appear to be part of the team. More face-to-face client time contributes to stronger and more successful vendor/client relationships.

Shared Office/Hoteling

Many large companies who employ a virtual or mobile workforce are making significant cost savings by moving to a shared or *hoteling* office model for their employees. Hoteling is the sharing of office space by employees who spend limited time in the office. For example, if a company has four virtual team members in the United States who spend much of their time traveling to the United Kingdom, China, and India, those employees can share the same office space as long as they are scheduled at different times. The office is made available on an as-needed basis and is available to the employee who has scheduled the office space for that period.

The advantage is that the employee has the use of a well-planned office, with all the necessary technology available at his or her fingertips. This will include a landline phone, a laptop port or docking station (assuming all four employees have the same make and model of laptop), Internet connectivity, and all office supplies.

Alternatively, the company might designate a specific number of offices or cubicles available for hoteling on a "first come, first served" basis. Rather than scheduling these spaces in advance, each virtual worker chooses a cubicle or office for the day as he or she arrives at the office. The facilities might not be as personalized, but will be adequate for a few days or weeks at a time.

This type of shared office setup is very common in consulting organizations with a large percentage of virtual workers. Some organizations set up one large office with space for three or four people to work at the same time. This setup limits privacy even more than working in a cubicle, but it offers a comfortable and adequate place to work for visiting or occasional team members. It also provides a great opportunity for the virtual workers to interact with the local team members.

A shared office is not the best location for virtual workers who find it difficult to work in busy environments. The shared office is more commonly a cubicle, which means the worker has limited privacy and not much protection from the noise going on around the office space. No door and no walls means no peace and quiet. For someone used to a quieter environment, the hustle and bustle of the shared office might be very distracting, making it difficult to concentrate. Managing complex negotiations via a conference call might also prove to be very challenging. It is hard to negotiate effectively while also trying to keep your voice low so as not to disturb other employees working in nearby cubicles.

Bus, Train, or Airplane

Many virtual team members spend a considerable amount of time in transit on a bus, train, or airplane. All of these interim virtual-office locations can provide an adequate work environment for short periods of time. If a number of hours or days are spent traveling each week or month, there is a potential to lose a lot of valuable work time while in transit. This time does not have to be wasted. Working while traveling can also reduce the boredom of the trip. A 12-hour flight can seem to go on forever if you do not have much to keep you occupied!

If you have Internet access via a wireless connection or cell phone service, you can easily turn travel time into productive work time. Internet access is becoming a standard service offered on many flights throughout the world. The cost can be a bit expensive, but could be well worth it if it makes the in-flight time more productive. Many airlines also have power outlets located between the seats for passengers to plug in laptops and other electronic equipment. This is a great improvement from the day when you had to bring five charged laptop batteries with you on a long-haul flight so you didn't run out of juice halfway there! With in-flight Internet, you no longer have to wait until you get to your hotel to read the 75 emails that arrived while you were en-route.

Even trains and commuter buses are offering wireless Internet so that commuters can start work before they get there. If WiFi is not available, it is possible to use a subscriber-based wireless service or a cell phone to access the Internet, so there are no excuses for not making the best use of travel time. Using a cell phone for Internet access, however, could get rather expensive if you need to stay connected for many hours. In that case, you'll need to be especially careful to work smart, connecting to the Internet as needed to download necessary emails or files, and working offline until you are ready to reconnect.

Airport (or Other Transit Station)

Virtual workers often spend a fair amount of time waiting around in airports or other public transit stations. A variety of Internet access options are available at airports:

- Internet kiosks
- Business centers
- Airline Lounges
- Wireless service (WiFi) hotspots

Internet Kiosks

Internet kiosks are free-standing computer kiosks offering Internet access. Many of the kiosks are located inside caber cafés, which makes it easy for the traveler to eat, drink, and check email at the same time. Some kiosks are free, while others charge for the service. Some caber cafés are also WiFi hotspots, offering wireless access for those who prefer to use their own laptops rather than the computer kiosks.

Business Centers

Business centers offer a variety of services in a private office setting. "Laptop Lane" is a service offered in many airports. This includes workstations connected to a T1 line or the ability to plug in your own laptop. These spaces are much more comfortable and private than the Internet kiosks. Here, there are power outlets to recharge your laptop, phone, and PDA. You can also make use of printers, fax machines, and conference-ready phones. Most business centers charge a fee, but it can be well worth the cost to be connected to a TI line, rather than using the less reliable wireless Internet available in the airport terminal. The peace and quiet, together with the ability to conduct real business, is another plus, especially if you expect to be waiting in the airport for a number of hours.

Airline Lounges

Airline members' lounges offer Internet access to travelers who have access to them. Many airlines charge for the Internet access, and costs vary. If a members' lounge is the only place in the airport with wireless Internet, it might be possible to use it even if you do not have access to the lounge. It is hard to restrict the wireless range to stay inside the walls of the lounge, so you could try sitting outside to see if you can pick up the signal. If there is a charge for the service, you will still be charged, but it might be preferable to sitting in a noisy caber café!

Wireless Service

Wireless access in airports is becoming more and more common. Unfortunately, in many locations, the service has a bad reputation for being unreliable and slow. In locations where the service is offered free, you don't have much ammunition for complaints. There are usually other options available that offer greater reliability and speed, but you might be required to pay a fee for those. Logging on while sitting at the departure gate and responding to emails until the very last second before boarding gives you a great opportunity to waste as little valuable work time as possible. If you can stay productive while traveling, you will not have to spend as much time working in your hotel room or at home the evening after you arrive at your destination.

Commuters in train and bus stations are also eager to be working while they are waiting. The number of options available to bus and train travelers might not be as extensive as at airports, since passengers do not tend to have such long wait times. However, it is usually possible to find a caber café or Internet kiosk somewhere nearby, no matter what kind of terminal you are traveling from.

The Car

Hopefully, not too much work is being done while you are driving! It is very common to see drivers on their cell phones. However, it is also very common to see those drivers driving erratically or dangerously. They are distracted, not paying attention to anything going on around them, possibly stressed by the phone conversation, and, if not on a hands-free phone, have only one hand available for driving. In many countries outside the United States and many states in the United States, it is illegal to use the phone while driving, or illegal to use a phone that is not hands-free. These laws were put in place for good reason. Talking on cell phones causes too many accidents and is not conducive to driving with due care and attention. A driver who is driving and taking part in a phone conversation is not paying sufficient attention to either task. It is a good idea to check the local laws regarding in-car cell phone use before traveling to new destinations. Otherwise, you could end up with a hefty fine for chatting to your client while en route from the airport!

Having said all this, many virtual workers spend hours driving and talking on the phone. If this is a reality for you, you would be well advised to get a hands-free phone installed. The distraction of the phone conversation is still there, but at least you have both your hands free for driving.

It is also common to see drivers checking email on their PDAs while driving. Mostly, this happens when sitting in a traffic jam, but some people do it while driving at 70 mph on the freeway! Just as some people can be observed reading a newspaper or applying make-up while driving at high speeds, some will be using their thumb and forefingers to send email messages to their coworkers.

You can even buy cell phone accessories that allow people to use a cell phone while driving a motorcycle. As if driving on the freeway wasn't scary enough already!

Small Local Office or Corporate Office

Let's not forget that some virtual managers and team members work in a local or corporate office. The worker has a permanent space in the office location, but works remotely from all or some of his team members. For global managers, this is quite common. The global manager is located in an office in New York or London, and coordinates with team members in other countries on a daily basis. You do not have to be working from a virtual office to be a virtual manager.

Virtual managers who work in a local or corporate office often manage hybrid teams. Some of the team members work at the same location as the manager, while others work virtually. The virtual team members might work in a satellite office with coworkers, or from individual home offices where they are remote from each other as well as from the corporate office.

Creating the Virtual Team

When creating a virtual team, be sure to consider the special qualities and skill Sets that a virtual team member requires to be successful. Virtual team members need to be comfortable working independently, but also need to have a strong teamwork ethic. Working together from a distance can be challenging, and a virtual manager must consider the special qualities required to be successful in a virtual environment when choosing team members. The personalities of the team members will determine the team dynamics, so this also needs to be an important consideration.

Creating the virtual team requires good process and careful thought. The manager will need to do the following:

- ➤ Choose team members.
- ➤ Interview team members.
- ➤ Consider the team dynamics.
- ➤ Consider the personalities of the virtual team members.
- ➤ Evaluate the abilities of the team members.

Choose Team Members

The first step in creating a virtual team is selecting the team members. The potential virtual team members who are the most qualified from an academic perspective might not be good virtual-team material. This can be a problem whether you are hiring from outside of the organization or from the internal employee pool. Either way, you need to have a clear idea of what you need to make your team successful. Remember that you will be operating in the real world and not an ideal world, so make sure that you have realistic expectations! If your organization has recently "gone virtual," it is unlikely that many of the internal potential candidates will have virtual experience. If your team members are all being recruited from within the organization, be prepared to do some training; you are not going to be able to instantly create the ideal team from the pool of resources available. In this situation, focus on hiring for skills and potential rather than for experience. (Specific skill sets for remote team members are covered in chapter 2 and appendix A.)

Regardless of whether you are recruiting internally or externally, you need to have a solid hiring or team-creation plan. Start by identifying what skill Sets you need for the team, and prioritize each as "critical," "desirable," or "nice to have." Be honest with this prioritization. If you list a skill as critical, it means you will not hire someone unless they have that skill. You might want to categorize some of the requirements as "either/or," meaning that the applicant must have one or the other, but you will not insist on both.

Next, you need to identify the relevant work experience, areas of knowledge, and depth of knowledge required for each position on the team. A team composed of all senior people might seem appealing, but in reality, a 100% senior team does not often work well. The tasks that a senior person finds boring are often very interesting stretches for intermediate team members. Similarly, the tasks that intermediate team members find less than interesting can be ideal for more junior members. If you can assign tasks relevant to team members' ability levels and areas of interest, you will have a well functioning, happy, and effective team. Educational background should also be a consideration. Some companies will not employ someone if they have a degree from the "wrong" school. This becomes less of an issue when hiring more senior employees, but for junior and intermediate employees, there can be quite a class system applied to applicants based on what university he attended or what degree she has. This might be a good way of reducing the pile of résumés on your desk, but it is not always the best way to find the most talented and creative team members. Hiring based on intelligence, potential, personality, and attitude will be far more effective than hiring based on the university attended.

> Hiring based on intelligence, potential, personality, and attitude will be far more effective than hiring based on the university attended.

Now that you have created your list of positions, skill Sets, and level of seniority, you are ready to create your staffing plan. The staffing plan is composed of the following areas:

- General information
- Staffing process
- Goals, objectives, and timelines
- Staffing profiles
- Skill Sets and requirements
- Organizational chart

The first three sections are shown in Figure 3.1. A full copy of a staffing plan is included in appendix B.

The staffing profile should identify each team member, the job level, type of employee, and approximate salary.

A staffing profile is shown in Figure 3.2.

Next, you need to complete the skill Sets and requirements table. This should include a high-level job description and the key skills required for each position. The detailed job description document will include a more comprehensive list of skills and responsibilities. Figure 3.3 shows the skill Sets and requirements table.

Staffing Plan - Virtual Team

General Information

This staffing plan identifies the staffing needs and skillsets for the Virtual Team. This document was created by John Smith on October 31st.

The team or project is scheduled to be created on January 1st with no plans to disband the team in the foreseeable future.

Staffing Process

1. Staffing plan is created by the team manager.
2. Plan is approved by Department Vice President and CEO.
3. Requisitions opened and posted internally and externally by human resources.
4. Internal resumes sent directly to hiring manager.
5. External Resumes
   a. Screened by human resources before sending to hiring manager.
   b. Hiring manager requests human resources to do pre-screening phone interviews.
6. Hiring manager conducts initial phone interview .
7. Short listed candidates bought to corporate office for round of face-to-face interviews.
8. For successful candidates - verbal offer made.
9. Offer documentation prepared and sent overnight.
10. Signed offer letter received.
11. Human resources begin new hire process.

Goals, Objectives and Timelines

The manager of the team is John Smith. The following objectives and timelines have been identified:

- Staffing plan completed by October 31st.
- Plan submitted and approved by November 7th.
- Hiring requisitions opened by November 8th.
- Positions posted internally November 8th.
- Positions posted externally November 8th.
- Initial phone interviews completed by December 5th.
- Onsite interviews completed by December 31st.
- First offer made by January 4th.
- All positions filled by February 28th.

Figure 3.1: Staffing plan

Staffing Profile

The team will comprise 5 permanent team members with a total annual salary of approximately $525k and one consultant for 2 quarters at an approximate cost of $50k.

The team needs some very senior personnel due to the complexity and high dollar value of the projects and the high profile clients for whom the projects are being implemented.

Dates Required	Title (Personnel Category)	Job Level	Terms	Rate
Immediate - Perm	Manager/Director	Senior	Full Time Virtual Employee	$150k
Immediate - Perm	Professional Services Project Manager	Senior	Full Time Virtual Employee	$120k
2nd And 3rd Quarter Only	Professional Services Project Manager	Intermediate	Consultant (Virtual)	$50 Hour
2nd Quarter - Perm	Implementation Engineer	Intermediate	Full Time Virtual Employee	$100k
Immediate - Perm	Software Engineer	Senior	Full Time Virtual Employee	$110k
Immediate - Perm	Software Engineer	Junior	Full Time Virtual Employee	$65k

Figure 3.2: Staffing profile

Skillsets and Requirements

Resource Title	Job Description	Source	Job Level	Skills	Resource Name
Manager/Director	Virtual manager working from home office. Responsible for managing virtual team responsible for development and implementation of projects.	Internal	Senior	10+ years management experience. 5+ years working in a consulting organization. Experience with managing a virtual team. Proficient with the following tools: • A • B • C	John Smith
Professional Services Project Manager	Virtual manager working from home office. Responsible for managing approximately 5 simultaneous projects for multiple clients. Requires 50-70% travel.	Internal	Senior	Experienced senior project manager. 10+ years in consulting role. Excellent communication skills. High level of technical expertise in "x" technology. Proficient in the following tools: • A • B • C	TBD
Professional Services Project Manager	Virtual manager working from home office. Responsible for managing approximately 5 simultaneous projects for multiple clients. Requires 50-70% travel.	External	Inter-mediate		TBD
Implementation Engineer		Internal	Inter-mediate		TBD
Software Engineer		External	Senior		TBD
Software Engineer		Internal	Junior		TBD

Figure 3.3: Skill Sets and requirements table

You will also need to provide a full job description for each of the positions listed in the staffing plan. The job description should include a detailed list of the tasks required for a team member to be effective in this job. This should include the skill Sets required for setting up and maintaining a virtual home office, if necessary. It should also include administrative tasks and skills required for using specific computer programs.

Identify how much and what type of communication will be required from the team member. Make sure to think about a virtual mentoring program if you are going to have senior and junior job levels. Define which senior team member positions need to be responsible for mentoring which intermediate and junior team members. If you wait until after you have hired your team members to make these decisions, your new employees might feel that their job descriptions changed considerably from the time of the interview to the day they started work! This is not a good way to start building your new team. The full job descriptions you create should be used to prepare the external job description (used for hiring) and the internal job description (given to the employee at the time of hiring). An example job description form is shown in Figure 3.4. A blank copy of the form is included in appendix B.

If you are choosing team members from an internal pool of employees, your options are more limited. However, you have some distinct advantages over hiring from outside:

- The hiring process is much quicker and cheaper.
- There are lower or no travel costs for interviews (unless employees are remote).
- You do not have to go through piles of résumés.
- Team members are already familiar with the company's policies and regulations.
- The hiring process is less stressful for you and for potential team members.
- You probably know something about the skill Sets and personality of an applicant before the interview.

Job Description - Virtual Team

Requisition Number :	1234
Job Title :	Virtual Project Manager
Job Level :	Manager
Functional Discipline :	Project Manager
Job Type :	Fulltime-Regular
Job Category :	Consulting
Dept Group :	Business Consulting Group
Travel % :	75%
Travel Type:	Domestic and International
Languages:	English plus Spanish or Portuguese
Country :	USA
State/Province :	East Coast preferred
Work Location:	Virtual - home office
Office Location :	Corporate office: Los Angeles
Functional Job Description :	Project Manager for multiple onsite client implementation projects worldwide
Job Description, Duties And Responsibilities :	The Project Manager will manage projects up to $40M. Will develop and manage the project plans, schedules and budget in consultation with the program director. Manage the project budget from project inception to completion. Obtain all required internal and external project approvals. Determine the appropriate project resources and organize the selection of team members and vendors. Represent the organization's interests throughout the project.
Experience/Qualifications :	10 years project management experience; 5 years in consulting organization. PMP or equivalent.

Figure 3.4: Job description form

When hiring internally, you might be limited to team members not currently assigned to a team or project. Your availability pool might be quite small, and the skill Sets available not as rich and varied as you would like. If other managers are also looking to create new virtual teams, you might be competing with them for the best people. If this is the case, you need to do a great job of marketing your team and yourself to the prospective team members, to convince them that they will enjoy working on your team more than anyone else's.

The majority of employees who leave their jobs leave because of their relationships with their direct managers. A very small percentage leave because they want more money, a bigger office, or do not enjoy the work. The manager is the person who can make people happy or miserable at what they do. Most people would prefer to be

> The majority of employees who leave their jobs leave because of their relationships with their direct managers.

assigned more boring work with a really great manager than have interesting work with manager they dislike. As a manager, this means you need to be selling yourself as much as you are selling the team and the project to prospective employees. You, the manager, are the one who decides how happy your employees will be in their jobs!

You are unlikely to get a perfect match of team member skills to your initial list, but you will most likely find that what you lose in one area, you make up for in another. For example, you might hire a project manager who does not possess the required number of years of virtual management experience you had specified in the job description. Some desirable skill Sets that she does possess are good project management skills, exceptional verbal and written communication skills, and two years of process management experience. Her combination of skills can be utilized in multiple areas of the organization.

Interview Team Members

Before you interview a team member, make sure you have prepared the necessary non-disclosure agreements and discussed the interview process with your human resources (HR) department and any additional team members or managers who will be involved in the hiring process. You should definitely have at least one face-to-face interview with a candidate before making a final decision. Ideally, you will also conduct at least one phone interview. If the new team member will be working virtually, you need to have a good sense for how well he or she communicates virtually, so try a few communication methods to see how well the candidate measures up. Email is a great way of judging a candidate's written communication skill, and it can be done prior to scheduling an in-person interview. Using email as part of the prescreening process could save you a lot of time and expense interviewing candidates who might not be suitable to work remotely.

If you are interviewing multiple candidates, it is a good idea to set up an "interview day" and conduct all interviews then. This way, you can arrange for the team members who will be involved in the interviewing to travel to a central location to conduct the interviews. You will save travel costs by conducting all the interviews consecutively.

A great way to gauge candidates' suitability for virtual work is to set them an assignment to be completed prior to the interview. You could give them some guidance on the assignment, but design it so that the candidate has to be resourceful to complete it. Make it small, of course. You cannot set someone a week-long task when they are not even working for you yet!

The type of assignment will depend on the nature of your business and the position for which the candidate has applied. If the role is in research, for example, set a small research assignment. For a project management position, ask the candidate some hypothetical questions via email about what actions he or she would take in specific situations. For a software engineer, set a task that requires finding the solution to a problem. For a team member who will working out of a home office, ask what he or she would do in the event of a power outage or Internet outage at home. Does the candidate have alternative workspaces in mind where he or she could work for a few hours or days?

Have a list of questions prepared to ask the candidates, and compare your list with the other interviewers' questions. There is no point in having 10 people ask candidates the same 20 questions. With some planning and coordination among the interview team members, a candidate could be asked 200 questions, which will give the team a much broader understanding of the candidate's skills and knowledge.

Set interview team objectives before the interviews. Make sure that each interviewer knows what he or she is trying to find out about each candidate. Prepare evaluation sheets and schedule a debriefing session to take place either after each interview or at the end of all candidate interviews, if they are being conducted in the same day or two. Make sure that interviewers complete their evaluation sheets immediately after each interview. Otherwise, they will forget things or start to get candidates mixed up.

Below are some examples of interview team objectives:

- ▸ Evaluate knowledge and skill Sets required for the specific position.
- ▸ Evaluate domain knowledge and experience.
- ▸ Evaluate technical knowledge and experience.
- ▸ Evaluate the ability to set up and maintain a virtual workspace.
- ▸ Evaluate the ability to work and think independently.
- ▸ Evaluate resourcefulness.
- ▸ Evaluate level of team orientation.
- ▸ Evaluate personality and attitude, and ascertain whether the interviewee would affect the team dynamic positively or negatively.
- ▸ Evaluate the candidate's level of honesty and self-motivation.
- ▸ Sum up your overall impression and make a recommendation.

You might not want to assign every objective to every interviewer. For example, you might want to ask the most technical interviewer to evaluate the candidates' technical ability and appropriateness for the job. Similarly, ask the person most able to evaluate domain knowledge to cover that objective. For example, a project manager would evaluate a candidate's project-management knowledge, abilities, and level of skill.

Here are a few ideas for interview questions:

- What can you tell me about your previous experience?
- Describe a situation, project, or outcome about which you feel especially proud.
- Describe a situation that was not successful, and why it was not successful. What changes did you make as a result of that situation?
- What is the most difficult project or task you ever worked on?
- What can you tell me about this industry?
- What can you tell me about our particular organization? How did you gain this knowledge?
- Talk about the most difficult person you have ever worked with. How did you handle the situation?
- What was the best or most interesting job you ever worked on, and what made it that way?
- Why are you interested in this position?
- What value do you bring to this position?
- What three words describe you?
- If I asked your previous manager to tell me one thing that you could improve on, what would he or she say?
- If I asked your previous manager what your best attribute is, what would he or she say?
- Do you prefer working alone, or on a team? Why?
- What do you think is the biggest challenge in working virtually?
- What is your definition of virtual teamwork?
- What makes a virtual team successful?
- What makes a project successful?
- What makes a virtual employee successful?

- ► What do you expect from your manager?
- ► What do you expect from your team mates?
- ► If we give you this job, what will you do in your first week?
- ► What is the first major change you think you will make?
- ► What level of importance do you put on documentation?
- ► What level of importance do you put on status reports and status meetings?
- ► How important to you is face-to-face time with other team members?
- ► How often do you think team members should meet in person, in an ideal world?
- ► Is the customer always right? If not, how do you tell the customer he or she is wrong?
- ► How would you manage a virtual conflict?
- ► How would you set up a virtual workspace? What tools, equipment, and knowledge would you need?

These questions should be personalized for the specific interview, but you get the general idea. One person does not need to ask all these questions. Split them up among the interviewers, and ask a few each. Write down the answers while the candidate is answering. If you wait until later, you will forget what was said, or which candidate gave which answer. You will need your notes to help with the evaluation. You should ask all candidates the same basic questions, so that the comparison is apples to apples, but you do not need to stick rigidly to the list. If a candidate says something that you think should be explored further, ask probing questions to ensure that you get a full answer. If a previous answer has already addressed a question, do not ask it again. The candidate will think you have not been paying attention.

It is extremely important during the interview process to assess the candidate's level of honesty, integrity, independence, confidence, and self-motivation. Without these qualities, the candidate will not be a successful remote worker. When team members work together in one location, it is not necessary for every team member to have similar levels of motivation or ability to work independently. This is not the case for remote team members. Every member of the team needs to possess these qualities in order for the team as a whole to be successful.

Honesty, of course, should be sought for all employees, local or remote. No manager wants to employ someone who is dishonest. However, in a local environment, it is easier to recognize the signs of dishonesty in an employee. The fact that the person's actions can be seen reduces the chance that employees are not doing what they say they are doing. Dishonesty goes beyond telling outright lies. It also incorporates not telling the whole truth or withholding information that should be shared. Though the virtual manager can put checks and balances in place to monitor employees' productivity and contributions, it can still take a lot of time to confirm suspicions about an employee's level of honesty. For example, if an employee is not working when she is supposed to be, how does the manager prove this? She might give lots of great excuses about why she was not answering emails, instant messages, or phone calls. In a local environment, you can check to make sure the employee is in the office. The virtual manager does not have this option. Virtual workers need the highest levels of honesty and personal integrity if they are to be good-quality team members.

Never believe someone who tells you he has never worked on anything that has been unsuccessful. That is only possible if he has never taken risks. Never believe someone who tells you she has never worked with anyone who was difficult. If the candidate has never worked with anyone who is difficult, perhaps she is the difficult one! Never believe someone who tells you he has never worked on a difficult task or project. This would imply that he has never been challenged and has only ever worked on easy tasks. Most importantly, never believe someone who tells you that she has nothing to improve on. We all have plenty of things we can improve on, and no matter how much we improve, there will always be more! Self-awareness and honesty are valuable assets; make sure you know how to evaluate these qualities.

After the phone and the face-to-face interviews, you should complete an evaluation form for each candidate. It is important to complete an evaluation for both the telephone and the in-person interview, as your impression might change after interviewing in person. An example interview evaluation form is shown in Figure 3.5 and is also included in appendix B.

Interview Evaluation Form

Candidate's name	
Position Applied For	
Interviewer's Name & Title	
Interview Date	

Evaluation: 1 is highest 5 is lowest. Circle appropriate number.

Has knowledge and skillsets required for the specific position
Evaluation: 1   2   3   4   5

Description and comments:

Has domain knowledge and experience required
Evaluation: 1   2   3   4   5

Description and comments:

Possesses technical knowledge and experience required
Evaluation: 1   2   3   4   5

Description and comments:

Ability to work and think independently
Evaluation: 1   2   3   4   5

Description and comments:

Resourcefulness
Evaluation: 1   2   3   4   5

Description and comments:

Level of team orientation (teamwork)
Evaluation: 1   2   3   4   5

Description and comments:

Personality and attitude and the affect candidate would have on the team dynamic
Evaluation: 1   2   3   4   5

Description and comments:

Summary (overall impression and recommendation to hire)
Evaluation: 1   2   3   4   5

Description and comments:

Figure 3.5: Interview evaluation form

Consider the Team Dynamics

In addition to considering the obvious aspects of recruitment, such as required skill Sets, previous experience, and seniority of team members, you also need to think about team dynamics. As we have mentioned before, the team will become an entity in its own right, with a personality unique to that team. All teams are different. What makes them different is the combination of personalities in them. That unique combination creates the *team dynamic*.

Creating a team is like creating a new recipe. If you use sugar instead of salt, the dish will be sweeter. If you use lemon instead of honey, it will have more zing. It is not right or wrong to choose to make something more sweet or more salty, more creamy or more tangy, it is just different. Teams are just like recipes; if you change or add just one ingredient, you might create a completely different result.

Before starting the recruiting process, give some thought to the type of virtual team dynamic you wish to create. If your team is working on innovative new products in emerging market spaces, you will want a team dynamic that is high-energy, creative, and very entrepreneurial. On the other hand, if your team is primarily assigned to work with legacy mainframe clients for support and maintenance, you will want a team that is solid, steady, and comfortable working with clients who are slow to adopt new technologies and processes. If the team needs a lot of collaboration on projects, as with a design team, you will need a collaborative and creative dynamic. The same team dynamic would not work well for these very different types of teams. No matter what type of work your team will be doing, it is imperative that each team member is team-oriented. This is essential to the success of a virtual team. Independent "superstars" who want to go off and save the world single-handedly are not going to help a virtual team be successful.

Once you have figured out the type of dynamic that would be ideally suited to your team, you can start to think about the combination of personalities and attitudes you need to achieve that dynamic. This should not be hit and miss. You don't just hire someone because he or she has the basic skills you need. You should hire a person who will be a good fit for the team and who can help to create the team dynamic you need to be successful!

Consider the Personalities of the Virtual Team Members

Personalities, as mentioned in the previous section, are a critical ingredient to your recipe for a great team. You also need to consider your own personality and how well you interact with other personality types. A team composed of all the same personality type is going to be pretty boring and not very strong. Sometimes, you need a little bit of something else to shake things up a bit. You need to add a bit of spice to the recipe to make it more interesting. A combination of personalities that complement and balance one other is ideal. If you can get a good mix, you will find that the team members will keep one another motivated and challenged.

If your team members are all very smart and rather forgetful, easily lose track of time, are very disorganized, and go into way too much technical detail even when asked a simple yes-or-no question, you are going to be in a whole heap of trouble. Who on this virtual team of "mad professors" is going to keep things on track? Who will be the voice of reason when nothing tangible is getting accomplished? Who will be communicating with clients in a straightforward, nontechnical manner? Someone needs to be organized and planning ahead. Ideally, all the team members will be organized and, if not planning ahead, at least working to the plan. You need team members who can finish their tasks on time and help keep each other on track, and who are working on the right assignments and not something they just thought might be interesting! Likewise, a team made up of organizers with limited creativity or innovation is not going to be very successful, and its members won't offer each other much inspiration. A well-blended team, whose members challenge and support each other, will be motivated, inspired, and productive.

> A well-blended team, whose members challenge and support each other, will be motivated, inspired, and productive.

Evaluate the Abilities of the Team Members

Once you have hired your staff and created a team, you need to do a deeper evaluation of each team member's abilities. If you did a good job building a diverse and well-balanced team, you should find that where some team members are lacking, others will excel. It always takes time for team members to ramp up and for the group of people you hired to come together as a well-oiled team. The manager is the most important ingredient in making a team successful. If the manager is working hard to build rapport with each team member, and to help the team members build rapport with each other, the team will bond and will become highly productive and successful.

Remember, when a team is virtual, the primary link that each team member has with each other is through the manager. The manager must work hard every single day to keep the team motivated, strong, and happy.

Defining Virtual Team Roles and Responsibilities

Each team member should have the following individual documents that describes the employee's job, the employer's expectations of the employee, and the employee's own expectations and goals:

- A detailed job description
- Annual or biannual performance objectives
- A growth and development plan

In addition to these individual documents, there should be a shared "roles and responsibilities" document detailing the team roles and responsibilities. This document should be created as a shared document, rather than as individual documents for each team member, because it benefits the entire team if everyone knows who to go to for what.

The roles and responsibilities chart is also the place where you would define some of the day-to-day responsibilities that are implied by the other three documents, but might not be clearly stated. For example, these responsibilities might include creating weekly status reports and attending the weekly virtual team meeting. These tasks are implied in other process documents, but are too detailed and specific to be included in a job description, objectives document, or growth and development plan.

Figure 3.6 shows an example of a roles and responsibilities chart. (A full copy of the chart is included in appendix B.) The chart could easily be expanded to include process ownership, or meeting ownership. Whatever functions are important to your specific team should be captured and assigned on the roles and responsibilities chart.

Roles and Responsibilities

Name	Title	Primary Role	Backup Role	Projects	Document / Webpage Owner	Report Owner	Go To Person For
David Johnson	Snr Project Manager	Project Manager	Backup for Melanie Swan, Team Manager & June Zhang Implementation Manager	ABC, JMT Corp,	ABC, JMT and team calendar	Weekly status, weekly client status, monthly budget report	Project Management, ABC, BRM Technology,

Figure 3.6: Roles and responsibilities

The roles and responsibilities chart should be easily accessible to each team member, preferably via the virtual team's Website. The more well-defined each person's role is, the more effectively the team will work together. It will be clear from looking at the chart if there is someone on the team with no backup, or if a key document does not have an owner.

Understanding Interaction Styles

Every person has his or her own distinctive style of interacting with others. This interaction style encompasses many aspects of a person's personality, including typical behaviors, communication, reaction under pressure, motivators, and demotivators. A person's style influences what makes him or her comfortable or uncomfortable, and determines how he or she deals with conflict. Does the person run away from conflict, or confront it and tackle the problem head-on? Is he or she usually the one creating the conflict, the victim of the conflict, or the person who steps in and tries to smooth things over? Understanding different styles of interaction is important in understanding your team members. It is also important in understanding yourself and your own behaviors. We all have positive and negative behaviors. Being aware of them is the first step in learning how to leverage and adapt them to give you the most positive results.

If you want to become more skilled at interacting with different styles, you first need to understand what they are and how they interact with each other. Most of us act and react in very predictable ways. This pattern of normal behavior defines a person's style. Sometimes, someone will behave in a way that is described as being "out of character." Recognizing this is an indication that you have an understanding of that person's normal character or style. The way other people perceive you might not be how you perceive yourself, but it is this external perception that indicates your interaction style. It is how you *interact* with others.

Many organizations use the style characteristics developed by David W. Merrill, Ph. D. These profiles use level of assertiveness versus responsiveness to determine style. They define whether a person is more task-oriented or more people-oriented, more likely to ask or more likely to tell. The four main interaction styles are:

- ► Analytical
- ► Driver
- ► Amiable
- ► Expressive

You might predominantly demonstrate the characteristics of just one of these styles. More often, however, a person displays a combination, with one style being dominant and one or two others playing less dominant roles. You might well find that what you think is your style is different from how your team members would define your style.

Analyticals like to analyze. They like lots of data in order to make decisions. Analyticals are very logical, precise, and literal. They will arrive on time for meetings and expect them to finish on time. They are organized, dependable, and process-oriented. Analyticals can sometimes be over-analytical to the point that there is never enough data to make decisions. When a problem arises, the analytical tends to try to distract attention away from it. He or she wants to deal with data that has no emotion attached, not issues that can become highly emotional. The analytical tends to avoid confrontation.

Drivers are highly motivated, strong-willed, and independent. They are persistent, and they like to get their own way. Drivers like to get results. They don't see the need for process and feel that they are able to get results without it. Drivers can be quite confrontational if they feel you are trying to prevent them from meeting their goals. Drivers are not always the best team players. They are driven by personal achievement and financial reward.

Amiables like to please. They are good listeners. They are supportive, cooperative, and strong team players. Amiables are peacemakers. They are also looking for acceptance from their team mates. They will often yield to others' viewpoints so as not to offend anyone. They would rather have harmony than results. Amiables are very people-oriented, which means tasks often take a back seat. The Amiable will avoid conflict at all costs.

Expressives are outgoing, sociable, enthusiastic, and have oodles of positive energy. They are good at influencing others and can be very persuasive. Expressives enjoy team events and usually dislike working alone. Expressives can be opinionated and egotistical. They need a lot of attention and praise. When there are problems, the Expressive becomes very confrontational, and will finger-point and blame others. Expressives often display extreme emotion.

Interaction Styles and the Virtual Team

An Analytical could be a great fit for a virtual team, as long as she can deal with moving into unknown territory and not having the time to analyze all the data before making decisions. The Analytical will not forget to call in for the weekly team meeting, and she will always be on time. However, if there is a problem, she will avoid your phone calls and might just email you to tell you she is too busy to deal with anything else right now. If the Analytical does not have enough data, she might procrastinate and refuse to make or accept decisions. She will apply logic to the decisions that are being made, and can be a great asset in helping keep you all on track and moving in the right direction. She will notice the minute you get off course!

A Driver will set the standard for getting results on your team. The *way* he gets the results, however, might not quite live up to your standards. He believes that the end justifies the means, which can lead him to stray from the approved and accepted ways of accomplishing his goals. If there is a bonus attached to the results, he will show no mercy, doing whatever it takes to get that bonus. The Driver works well in a virtual setting, as he is self-motivated and very independent. However, this can sometimes mean that he goes it alone and forgets that he is part of a team. You will be constantly reining him in and trying to get him to follow process. He won't like submitting status reports, as he dislikes process. He likes to do things his own way, and he will try to get others doing things his way, too. If the Driver thinks his fellow team members are slowing things down or are risking success, he will push hard to get everyone back on track to ensure success. He is driven by excellence, and so can be a great motivator for other team members.

An Amiable likes to please and wants everyone to be happy. She might find it a little difficult working in an isolated environment, as she likes to keep tabs on everyone to make sure they are all OK. Amiables are very people-oriented and like to have personal contact with others. If there is sufficient virtual contact, an Amiable could well thrive in a virtual environment. The Amiable might not fare so well in a client environment, however, as she will tend to agree with everything they say and might end up committing to a lot more than she should. The Amiable will be proactive in keeping in touch with other team members and will constantly be coming up with great ideas on how to make team meetings more fun and participatory. Everyone will like the Amiable, who will always make herself available to help others out, even if it means she has to work late into the night finishing her own work!

An Expressive working on a virtual team is going to struggle with isolation if he is working out of a home office most of the time. If he is traveling most of the time and spends most days onsite with clients, he will get the attention he needs to be productive and to keep his energy positive. Clients will likely respond well to the Expressive, who will be talkative and sociable and bring a lot of energy and excitement to onsite meetings. If there are problems, however, don't expect the Expressive to accept any responsibility. He will find a way to make it someone else's fault. He is easily moved to emotional outbursts and has no qualms about personally attacking someone else's ability or integrity. The Expressive will liven up conference calls with the team and will add an element of humor into the proceedings. He will be the life and soul of the party at face-to-face team events.

None of the styles is right or wrong, and none of them is better than the others. They can all function well on virtual teams, but you have to be aware of their different strengths and weaknesses and make sure that you are managing each person in a unique way. The key is to leverage these diverse strengths and personalities, using them to create a strong and motivated team.

Think about your own interaction style and what kind of manager you are because of it. Be aware of your own strengths and weaknesses, as well as those of your team members. Think about how you respond to others when you are under stress and how they respond to you when they are under stress. Be aware of the negative tendencies associated with each style, and learn to recognize when one of your team members is exhibiting a negative style behavior. This could be an indication that the person is becoming stressed and needs help. By learning to recognize these signs, you can more quickly and accurately evaluate a situation as soon as it occurs. If you know the style of each team member, you can be on the look-out for telltale signs that trouble is brewing. You can be ready to take action even before the team member tells you there is a problem.

Learning Styles

In addition to interactive styles, everyone has what is generally referred to as a learning style. The three styles are:

- ‣ Visual
- ‣ Auditory
- ‣ Physical (kinesthetic)

Each of us possesses elements of all three styles, but will have one style that is more dominant than the others. The more dominant style is what is referred to as the learning style.

Visual

Visual learners learn by seeing. They learn well with demonstrations, visual presentations, and reading. They remember what they see. You can recognize visual learners by the things they say:

- ► "I see that we have a problem."
- ► "That looks good now."
- ► "I get the picture."

Visual learners might have a hard time working on a virtual team, where they cannot see what is happening, but only hear it. The visual learners might not remember much about what happened in an audio conference, but if he reads the minutes, everything will become clear. He needs to see things in writing as well as hear about them. He learns well from seeing presentations. You might be unable to give a presentation to your team in person, but you can give an online presentation. If it is accompanied by an audio conference, you can answer questions in real time. This will enable the visual learner to really understand the points you are trying to get across. Alternatively, you could email the visual learner the presentation. He will be quite happy to watch it without the real-time audio. However, this does take away the ability to answer questions on the spot, which can be a significant learning aid to all types of learners.

The visual learners will most likely be paying little attention during conference calls. He will mute his phone and be reading and responding to emails rather than listening!

Auditory

Auditory learners learn by hearing. They respond well to verbal instructions. They learn most effectively by listening to directives, listening to recordings, and attending seminars. They remember what they hear. You can recognize auditory learners by the things they say:

- "It sounds like we have a problem."
- "That is music to my ears."
- "That rings a bell."

An auditory learner would rather call you than send you an email. She doesn't like reading emails, and likes writing them even less. She will save up what she has to say for the team meeting, so you had better be listening. She is unlikely to follow up with a written synopsis. She forgets a lot of what she sees, so if you email her about something important, be sure to follow up with a verbal conversation about it, too. She will likely have forgotten most of what she read within an hour or two.

The auditory learner, like the visual learner, will benefit from an online presentation, but she needs to hear the audio. Don't just send her the presentation in email; she is unlikely to watch it. The auditory learner will not be multitasking during your audio conferences. She will be listening and participating.

Physical or Kinesthetic

Physical or kinesthetic (tactile) learners learn by doing or touching. They learn well by having direct involvement in the activity, role-playing, or participating physically in some way. They often remember things based on how the experience made them feel, rather than what the experience was. You can recognize kinesthetic learners by the things they say:

- "I get the feeling that we might have a problem."
- "That feels right."
- "That touches a nerve."

Kinesthetic learners learn by being part of the process. They can learn by reading emails and by writing them. They can learn from audio conferences, but only if they are participating in them. If they do not get an opportunity to join in with the conversation, they will find it harder to remember what was discussed. If the topics discussed created feelings of strong emotions, the kinesthetic learner will remember the meeting even if he or she did not participate. The kinesthetic learner will likely be fidgeting or doodling while participating in a meeting. Sitting still is not usually an option.

Communication Preferences

We have established that everyone has a learning style, and that this style is closely related to our communication preferences and styles. An auditory person, for example, will be quite happy communicating by phone. A visual person will be more comfortable communicating face-to-face or via a video connection. Kinesthetic people can be more tricky to figure out. They like to meet face-to-face, as they have a tendency to touch someone's arm while talking, or pat someone on the shoulder while shaking hands. However, a kinesthetic can also be quite comfortable writing emails, as the physical act of writing fulfills the need to be physically involved in the activity.

Add into this mix the interaction styles and perhaps some cultural idiosyncrasies, and you start to get a much better understanding of what and how people communicate. For example, Analyticals are generally happy as long as you send them lots of data. It might not matter if it is via email or via the phone, as long there is enough information for them to analyze and process. On the other hand, Expressives tend to like face-to-face communications, as they are quite visual in their style of communication. They use how they look to increase their communication effectiveness. They like to make an impression, and it is much harder to do this on the phone than in the same room. In this situation, a Webcam might be the perfect tool.

Virtual workers need to be comfortable with all methods of communication, but you will notice that people will gravitate to their preferred methods when it doesn't matter which they use. If you know that Jason prefers to talk on the phone rather than via instant messaging, it would be advantageous to use this communication method with Jason whenever appropriate. Likewise, if Julie prefers to communicate via email, then use email whenever possible. If you can adapt your behavior to the style of each team member, you will be able to build rapport and teamwork very effectively, even in a virtual environment. Each team member will feel that he is in tune with the boss. This cannot happen if your behavior always mirrors your own style. The ability to adapt in this way is what we refer to as *situational leadership*. It does not involve changing your own style; it is not possible to do that. It involves adapting your method or style of communication to match the person with whom you are communicating.

Managing a Team Split between Two Locations

Managing at team that is split between two office locations has its own unique challenges. It is very easy for a split virtual manager to focus too much attention on the local manager role, and forget to allocate an adequate amount of time to the remote team members.

If you are managing a split virtual team, you should plan your time so that it is shared appropriately among all team members, regardless of their location. If you have a local team of 18 and a remote team of two, it is very likely that the majority of your time will be spent with the local team. Your time will not necessarily be split between the two parts of your team based on the percentage of team members in each part. For example, it is possible that the two remote workers will be working on assignments that require more of your time than the local workers. Thus, you might spend 50% of your time with the remote team, even though it comprises only 10% of your workforce. Also, since over 80% of communication is nonverbal, you need to spend more actual time communicating with the remote team members to achieve a level of communication comparable to what you have with your local team.

Split teams often fall into the "us and them" trap. This is where the team splits along geographical lines into factions that act as though they are at war with each other. They don't usually try to actually kill one other, but they work against each other rather than alongside each other. The team members become uncooperative and unhelpful, and spend as much time as possible apportioning blame onto the other half of the team for the latest issue !

The only person who can prevent this from happening is you, the manager. It is extremely important that the team is managed proactively, and that any conflicts or distant rumblings signifying disaster are dealt with quickly and effectively. You are not going to be aware of these issues unless you are actively looking for them. Staying alert and keeping tabs on the general mood and morale of the team members is the only way to actively manage this. You must remember to keep tabs on the remote workers as well as the local ones. If you don't know how the remote team members are feeling, ask them. Be honest about what you observe and what you hear. Do not pretend it is not happening. Don't fool yourself that this would never happen on your team because your team members are all very mature and experienced. It will happen on any team if it is allowed. Ignoring these types of problems is tantamount to condoning them. Building teamwork is about building respect and rapport among the team members. As soon as the "us and them" war starts, it is hard to get things back on track again.

How do you effectively manage a split team and avoid a geographical conflict? First, you need to acknowledge that there are cultural differences between the teams. Any two teams in different locations will have cultural differences. This is team culture we are talking about, not nationality or regional culture, although those can add to the mix! Your team members need to discuss the cultural similarities and differences between the locations. You should decide which cultural aspects of each you all like the most, and adopt them for both parts of the team. You should talk openly and honestly about the cultural differences that will remain between the two parts of the team. Discuss how the team can avoid misunderstandings and how you can build strong teamwork, so that you are always supporting and helping each other and not fighting against each other. Talk about the perceptions that each part of the team has about the other. Talk about what it is that creates animosity. If you can get your team members discussing these things, they will quickly realize how many similarities there are between them and how silly some of their prejudices were.

People have the same fundamental needs, no matter where they are from or where their managers are located. Their fears stem from those fundamental needs, and fear is what causes rifts in split teams. Both factions have the same fears. They fear that the other team is getting more attention, is more highly valued, is more highly paid, is trying to make them look bad, is trying to blame them for something, is getting more interesting work, has an easier job, works fewer hours, and so on. It is like basic sibling rivalry. There is no real substance to the fears, just as there is no substance to the feeling that you must prove yourself better than your siblings. Still, something inside you drove you to blame your brother for breaking Mom's favorite vase, or to tell Dad that your sister was drinking with her friends last night when she was supposed to be at Bible Study!

When split teams start to bicker and fight with each other, they are doing exactly what siblings do. You need to deal with the problem swiftly. You must make it absolutely clear that the behavior is unacceptable and that you expect a higher standard of professionalism from your team members. Your team members will respect you, and each other, if you set the ground rules and make sure that everyone understands what your expectations are from each of them.

Setting Goals and Objectives for Team Members

It is important to set reasonable goals and measurable objectives for all your team members. Goals are high-level requirements that are usually not measurable. Objectives are detailed requirements that are measurable.

For virtual team members, it is vitally important that the goals are clearly understood and that the objectives are unambiguous, well-defined, and measurable. Most important, document the objectives and ensure that both you and the employee sign them. That way, there is no question that you both agreed to them.

If you have a team composed of virtual employees, set some goals and objectives for the team members that relate to their virtual world. For example, communication is key to virtual employees, so set goals and objectives that help them to increase and improve their communication skills.

If the goal is to "improve communication skills," the objectives that accompany the goal could be something like these:

- Attend at least one internal or external virtual communication class.
- Present at least one online virtual sales or training class.
- Set up and present one virtual kick-off meeting.

You need to be confident that you are able to effectively measure and verify the objectives you set for team members whether or not they are in the same geographical location as you. If it is not possible to evaluate performance on a particular objective for a virtual team member, then you should not be setting the objective. If the objective is ambiguous or vague, you cannot expect the team member to be able to achieve it. The more you can avoid vagueness and replace it with clarity, the more you will be able to measure performance effectively.

If you are managing salespeople, it is relatively easy to set objectives. These people are generally measured on financial success, such as number of contracts signed or renewed, or on revenue. Regardless of a team member's primary objectives, try to set some development objectives, in addition to the financial ones. These could include increasing communication, post-sales skills, and effectiveness.

One objective we would recommend for everyone on your team, no matter what their position, is to improve conflict-management skills. All jobs at all levels and in all industries have some stress and conflict associated with them. The conflict might come from inside or outside of the organization. Regardless of where a problem arises, it is a very valuable skill to know how to recognize conflict and manage it so that it does not escalate into a huge problem.

If possible, have all your team members attend the same conflict-management training (not necessarily at the same time). They will then all be speaking the same language as they use the skills they learned to communicate with each other and to avoid creating conflicts. Conflict that arises on a virtual team often grows slowly and create grudges that are harder to eradicate than on a traditional team. It is not as obvious that one person is annoyed with another when you cannot observe them ignoring each other in the elevator or the lunchroom. Virtual workers are not likely to call the boss every time they have a little disagreement with someone else on the team. However, those little disagreements can fester and grow into something that can poison the team. If the team members do not know how to manage and resolve conflict, you will have a very difficult time running around putting out all the fires as they start.

Managing Performance and Performance Reviews

The key thing to remember when managing performance is to *manage* performance! Don't wait until a week before writing the formal performance review to give any thought to how well each team member has performed, or to review what objectives you gave them six months ago! Managing performance means talking regularly with every team member about their objectives, and helping them stay on track with achieving (and hopefully exceeding) them.

> The key thing to remember when managing performance is to manage performance!

Ask your team members to write their list of objectives on the whiteboards in their offices, or to print them out in large print and pin them up in their offices. Each team member should know what his or her objectives are without having to refer to the objectives document.

Ask your team members to write a short description each month of what they did in the month toward meeting their objectives. Discuss this in one of your regular one-on-one meetings with each team member. When it comes time to write reviews, you should know each team member so well that it should not be a struggle to document how well each one met his or her objectives. This is even more important for virtual team members. You cannot see what they are doing.

The only way you will know how well each of them is doing is to have an ongoing dialogue about performance objectives.

It is customary in many companies for employees to write self reviews and to ask one or two peers to also provide review feedback to the manager. It is a good idea to have virtual workers write self reviews. It is also an excellent idea for you to solicit feedback from each team member about the other team members' performance. It is not necessary to ask for written feedback. In fact, written feedback is not usually very helpful to the manager, unless it addresses specific questions that the manager has about each employee. Written peer feedback often ends up being a waste of the team member's time. Instead, schedule an hour of phone time with each team member, and use that time to ask specific questions about each team member that relates to his or her objectives. Communication among team members is vitally important to the success of your team. Questions related to the quality, timeliness, quantity, and appropriateness of each team member's communication will give you some valuable insight into how well each team member is integrated into the team and what his or her contributions have been to the team.

Regular feedback is vitally important. Do not tell team members they are "doing a great job" if they are not. Tell them precisely what they are doing that is great and what they need to improve on. When you write a performance review and present it to an employee, there should be no surprises—negative or positive.

Employee compensation is usually tied to performance ratings. Therefore, make sure you are giving your team members every opportunity to get a high performance rating. You can do this by keeping them on track and giving regular feedback on the assigned objectives as well as their overall job performance.

Personal Development Plans

The employee objectives documents and the job description describe what the company expects from the employee. The personal development plan should describe what the employee expects from himself or herself and from the company. Many companies do not work with employees on creating personal development plans. The company and the manager are both so focused on what they want from the employee, they forget that the employee has goals and objectives, too.

A personal development plan is valuable for many reasons. First, it makes employees feel that you truly care about what they want and that each employee's opinions and ambitions are valued. The plan helps employees figure out what they really want. It helps you to understand your employees better. It helps you to decide on the development priorities for each employee, not only for the position the employee holds now, but also for the one that he or she wants to move to next. The personal development plan also helps you understand which employee is best suited to which task or project. It is a misconception that because someone is really good at something, he or she wants to be asked to do it over and over again. People get bored doing the same thing, day in and day out. They want to learn and grow. They want to be challenged and work on hard problems. They will never get to do that if you always assign the person with the most experience in a particular area to that task!

A virtual team member's hopes, dreams, and ambitions are not likely to be discussed during the course of everyday phone conferences. Locally, you can hear idle chit-chat that gives you an insight into the motivations, interests, and ambitions of team members. Virtually, you don't hear those things by passing by in the hallway or by overhearing someone talking in the cafeteria.

How, then, will you find out what motivates each person on your team? Do you think they are all motivated by the same thing? Do you think they are all like you, and have the same likes and dislikes as you? Of course not. How do you know what motivates them or what they like or dislike, if you don't ask them?

Here are some key questions that you can ask your team members to gain insight into their needs and motivations:

- What are your short term goals? (What do you want to achieve in the next 1 to 2 years?)
- What are your longer term goals (2 to 5 years)?
- Do you have a well-defined career plan?
- How many years do you see yourself working in the position you are in now?
- What do you think your next step will be?
- What do you consider to be your most valuable skills or assets? (What are you best at?)
- What do you consider are the things you need to improve on?

- What new skills or knowledge would you like to learn in the next 1 to 2 years?
- What kind of things do you enjoy working on most?
- What kind of things do you enjoy working on least?
- What three things motivate you most (money, time, praise, outings, travel, challenging work, etc.)? How would you prioritize them?
- What expectations do you have from your manager in helping you meet your goals?

The answers to these questions will vary among your team members—probably more than you would imagine. Use this information to help your team members meet their goals. You might be able to use some of this information to set performance objectives for team members. It is great if you can get your team members to document this information by completing a form, but some people find it very hard to write these things down. Some of your team members will have never even thought about these things before, and it might take them some time to figure out what they want. Give them time if they need it, but not too much time. If they are not able to document their own plans, you can meet with them, ask them questions, and document what they tell you. Remember that these plans are personal and confidential. They should not be shared with anyone else.

Personal development plans should be reviewed and updated at least twice a year. People change, they grow and develop, and their growth and development plans need to be updated to reflect those changes. Major life changes can change personal goals a lot. Someone who was primarily motivated by travel when single might be primarily motivated by money when married with twin baby boys! Once a personal development goal has been achieved, it should be removed from the plan and replaced with a new goal. A personal development plan can be changed whenever the person who owns it wants to change it. These plans are not designed to be for life!

All virtual managers should complete their own personal development plans. Even if it is not shared with your manager, it is a great exercise to go through for yourself. It will give you some additional insight into your motivations. It will also give you a better understanding of how difficult it can be to create a personal development plan. If you can share your plan with your own manager, even better!

Employee One-on-Ones with Manager

Schedule regular one-on-one time with each of your team members. Once a week is ideal, but if you have a large team, it might need to be every two weeks. Both parties should plan for the meeting and be prepared to discuss status, ask questions, and give and receive feedback. For virtual team members, these meetings should be by phone. Remember to email any written documentation that you wish to discuss prior to the meeting, so your team member can be prepared.

Try not to make the one-on-one a status meeting, where you go through a big list of tasks and get a verbal report on whether each one is completed. You could do that in an email! One-on-one meetings with virtual employees is precious time. Make the best use of it by talking about key tasks and issues, and by talking more generally about how the employee is getting on. Use the time to discuss the employee's objectives and personal growth and development plan. Remember to ask for feedback, not just give it. Here are some examples of questions to ask in a one-on-one:

- ► Is there anything that I can do for you?
- ► Is there anything generally that you think I could do better to make your job easier or more enjoyable?
- ► Do you have feedback on any other team members or people we interact with that you think would be good for me to know?

With the last of these questions, make sure the meeting does not turn into a general complaints session about others. Set clear guidelines about what you mean by "feedback." The three Cs are helpful in this respect: Ask for feedback to be clear, concise, and constructive. Make sure that the feedback you give also meets the three Cs criteria.

> Never give negative feedback via email, no matter how constructive you think it is.

Virtual one-on-ones should be conducted by phone. Instant messaging or email one-on-ones are not going to be effective. Never give negative feedback via email, no matter how constructive you think it is. Negative feedback in an email is guaranteed to be destructive.

Document your one-on-ones. Make note of anything that was agreed to or any action items taken by either party. Follow up with an email noting any action items, so you can be confident that you both finished the meeting with the same understanding of next steps. Be sure to follow up on action items at the next meeting. Always document virtual meetings, whether they are scheduled or spontaneous. Most people do not remember a lot of what they hear, and as you cannot see who you are talking to, you should make notes so you don't forget what you talked about or what you agreed to.

Virtual Coaching

If you have created written objectives and personal development plans, and hold regular one-on-ones with each team member, you will have a pretty good idea what level of coaching each person needs. You cannot coach someone unless you know what it is you need to coach him or her on. Don't try to teach someone something he or she already knows, or even worse, something that person knows more about than you do!

Coaching needs to be personalized and unique for each person. If there are things that the whole team needs help on, talk about it in a team meeting and follow up with individual help for any team member who needs it. Coaching is talking to team members about situations or decisions and helping them visualize how they could have done something differently to achieve better or different results. Coaching is leading by example and helping each person to develop skills in his or her own unique way.

If you want to coach, make sure you know what you are talking about! For those things where you have limited knowledge or experience, draw on the help of others, either on your team or outside of it. Coaching over the phone or via email can work very well. If your team members trust you, they will call you when there is a problem and ask for help in resolving it. Help them to figure out what to do. Don't ignore them. Don't manage them like a sergeant major, demanding they do this or that. Work with them to help them find a solution that works for them. Think about the person's interaction style and learning style when coaching. You cannot make an Amiable behave like a Driver or an Expressive behave like an Analytical. Take this into account when coaching your team members. Coaching someone to do something the way you would have done it might not always be appropriate.

When you lack face-to-face communication, you need to rely on your knowledge of a person's style to know how he or she will react in certain situations.

You can't always be there to save someone at the last minute, so use coaching to give the team member the tools needed to be successful, and then encourage that person to use his or her own style to its best advantage.

Virtual Training

Virtual training is a way of learning very different from that of a traditional classroom where all the participants and the instructor are present. Many elements are missing from virtual training that are taken for granted in a classroom setting. The instructor has to use creativity and intuition to replace what is missing. It is like losing one of your senses. The other five senses have to improve to compensate for the loss of one!

There are different levels of "virtual" in virtual training. It could be that the instructor is the only one working virtually, and all the participants are in the same room. Alternatively, the instructor might be in a classroom with some participants, while others are working virtually. Then there is the absolute virtual situation, where the instructor and all the participants are virtual, and no two people are present in the same room. By far the most challenging situation is the last one. If every single person is remote from the others, it creates a feeling of isolation and distance for everyone. The challenge for the instructor is to pull the group together to make them feel like a class.

An instructor is used to being in a classroom full of participants. Instructors feed off the energy in the room, taking cues from the training participants by reading their body language, and gauging the level of frustration or excitement with the material being taught. The instructor can easily tell when the class needs a break, or when the pace is too fast or too slow. In a virtual training environment, unless the training is being conducted via video, the instructor cannot see the participants. This can make the instructor feel very isolated. Trainers are used to walking around a classroom, maintaining eye contact and making sure that nobody is falling asleep! When working virtually, the trainer is most likely sitting in front of a computer and talking to a telephone. It is very difficult to feel energized and enthused when you feel like you are talking to yourself! The trainer cannot see when people are yawning or getting distracted by email, phone, or other things going on in the participant's environment. He or she cannot see when someone has left the room. This can be a problem when the trainer gets to a really important part of the session, where everyone should be giving the training their full attention. In the classroom, the trainer can wait to impart the critical information until everyone is present and attentive. This is not so when working virtually.

The instructor is also challenged when using a half-duplex audio conferencing system because when he or she is talking, the other lines are automatically muted. The virtual trainer needs to leave lots of breaks and pauses in the presentation to allow participants to ask questions. If the class members are working on some exercises, how does the instructor know if they are all finished? He or she has to ask them and trust that they are telling the truth. You might wonder why participants would not tell the truth. How would you feel if you were participating in training with a group of strangers, or a group of your peers, and the instructor asks if everyone is finished and you hear everyone else say "yes"? You might not want to be the one that holds up the class, so you just say "yes" as well. Or you simply keep quiet rather than piping up with a "no." It could be that half the people who said "yes" were not really finished at all. It is very difficult for the instructor to give individual attention to one participant when talking into the microphone so everyone can hear. In the classroom, the instructor can take one student aside and quietly help him or her while the rest of the class continues working.

Let's talk more about how the participants feel in a virtual training session. They are feeling just as isolated as the instructor. They are in training with a group of people they cannot see, and they might feel a bit intimidated by the other participants. Perhaps one attendee is asking really insightful questions in a very confident way. The others might feel that the person is more intelligent than themselves. They might feel that their own questions will sound stupid, so they don't ask them.

How easy is it to get distracted when participating in training while sitting at your desk? Most people would say "very easy!" Unless the participants are determined to give the instructor their full attention, they are going to get distracted by all sorts of things. The problem is that the instructor will have no idea that someone is not paying attention. The instructor might think he or she is being very clear and concise, not realizing that one of the participants is on the other line talking to her mom, and another is reading emails. If participants are working from home, there could be any number of additional distractions, such as family members wandering into the room asking questions, the dog needing to be let out, or perhaps laundry or dinner is also being worked on! Our lives are full of distractions. Classrooms are great places to get away from them. If a few participants are constantly being distracted and not following what is being taught, there can be all sorts of repercussions. First, they will not be following the training and will most likely start asking questions that would have been unnecessary had they been paying attention. This could slow down the rest of the group, who will get bored waiting, and might then also start doing unrelated things to fill in the time. Before you know it, the training is a complete disaster.

In a classroom setting, the instructor will work with the group to build rapport and teamwork. After a while, the attendees feel like they are "in this together." They tend to feed off each other's enthusiasm or skepticism, and if one person asks a question, others might pick up the thread and start to ask related questions. The person who asks the intelligent and confident-sounding questions might be very pleasant and smile at the other people in the room, making them feel comfortable so they are less intimidated by the question and more interested in the instructor's answer. It is not easy to build this kind of rapport over the phone. It is especially difficult in a short time period. If you speak to someone on the phone every day for six months, you are likely to build some rapport. If you are in a shared virtual training with 15 other people for two hours, it would be nothing short of a miracle if you were able to build rapport with the instructor or any of the participants!

Another very important aspect of the classroom setting that is missing in virtual training is the side conversations that occur. Someone might mention that she saw a movie last night and get into a discussion about that. Another participant might need to leave early, as his child is performing in a school play that evening. These small and seemingly insignificant side conversations play a huge role in building rapport and making the group feel more comfortable. That comfort level is conducive to a successful training session with high attendee participation and enjoyment.

The instructor needs to develop strategies for dealing with virtual training attendees. Asking specific attendees questions rather than asking an open question that anyone can answer can help to keep the attendees alert. Asking each attendee in turn for the answer or solution to specific exercises will help the instructor know who is following the discussion and who is completely lost. If attendees think they might be asked a question, they are more likely to pay attention. The instructor can ask participants to send an instant message if they need to leave the room. This will help the instructor keep track of where people are.

We have talked about a few things that are missing in a virtual training environment, but there are also some pretty significant advantages. The first one is financial. It is often too costly to have all participants travel to a training center for classroom training. It can mean the difference between spending a few hundred dollars or a few thousand dollars! Virtual training might not be your first choice, but it is definitely preferable to no training at all. Another advantage is no travel time, which can also be a significant cost saving. There is no jetlag for attendees who have changed time zones, and no participants absent or late due to flight or road delays. Online training allows more flexibility in when the training is taken. The instructor can run classes at different times and on different days to accommodate various schedules and time zones.

As another benefit, consider the person who feels embarrassed to speak up in front of the whole class when he does not understand something. This type of person might feel more comfortable in a virtual training setting, where none of the other participants can see him. He might be more inclined to ask questions if he does not feel embarrassed about everyone looking at him when he speaks.

How to Make Virtual Training Successful

In a classroom situation, it often works well to run a day-long class or a week of day-long classes. The attendees are focused and have minimal distractions to prevent them from getting maximum benefit from the intense training. For virtual training, however, this intense "total immersion" training does not work well at all. Keep training sessions to approximately two hours to be most effective. Four 2-hour classes will work much better than a single one-day class.

Where possible, have team members work together in the same room. For example, if the instructor is remote from the participants, and there are five people who work in the same location, the instructor should arrange for those five people to attend the training in the same room. This way, they will be able to focus more attention on the training. They will not be so easily distracted, and they can help each other if someone is confused or needs help with one of the exercises.

Video conferencing is a great way of making virtual training more effective but this only works well if the participants and instructor are in no more than two locations. Otherwise the instructor will have a screen full of video screens showing the participants. That will make it hard to focus on the training! If participants are in multiple locations, it is a great idea for the instructor to be on video or a webcam. It can make the participants feel much more involved in the training process if they can see the person presenting to them.

Keep the classes as small as possible. It is very difficult managing a virtual training session when there are a lot of participants. It is hard for the instructor to keep tabs on everyone and ensure that they are all engaged and following what is going on. With a small group, there is more time for everyone to ask questions or make comments without it cutting into the class time. If the session is only two hours, there is not much time to allow for delays.

It is important that the instructor acknowledge each person as he or she enters the training, whether this is in person, online, via audio conferencing, or via video conferencing. Attendees need to know that someone knows they are there and cares that they are sitting, waiting for the class to begin. When all attendees are present, it is polite for the instructor to either introduce everyone or to ask them to introduce themselves. The instructor should also do a personal introduction. Without these introductions, participants will feel even more isolated. It helps to know that there are other people involved in the training and to know who they are, where they are located, and why they are doing the training. The instructor should make sure to know who is in attendance so that he or she can check in with them from time to time.

If possible, let the training participants work on exercises outside of the training session. This gives them more time to work on the exercises, so they do not feel rushed during the class. This is a double-edged sword, though. Having after-class assignments takes the pressure off having to complete them quickly, but it also means that a student who runs into problems cannot ask the instructor for help until the next training session. This is where it is ideal for training participants to work together. If they work in the same location for the assignments as well as for the classes, they will be able to help each other if someone gets stuck.

The instructor must share the rules of the training at the beginning of the virtual class, just as for a classroom training. The rules will be slightly different, but just as important. Some examples of the rules are as follows:

- Turn off cell phones
- Mute the phone unless you are speaking.
- Do not interrupt when someone else is speaking.
- Do not put the line on hold. Otherwise, the team will have to listen to the on-hold music, which is distracting.
- Say your name before you speak, so everyone knows who is speaking.
- Close email programs, instant messaging, and any other programs that might distract participants from the training.
- Turn off computer speakers.
- Do not multitask. Pay attention to the training, so the instructor does not have to repeat anything.
- If you need a break, let the instructor know.
- If you do not understand something, let the instructor know. Chances are that someone else doesn't understand, either.
- If you step out of the room and miss something, do not ask the instructor to repeat it. Email the instructor after the class to ask questions about what was missed.

The trainer should check in with each attendee from time to time to make sure everyone is still there and that they do not have any issues. Calling people by name and asking each person personally can make all the difference. If the class is very large, this might not be possible, but for four or five participants it should be manageable.

Online Training Tools

The Webinar is a great tool for online training. It allows the instructor to interact with the attendees during the training session. Used in conjunction with audio or video conferencing, this type of training can be very successful.

Online meeting software used in conjunction with audio conferencing can also be a very effective conduit for learning. You can set up quick and easy training sessions with your team members using a PowerPoint presentation, a Web meeting tool, and a dial-in number. You don't have to get hugely sophisticated to make it work well.

Prerecorded presentations that include audio and online slides can also be quite effective. These presentations do not have a live instructor involved in the training, so there is no interaction between participants and instructor. The advantage of this type of training is that it can be viewed at any time. It can be paused, stopped and started, and watched over and over again. This type of training is best used for low-complexity material. It is an ideal tool for training on processes and procedures or other internal company training.

Managing Global Teams

Imagine a team that has its workforce based in one country—let's say the United States. The workforce is composed solely of U.S. citizens, and it has just started to conduct a large percentage of its business internationally. The team has no international experience, but is very knowledgeable about the company's products and services. What kind of difficulties is the team likely to encounter, communicating with its new clients overseas? Will the team members be aware that they need to develop cross-cultural skills to be effective? How does the manager teach her team members to communicate effectively and set appropriate and realistic client expectations, when she is unsure of how to do these things herself? What can the manager do to ensure her team is successful? If she is asking herself these questions, she is part of the way there. A manager who assumes that there will be no communication issues because the clients all speak English very well is going to be in for a lot of surprises!

Jet-setting around the world as a manager for an international team sounds very cosmopolitan and trendy. However, there is a lot more to it than buying an airline ticket, making a hotel reservation, and packing your international power adaptor. Global business requires a different approach to management, and not many companies manage to do it well. The biggest problem is that people tend to apply the same management approach and style to global business as they do to domestic business. It doesn't work.

International Business and Global Marketspaces

The 21st century is all about globalization. You hear about it everywhere: international sales, international conferences, outsourcing, and offshoring. Doing business internationally has multiple challenges. Making the decision about whether international business is the right choice for your organization takes some careful research and thought. If you decide that it is the right choice, you need to figure out how to position your company, your products, and your employees to be successful. Both strategic and tactical challenges need to be taken into consideration, and planned and managed appropriately.

Going global can be an excellent choice for an organization. It can lead to rapid growth, open up a plethora of new business opportunities, and have a very positive effect on the company's bottom line. Realizing the full potential of overseas operations, however, requires a commitment to change. For example, you need to consider the required changes in the way you do business, your processes and procedures, management styles, employee skill Sets, and attitudes. Depending on the scope of the globalization, the changes might be minor or drastic. Drastic changes that permeate your whole organization will be expensive. It might take years to recoup the costs. All these things need to be taken into consideration when preparing your organization for globalization.

The Global Decision

Companies choose to start doing business internationally, or to move specific business functions overseas, for various reasons. Some companies move into the international arena to gain a competitive advantage and stay ahead of the competition. Others are trying to keep pace with competitors who are already doing business internationally. Other reasons for doing business overseas are to reduce costs, increase revenues, expand into new markets, support existing clients who are doing business overseas, or support a merger or acquisition. No matter the reasons for the globalization, there are multiple options available on how to become global, all of which have their own unique advantages and disadvantages.

When moving into international markets, carefully weigh the pros and cons of locating representatives overseas versus managing your overseas business completely from your home country. If you have decided to outsource, you need to decide whether to outsource domestically or internationally. For offshoring projects, you need to consider whether it makes more sense to outsource the work or to set up your own offshore office or factory. If you are selling to clients over-seas, you need to determine whether it is more financially viable to employ local salespeople in those geographically regions, contract with local companies to represent your business in those regions, or manage your international business from your home country. These decisions will be based on how much overseas business you are doing, how important local representation is in those regions, the level of expertise required to manage an overseas operation, and whether you have that expertise in your existing employee pool or would have to go outside the company to find it.

No matter what option you choose, there will be costs associated with it. While most companies do a pretty good job of estimating the direct costs of do-ing business overseas, many underestimate or do not even acknowledge the indi-rect costs. For example, the cost of leasing premises, hiring staff, purchasing equipment and services, and generally setting up and running the overseas opera-tion are not difficult to estimate. What often gets overlooked are indirect costs like these:

- The increased amount of management time required to manage or coordinate with the offshore office
- The cost of training existing staff in cross-cultural communication
- The costs of misunderstandings or misinterpretation, including the cost of rework and time spent managing the fallout from the issue
- The increased costs of employing staff domestically with experience in managing offshore teams or projects
- The increase in communication and travel costs

Before You Start

Any company that moves into the global marketplace has to be prepared to make some changes in the way it does business. Business practices that work well in the United States might not work in Asia or Europe. Sending employees out into those regions with no specialized training is likely to end in disaster. For this reason, many com-panies open regional offices and employ local people. Understanding the local customs, business etiquette, and decision-making process is vital to success.

> Any company that moves into the global market-place has to be prepared to make some changes in the way it does business.

Expecting to solve all your global business problems by opening a satellite office is not very realistic, however. You have essentially replaced the challenges of working directly with your customers with the challenges of working with your remote (regional) employees. You need to build strong working relationships with those employees, and you are going to be unable to do that without a solid understanding of the cultural differences that exist among the different geographical regions.

This is where training is vital. Employ the services of a cross-cultural training organization to come in and train your team members. In addition, consider employing someone in your home office or home region who has first-hand experience working in the overseas region where your office or outsourcer is located. This person can act as a conduit for information between the two offices, helping enormously with the quality and clarity of communication. Everyone on your team who will be interacting with employees in another geographical region must understand the cultural differences and similarities between the two locations. If you try to save money by employing the regional expert but not offering cultural training to any of your other team members, it will likely come back to haunt you at some time in the future. If you do not position your employees in each location to be successful, you are setting them up for failure. Good intentions are not going to be sufficient without a good understanding of what needs to be done to be successful.

With the rise in globalization, one would think that the various people of the world would feel a tighter bond with each other; a cross-cultural, global village of teamwork, participation, and mutual respect. Unfortunately, this does not seem to be the case. In many instances, globalization has caused uncertainty, insecurity, and mistrust. The global utopia has not been realized. Globalization has led to as many problems in the world as it has to solutions. There is uncertainty and fear everywhere. In the United States, workers are fearful when they hear of information technology jobs being moved abroad. In the countries where the IT jobs are moved, employees might appreciate the opportunity to get good jobs locally, but they are also uncertain about the future. If the financial benefits of being in that country start to decline, the parent or outsourcing company could easily pull out and move operations elsewhere. In some regions of the world such as India, there are already rumblings about the increasing costs of employing staff. The world of outsourcing has become so competitive that companies are having to pay higher and higher salaries to attract and retain their high-performing employees. If the costs continue to rise, it might end up being as cheap to outsource work within the United States or Western Europe as it currently is to outsource to areas like India and Eastern Europe. You need to take all this into consideration when you are planning the execution of your global strategy. Many of these issues feed into the indirect costs mentioned in the previous section. Effectively managing employee uncertainty and angst will take time and effort on your part. During times of uncertainty, change, and upheaval, your team will probably not be working at optimal levels. Productivity and quality are likely to suffer. The more closely you manage the situation, the more quickly your team members will settle down to normal operations.

Imagine for a moment that you have the cultural differences figured out, everyone on your team gets along with everyone else, and all the employees understand one another, even though they're located in different countries. What about the laws in those countries? Someone in your organization must be responsible for knowing what is allowed and what is not allowed. You need someone who is knowledgeable in international law and how it applies to your international business. There are different trade agreements with different countries, and there are different laws in each country. If you are doing business in 20 countries, you might have 20 different sets of laws to understand. Something that might be legal in the United States might be illegal in a European Union country, and vice versa.

> International business is not as simple as opening an office in Japan and making sure that you have some bilingual employees!

International business is not as simple as opening an office in Japan and making sure that you have some bilingual employees! You need the legal expertise to ensure that you understand the business and human-resources laws in the countries in which you will be doing business. You can either employ someone with international law expertise directly, or you can contract the services of an international law firm to manage and advise your organization. Many law firms offer these services. If you are planning to do business in multiple countries, you need expertise in the laws of those countries. That could be hard to find from one person. Contracting with an outside law firm is a good option if the amount of advice you need is going to vary from month to month. It might not be financially viable to hire a full-time employee (or team of employees) if you only need their services from time to time.

Other things to consider when setting up shop in other countries are tax law, employment law, working hours, vacation time, paid public holidays, and benefits. Your employees in the United States might be legally entitled to just one week of vacation but are given two or three weeks. Your employees in France might legally be entitled to five weeks vacation but need to be offered six or seven weeks in order for your employee package to be competitive. Then there are paid public holidays. These are referred to by different names in different countries. The most common are *bank holiday*, *public holiday*, and *legal holiday*. The paid public holiday is one recognized by the state and for which employees are generally given paid time off. Some countries have so many state-recognized holidays, however, that employers have to choose a certain number to give their employees as paid time off. In the United States, it is common to offer between nine and 11 paid holidays per year. In the United Kingdom, this number can be as low as seven days, although many employers give additional time off between Christmas and New Year's Day. Public holidays can be broken down into two types:

- Religious holidays reflect the dominant religion in a country (Christian, Jewish, Hindu, Islamic, or Buddhist, for example).
- Secular holidays are politically or historically specific to a country or region. For example, many countries have a Labor (or Labour) Day, although the day has different names in different countries.

Many religious holidays are shared among different countries, as are many secular holidays.

Employee benefits vary from country to country, too. In the United States, it is expected that most employers will offer health insurance benefits. In countries where there is a national health service (socialized medicine), this is not an expectation that most employees have. In some countries, employees at a certain level expect to receive the benefit of a company car. In other countries, this would not be an expectation. Childcare benefits also vary from country to country, and time off for sickness, disability, or pregnancy also differs among countries. Do not assume that all employees who work for the same company receive the same benefits, or that because employees work for an American company, they receive the same benefits as the American employees. Labor laws are different in other countries, and any employees living and working in those countries are subject to those laws. Those laws include legal maximum working hours per week and overtime payments.

There are lots of things to consider not only in making the decision to do business internationally but also in *how* you do business internationally. One reason for the popularity of outsourcing is that by contracting with an international company to supply specific products or services, the client (you) is not responsible for the employees of that company in any way. You need no understanding of international labor laws or religious holidays; you pay the outsource company, and they take care of the day-to-day management of their own employees.

Time Differences

Working with team members or clients in different time zones can be very confusing. Dealing with just two different time zones, yours plus one other, is not usually too much of a problem. Dealing with five or six time zones, however, can get very tricky when scheduling meetings that are not at completely unsociable hours for at least one member of the team. It is challenging enough just trying to schedule meetings that work for everyone in the U.S. time zones! Starting work an hour or two early or staying an extra hour or two at the end of the day is acceptable from time to time, but not if it is necessary to do both on the same day. If this is required on a regular basis, you could soon find that you and your team members are working way too many hours and are starting to feel tired and burned out. This will lead to unhappy and unmotivated team members and a high rate of attrition.

It is not always possible to hold a team meeting that includes all geographical regions. You might find that you have to hold the same meeting two or three times to include different time-zone groups. There are some creative ways of making this work without continually having to do the same thing several times over. It takes some planning, but once you have a structure in place, it is possible to minimize, though not totally eradicate, the need to repeat meetings.

First, identify the geographical regions where each team member is located. Then, figure out what time zones apply to each region, and the specific time zone for each team member. You also need to understand which team members are in locations that have daylight savings time, and when it starts and ends. There are some great Websites for finding the time zones of cities and countries around the world. Here are two we recommend:

▸ www.worldtimezone.com
▸ www.timeanddate.com

For communication purposes, consolidate your regions into three or four major areas, for example:

▸ North America, Latin America, and Caribbean (NALAC)
▸ Europe, Middle East, and Africa (EMEA)
▸ Asia Pacific (AAP)

You can split your team into regions that work well for you depending on the exact locations of your team members.

Before you start scheduling meetings, it is a good idea to create a spreadsheet of team members with regions and time zones, so you don't have to go through the process of figuring this out every time you need to schedule a meeting. An example time-zone spreadsheet is shown in Figure 4.1 and is also included in appendix B.

Name	City	Country	Region	Time Difference	Start No Earlier Than (PT)	End No Later Than (PT)	Notes
Bruce	Auckland	Australia	AP	+18hrs	2pm		Mon-Thurs
Cindy	Osaka	Japan	AP	+17hrs	3pm		Mon-Thurs
Amir	Jakarta	Indonesia	AP	+15hrs	4pm		Mon-Thurs
Ravi	Bangalore	India	AP	+13.5hrs	5.30pm		Mon-Thurs
Richard	London	UK	EMEA	+8hrs		10am	
Karli	Istanbul	Turkey	EMEA	+10hrs		8am	
Alan	Honalulu	Hawaii	NALAC	-2hrs	10am		
Jeanne	San Diego, CA	USA	NALAC	0	8am	5pm	
Enrique	Sao Paulo	Brazil	NALAC	+6 hrs		11am	
Maria	Manaus, Amazonas	Brazil	NALAC	+4hrs		1pm	
Chuck	New York	USA	NALAC	+3hrs		2pm	

Figure 4.1: Team time-zone spreadsheet

If you have team members located in regions where the time difference is 10 to 14 hours, someone is going to have to be on a conference call outside of normal business hours. Try to minimize the impact of these out-of-hours calls by working them into your schedule or your team members' schedules. This can be accomplished by changing your working hours once a week or month so that you come into the office late and work late. For time differences of 15 or more hours, it will be a different day of the week for at least one meeting attendee. For meetings with team members in countries that are more than half a day ahead of your time zone, a call late in your day is the next morning for them. If you are in North America, for example, you should not schedule calls to Japan on Friday afternoons—it will be Saturday morning there, and the office will be closed!

> If you need to meet regularly with team members in all regions, it is important to take time zones into account when scheduling meeting

If you need to meet regularly with team members in all regions, it is important to take time zones into account when scheduling meetings. Using the team time-zone spreadsheet in Figure 4.1, you will be able to group your team members into regions that make sense for your meetings. For some meetings, you will be quite limited in the time of day you can meet. For those cases, it is advisable to set up recurring meetings, so that you are not struggling at the last minute to find a time when everyone is available.

Suppose you are located in North America in the Pacific time zone (on the West Coast), and you are scheduling a meeting of the NALAC region. You need to take into account the various time zones that apply. Your team members on the East Coast are three hours ahead, so meetings with those people should ideally be scheduled to finish no later than 2:00 PM (Pacific Time). Your team members in Brazil are four and six hours, ahead so the meeting should end no later than 11:00 AM (Pacific Time). Perhaps you also have a team member in Hawaii, two hours behind, which means you should meet no earlier than 10:00 AM (Pacific Time). So, you need to schedule your meeting to occur from 10:00 to 11:00 in the morning, any day from Monday to Friday. It might make sense to add the team member from Hawaii to your AP meetings instead of your NALAC meetings. You could then schedule your NALAC meeting to start at any time before 10:00 AM (as long as you finish by 11:00). If the focus of the Hawaii team member is primarily on North America, however, you might not want to switch him or her to a meeting focused on the Asia Pacific area. There are multiple options, and as long as you have planned appropriately, you should be able to figure out a good plan that works for everyone.

One suggestion might be that you hold a weekly conference call rotating through the three regions, so that you meet with each region every three weeks. If you record the audio of the conference, you can make it available to the other team members, so they are aware of what has been discussed. This will reduce the need for out-of-hours meetings while still allowing your team members to stay up to date with current status.

Don't forget that daylight savings time can really mess up people's calendars. Be sure you are using calendaring software that will adjust times based on daylight savings. Otherwise, you need to make a note of these time differences and remind your team members to update their calendars at the appropriate times.

Managing Language Differences

Managing language differences sounds easier than it is! There are many different aspects to language that have to be considered, including these:

- Communicating effectively with people for whom English is a second language
- Translating
- Speaking clearly
- Listening and understanding
- Gesturing
- Asking questions

Communicating Effectively with People for Whom English Is a Second Language

When working on global teams or engaging in international business, remember that English will be a foreign language for many of the people with whom you associate. Do not assume that someone understand English well, just because that person is able to express thoughts well in English or speaks without a heavy accent. For many people, it is much easier to learn how to speak a foreign language than it is to understand when someone else is speaking in that language.

Have you ever traveled to a foreign country armed with a few key phrases to help you get by? You probably learned how to ask for directions, purchase a train ticket, ask what time it is, find out the price of something, order a drink, and so on. The phrases you learn might work really well in a beginning Spanish class or conversational French class, but what happens when you find yourself in Paris and ask for directions? The person you ask assumes that you understand French, because you asked for directions in French. He or she then starts talking at a hundred miles an hour, pointing and gesturing and smiling, and you just stand there, nodding your head and smiling back. The person is being very helpful and giving a really thorough explanation, so you thank him or her effusively ("Merci, merci beaucoup"), and go on your way with absolutely no idea what the person was talking about. You are none the wiser as to where you are or where you need to go, and you suddenly realize that what you really need is a map, not conversational French! In your French class, the person you practiced with always answered very succinctly, so you knew that you should go straight and then turn left at the end of the road, and there you would find the metro station. The French person you spoke to had no idea, of course, that you did not understand a single word that was said. He or she heard the question, saw you smiling and nodding, heard your heartfelt thanks, and assumed that you knew exactly where you needed to go. It is very easy to misinterpret a few words spoken in our own language as fluency in the language.

The extent to which your associates understand English might vary widely. Some might be able to read and write in English exceptionally well, but might not have mastered the spoken word. Do not assume that because you understand each other well in email, you will also do so in person. Some people might be shy about speaking, as they are nervous about making a mistake. You might find that the quietest person in a group understands and can speak English better than the others. That person is just embarrassed and afraid to speak.

The most important thing to do when hiring employees for whom English is a second language is to arrange for weekly English as a Second Language (ESL) lessons. These lessons are essential in helping non-native speakers understand and be understood. ESL lessons will help to increase employees' confidence in asking for clarification when they do not understand something that has been said. These lessons will also help to increase speaking, listening, and comprehension skills. If employees have very heavy accents that make it difficult for them to be understood, ESL lessons will prove invaluable in helping them to enunciate words clearly so they are better understood.

Take the time to talk to every employee and evaluate for yourself their levels of skill in writing, speaking, and understanding English. Give feedback. If someone is afraid to speak, encourage him or her to speak. Ask that person to speak more loudly, so he or she can be heard. Give encouragement and give praise for effort and improvement. Most importantly, make sure that your other team members are not laughing at the non-native speakers or making jokes about their pronunciation or use of the language. It can be very embarrassing to feel that others are laughing at you.

Translating

Translating from one language to another is not always as straightforward as you might think. If a translator is highly proficient in one of the languages and not quite as proficient in the other, the translation might leave a lot to be desired! What you are trying to communicate might be interpreted in a way different from that which you intended. Translation gets to be quite tricky once you add in a few analogies, colloquialisms, and perhaps a sprinkling of humor. Add these together, and you can easily end up with a totally different message being delivered by the person doing the translating. If possible, ensure that anyone performing translation duties is highly proficient in both languages. If you know this is not the case, ask questions to make sure your translator is translating accurately. Use active listening skills to repeat back what you heard, using slightly different language or an example, so that the translator can confirm that the meaning conveyed was accurate.

Remember that the same language is not always the same language. This can create its own unique problems with translating, but it is often overlooked. For example, there is a big difference between British English and American English. Likewise, there is a big difference between Castilian Spanish and Mexican Spanish. The Italian spoken in Milan is very different from the Italian spoken in Sicily. Just because a language is nominally the same does not mean that a speaker of one variant will understand a speaker of the other. If a translator from Spain who has lived and worked in the United Kingdom is translating between someone speaking Mexican Spanish and someone speaking U.S. English, there might be mistakes due to the differences in the two Spanish variants and the two English variants being translated.

Translation is not always something that happens externally. Someone who is learning a new language mentally translates everything read or heard into his or her native language. If you have ever studied a new language, you will remember that feeling of your brain hurting from the constant translations going back and forth in your head. It can be exhausting. As a person becomes more proficient with a new language, he or she can understand it without the continual mental translation back and forth. However, it is still hard to understand when conversing with people who are using a lot of analogies, acronyms, and colloquialisms.

Add into this mix the virtual nature of the communication: crackly phone lines, people not speaking loudly enough, typing going on in the background, and perhaps a few side conversations going on in the corporate office meeting room. It is not surprising that a lot of what has been discussed has not been fully understood by all meeting participants!

The manager must coach team members in speaking clearly and concisely, and ask them to be considerate of others when using colloquialisms or slang in their communications. The native speakers should be encouraged to ask if everyone has understood what has been said. Even more valuable would be for the speaker to be aware of when he or she is using nonstandard English and to explain the expressions being used. All team members should be encouraged to speak up and explain nonstandard expressions that are used by others, to be sure non-native speakers are not losing the thread of what is being discussed. This commitment to speaking clearly and explaining colloquialisms not only helps the non-native speakers to understand the conversation, it also helps them to learn more slang, which will in turn help them to increase their depth and breadth of understanding of the language. Once non-native speakers start to understand slang, they will start to become a lot more confident speaking a second language.

The manager should also coach non-native speakers to ensure that they are speaking up and asking for clarification when they do not understand what is being said. It can take some time before team members feel confident enough to do this, but as each person gains confidence, he or she will be more inclined to do so.

Speaking Clearly

To ensure that you have the best chance of being understood, you need to learn to speak clearly, slowly, and concisely, while avoiding colloquialisms and slang. If someone does not understand you, do not be tempted to speak more loudly, and do not get irritated if you have to repeat yourself. Not understanding another language is not the same as being hard of hearing, and it is not something that is done to be intentionally annoying! If you treat others with rudeness and disrespect when they ask you to repeat what you said, they will stop telling you when they do not understand. You could end up creating a lot more serious problems for yourself!

Be patient. If you need to repeat yourself, try slowing down and enunciating your words more clearly, and try saying the same thing using different words. It could be that one or more of the words you used were not familiar, and that is what caused the confusion.

Remember to summarize the key points simply and clearly. If someone else has spoken, and you suspect that he has not been fully understood, summarize what has been said for everyone's benefit. It is better to summarize now than to find out later that some people did not understand.

Keep sentences short and to the point. Avoid long, drawn-out, and complex sentences. Short, concise, and to the point will be most effective. Ask meeting attendees regularly if they have understood the issue or the point being made, and be prepared to summarize again if you get feedback that indicates there was a lack of understanding.

Audio conference calls can include all kinds of additional roadblocks to comprehension: different accents, uncertainty or lack of confidence with the language, people speaking very quietly, people speaking fast, noise on the line, someone typing or talking in the background, someone on a cell phone, a delay or echo on the line, and so on. Audio conferences also lack the face-to-face clues, such as body language and gestures, that aid comprehension. Virtual meetings can be difficult at the best times. It is very easy to end up in a situation in which less than half the attendees have understood what was being said.

When giving formal presentations, improve comprehension by using graphs and charts. This is especially helpful when communicating technical or complex material. Technical terms can be confusing to non-native speakers. Technical jargon is not generally learned in English classes. If you need to use acronyms and company-specific language, make sure that you include a description of what the acronyms or expressions mean. When giving virtual presentations, don't forget to send a copy of the presentation to the remote attendees ahead of time, so they can follow along. Alternatively, conduct the entire presentation virtually, and use desktop-sharing technology in conjunction with an audio conference to present to the meeting attendees.

Document meetings with minutes. Non-native speakers who understand written English better than spoken English will find minutes especially helpful in ensuring that they understood the content of the meeting and the key decisions and actions that came out of it. Ensure that you are avoiding using colloquialisms, slang, and jargon when writing minutes, so they can be easily understood by everyone. Document briefly what was discussed, key points, and action items, and include a summary. The summary can be beneficial to others in understanding what you consider to be the most important aspects of the discussion. Meeting minutes also help to fill in the gaps for anyone who had trouble hearing or comprehending what was being said during an audio conference for all the reasons mentioned earlier.

Listening and Understanding

Listening is as important as talking. Ask questions, and be patient while waiting for an answer. Non-native speakers are not usually as concise or confident in their communications as native speakers. They might "beat around the bush" a bit in their explanations because they do not have the range of vocabulary in English to say what they want to say. It can be frustrating trying to find the right words, and even more so if the listeners are sighing and fidgeting and making it obvious that they are impatient to get the answer quickly! This can be especially difficult on the phone. If you keep speaking while the person is mentally composing an answer, or interrupting if the person is going a bit slow, you are going make it impossible to get any good quality communication between you.

Make sure that you listen carefully to what is being said and that you understand what is *meant*, not just the words that are being used. People from cultures that are super-polite will be hesitant to disagree with you, as it is considered disrespectful. You need to pay attention to what is being said and how it is being said, and be prepared to ask the right questions to draw out the answers that you need. For example, if you hear a team member agree that it is OK to delay a shipment to a client, but the agreement does not sound very enthusiastic, you could try asking some probing questions. For example, suppose your first question was "José, what do you think about us delaying the shipment to XYZ company so that we can secure this huge contract with ABC company?" The answer you get might be "Yes, that would be OK."

Is it really OK, or is José agreeing with you because he thinks you will do that anyway, so why disagree with you and make you think badly of him? Or is he agreeing because he doesn't want to contradict you in front of your colleagues and make you look bad? Or is he agreeing with you because you are the boss, and he thinks he is supposed to say "yes" to whatever you say? Or is he agreeing with you because he really does agree with you?

You could try asking some probing questions such as these:

- "José, what do you think XYZ's reaction would be if we had to delay their shipment by two weeks?"
- "What is XYZ's timetable for implementing the project?"
- "What concerns do you think XYZ will have if we delay the shipment?"
- "How do you think a delay at this point will affect our relationship with the customer?"

These questions are not asking for agreement, they are asking for information. You are not putting José on the spot by asking him to agree or disagree with you. You are merely asking for his opinion about the client. He can easily answer these questions without fear of offending you. It is much easier to answer specific questions like these than to answer a more general question that requires a lot of thought. There might be many aspects to a more general question that are not easy to put into one thought.

Listen carefully to what you are being told. Use active listening skills to repeat back what you have heard, and get confirmation that you understood correctly.

Gestures

Gestures can be dangerous, so beware! Gestures can mean completely different things from country to country. In Japan, for example, a bow is considered polite and respectful. A British person who bows to you is likely being sarcastic and feels that you are being too aggressive or pushy.

In Italy, flicking your fingers forward across the chin is an insult, whereas in the United States, it might just be that someone had an itch under the chin. Holding up the middle finger in the United States is a rude gesture, as it is in

Malaysia and Singapore. Holding up two fingers in the United Kingdom, with the back of the fingers toward the other person, is a very rude gesture. In the United States, this gesture might be used to signify victory or the number *2*. When the French hold up two fingers, it means three—they count the thumb even if it is not held it up. In the United Kingdom and United States, holding a finger to the lips signifies that you want someone to be quiet. In France, they hold up the index finger, which in the United States might be construed as being asked to stop whatever you are doing, or that you are in trouble. The thumbs-up sign means "good" in the United States, but is a rude gesture in some Islamic countries. The *O* sign, using thumb and forefinger, means "OK" in the United States, but is a rude gesture in some Latin American countries. In Japan, the gesture for "come here" looks like the gesture for "go away" in the United States Confused yet? You never really know how a hand gesture will be interpreted, so be very careful about how and when you use them.

Virtual workers do not get the benefit of hand, or other, gestures. If some people are in a room together, it is polite to interpret gestures for anyone listening by phone. You will not need a running commentary on every single movement that everyone makes. However, if a gesture is used in place of words, you should let the listeners know. For example, you might say "John is giving us the thumbs up so that means, yes, we can go ahead with the plan," or "Jane is scratching her head. She is not sure."

Asking Questions

When communicating with non-native English speakers, try not to ask "either/or" questions. They are confusing, and it is difficult for the listener to know if you are asking a question or making a statement. A listener who thinks you are asking for agreement might just say "yes," and not truly understand that what you wanted was an opinion one way or the other. For example, avoid a question like "Do you think we should fly to China next week to close the deal, or do you think we should focus on the clients in India first and deal with China later?" Instead, try asking two separate questions. First, ask "Do you think we should fly to China next week to close the deal?" Wait for an answer before asking your question about the clients in India. Or make a statement, "I am not sure if we should make China or India our priority next week. Do you have an opinion on which one we should focus on first?"

You should also avoid negative questions, like "Don't you think we shouldn't do that?" Instead, ask "Do you think we should do that?" It is hard to know how to answer a negative question, even if you are a native English speaker. Do you answer negatively or positively if you agree? You can avoid confusion by clearly asking what you want to know.

Managing Cultural Differences

In the world of business today, cultural diversity in the workplace is inevitable. This diversity can enrich or impede teamwork. It can have a positive or negative effect on productivity, morale, and results. The person who has the most influence over the impact of cultural diversity on a team is the manager.

Global team-building can be extremely challenging, but when it is done right, it can lead to amazing results. A team made up of individuals who understand and embrace each others' differences are able to use those differences to be highly effective and successful in the global marketplace.

There are many challenges managing teams who are as diverse in nature as they are in geographical location. It is important that the "host" team—the country that houses the company's headquarters—not see itself as the yardstick by which the other teams or individuals should be measured. Global management and teamwork does not mean teaching everyone else how to act "American" or "British." It is about nurturing and blending the global team into a truly international entity, with a culture and identity of its own.

Many different areas contribute to cultural differences, for example:

- Family
- Religion
- Nationalism
- Education (the system and the importance)
- Separation of personal and business life
- Politeness and etiquette
- Personal hygiene, cleanliness, and appearance
- Social status
- Values
- Communication
- Ethics

All of these areas have different levels of importance culturally, as well as personally. Their importance and priority will differ from culture to culture. The mixing and matching of these beliefs, approaches, and attitudes create an incredible complexity. Not surprisingly, spending too much time pondering cultural differences can make your head spin.

Consider how you, as a global manager, can use cultural differences to your advantage. First, you need to recognize that there are differences. You need to accept that on a global or multinational team, it can take years to understand what all the differences are. Most important, it is critical to the success of your team for your team members not to interpret others as "weird" or "wrong" because they are different. You need to work with your team members to ensure that there is mutual respect among them, regardless of their differences. No matter how great the differences, there are always similarities. The similarities create the commonalities that link us to each other and create bonds, rapport, and friendship.

It is fairly normal for people to ignore cultural differences. They pretend the differences are not there, avoid talking about them, and hope that they will go away. Some people think that perhaps when someone gets more used to dealing with, say, Americans, he or she will start to act more like one, or will realize that the non-American way of doing things is wrong and will eventually change his or her behaviors and attitudes to the "right" ones.

If differences are ignored, things will deteriorate quickly. This is why many global teams struggle with success. The managers are managing the same way internationally as they are locally, and it doesn't work. The local team might be happy, but the international members of the team (whether they work locally or globally) will not be happy. They may feel they are viewed as being not as good or as valuable as the local team. You need to manage this. You need to ensure that the diversity on your team is valued and respected. The more your team members understand about each other, the more likely that the cultural differences will be recognized and appreciated. The cultural training discussed earlier in this chapter is an ideal foundation for you to build on.

Socially and professionally acceptable behaviors differ greatly from culture to culture. For example, there is a big difference in how people from different cultures view time, and the value that is placed on time. The British and Japanese will be offended if you arrive late for a meeting, and will be even more insulted if you do not apologize for your lateness. Americans, on the other hand, view five or 10 minutes late to be almost the same as "on time." In Latin American countries, 30 minutes or an hour late might be considered acceptable. In some cultures, not turning up at all is quite common, and hardly anyone seems to get upset about it.

As the manager of the team, it is your responsibility to set the rules and guidelines for the team. What the team members do in their own personal lives is their business, but what they do during the course of their work is your business. Set rules for timekeeping, and insist that your team members demonstrate respect and courtesy for others by being on time for meetings and completing and delivering assignments on schedule. Team members should not be expected to accept behavior they find offensive or disrespectful, to accommodate one member's culture. A team must create its own rules of conduct that are acceptable to everyone on the team.

> In some cultures, not turning up at all is quite common, and hardly anyone seems to get upset about it.

Communication styles differ from culture to culture. For example, Americans tend to be more aggressive and louder in their communication than the Japanese. Americans tend to want everything done yesterday; it is all about speed and signing on the dotted line as quickly as possible. Asians tend to be more interested in the details, and want time to consider all the options before making a decision. They do not want to be rushed or bullied into making a quick decision. The decision-making process is very different in different countries. Not only can it take longer to make a decision in some cultures, but the attitude toward changing one's mind can differ greatly. One person might feel that because a decision was made everything is settled, while someone else might feel that a decision means nothing, and it can change multiple times before it is settled.

On your own team, you need to ensure that everyone understands the decision-making process. This includes identifying the decision-maker, defining at which point a decision has been made and is final, and having a clear process for requesting a decision be reviewed or reevaluated. If you are making decisions and nobody is acting on them, the decision has no value. If your team members are making decisions that are inappropriate for their positions on the team, you are going end up in chaos, with everyone going in a different direction, following their own individual guidelines.

When working with overseas partners or clients, make sure that both you and your team members understand the differences in culture that might affect attitudes toward decision-making. If you are doing business with an international client, for example, you will need to be prepared to adjust your behavior and attitudes to match that of your client, or perhaps meet somewhere in the middle. Work with your team members to define strategies for managing expectations for international clients. Do not make assumptions. If you are not sure about expectations, ask.

The Stages of Cultural Adjustment

Culture shock can have a huge impact on individuals, teams, and companies. Following a move to a new country, the cultural stages of adjustment can sometimes be quite painful. You need to work with the members of the team who have moved from other countries to help them understand that adjusting to a new culture takes time, and that it can be very difficult being in a situation where nothing feels familiar or comfortable. It takes time for people to adjust and integrate into a new culture.

There are four major stages of cultural adjustment:

- ▸ Honeymoon—enthusiasm
- ▸ Conflict—hostility
- ▸ Integration—adjustment
- ▸ Adaptation—home

Honeymoon Stage

During the honeymoon phase, newly transplanted team members will feel enthusiastic and excited. Everything is new and interesting. It is like visiting a new place on vacation, where you can't wait to see and experience everything that is new. During this time, your team members will be happy and eager to please. They will likely smile and nod in agreement enthusiastically. It is possible that they are doing this out of eagerness, not out of understanding. It is important that you are aware that they might not fully understand what is being communicated. Don't confuse enthusiasm for comprehension. Be sure to follow up, and explain things multiple times if necessary. Team members in this phase are unlikely to tell you that they do not understand something, as they do not want to disappoint you.

Conflict Stage

During this stage, the transplanted team members have lost their initial euphoria. They are starting to feel overwhelmed by the lack of familiarity and comfort with people and things around them. They will be feeling homesick and yearning for family and friends. They will start to feel hostile toward those around them. They will be frustrated with trying to speak and understand a second language. They will be feeling anxious, isolated, confused, and possibly angry. At this stage, these team members might start to withdraw and stop communicating with their peers. They might start to complain about the way things are done in the host country. The quality of their work and productivity might decline. They might get angry or sad about seemingly unimportant things.

Your team members are experiencing culture shock. The good news is that this is a temporary stage, and they will get through it. They need support and understanding while going through this bleak time. Speak to them about how they are feeling. Let them know that their emotions and frustration are normal, and that things will start to get better as they adjust. Emotionally, the honeymoon stage is the highest point and the conflict stage is the lowest point during cultural adjustment. The difference between the two can be huge. Going from feeling on "top of the world" to feeling lower than you have ever felt, in a very short time, is very difficult. It can also be very frightening experiencing these extremes of emotion if they have never experienced before.

Integration Stage

The integration stage of adjustment is a huge relief after going through the conflict stage. Your immigrant team members will start to feel more relaxed and comfortable in their surroundings. They will feel more confident with the language, and will not feel so exhausted by the effort to think and speak in it. They will be happier, and will start to demonstrate more humor. Small mistakes that made them upset or angry during the conflict stage might start to seem amusing. They might make jokes about their misunderstandings or mispronunciations, rather than feel embarrassed by them. They will also have started to make friends and have more active social lives. Since they will be happier, their productivity and quality of work will start to increase. They will still feel at times like strangers in a strange land, but generally, they will be feeling more comfortable.

At this time, these team members need lots of encouragement and praise. Tell them how pleased you are with how well they are settling in. Provide positive feedback on the progress they are making to increase their knowledge and understanding of the work. Start to challenge them by giving a little more responsibility, so they know you have confidence in their abilities.

Adaptation Stage

When your team members reach the adaptation stage of adjustment, they feel at home both in their own culture and in the new one. They have learned to function well in both, and feel comfortable and sure of themselves. They are settled and happy. This is not the euphoria felt during the honeymoon stage, but it is a pleasurable feeling of confidence and self-assuredness in their roles.

At times, some of the stages of adjustment might be repeated. Your team members might lapse back into the conflict stage and have to progress back through acceptance again, or they might repeat the conflict and acceptance stages a few times before reaching the adaptation stage. A visit home can spark a recurrence of homesickness and a relapse to the hostility stage. The hostility might not last very long, but it is still very real. These relapses can continue to occur after family visits for years after the initial move to a new country. The most important tool to getting through the stages of adjustment is the support and understanding of others. Ideally, your team members will be able to discuss their feelings with others who have been through the stages of adjustment and understand them. Often, just knowing that you are completely normal can make you feel a lot better about yourself!

Building Teamwork in a Global Environment

Building a successful global team requires recognizing and understanding some of the key cultural differences among team members. How do you do this? Start by asking everyone on the team what they know about the other cultures and what they think is important to each culture. Each team member can also talk about what is important to him or her.

You could have a brainstorming session with your team, during which members write down their ideas and discuss them, or you could meet more informally to talk about it. It is recommended that you document what you discuss. The team should talk about every point that is raised, so that everyone has a common understanding of why an opinion or stereotype exists, and what it is based on.

For example, someone from Japan might state that Americans are viewed as aggressive and rude. There could be discussion about what this means. Ideally, the result will be a discussion about the differences in business etiquette between Japan and the United States, and an explanation that being a "go getter" and fighting hard for what you want and what you believe is considered admirable and respectable behavior in the United States The Japanese team member could explain how things are done differently in Japan, and what is considered respectable behavior there.

A British team member might comment on the Mexican culture of promising things tomorrow and then not being able to deliver. The resulting discussion about the reason why a promise is made will most likely reveal that it is because the person wants to be able to deliver tomorrow. He has the intention of doing so, if at all possible. He might know that, barring a miracle, it is not going to happen tomorrow, but he wants to make the other person happy, so he states that he can do something when in reality he just wishes he could do it. He knows that there will be a problem tomorrow, but he can deal with that then. In the meantime, perhaps the person he made the promise to will forget, and he will get an extra day to complete it anyway. Then, if it is still not done, he can promise "tomorrow" again, and make the person happy one more time! And so it goes on.

The result of these discussions should be a common understanding and respect for the behavior and culture of each others' countries. The most important lesson to learn is that nobody is intentionally trying to behave badly. Every culturally based behavior that appears to another to be negative is based on a desire to do something positive. Based on the discussions, the team chooses some objectives or behaviors that are crucial to the success of the team, and every member commits to them. This agreement should be documented and will become the teams operational objectives. Here are some examples:

- Team members will not agree to, or offer, deadlines they know they cannot meet.
- Team members will behave with respect toward others in meetings and will not interrupt or raise their voices.
- When team members are asked for an opinion, they will be honest and open in the meeting and not express different opinions outside the meeting.

You are not removing culture from the team. You are blending the cultures together and creating a shared culture that works for everyone.

It is important to recognize cultural celebrations across the team. As discussed previously, team members working in other countries might have different company-paid holidays than their counterparts in the United States It is a good idea to talk about those holidays and to discuss their significance. Also be sure to recognize holidays that might not be public holidays (with paid time off), but are important in particular countries for social or religious reasons. Some examples of these are Halloween, Guy Fawkes, Ramadan, Valentine's Day, April Fool's Day, Eid, and Yom Kippur.

It might seem unimportant to you that your counterparts or clients in another country are celebrating a festival, when it is just an ordinary week where you are located. However, it is important to be aware of these events for several reasons. First, there might be less focus on work and more focus on the imminent festivities at these times. Also, there might be more people taking vacation time and providing less coverage to accomplish all the scheduled or anticipated tasks. This is true in the United States during the week of Thanksgiving, in the United Kingdom during Christmas and New Year, and in many European countries during the Easter holiday. It is important to be aware that during Ramadan, Muslims do not eat during the hours between sunrise and sunset. It is not very polite to be talking about what a delicious lunch you had today when conversing with someone who is fasting. Fasting takes a lot of willpower and self control. It can also make the person tired and less focused. How would you feel if you had not eaten for 10 hours, and then you were asked to work late to attend a phone conference with a team in another time-zone, meaning you would miss eating with your family that evening? How would you feel if your boss in China wanted you to be on a conference call on Thanksgiving or Christmas day? It is polite for team members to acknowledge these festivities, and not behave as though they do not exist.

It is a fun team exercise to put together a schedule of events that you will recognize as a team. You can choose one festivity or event from each country or, if you have too many countries, choose one from each region. You will not necessarily get the day off work on those days, but you can find a way to celebrate them together. Perhaps in the United States, the event chosen will be Thanksgiving. You could have a team event or team day in November focused on

Thanksgiving. You can talk about what the holiday means to you, and perhaps everyone on the team can share something they are thankful for.

It is a nice gesture to celebrate birthdays for everyone on the team. Be aware, however, that birthdays are not celebrated in the same way in all countries. The Chinese, for example, do not traditionally celebrate the actual day on which they were born. When they are born, they are one year old. On the first new year after they are born, they become two years old, and then they add an extra year each new year. It is a very different way of celebrating and gives a whole different importance to the Chinese New Year celebrations.

There are many cultural activities in which the team can participate together. The cultural diversity of your team can enrich your team members on a personal as well as a business level. You can make your celebrations truly international!

CHAPTER
5

Outsourcing

Contrary to the popular belief that outsourcing is a new trend that started in the latter half of the 20th century, it is in fact an established trend that has been around for centuries. Significant changes in industry began during the Industrial Revolution. Cottage industries started to be replaced by factories, and the way goods were manufactured changed dramatically. Instead of the production of goods being completed by one family or one community, it was split into separate processes, each completed by a different factory or community focused on streamlining that specific process. The emphasis was on increased speed and higher productivity. Many raw goods, like cotton, were imported from other countries where labor was cheap. The raw cotton was sent to a factory to spin it into yarn, and then the yarn was sent to another factory to be woven into cloth. These changes signified the early beginnings of outsourcing, which has become a driving force in the global economy of today.

Offshore outsourcing of the manufacture of clothing, fashion accessories, household goods, and electronics has seen huge growth since the 1970s. The auto industry followed suit in the 1980s, and even the film industry started to move a lot of production from Hollywood to Canada in the 1990s! The 1990s also saw call-center offshore outsourcing becoming a trend. By the year 2000, other IT functions such as software engineering were being outsourced.

Not all outsourced work goes abroad. A lot of outsourcing is done locally or regionally. For example, many companies today outsource payroll services to large payroll companies. Doctors outsource the answering of phones to answering services and out-of-hours home visits to "locums." Cleaning and housekeeping services are outsourced to professional companies, both for the home and the office. A fairly new phenomenon is the emergence of farmsourcing or farmshoring. This is a domestic alternative to offshoring, where the work is outsourced to rural, underdeveloped parts of the United States Farmsourcing can offer significant cost savings to companies—in some cases, the savings are comparable with offshoring to countries such as India or China.

In today's business world, it is hard to find an organization that does not outsource at least one business or technical function.

The Decision to Outsource

Many companies are making the decision to outsource both core and non-core activities. Some of this work is outsourced to companies in the same country or region, and some of it is outsourced abroad. Outsourcing overseas is generally referred to as offshore outsourcing or offshoring. Outsourcing domestically is often referred to as insourcing or farmshoring. The specific business reason for outsourcing goods or services might vary, but it is almost always based on the need for cheaper, faster, or more efficient goods and services.

When evaluating the available outsourcing options, there are some important elements to consider before making a final decision:

- *Why do you want to outsource?*—There are many reasons why companies outsource, including cost savings, efficiency, lack of expertise in-house, the volume of work is not enough to need a full-time resource, or the work is sporadic or seasonal. The decision to outsource is often based on more than one factor. Define what is important to you so you can more effectively evaluate the outsource decision as well as each outsource vendor.

- *What are the cost savings of outsourcing?*—Cost is often an important factor in the outsource decision. It is important to define the exact savings so they can be compared to the direct and indirect costs that will be incurred in other areas.

- *Are there any one-off or recurring setup or maintenance costs?*—These costs are often overlooked in the calculation of cost savings. If it is going to take you five years to break even after paying setup costs, you need to consider whether the outsource relationship will last that long. If you change outsource vendors, you will very likely have to pay these costs again, and setup costs are not refundable.

- *What additional costs will be incurred for managing the outsource relationship?*—This will include things like increased management, travel, communication, shipping, additional equipment, and training costs. There could also be increased personnel costs related to such things as employees working different shifts to allow for time-zone differences, or the hiring of bilingual or multilingual employees.

- *How much risk can you afford for the project?*—This is key to making an informed outsource decision. It is almost impossible to outsource without increasing risk. If you no longer have direct control over the resources or process, there is increased schedule and quality risk. The increased risk might lead to an increase in costs or a decrease in customer service.

- *How important is quality?*—Depending on the nature of the work, maintaining quality might be challenging or very straightforward. For some outsource work, the client can see at a glance if the product meets expectations, and can accept or refuse it. For others, particularly for service work, quality is harder to measure and control.

- *How important is schedule (timeliness)?*—Some work is driven by schedule, while other work is not. Timeliness might be more important than quality and less important than cost, or vice versa. Make sure that you understand your priorities and that you make your decision based on them.

- *Who will manage the outsource project?*—Perhaps you or one of your employees need to be heavily involved in managing the outsource project. On the other hand, you might be quite happy for the outsource company to manage the entire process, and just deliver the final product to you at the end. This decision will be based on the nature of the work and your level of confidence in the outsourcer.

- *How independently can the outsourcer work?*—If the outsourcer is unable to make any decisions or deal with any problems without your involvement, and you have a 12-hour time difference, you could have a problem. If the vendor has to keep stopping and waiting for you or one of your team members, the work could slow down considerably. If, however, you plan to manage the outsourcer very closely and want to make all the decisions, you might not want them to work very independently.

- *Does the work have to be performed to an exact specification or process, or can the outsource company use its own specification or process?*—This is vital to the success of an outsourcing project. You must be clear in your own mind about who is going to own the specification and the process. If all you want is a final product, you could let the outsourcer own the whole process. Do you need to know if they change their process? Will it affect your processes? If you own the specification, you must have someone assigned to manage that with the outsourcer. If you own the specification and you update it, does that affect the setup or ongoing costs you pay to the outsourcer?

- *Is the outsource process scalable?*—If your business is growing, or if the work that you outsource might increase, you need to know whether the outsourcer is able to scale its business to align with your growth. Make sure that you understand the limits of the outsourcer, so you can plan appropriately.

- *Is the outsource process extendable?*—You might want to consider outsourcing additional work later if the outsource project works well. Knowing what the outsourcer can do to accommodate those needs is important.

- *If the processes are scalable and extendable, will there be additional costs to change the scope/size of the project?*—There is not much point in having a scalable and extendable process if expanding the scope means the outsourcer is going to charge the same setup costs as a new project.

- *How flexible is the outsourcer in its ability to adapt to changes in your business?*—In some industries, companies need to be able to adapt quickly to changes in the marketspace that affect the way they do business. If key functions are outsourced, you need to evaluate how this might affect your ability to act quickly and adapt to market changes.

- *How much time and effort will you and your team members need to invest in the outsource company?*—If your team needs to spend a lot of time getting the outsourcer up to speed, training the employees, and offering ongoing support, the time invested needs to be considered in the return-on-investment equation. If the outsource relationship is not likely to be long-term, the investment might not be worthwhile. There is also a danger that the training you give to the outsourcer might benefit them more than you. For example, what if they use that newly acquired knowledge or expertise to sell services to your competitors?

- *Does the outsourcer understand your business as a whole, or just the portion of work you are outsourcing?*—This is an important question. Not only do you need to know how much the outsourcer understands about your business, but you must also have a sense for how much you think the outsourcer should understand about your business. It might be critical that the outsourcer knows your business inside-out. On the other hand, it might be important that the outsourcer has as little knowledge as possible of proprietary information.

- *What are the hours of operation?*—It might be important to you that the outsourcer is available during business hours in your time-zone. Outsourcers in other time zones may work shifts to ensure full coverage. Alternatively, you might decide to outsource domestically to avoid significant differences in normal business hours between you and the outsourcer.

- *Is anyone available outside normal business hours?*—If you outsource in a region where the time difference is substantial, you need to know who is going to be available to answer your questions during your business hours. Will the outsourcer be available during your business hours, or do you need to be available during their business hours? You are the client, so you need to decide what will work best for you.

The answers to these questions will help you understand what you need from an outsourcer and whether the work you are planning to outsource is a suitable outsource project.

Defining why you want to outsource will help you evaluate the suitability of the work for outsourcing and the suitability of each outsourcing option you are considering. For example, suppose cost is the prime motivator. If you find that the cost savings from outsourcing a specific function are outweighed by the increased costs of additional prep work, packaging, shipping, or management, then outsourcing might not be the best choice. If you cannot afford any increased risk for the project, and quality and timeliness are more important than cost, you need to ensure that the outsourcer can provide the quality and timeliness you need. If you do not have the management expertise within your organization to manage an outsource relationship, you should consider outsourcing self-contained projects or functions that do not require ongoing management, so that you do not have to hire an experienced vendor manager to manage the relationship.

If your organization is growing and expanding into new markets, you need to be confident that your outsourcer can grow and expand with you, and that the costs of that expansion will not be prohibitive. It can be very expensive to change outsourcers. Sometimes, the nature of the work requires payment of substantial setup costs, or there is a lot of training involved in getting the outsourcer up and running. These costs need to be considered when choosing your outsource vendor. Never assume that everything will run smoothly. Make sure that you have contingency plans in place, and that you understand the costs and the effort involved in making changes to existing agreements, terminating agreements, and creating new ones.

> Many companies outsource to enable them to stay competitive in the business marketplace.

If the work requires a lot of interaction and face-to-face time, it might be more cost effective to outsource domestically or keep the work in-house. If your business model changes often, or you need a lot of control over the way the outsourcer works, the offshore office might be a better option than an offshore outsourcer.

The decision to outsource services should not be taken lightly. Reducing costs is a positive aspect of outsourcing, but it might come at a high internal cost. Underestimating how much management the outsource vendor will need could lead to all sorts of problems down the road. The savings from the lower costs of outsourcing must exceed the increased costs of management and the risk associated with this model, or it will not be economically viable.

It often doesn't make sense for large companies to keep all business functions in-house. Companies that want to be innovative and streamlined often want to focus on their core strengths. That leads to the decision to outsource non-critical functions to other companies. More recently, companies have been making the decision to outsource some of their core activities as well as their non-core activities. For example, many technology companies are outsourcing software development both domestically and abroad. Outsourcing work to regions where living costs and pay rates are lower can lead to much more attractive profit margins for companies located in high-cost regions.

Many companies outsource to enable them to stay competitive in the business marketplace. Suppose a company's competitors are outsourcing customer-support functions to offshore companies, decreasing the costs of that support by 600%. This enables the competitors to offer their goods and services at a lower cost while maintaining the same, or better, profit margin. As more and more companies move to this model, it gets harder and harder for companies to remain competitive unless they follow suit.

There is a lot of pressure for publicly traded companies to keep stock prices high. Shareholders push very hard for those companies to decrease costs and increase revenues. For many public companies, there is no choice but to consider outsourcing to reduce costs. Outsourcing allows companies to make huge savings in a very short time frame—a very tempting opportunity.

Smaller businesses often cannot afford to maintain every single business function in-house. If they did, they wouldn't be small companies! Focusing on the core expertise of the employees and outsourcing other functions is a successful business model for many small companies. Virtual companies generally keep full-time employees to a minimum and outsource or contract a lot of the work. There is no point in hiring employees if there is not enough work to keep them busy all the time.

Offshoring

There are two different types of offshoring. The first is offshore outsourcing, where an outsource company in the target country is contracted to provide specific services. The second is an offshore office, where the parent company opens an office in the target country and directly employs the staff at that company. Both of these setups are referred to as offshoring, and companies have to decide which option is best for them.

Offshore outsourcing has the benefit that once the work is complete, the company outsourcing the work has no further obligation to the employees who worked on the project. The offshore office, on the other hand, has to be maintained even if work gets slow for a while. The advantage of the offshore office is that the employees are not working for other companies at the same time. The parent company sets the priorities and knows which employees are working on each project.

Offshore Outsourcing

Offshore outsourcing can be very successful, but it is not always as simple as finding a company that can perform specific functions and then leaving that company to get on with it. You need a way to measure the effectiveness of the off-shore company. If you cannot monitor and measure the quality of the service being provided, you will be unable to evaluate the effectiveness of the outsourcer. You need to have confidence that the outsourcer is meeting your expectations. Make sure that you have a plan in place to monitor what is being done, and assign responsibility for the monitoring to a resource either at your own company or at the outsource company. The monitoring should continue for the life of the outsource agreement. Do not simply monitor efficiency for a few months and then stop because everything seems fine. It is often after a few months when the complacency sets in and, if you are not keeping an eye on what is going on, it could be too late by the time you discover that you have a problem.

> Offshore outsourcing can be very successful, but it is not always as simple as finding a company that can perform specific functions and then leaving that company to get on with it.

To accurately measure performance and results, you need to collect metrics. Think about how you will collect them. Asking the outsourcer to provide information that cannot be verified is not a recommended model. Make sure that there is some verification of results by you or someone on your team.

When evaluating the costs and efficiency of an outsource project, it is important to also take into consideration the effects of the economy, exchange rates, inflation, skills availability, market pay rates, and salary trends in the outsourcer's region. For example, if pay rates are increasing rapidly, the outsourced work might become a lot more expensive after the initial contract term has expired. If the local currency is getting weaker, and the currency in the outsource region is getting stronger, the costs of the project in real terms could increase considerably in a short time frame, which could severely impact the desirability and profitability of offshore outsourcing.

The logistics of day-to-day management and operations must be taken into account when deciding to offshore and when choosing the offshore vendor. Many large offshore companies handle offshoring for multiple companies, so there might be conflicting priorities. Situations might arise in which it is unclear who is responsible for the additional costs. For example, if you send someone to India to train customer-support representatives and, two months later, half of the original team has either left the company or moved to other assignments, someone has to train the new employees. Should that be the responsibility of your company or the outsource company?

To understand the time and costs of the project, it is important to define the following:

- *Where does the responsibility lie for the initial training of the offshore employees?*—This is very likely to be the client. It would be wise to build into the contract some provision for additional training at some time in the future for new employees and for training for changes in the business. The contract should define who is responsible for covering the costs of the training and the travel expenses.

- *Which company is responsible for ongoing training or training of new hires?*—There are many options. For example, your company could train some of the outsource employees and expect them to train new hires; the new hires might be sent for training to your facility (define who covers those costs); or you might send a trainer to train the new employees onsite (again, define who covers the costs).

- *Who is responsible for ensuring that the number of people who are supposed to be assigned to your company are, in fact, assigned and working for you?*—This is a similar problem to the one you have with managing virtual employees. How do you know what they are doing? With outsourcers, you need to set up a system that gives you appropriate visibility into what is being done and by whom. For some outsource agreements, you might not care who is doing what as long as you receive the final product on time, and it is of acceptable quality. For other projects, you might want a list of the employees assigned and the ability to speak directly to each of them as required.

- *Who is responsible for the quality assurance of the product or service?*—If a problem is found, what is the process for resolving it? How long will that process take?

- *Who controls whether team members are moved to other teams?*—Is it you or the offshore company?

- *How many, and which, team members must be bilingual in your company and the outsource company?*—If only one person on the outsource team speaks English, and that person is out of the office or leaves the company, you could find yourself in a situation where you are unable to communicate with the outsource team.

These are all very important questions that must be answered. The final decisions must be included in the outsource agreement before the contract is signed. It could become very costly if you find out three months into your contract period that you are responsible for covering the training costs of new employees, or that the offshore outsourcer is not required to maintain a team with any English speakers.

Offshore Office

Opening an offshore office has just as many advantages and disadvantages as the offshore outsourcing model. If the offshore office is not working, it is much more difficult for the parent company to disentangle itself from the offshorers. The parent company has to deal with employment law, vacation time, employee training, and benefits. Just because the team in India are direct employees of your company does not necessarily mean that they will be less transient than the employees of the outsource companies. In regions where there is a lot of work, there is a lot of competition to attract skilled workers, and people tend to move from job to job more often.

The offshore office has the same issues around day-to-day management, status reporting, quality, and efficiency as an offshore outsourcing company. For example, you must decide whether to send members of your existing management team to work in the offshore office (temporarily or permanently), or whether to train local employees to manage the office. The danger with sending existing employees to work in the offshore locations is that you might find yourself offshoring the work, but paying the same salaries as in the United States.

The offshore office does has the huge benefits of you setting the priorities of the team, having a lot more control over who is hired, and deciding what each person is assigned to work on. It is easier to build teamwork when you have direct access to the employees than it is with the relatively unknown staff of an outsource company.

You still need to answer a lot of the same questions for the offshore office as you would for offshore outsourcing, such as with whom responsibility for training lies. Paying to fly someone from the United States to Australia or Russia every time a new employee is hired could become very expensive. You need to decide which language skills are required and how quality and productivity are measured. The difference with the offshore office is that your organization has managerial and financial responsibility for the day-to-day activities and results of the offshore team.

Offshoring changes the business landscape considerably. Some believe that this leads to positive outcomes, like a more global environment and better opportunities for people living in developing countries. Others believe it has a negative impact by moving skilled jobs elsewhere, creating local job shortages, and decreasing quality, innovation, and long-term success. Whatever the belief, the reality is that offshore outsourcing is changing the way we do business by changing the balance of power from business, technology, and social perspectives. Many regular working people in poor, developing countries now drive around in BMWs, talking on cell phones and sending emails via PDAs. This would have been almost unheard of 20 years ago. The global economy and offshore outsourcing enables more people to buy high-cost consumer goods, thereby increasing and expanding global consumerism as well as the profits of companies that sell those consumer goods. The world is changing, and offshoring is driving a lot of that change.

Domestic Inshoring and Farmshoring

Domestic inshoring and farmshoring are also big business. There are many reasons why offshore outsourcing is not a feasible or desirable option for some companies. Some companies need to keep their work onshore for marketing or business reasons. A U.S. company that prides itself on being "made in America" would find it difficult to offshore work without completely changing the company's image.

Companies that work on a lot of government contracts are often restricted to domestic outsourcing only. Many government contracts or government-regulated work prohibits offshore outsourcing. Depending on the nature of the work, some of those contracts might require that the work is restricted to U.S. citizens, and that those citizens must also have security clearances. For companies involved in these contracts, domestic inshoring or farmshoring might be a cheaper alternative to keeping the work in-house.

Some companies resist the urge to offshore for moral reasons or due to long-term business concerns. Some feel that it is important not to outsource too much work offshore because of the negative impact on the domestic workforce.

> Companies that work on a lot of government contracts are often restricted to domestic outsourcing only.

Some believe that if offshoring continues to accelerate at such a high rate, there will soon not be enough trained workers in the United States to do the work if it needed to be brought back onshore. There is a fear that if technology jobs are perceived as becoming scarce, students will be reluctant to continue working toward technical degrees. The long-term impact of this could be an expertise gap in the domestic workforce. Some would argue that manufacturing of clothing, household goods, and automobiles have been offshored for many years, and yet there is still an abundance of jobs in the United States and the economy has not collapsed as a result of the offshoring. Which of these opinions is correct, we cannot say. There appear to be valid arguments on both sides!

Datacenter outsourcing, or sharing, is a growing trend. Some companies have seasonable demands for disk space or computing power, which makes outsourcing all or part of their datacenter needs very desirable. Building and maintaining a datacenter can be very expensive. Finding the skill Sets needed to maintain and back up the systems can add a lot of additional overhead, both in terms of resources and space.

Payroll and human resources have been outsourced by many companies for years. Accounting and legal services have also been increasingly outsourced by many U.S. companies over the past decade. Traditionally, this work has been outsourced domestically.

Farmsourcing is a relatively new term used to describe the outsourcing or re-locating of jobs to rural areas of the U.S. companies are tapping into a highly skilled workforce located in areas of the country with a much lower cost of living, and therefore demanding much lower salaries. The cost of living in San Francisco or New York, for example, is much higher than some rural areas of Arkansas, Virginia, or New Mexico.

> Farmsourcing is a relatively new term used to describe the outsourcing or relocating of jobs to rural areas of the United States.

Farmshoring has some huge advantages over offshoring. Many offshore disadvantages, such as language differences, cultural differences, and employment law are nonexistent for U.S.-based outsource companies. A "battle of the outsourcers" is beginning, in which companies that wish to outsource now have a choice whether to do so internationally or domestically. It will be interesting to see what effect this new onshore competition will have on the huge growth of outsource cities like Bangalore, India and Shanghai, China.

Unique Challenges of Outsourcing

Outsourcing can have a very positive impact on company financials. The decreased costs associated with outsourcing give companies the ability to launch more projects and accomplish more in the same time frame. However, outsourcing involves some unique challenges that you must understand and accept.

An important thing to consider when embarking on an outsource project is the impact on the existing employees. When employees hear that some functions or projects are being outsourced, they often start to feel nervous about their own jobs. If there have been layoffs to support the outsourcing, this problem is intensified. Companies often decide to outsource a whole division of the company, such as customer support or software engineering. This can result in hundreds of layoffs. Even if no jobs have been lost due to an outsourcing project, it can still create unease in the existing workforce. Employees fear that a trend is developing, and that perhaps their department or function will be next.

When outsourcing part of the work while retaining some domestic team members, ongoing communication and teamwork issues will need to be managed

> More than half the U.S. companies that have outsourced in recent years have brought the outsourced work back in-house within the first five years.

closely. Cultural differences between the teams, possible language differences, and general mistrust can lead to tension, lack of effective teamwork, and in some cases, destructive behavior.

More than half the U.S. companies that have outsourced in recent years have brought the outsourced work back in-house within the first five years. The majority of the failures occur in the first two or three years. Companies might decide to stop outsourcing for many different reasons:

- The outsource agreement was designed to be a short-term arrangement.
- The economy changed, such that outsourcing was no longer a financially viable option.
- The political situation in the outsource country was such that the client no longer felt comfortable or safe doing business there.
- The client was unable to successfully manage the relationship.
- The vendor was unable to deliver on the agreement.
- The quality of the service or product was not deemed acceptable.
- The project failed due to misunderstandings or inability to agree on the terms of the contract.
- The outsource vendor increased costs.
- The outsource vendor was not able to make the investments in technology needed to continue supporting the client.
- The client felt it was losing control of a key part of its operation that should be controlled in-house.
- The client felt it had gained efficiency at the cost of innovation.
- The client felt that managing the outsource contract took so much time, it could just as well perform the function in-house.

The list could go on. There are as many different reasons that companies run into trouble with outsourcing as there are reasons for people running into problems in their marriages. The key to outsource success is careful and attentive management of the project or function, combined with a strong working relationship between the client's and vendor's project managers, and between the companies involved in the outsource agreement.

Assigning a manager to an outsource project who is experienced in outsource or vendor management will significantly increase the chances for success. A vendor manager needs to spend adequate time working with the vendor remotely and also spending some face-to-face time with them. A formal statement of work or other written contract with the outsource company will ensure that there are no misunderstandings about expectations or contractual obligations. Combine this with a strong manager, who can work with the vendor to keep the project on track and maintain a strong working relationship, and you have the potential for a successful outsource project!

> The key to outsource success is careful and attentive management of the project or function, combined with a strong working relationship between the client's and vendor's project managers, and between the companies involved in the outsource agreement.

As a virtual manager, you need to be flexible when dealing with and managing vendors. You will need to demonstrate situational leadership skills and adjust your management and communication styles to that of the vendor or situation at hand. You should insist on support from your senior management in addition to appropriate professional resources for contract creation, negotiation, and finalization.

Managing Outsourced Projects

It is important to understand what type of management you are going to need for an outsourced project before you engage the services of an outsourcer. The project might be outsourced domestically or internationally, it might be a product or a service, it might be a specific one-off project or an ongoing business function. You need to take into account the management, language, and communication skills required, and how much actual management time your project needs.

For example, if your outsourcer is located in a different country and time zone, you will need to take communication practicalities into account. The most obvious of these is that you will have limited face-to-face communication with the outsource team, and you might have to be creative with your work hours to accommodate phone conferences. You also need to learn about any cultural differences that could hinder communication or comprehension between you and your outsourcing partner. For example, while you probably won't be able to learn to speak Hindi or Urdu, you can learn what your Indian outsource partner considers polite and rude. If it is a large project, you might decide to hire a bilingual project manager who understands the cultural differences and can improve communication.

Some companies have a vendor management department or an outsourcing management department. The role of these departments is to be the communication channel between the client manager and the vendor manager, and to support both effectively for positive results. Communication is the key to success in this role. This added level of management can help solve a lot of problems if the middle managers are communicating effectively and in a timely manner, but also has the potential to merely create another layer of bureaucracy to the process. If you need a full-time project manager to manage a project (or projects) outsourced to China, for example, hire a strong project manager who speaks the Chinese language you need (typically, Mandarin or Cantonese), and who possesses vendor management experience, and cut out the intermediary. This might not always be possible, but in many situations, less is more!

For some projects, you will want to have visibility into the specific resources working on your projects. For others, you might not know or care who is assigned to do the work, as long as the outsource company meets its deliverables.

Specific Project Outsourcing

Specific project outsourcing can be split into two separate categories:

- ‣ Product development, such as a software engineering project
- ‣ Outsourced services, such as a marketing campaign

Product Development

Product development projects usually require a lot of involvement from you in their planning and design phases, and less involvement in the development and execution phases. This type of project can sometimes require a lot of day-to-day management, especially if the outsourced product is part of a larger project that will require integration and testing as the project progresses. If specifications for in-house work need to be aligned with specifications for the outsourced work, there will need to be close communication between developers on each team.

If you are managing an outsource project and are also managing your own local or virtual team, it can be tempting to focus on your direct-report responsibilities and just let the outsourcer get on with it. If the outsourcing piece is self-contained, and you have a high level of confidence that the outsourcer will deliver to specification without much management, this might be an appropriate way to balance your time. If, however, you simply assume that the outsourcing employees know what they are doing without having much insight into their abilities or any experience working with them, you might well run into problems.

You might feel it is almost impossible that the outsourcer will not deliver to specification, if you have a contract that defines exactly what you expect. In theory, this sounds great, but plenty of things can go wrong. For example, your interpretation of the contract and the technical specification might be different from that of the outsourcer. Sometimes terminology is used in different ways in different companies. Sometimes translation changes the meaning of the specification. Be sure to check that the outsourcer is making the progress you expect, and take a look at the product as it is developed. Otherwise, you might end up with a big shock at the end of the project.

When you hire a new employee, you describe the job in detail before, during, and after the hiring process. You document the requirements of the job, give the employee a job description, write up formal objectives, and tell him or her more than once what the desired results are. Would you leave the employee with all this information, and not check in for a few months, or only check in when you need input for a performance evaluation? Of course not! In the same way, you should not leave your outsourcer with a specification and hope for the best.

Early in the project life cycle, you should draw up a project plan with the outsource project manager. In it, you agree on specific review and validation points throughout the project. You need to define what you expect to see at those milestones. Then, you will need to spend time reviewing and providing feedback to the outsourcer. For software projects, this might involve design reviews, code reviews, and prototypes.

Outsourced Services

Services outsourced for a specific project that is not ongoing work are generally self-contained projects. They do not require the level of management needed for a product development project. These types of projects are usually outsourced to professional companies who have the expertise to perform the contract work without too much involvement or management from the client.

An example of an outsourced service project would be a marketing campaign. Though a marketing campaign requires checkpoints and sign-offs at certain stages of the project, the outsource company would rarely ask you for guidance. It is most likely going to be presenting options and asking you to choose one or more of them. Other kinds of service projects that are often outsourced include process improvement projects, technical infrastructure projects (datacenter or disaster-recovery planning, for example), and recruitment.

These projects involve more hands-off management. You need to be responsive and communicative, but not involved in day-to-day management, review, or validation of work. These projects are also usually quite straightforward to measure. The vendor either delivers what was contracted or does not. There is less potential for a specification to be misinterpreted or a contract to be misunderstood.

Ongoing Business-Function Outsourcing

Ongoing business-function outsourcing can be divided into two separate categories:

- Product development, such as manufacturing
- Outsourced services, such as customer support

Product Development

Outsourcing ongoing product development might require a lot of initial setup time to get the processes and procedures well defined. Generally, once the setup is complete, the outsource company manages its own processes, and the products delivered to you will either pass or fail a quality inspection. The quality inspection might also be performed by the outsource company, so your involvement might be minimal.

Always maintain regular contact with outsource companies, regardless of the amount of management hours you need to spend on the work. This type of outsource relationship needs strong customer/vendor relationship management to be successful. Maintaining a good-quality relationship with the vendor is critical to ensuring that things continue to go well. When there are problems, the strong working relationships you have built with the vendor managers will help you to get resolution more quickly, and with less conflict and stress.

Make sure you are checking the quality of the work from the outsource company regularly, even if they are responsible for quality testing and inspection of the product. Visit the outsource company from time to time, if possible, to observe the manufacturing process and to meet face-to-face with your contacts.

Outsourced Services

Outsourcing services, such as customer or technical support functions, usually need more ongoing management than functions such as accounting, billing, or payroll where, once the initial systems are in place, the work is very straightforward. Customer support functions usually require an up-front investment in training and the definition of processes such as escalation procedures and reporting.

If you have been involved in training the outsource workers, you might have an agreement that your outsource team is dedicated to working for your company. Even when this is the case, your outsourcer probably has many clients, and at times your team members might be reassigned to work on contracts for other clients. It might be that you do not care who is assigned to your project. If you do care, however, you will need to spend sufficient time monitoring the outsourcer to be sure that you are receiving the coverage that you expect and have contracted for.

Customer support services will require some level of reporting back to you. For example, you will want to monitor average wait times and call length times for customers calling in. You will also likely want to categorize and monitor the types of calls being received, so you can identify product or service issues and update operator scripts. This type of management takes time. Lack of attention to what the outsourcer is doing can lead to a lot of problems down the line.

Building Relationships with Outsource Vendor Managers

It is important to build strong working relationships with the vendor project manager for any outsourced project or business function. Consider this person to be a member of your team, and give the relationship the time and attention it deserves.

Set up a process for daily or weekly reporting from the project manager, and schedule regular one-on-one meetings to discuss status, risks, and issues. In an ideal situation, you will meet in person with the project manager at least once before the outsource project begins or in an early phase of the project. If you can also meet with the team assigned to your contract, even better. This might not be possible, but anything you can do to get closer to the outsource team and to have high visibility with its members will help minimize problems and add to the success of the project.

When you have team days with your team members, invite the outsource project managers if you are able to do so without revealing any confidential or proprietary information. If you hold all-hands meetings from time to time, invite the vendor project manager and key team members to attend.

You can add a personal aspect to your relationship with the vendor project manager by adding him or her to your instant-messenger contact list and sending a "hello" every now and then. All the tricks and tips you use to build strong relationships and teamwork with a remote team can be used with outsource vendors to achieve the same results.

Remember that all vendors are different, just as all people are different. The outsource project manager and team members will have different interaction styles, learning styles, and communication preferences. The vendor organization will have its own company culture in addition to a national and regional culture that will most likely be different from yours. You need to learn what these styles and cultural differences are and use them to help build strong teamwork and cooperation.

Importance of the Statement of Work and Outsourcing Contract

When projects are outsourced, you must carefully document the work being contracted to the outsource company. The Statement of Work (SOW) defines the work tasks and deliverables that the outsourced company is being contracted to provide. The Statement of Work should be very clear, concise, and unambiguous. It is especially important to be aware of the language used when you outsource work to a foreign company. It is also important to understand the laws in those countries. Anything in your contract that is out of compliance with a country's laws will not be enforceable.

An example Statement of Work is shown in Figure 5.1. A full copy of the document is included in appendix B.

Statement Of Work

1. *Introduction*
   1.1.   Objectives
2. *Project Scope*
   2.1.   In Scope
   2.2.   Out Of Scope
3. *Period Of Contract*
4. *Specific Tasks*
5. *Schedule Of Deliverables*
6. *Completion Criteria*
7. *Fees And Payments*
   7.1.   Fees
   7.2.   Payment Not To Exceed
   7.3.   Payment Terms
8. *Roles And Responsibilities*
   8.1.   Vendor (Outsource) Company Responsibilities
   8.2.   Client Responsibilities
   8.3.   Conflict Of Interest
   8.4.   Key Contacts
   8.5.   Reporting Requirements
9. *Assumptions And Constraints*
10. *Staffing*
    10.1.   Staffing Plan
    10.2.   Physical Location
    10.3.   Workers Citizenship
    10.4.   Security Clearance
11. *General Provisions*
    11.1.   Change Process
    11.2.   Cancellation/Termination Terms
    11.3.   Renewal Terms
    11.4.   Disputes
    11.5.   Delays
    11.6.   Legal Compliance
    11.7.   Intellectual Property Rights
    11.8.   Security
    11.9.   Inspection And Acceptance

Figure 5.1: Statement of Work

The SOW generally contains the following elements:

- Introduction
- Objectives
- Project Scope
- Period of Contract
- Specific Tasks
- Schedule of Deliverables
- Completion Criteria
- Fees and Payments
- Roles and Responsibilities
- Assumptions and Constraints
- Staffing
- General Provisions

Introduction

The introduction of the Statement of Work gives an overview of the project or functions to be outsourced, including the project timelines. It includes the business case for outsourcing, in addition to information about the selection criteria for choosing a vendor. This section also identifies the client and the vendor who are entering into this agreement.

Objectives

The objectives are the measurable outcomes of the project. They can be financial, organizational, process, business, or technical, or a combination of these.

Project Scope

The project scope should include a detailed description of the work or tasks that are "in scope," in addition to the work and tasks that are "out of scope." If a project is very complex, the scope might include diagrams and specifications to ensure that it is clearly understood by both parties. For example, an outsourcer might be contracted to provide specific pieces of functionality within a project, but not for the entire project. Likewise, the vendor might be contracted to provide customer or technical support for specific products that the client owns, but not for all products. The scope should also include the timelines for each service.

It is important to document anything specifically excluded from the outsourcing agreement. This will ensure that there is no confusion about the expectations for the client or the vendor. It is particularly important to indicate out-of-scope items if the payment for the contract is by the hour or amount of work completed, and not a fixed amount. The client does not want the vendor invoicing for time spent on tasks that are not within the scope of the contract. The outsource company generates its revenue from the services it performs. The more services performed, the more it can charge the client. If the client is not clear about what is excluded, one phone call from a project manager in a few months' time might cause the outsourcer to start providing a lot more than was required.

Period of Contract

The duration of the Statement of Work might vary from several days to many years. The SOW should define the duration or time frame of the agreement. This includes the start date, the end date, and any dates that are specifically not included. If the contract is set to automatically renew, the terms of the renewal must also be documented in the Statement of Work.

Specific Tasks

Include a detailed description of all the tasks that the outsource company is contracted to perform. For example, if the outsource company is providing customer service, its list of tasks might include the following:

- Staff the call center from 8:00 AM to 6:00 PM PST, Monday through Friday, excluding U.S. public holidays as defined in the staffing plan.
- Answer phones within 15 seconds maximum during peak hours, and 10 seconds in non-peak hours.
- Respond to emails within 24 (business) hours.
- Document all customer calls and emails in the call center's logs.
- Escalate customer issues to supervisors within 10 minutes if unable to resolve within 10 minutes or two emails.

Schedule of Deliverables

The schedule of deliverables should contain a list of major milestones and deliverables for the contract. For the example of a call center used in the previous section, this might include weekly or monthly reporting on the call levels, average call length, issue resolution time, and number of issues escalated.

Completion Criteria

The completion criteria is the measurable deliverable that clearly demonstrates that the tasks or projects have been completed. For a short-term outsourcing agreement, this could be the final deliverable, such as a piece of software, a database, or six new employees hired. For a longer-term contract, such as with a call center, this could be the monthly report deliverables showing that the level of service has been in line with the provisions of the contract.

Fees and Payments

The Statement of Work defines the outsourcing costs or fees. There are three basic types of fee agreements:

1. Fixed costs
2. Time and material costs (variable, based on hours or days worked)
3. A combination of fixed and variable costs

This section also includes information about terms.

Fixed Costs

Fixed-cost agreements are more common for longer-term agreements, where a fixed number of staff are allocated to the project. This type of agreement is typical for call-center or software engineering outsourcing. The client needs to know what the specific costs are going to be, up front. This type of agreement states that the work as specified in the SOW will be completed for an all-inclusive fixed price. The contract might include penalties if the work is not completed on time or if it does not meet the specified completion criteria.

Time and Material Costs

Time and material cost agreements are more common for short-term projects, especially for those where the client is not sure exactly what will be required to meet its needs. For example, if the client company wants to pay for some contract software engineers, but is not sure how long it needs to keep them, the company will be more likely to put in place a time and materials agreement.

Often, these agreements are put in place to resolve short-term problems. For example, a company might have a hiring freeze, but a key project cannot be completed without more resources. Alternatively, suppose a new facility is being built to house more employees, but before it is ready, there is an immediate need for coverage of some specific functions. Time and material costs are billed according to the actual time and expenses the outsourced vendor spends on the project. These types of contracts require more diligence on the part of the client to ensure that they stay within budget and that the vendor is providing the level of service expected within time spent. Sometimes, this type of agreement is put in place during the initial stage of an outsourcing project, as a prelude to starting a formal project with a fixed-price SOW.

Combination of Fixed and Variable

The final type of fee structure is a combination of the fixed and variable fee structures. Some specified amount of work is completed within the fixed price agreement, and any additional work is subject to time and materials costs. An example would be if a call center was seeing unusually high call rates, and the client wanted the outsource vendor to add additional staff for a short time until the problem causing the high call volume was resolved. The costs for these additional workers would be billed as time and expense costs.

Payment Not to Exceed

The "Payment Not to Exceed" section can be very important for any fee agreements that contain variable costs. If there is an upper limit on costs that must not be exceeded, it is documented here.

Payment Terms

The "Payment Terms" section defines when and how the client will pay the fees to the outsource vendor. For example, the fees might be payable monthly or quarterly. They might be required to be paid in advance or in arrears. The fees might be tied to specific deliverables. There might be penalties for late payment that need to be documented here.

Roles and Responsibilities

Roles and responsibilities should be documented in detail.

Vendor (Outsource) Company Responsibilities

Include the specific tasks for which the key members of the vendor team are responsible. This should encompass communications or expectations that fall outside the specific task and deliverables lists, for example:

- The project manager might be responsible for providing a weekly status report to the client project manager and escalating any urgent issues to the client company within a specified number of hours.
- The vendor might be expected to have representation at key project meetings.
- The vendor informs the client if any key personnel leave the team or if any new team members are added.
- The vendor sends a representative to the client's quarterly onsite meeting.

Client Responsibilities

The client also has specific responsibilities to the vendor. These can include the following:

- Provide training to the vendor.
- Give the vendor access to specific information contained on the client's internal network.
- Assign a project manager to the vendor as a single point of contact.
- Respond to urgent issues within 12 hours.

Conflict of Interest

This section should clearly define any conflict of interest issues. For example, if the vendor is in the same line of business as the client, or plans to move into that market space as a direct competitor, it must be disclosed here

If a principal of either company has a financial interest in the business of the other, these relationships or interests should be documented here together with any limitations or regulations that apply to that relationship or interest.

Key Contacts

The "Key Contacts" section of the Statement of Work lists the key employees and executives from each company and defines their role in the agreement. This section does not need to include the staffing plan, but it would include the executives or principals of each company who are responsible for signing the contract. It also specifies who is responsible for approving any changes to the contract.

Reporting Requirements

The "Reporting Requirements" section includes any company or regulatory reporting requirements. It could pertain to the actual work being completed or the staff members being employed to work on it.

Assumptions and Constraints

As part of the Statement of Work, many items will be assumed for purposes of the outsourcing agreement. For example, the SOW might assume that the vendor continues to exist in its current form. If the vendor is acquired by another company, then the old outsourcing agreement will become null and void and will need to be renegotiated. Less obvious assumptions might be related to the number of staff members assigned to the project, or specific individuals who will be assigned to the project. If specific individuals are required, it must be documented in the agreement, so that the outsource company does not replace one of those individuals with someone else. Another assumption could be that the vendor and the client need to agree on all resources assigned to the project.

Any known constraints should also be documented. For example, if the vendor is unable to add additional staff to the project due to space limitations, document it here. There might be technical or legal requirements that constrain the project in some way. For example, for a software project, the client might have a constraint that the code is written in a specific language or designed to work on a specific version of operating system or database. Any employment laws that might affect the vendor's ability to staff the project should also be documented here. These might relate to maximum hours that can be worked per week or minimum payments for overtime.

Staffing

The "Staffing" section includes a staffing plan that identifies the resources and skill Sets available for the project or outsource team. The staffing plan should be similar to the one included in chapter 3. Specific names are not usually included in the staffing plan. The outsourcing company usually reserves the right to substitute or change staff members when necessary.

The staffing plan should also include employee benefits, such as right to time off for sickness, vacation, or parental leave. Though the outsourcing company is responsible for covering the costs of these benefits, it is important that the client understands that the vendor is required by law to give each team member a certain amount of time off, regardless of whether it is paid or unpaid. This agreement should specify what amount of time off is acceptable before the vendor is required to hire a temporary replacement for a missing worker. In a time and materials agreement, this will likely not be a big issue, but for a fixed-fee agreement, this could become a bone of contention between the vendor and client if not properly documented.

Physical Location

The physical location of the outsourced workers needs to be defined in the Statement of Work. This will include the country in which they work as well as the actual location. It should identify if the workers are virtual or if they work in a local office. This agreement should also identify which country's employment laws will cover the outsource workers.

Well-written Statements of Work need to define all onsite and offsite work. Many Statements of Work have conflicts regarding this issue. Perhaps the customer wants to have the outsourced project manager onsite every day for the duration of the project, but the outsourcing company believes that the project manager will be virtual or offsite during the duration of the project. For many outsourcing companies, the location of workers is an area of potential confusion.

Worker Citizenship

Some outsourced projects might have citizenship requirements. For example, government contracts often require that the people working on them are citizens of that government's country, or they might exclude citizens of specific countries. The vendor might be required to perform certain checks to ensure that the workers are legally allowed to work in the country where they will be located. Any citizenship-related requirements should be clearly defined.

Security Clearance

Some projects require security clearance or background checks. This section of the document should document any security clearances required.

Many companies require various background or other security or technical requirements for workers on their projects. This validating of the appropriate clearance or approval is required for many projects. This approval process can take several days or months, and can have an overall impact on the resource staffing of outsourcing projects.

General Provisions

In addition to the previously discussed sections, a SOW also has a "General Provisions" section with several areas.

Change Process

Define the process for making changes to the project, the scope, or this agreement.

Cancellation/Termination Terms

Specify the terms for cancellation or termination of the contract. For example, what will happen if the vendor is acquired by another company, fails to deliver on the terms of the agreement, has a security breach, or has not been paid the fees in a timely manner by the client?

Renewal Terms

If the contract is renewable, define the terms of the renewal. There might be any number of terms relating to contract renewals, including pricing guarantees for renewals made in specific time periods. Alternatively, the contract might automatically renew annually unless the client cancels.

Disputes

The process for resolving disputes should be documented so that both parties are aware of the steps involved if there is a dispute. Often, companies want a set escalation procedure that must be followed before either party seeks legal representation in a dispute.

Delays

The impact on the contract of delays in meeting deliverables or paying invoices should be documented. Acceptable delays should be clearly defined, in addition to what will be considered unacceptable delays. If a delay will result in a penalty or interest payment, the terms must be defined clearly and unambiguously.

Legal Compliance

Any legal compliance regarding the implementation of the product or service should be documented. This should include employee rights compliance. Any government regulations in place in the country where the client is located, the vendor is located, the workers will be located, or the product or service will be sold or made available need to be clearly explained, together with any supporting documentation.

Intellectual Property Rights

Specify who owns the intellectual property rights and how those rights must be protected.

Security

Define any security concerns or requirements. These might be related to the safety and security of the staff or the property. They might include building security and network security. They might also cover security policies for passwords, firewalls, and physical access to the product or technology systems being used by the vendor.

Inspection and Acceptance

Define any work pertaining to inspection, testing, and acceptance of the product or service being provided. Include the specific measurements that will be used and who is responsible for conducting the measurements and analyzing the results. You should also identify who will sign the Statement of Work and the Project Completion form, which is a critically important part of the SOW. This form is signed by the client and the vendor when the terms of the SOW have been met satisfactorily. It signifies the official end of the agreement.

Time Management

The term "time management" is very widely used but, in reality, it is not possible to manage time. Time doesn't actually do anything; you cannot manage something that does not do anything and cannot be changed in any way. Time cannot be increased or reduced, and it cannot deliver anything. What we really mean when we talk about time management is *task* management—getting our tasks completed on time and managing our workload to fit it into the time we have available. It is important to make this distinction, so you understand that to manage your time, you must actively manage and prioritize your tasks. There are no secrets that will make time last longer, nor are there any magical formulas that will make you an instant success at time management. You need to learn how to prioritize and manage your tasks so that you can complete them successfully. You also need to learn to recognize problems. In this chapter, you will learn how to do these things.

The Importance of Time Management

Effective time management is an important factor in any team. It is of vital importance to team members working virtually. There are many unique factors to the virtual work environment that make it difficult to prioritize tasks and stay on track. Team members who work alone generally have less structure in their day-to-day activities. Less structure can make it harder to schedule regular tasks and to get into a groove with completing them on time. Frequent travel adds more complexity and even less structure to the equation, so it becomes even more critical that time is being managed proactively and that tasks are prioritized effectively.

If time is managing you rather than you managing your time, you will become less and less effective. Productivity will decrease, and an overwhelming sense of confusion will set it. You can get to the point where there is so much to do, you don't know where to start. You end up spending most of your time contemplating the problem rather than doing something about it. Meanwhile, you are getting more and more pressure to deliver. You start to feel overwhelmed. You have no idea how long it will take you to get each task accomplished, so are unable to commit to anything. Your coworkers, boss, client, and others to whom you owe deliverables get frustrated with you, and can't understand why you are unable to commit to something and get it done on time.

> Virtual employees working out of home offices can find endless distractions to take their minds off what they should be doing.

Staying focused and avoiding distractions are the keys to successful time management. Virtual employees working out of home offices can find endless distractions to take their minds off what they should be doing. The laundry might need doing, or perhaps they need to run to the store, or they really should clean the kitchen as the in-laws are coming over for dinner. There are no end of things that really need doing and, as the remote worker is already at home, it is very easy to stop work for a few minutes to take care of those things—especially if the work is overwhelming. If the worker cannot stay focused on what he or she should be doing, the distractions will take over, and work time will not be productive time.

The virtual manager and each virtual team member must develop high levels of skill in task prioritization and time management in order for the virtual team to operate smoothly and be successful.

Time Management for Virtual Managers and Remote Workers

Time management can be problematic for everyone on the team. There always seems to be too much to do and not enough time to do it. Each person must take responsibility for his or her personal time management. As the manager, you have an even greater responsibility. You must take ownership for not only your own personal time management, but also the team's time management. In addition, you must ensure that all of your team members are managing their time most effectively. You cannot just assume that each team member is managing to balance his or her workload effectively. First, you need to give your team members the appropriate training and tools to manage their own time. Second, you need to monitor progress so you are aware as early as possible if a team member is struggling to prioritize appropriately and stay on track with assigned tasks.

Working on shared tasks can be more time-consuming when working virtually. It can take time to email files back and forth and stop to wait for responses from other team members. In a local office environment, the team members could sit in the same room or could review the results together, rather than going through a time-consuming virtual review process. Having team members located in different time zones can slow things down a lot, too. Waiting for an email to be read or having a very small time window in which phone calls and real-time online meetings can be scheduled adds a lot of calendar time to completing a task, even if the actual time spent working on it is not affected. Plan for these delays, and add some contingency time into the schedule as part of your overall time-management process.

> Working on shared tasks can be more time-consuming when working virtually.

Work with your team members to help them estimate collaborative tasks as accurately as possible. Make sure that actual time and calendar time are both taken into consideration when estimating timelines for these types of tasks. Also take time differences and workload into account when allocating review and update time at each stage.

In a traditional, non-virtual environment, a certain amount of time management is accomplished as a result of the structure and processes of the team and the work. If everyone is in the same location and time zone, working the same hours each day, it is easy for the manager to have good quality (and often a higher quantity of) one-on-one time with each team member. You can meet face to face to set priorities either on an individual or a team level daily, weekly, or monthly. This can also be done virtually, but it requires a lot more effort and planning to accomplish. Make sure that you schedule regular one-on-one time with each team member and use the time as effectively as possible.

Local team members get to chat with their manager in the break room, between meetings, or when they meet in the elevator. A one-sentence question requiring a brief answer can be handled without a formal meeting and without taking additional time out of either person's day. The ability to swing by someone's office, stick your head in, and ask, "How's everything going?" might not seem particularly amazing, but it can have a very positive effect on the team member's morale and increase his or her ability to complete tasks on time. It is an ideal opportunity for the team member to say, "Things are going well, but I need some direction on these two tasks I am working on. Both are high priority, and I can only get one completed today. Which one would you like me to work on first?" When working remotely, if a team member called you once or twice a day to ask questions like this, it might be construed as an inability to work independently.

A lot of time-management issues can be resolved by staying in touch via instant messaging, which is the virtual equivalent to "sticking your head in the door." If some team members are working locally and others remotely, it can sometimes be more difficult to remember how important this daily check-in is for all the team members, not just the ones who you see each day. If you and your team members stay connected via instant messaging, and make yourselves available whenever possible so you can answer questions from team mates, it is possible to reduce some of the time drag inherent in virtual teams. Anything you can do to help smooth the process of exchanging information will contribute to greater productivity and fewer delays.

Team Time Management

At some companies, the manager has a team meeting at the beginning of each day or week. In it, team members report status and priorities for the current day or week. These meetings are so effective because every team member is present, and the manager can see everyone. It is much easier to tell if a person is overwhelmed and stressed out when you can see his or her face and body language. In the virtual environment, managers often skip these meetings or hold them with just the local team members. The justification for skipping the meetings can be that the manager feels he or she has a good handle on everyone's status, having checked in with each person individually during the week. Alternatively, the manager might feel that it is too difficult finding a time when everyone is available, due to schedule differences and time differences. These are terrible reasons (excuses, really) for not holding a team meeting. The real reason is more likely to be that the manager feels more comfortable holding local meetings than virtual ones. Virtual meetings can feel cold and impersonal. If you want to keep your team members on track, however, you need to talk about priorities and status in team meetings.

The team members need interaction with each other as well as with you. They need to understand what others are working on, and they need a common understanding of the day's or week's priorities. Business today is fast-moving and ever-changing, and priorities can change overnight. Your team members must understand any change so they can reprioritize their tasks and schedules accordingly. If every change is a last-minute panic, the entire team will be struggling with time management and will feel like they are late with every deliverable. Communication, teamwork, and time management are closely linked. They need to be managed in a holistic way to ensure you have a focused, cohesive, and effective team.

> Communication, teamwork, and time management are closely linked. They need to be managed in a holistic way to ensure you have a focused, cohesive, and effective team.

In addition to team time management, every team member needs to practice personal time management. As the manager of the team, it is your responsibility to ensure that each team member has the knowledge and tools to effectively manage his or her time.

Personal Time Management

Effective time management is essential to anybody who works in a virtual environment. As the manager of a virtual team, you need to be skilled at time management. Each of your team members also needs to develop the same level of skill. Time is a limited resource. Because you can't make more of it, you have to learn how to make the most of what you have. To work most effectively, you must learn how to get things done and how to plan for the future. You need to learn how to focus on the right tasks and not waste time working on small, unimportant ones. You must learn how to make decisions, take responsibility for those decisions, and communicate them to others in an appropriate and productive way.

Some negotiation might be necessary from time to time. Others will not always agree with your assessment of the importance or priority of tasks. Negotiation does not mean convincing others that you are right. It means listening to input, discussing ideas, and making the most appropriate decision based on the business need. Task lists, to-do lists, and personal schedules are subject to

change. Nothing is ever set in stone. In today's fast-moving business environment, the ability to adapt to, and embrace, change is a valuable commodity for an
individual, a manager, and a business.

To manage your time, you need to manage your tasks. To manage your tasks,
you need a way to identify, prioritize, and complete them on time. First, let's
identify the core requirements for a time-management process:

1. Identify the meetings and tasks to be accomplished.

2. Prioritize meetings.

3. Prioritize or rank tasks.

4. Schedule tasks.

5. Update and reprioritize as new tasks are added and others are completed.

6. Estimate and schedule tasks.

7. Track and complete tasks.

8. Communicate the progress and status of tasks in a timely manner.

Let's focus on one requirement at a time.

Identify the Meetings and Tasks to Be Accomplished

The easiest way to get started identifying meetings and tasks is to compile a list
of all the things you are responsible for doing. This should include regularly
scheduled meetings and tasks, plus other project-related or one-off tasks. Here
are some examples:

- Meetings (scheduling, agendas, minutes, attending, travel, and facilitating)
- Reports or documents
- Project deliverables
- Client communication
- Emails
- Status reports
- One-on-one time with direct reports
- Coaching and development of team members
- Professional development (self development)
- Training

It is a good idea to list the tasks in an Excel spreadsheet to start with, such as the example in Figure 6.1. Eventually, you will need to sort the tasks into categories, to determine the most effective way to manage and track them. A spreadsheet is the ideal method for this. (A sample task-management list is also included in appendix B.)

Your list will probably be much longer than the example in Figure 6.1. You might be surprised at just how many recurring tasks you have, and how much of your weekly work time is taken up with them. If you are responsible for running meetings, do not forget to add time for meeting preparation (scheduling the meeting and creating the written agenda) and for meeting minutes and follow-up. These tasks can take a considerable amount of time. If you do not allocate time to do them, you will not have adequate time to complete them. Do not skip agendas and minutes for meetings to try to speed up the process. It doesn't speed up anything! You will end up with badly run meetings that lack structure and results. They will not be productive or worthwhile.

Category	Priority	Task Name	Frequency	Start Date	Duration (hrs)	Due Date
Meeting		Team Meeting	weekly	Monday's	1	
Meeting		Client A meeting	monthly	varies	2	
Meeting		Client A meeting prep	monthly	varies	4	
Meeting		Client A meeting minutes/notes	monthly	varies	2 to 4	
Reports		Weekly Work Results Report (update daily - submit weekly)	daily	daily	0.5	each Friday 4pm
Projects		Project XYZ task 1	once	June 30th	20	Aug 31st
Client communication		Phone calls to clients	weekly		5	
Emails		Reading and responding to emails	daily		2	
Meeting		1x1 with manager				
Coaching and development		Weekly meeting with mentor	weekly	Monday	1	
Professional development		Time management training class	once	Sept 3rd	8	Sept 3rd
Filing		Filing paperwork backlog in office	once		4	
Filing		Weekly filing of paperwork	weekly		1	
Reorganizing office		Changing file system and adding new file cabinet	once		5	

Figure 6.1: Task-management list

In a nutshell, time management is not about doing everything as fast as you can; it is about doing everything as efficiently as you can. Speed and efficiency are not the same thing. Confusing the two will only add to your time-management headaches. The more predictive you can make your outcomes, the less surprises you will need to deal with, which equals more time to get your work done!

Prioritize Meetings

Before you can prioritize your meetings, you need to define your list of priority levels and how each level will be handled. Below is an example priority list:

- *Priority 1*—The meeting cannot be delegated. It is critical to the success of the business and/or project.
- *Priority 2*—The meeting is critical to the success of the business and/or project, but it can be delegated in an emergency.
- *Priority 3*—The meeting can be delegated.
- *Priority 4*—You do not need to attend this meeting unless there is an agenda item that is applicable to you. You should read the minutes of the meeting.
- *Priority 5*—You do not need to attend this meeting.

Go through all the meetings on your task-management list, and assign each one a priority. Then add, or update them, on your online calendar.

Most calendaring tools allow you to use labels to prioritize tasks and to define how your time is shown on the calendar (busy, tentative, or free). Microsoft Outlook, for example, has the following labels that can be used to help prioritize and sort your tasks:

- None
- Important
- Personal
- Vacation
- Must Attend
- Preparation Required
- Travel Required
- Birthday
- Anniversary
- Phone Call

You can also use the "Show Time As" function to allow you to schedule tasks on your calendar without showing the time on your calendar as busy. This is important on a virtual team, where you are most likely using shared calendaring. This allows your team members to see when you really are available, so they can schedule meetings with you.

After you prioritize your tasks, use the categorization labels to set the Priority 1 tasks as "Must Attend" and Priority 2 as "Important." For the rest, you could omit labels, or use the "Needs Preparation" or "Travel Required" labels to give you a quick visual of what you need to do to prepare for meetings. If there are any meetings that you can permanently delegate, do so immediately. Ask the meeting organizer to keep you on the distribution list for minutes, if you want to keep up-to-date with the outcomes of these meetings. Alternatively, you could change the meeting to "Tentative" on your calendar, and only attend if there is an agenda item that is of particular interest to you.

Always ensure that you have a delegate who can take your place at meetings when you are unable to attend. Everyone on the team should have a backup for meetings and any critical tasks. This is especially true for remote workers, who cannot pop into the office next door to ask a team mate to cover in a meeting for the few weeks while he or she will be on vacation.

When prioritizing the meetings on your task-management list, give some thought to the priority that each meeting should have for your team members. You will need to assist them with setting appropriate priorities for each of their tasks and meetings, too.

Prioritize or Rank Tasks

You have listed all your tasks and subtasks. You have included all the things you currently do, as well as the things that you (or someone else) thinks you should be doing. You have also categorized the tasks in a meaningful way. You have prioritized meetings on your calendar. Now it is time to prioritize your tasks.

First, you need to define your prioritization levels, as you did with your meetings. Below is an example of a five-level prioritization:

- *Priority 1*—The task cannot be delegated, postponed, or canceled. It is critical to the success of the business and/or project.
- *Priority 2*—The task cannot be postponed or canceled. It is critical to the success of the business and/or project, but it can be delegated in an emergency.
- *Priority 3*—The task can be delegated or postponed.

➤ *Priority 4*—The task can be delegated, and could also be postponed indefinitely.

➤ *Priority 5*—This is a low-priority task. This task probably will not be completed unless its priority changes.

Next, go through the list of tasks and add a prioritization level to each one. The task-management list will look like the example in Figure 6.2.

Category	Priority	Task Name	Frequency	Start Date	Duration (hrs)	Due Date
Meeting	3	Team Meeting	weekly	Monday's	1	
Meeting	1	Client A meeting	monthly	varies	2	
Meeting	1	Client A meeting prep	monthly	varies	4	
Meeting	1	Client A meeting minutes/notes	monthly	varies	2 to 4	
Reports	1	Weekly Work Results Report (update daily - submit weekly)	daily	daily	0.5	each Friday 4pm
Projects	2	Project XYZ task 1	once	June 30th	20	Aug 31st
Client communication	2	Phone calls to clients	weekly		5	
Emails	2	Reading and responding to emails	daily		2	
Meeting	2	1x1 with manager				
Coaching and development	3	Weekly meeting with mentor	weekly	Monday	1	
Professional development	2	Time management training class	once	Sept 3rd	8	Sept 3rd
Filing	3	Filing paperwork backlog in office	once		4	
Filing	3	Weekly filing of paperwork	weekly		1	
Reorganizing office	4	Changing file system and adding new file cabinet	once		5	

Figure 6.2: Prioritized task-management list

Schedule Tasks

The tasks on your task-management list are going to need scheduling and tracking. Remember to schedule time for tasks related to meeting preparation and documentation. If your tools allow, schedule these tasks with reminders, so you don't forget to do them. Try to schedule meeting-related tasks with some buffer time, in case you get delayed and run out of time to complete them. If you schedule time to create an agenda two hours before a meeting's start time, and are delayed by other tasks, you will have to run your meeting without one. If you have a weekly status report that must be submitted by Friday afternoon, you might want to schedule actual calendar time to work on that, too.

Make sure all your Priority 1 tasks are scheduled either on your calendar or on your to-do list, and that they all have completion dates assigned. Review your list of Priority 2 tasks. Since a Priority 2 task can be delegated temporarily, it is good idea to identify a primary and secondary delegate. Talk to the delegates to ensure that they are willing to be assigned temporarily to this task. You will likely need to reciprocate, and agree to act as a temporary delegate for some of their tasks, too. Add these tasks to your calendar or to-do list.

The Priority 3 tasks can be scheduled as tentative. Alternatively, you might decide that one of these tasks should be permanently delegated to another member of your team. In that case, you should hand over responsibility to that team member.

Priority 4 and Priority 5 tasks should be added to your to-do list and prioritized appropriately. Do not delete these tasks. Even though they are not critical to your success today, they might be, at some point in the future. For instance, suppose you are interested in doing some research or analysis of a particular business trend. It is an interesting, but not critical, task today. Six months later, the business trend has continued. It is now affecting the success or potential success of your business, and has become a higher priority task. Fortunately, you were tracking it.

Work with both your local and remote team members to help them prioritize and plan their tasks in the same way. There is no point in you being organized and on track if everyone else on your team is disorganized and late with everything. This is a great topic for an online presentation. (More information on prioritizing and delegating tasks is provided in the "Prioritizing Tasks" section later in this chapter.)

Update and Reprioritize as Tasks Are Added or Completed

You and your team members will have new tasks coming in every day, which will need prioritizing and adding to your task list. You do not need to continue to update the prioritized task-management list unless you want to do so. The main purpose of that spreadsheet was to prioritize all your existing meetings and tasks, so that you could get the foundation of your time-management process built. You can either use that as your main task list, or you can use a different task-management tool for managing tasks on an ongoing basis.

Task lists that are built into calendaring software, like the TaskPad included with Microsoft Outlook, have the added advantage of built-in reminders and scheduling. The great thing about using electronic reminders is that they will automatically update the time of each reminder to the time zone of your calendaring software. If you travel a lot, this can be very helpful. If you find yourself with a seven-hour time difference, for example, you would be seven hours early or late for each meeting or task unless your software updated to local time. For this reason, it is a great idea to send your remote team members to-do tasks electronically, if the tasks have due dates and times associated with them. As soon as the team member accepts a task into his or her list, the due date and time will automatically be changed to the equivalent local time.

Estimate and Schedule Tasks

To schedule tasks appropriately, you and your team members need to gain some experience and expertise with estimating them accurately. Early on, you will be using a lot of guesswork, but as you work in a more structured way, get into the habit of tracking how much time you spend on each task. This will help a lot in managing your tasks and ensuring that you are not committing to more work than you can accomplish. If you are using a task list or TaskPad to track tasks, move the ones you are planning to work on this week onto your calendar. By scheduling time to work on them, you will be sure to get them completed. A task list that just sits there and never gets looked at or worked on is not going to be much help in managing your time more effectively!

Track and Complete Tasks

Everyone on your team must track their tasks to be sure they are completed. A great way to do this is to use the "% Complete" function in Outlook's TaskPad. You can use this to produce status reports for your team members or your manager, and your team members can create reports for you. When you complete tasks, you need to schedule any follow-up tasks and ensure that those are also tracked to completion. A lot of people are very good at starting tasks, but not completing them. Owning a lot of partly completed projects will make you feel that you always have too much to do, and that it is overwhelming to accomplish everything.

If you have a lot of partially completed projects, schedule time to get them completed. If they are not important enough to work on, either hand them off to someone else or abandon them. If you abandon a task, you must consider it "cut," which is the same as "complete," in that you remove it from your list of things to do and never work on it again. Don't allow yourself to get emotionally tied to something because you spent a lot of time working on it. If it is no longer of importance, let it go. Remember to keep track of the actual time you spend working on each task, as well as the calendar time. It might have taken you four months to complete something, but you might have only spent three hours working on it, in total!

Communicate Progress and Status in a Timely Manner

There is no point in doing a great job and completing lots of amazing projects if no one is aware that you are doing it. Each of your team's tasks or projects that is of interest to others needs a communication plan. For high-priority, high-visibility projects, you need a list of stakeholders with whom you communicate status on a regular basis. Your team members need to be doing the same.

Meeting Time Management

What would happen if newspapers decided that typesetting their stories took too much time, so they would write them, but only print the headlines, rather than the whole story? If all you saw was a headline and a blank space, you would not know what had happened unless you were at the actual event being featured. This is how people feel about your meetings when you do not write minutes. If they miss one meeting, they get a headline with no story.

Why is it more efficient to spend 30 to 40 minutes writing and distributing minutes than to not write them? This is a good question. There is a good answer. Imagine if each newspaper customer had to call or email the reporter personally to ask about the story that went with the headline. The reporter could spend the whole day answering questions about the story, and be too busy to research the next story. If people started to call others who have already spoken to the reporter to ask what the story was about, they might get a scaled-down version of the story, with many important facts missing. By the time the story had been recounted a few times, it would hardly resemble the original story at all. Pretty much like the content of your non-documented meetings! By writing and distributing minutes, you can avoid lots of phone calls and emails from people trying to find out the status of whatever your meeting was about. In addition to the potentially inaccurate information being shared, it is also taking up a lot of other people's time relaying the story (or details of your meeting) to others, so everyone is getting behind with their tasks!

It is also important to understand that some people will exit a meeting with a different understanding of what was agreed upon than you have. As mentioned earlier in the book, it can sometimes to be difficult for participants to hear everything being said in an audio conference because the line is not clear, because too many people are talking at once, or because the participant is writing emails instead of paying attention. If you want a cohesive effort to accomplish your objectives, you need a common understanding of what they are. The non-attendees will be none the wiser and still working on the assumption that the status is the same as it was the last time they attended your meeting (which could be some time ago). Lots of wasted time and miscommunication can be avoided by allocating the time to document what was discussed and agreed to. You don't have to document every single word, but you should summarize the key points of discussion, the decisions made, the open issues, and the assigned action items (with required completion dates). Your meetings will run more smoothly, you will accomplish much more in a shorter time frame, and you will save a lot of time and energy by doing things right the first time.

Try not to schedule meeting prep time to occur immediately before the meeting. If an urgent meeting or task comes up, you will find yourself with no time to complete your meeting preparation. Some attendees of your meetings will decide whether or not they are required to attend based on the agenda topics, so it is important that there is an understanding of the purpose of the meeting beforehand. Other attendees will need to prepare for the meeting based on the agenda items so, as a courtesy, try to get the agenda out at least two days prior to the meeting.

It is standard practice to send out meeting minutes no later than three days after a meeting. For regularly scheduled weekly meetings, one or two days of lag time is ideal. It is always better to write minutes while the discussion is still fresh in your mind. If you are a really good note-taker, you will not have a problem with a two-day lag. If your notes are scant bullet points, however, and your memory is not excellent, those two days could make it difficult to recall exactly what was discussed!

Start and finish meetings on time. Don't expect your attendees to stay in the meeting past the scheduled end time. You must be respectful of others' time, just as you expect them to be respectful of yours. It is perfectly acceptable to excuse yourself from a meeting if it has run over time. You need to be sure that others' mismanagement of their time is not negatively affecting your own time management. You should be setting an example to your team members, so make sure you are not the one running open-ended meetings!

Time Management Tools

Many tools are available to help with planning and managing tasks, including ones you might already be using, like Microsoft Outlook or Microsoft Project. There are also a lot of task-management tools available for PDAs and included in virtual-management software applications. (Chapter 13 describes some of these tools in more detail.)

Remember, tools can assist you in managing a process, but they cannot create the process or *be* the process. Design your process first, and find the tools to manage it second. This will ensure that you have realistic expectations of what the tools can do for you.

Tips on Speeding Up the Process for Time-Consuming Tasks

Ask people which task wastes the most time on a daily basis, and most of them will tell you "reading, prioritizing, and clearing out my inbox." Email! What a great tool, but what an easy way to waste most of the day. This is an area where you can considerably speed up the process and make a lot more time for more important tasks.

There are features available in most email programs for sorting and prioritizing messages. You can automatically route messages to predefined folders based on the sender or the subject line. You can also add follow-up flags to messages, so that you do not forget to respond.

You do not need to read every single email that you receive on the day you receive it. Learn to scan the list of emails, and decide which need reading immediately and which do not. Schedule some time each day for reading and responding to emails. Schedule at least an hour for this task, although you might need more if you get a lot of emails or have just returned from being out of the office for several days. Ask the people who are sending you emails to be specific if they expect you to do something as a result of an email message. Ask them to add you to the "CC" line if it is for your information only, and to the "To" line if you need to read and respond. Make sure that you are doing the same thing. Do not assume that recipients of your emails know what you expect of them if you have not been clear in your request.

Your remote team members will appreciate some standards for how email is used, too. Knowing that they only have to read and respond to emails where their name is in the "To" line will save them all a lot of time reading and responding to emails unnecessarily. Often, three or four people are all tracking down the same information as a result of one email. If it is unclear who should be working on something in an email, ask your team members to send a "Reply to All" email to let everyone know if they are working on the issue. This will save other team members from spending time working on the same thing. Virtual teams need a lot of process and a lot of communication to keep things running smoothly and efficiently.

You can also save time by keeping lists of questions or tasks that you have for each team member, and talking about them in your regular one-on-one meetings instead of in emails. This saves a lot of email writing and reading time, as well as a lot of one-off phone calls. Alternatively, upload the notes to each team member's virtual workspace, if you are using a collaborative virtual-management tool to manage your work and projects. This will allow each team member to check in regularly and see what is new. Use emails for more urgent matters, instead of filling up each others' email inboxes with so much information that the important things get lost in the noise. Having said this, make sure that you use the one-on-one time effectively, not for the same things that you are planning to talk about in the weekly team meeting.

If you need to share the same information with a lot of people, or if there is a long, drawn-out email chain going around that is creating a lot of work for team members to keep up with, schedule a meeting to discuss the issue with all the interested parties. Having everyone spend one hour in a meeting discussing, understanding, and resolving an issue is a much more effective use of time than having each person spend two hours per day for two weeks reading and responding to emails about the topic. It is truly amazing how many times those long, drawn-out email discussions go on for a painfully long time with no resolution in sight. They just go around and around. The worst thing about this scenario is that some people start to "Reply to All," but decide to delete some of the recipients and perhaps add new ones. This leads to different threads of the original discussion going on that others are not aware of. It can get to be a big confusing mess, with nobody sure who is driving the issue to resolution or who is responsible for doing something about it.

Prioritizing Tasks

We have already discussed how to prioritize, schedule, and track tasks, but what if you have so many tasks that all seem important, and you have no idea how to rank them? Which one do you work on first? Which one goes to the bottom of the list? There are various methods available for prioritizing tasks. These range from very simplistic comparison systems to very complex weighting systems.

One method for prioritizing tasks is referred to as the forced-pair comparison process. This is a very simple process for prioritizing projects. It allows individuals or groups to rank lists of candidate tasks or projects.

Forced-Pair Comparisons

The forced-pair comparison prioritization method works well for fewer than 20 items.

This method requires the use of a grid, as shown in Figure 6.3. (A full-page copy of this grid is included in appendix B.) The example in Figure 6.3 compares 10 items.

If you need to prioritize more than 10 tasks, you can easily create a larger grid using Microsoft Excel.

1 -- 2									
1 -- 3	2 – 3								
1 -- 4	2 – 4	3 -- 4							
1 -- 5	2 – 5	3 -- 5	4 – 5						
1 -- 6	2 – 6	3 -- 6	4 – 6	5 – 6					
1 -- 7	2 – 7	3 -- 7	4 – 7	5 – 7	6 – 7				
1 -- 8	2 – 8	3 -- 8	4 – 8	5 – 8	6 – 8	7 – 8			
1 -- 9	2 – 9	3 -- 9	4 – 9	5 – 9	6 – 9	7 – 9	8 – 9		
1 – 10	2 – 10	3 – 10	4 – 10	5 – 10	6 – 10	7 -- 10	8 – 10	9 -- 10	
Item Scores									
1	2	3	4	5	6	7	8	9	10

Figure 6.3: Forced-pair comparison grid

To get started, you need to do the following:

➤ Generate a list of items to be prioritized.

➤ Number the items for identification purposes.

➤ Using the grid, compare each item with the other items on the list, circling the item that is the more preferred of the two. You must make a choice for each pair.

➤ Count the number of times each item number was circled, and enter its score on the bottom line of the grid.

➤ Rank the list using the scores you have derived. The item with the highest score is number 1. The item with the second-highest score is number 2, and so on. In case of a tie, you can either do a mini-grid for the tied items, or refer to your original preference when you were circling the items in the grid.

➤ Use less than a full grid for fewer than 10 items; expand the grid for more items.

This method is more easily understood using a real example. Suppose you want to decide where to go on your next vacation. First, you generate a list:

Seven Places I Have Always Wanted to Go But Haven't

1. Bali

2. Nevis & St. Kitts

3. Australia

4. Fiji

5. Tortola

6. Singapore

7. Tahiti

Then, using the grid, you compare each item with the other items on the list. You add up each time each number was circled, and put this in the "Item Scores" section at the bottom of the table. Sample results are shown in Figure 6.4.

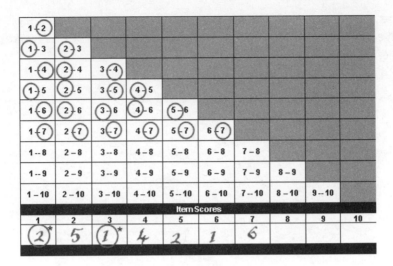

Figure 6.4: Forced-pair comparisons results

This example includes two ties that need to be broken. Items 1 and 5 are tied with two points each, and items 3 and 6 are tied with one point each. The ties can be broken merely by referring to previous choices made between those items in the grid. Look at the box where item 1 is compared to item 5 in the first column. You'll see that the choice was item 1. Then, look at the box where item 3 is compared to item 6 in the third column. Item 3 is circled.

Here, then, is the resulting prioritized list:

1. Tahiti (1)

2. Nevis & St. Kitts (2)

3. Fiji (3)

4. Bali (4)

5. Tortola (5)

6. Australia (6)

7. Singapore (7)

There are other methods for prioritizing tasks that include weighting items based on certain criteria. The forced-pair method is quick and easy. It takes very little time, but can add a lot of clarity to the process!

Virtual Teamwork

As soon as you have chosen team members and assigned them to your team, you need to start building teamwork. Teamwork is what transforms a group of individuals working independently to achieve their own goals into a team working collaboratively to achieve the team's goals. As we have mentioned before, you, the manager, are the glue that holds the team together. You are the common link between the individual members of the team. You are the nucleus around which the team revolves. You must drive the effort to build strong and collaborative teamwork.

A strong team with a high level of teamwork is:

- ➤ Happy
- ➤ Energized
- ➤ Innovative
- ➤ Creative
- ➤ Collaborative
- ➤ Honest
- ➤ Effective
- ➤ Productive
- ➤ Supportive
- ➤ Successful

These team qualities create teamwork, and teamwork creates these qualities. If you are part of an awesome team, it doesn't matter how big or hairy the problems are. The process of getting where you need to go will be inspiring!

Discovering Commonalities

Some people are excellent party-givers. You turn up at their house, and everything flows easily: conversation, beverages, friendship, fun, activities. It seems as though everything just magically falls into place and happens at the right time to make the party perfect. Well, perfect parties are no accident! The hosts spend considerable time planning, preparing, and managing the party to make it a success. The thing that makes is so successful is that the hard work is transparent. It seems as though the hosts are just wandering around, chitchatting with everyone and having a nice time.

The most important part of the hosts' interaction with their guests is to introduce the guests to one another in a way that influences them to want to converse beyond the customary, "Hello, I am pleased to meet you." If the guests at a party feel connected to everyone else, rather than feeling part of a small clique or on their own, then the hosts have done a fine job of building rapport. This is accomplished by using introductions to help the guests identify commonalities that exist between them.

For example, if you introduce two couples to each other, you might say something like, "Steve and Julie, I would like you to meet John and Angie, old friends of ours who have just moved back to the area. Their daughter has just started middle school and she plays the piano." To John and Angie, you might say, "Steve and Julie have a daughter the same age as Emily, and she is also very musical. Julie and I work together at the bank." You have given them a few key words and comments that should be helpful in getting the conversation going. This kind of communication is inclusive.

Suppose, on the other hand, you just introduce the couples by saying, "Steve and Julie, meet John and Angie. Oh, excuse me—I have just seen my best friend arrive. I must go and chat with her. Help yourself to food and drinks." This is not conducive to building rapport or finding commonalities. It is almost guaranteed to lead to a polite "nice to meet you" before they go in search of their respective friends.

The same principles used in throwing a great party can be used to help your team members get to know one another and to build rapport. It can take a little time, as initially, you probably don't know much about your team members, either. With virtual teams, you need to be creative in finding ways to help people identify commonalities. You must find commonalities with each team member, and then help them share information with each other so that a commonality links each of them to someone else. It is unlikely that you will all initially share the same commonality. Over time, however, you will create some. For example, you will share experiences, projects, business trips, and meetings. Hopefully, at least one shared experience will be memorable!

> With virtual teams, you need to be creative in finding ways to help people identify commonalities.

A great icebreaker for a virtual team meeting is to ask everyone on the team to share one piece of information about themselves that other meeting participants will not already know. Just this one piece of information about each person can result in a lot of common links and can spark some offline conversations among team members. Once the network of commonalities has started, it will grow and weave itself together until it becomes a strong web of connections. When you have a web, you will know you have created a team, and not just a group of individuals who work for the same manager!

Creating Trust

You cannot demand trust from your team members, nor can they demand it from you. Trust and respect have to be earned, and they must be earned honestly! The virtual team needs to have trust and confidence in itself and its manager. Creating and maintaining trust creates a positive working environment for everyone on the team.

To create an environment where trust can thrive, you must ensure that every member of the team feels valued and appreciated. Each team member should feel comfortable speaking openly and honestly about issues, both with you and with other team members. Each team member should feel that he or she is entitled to have an opinion and that the opinion will be listened to and taken into consideration. This does not mean that you have to agree with every opinion; it means that each team member has a voice and has equal rights to be heard and to contribute to discussions.

Speaking openly and expressing opinions does not mean that team members have carte blanche to say whatever they please to whomever they please. The manager must ensure that communication among team members is respectful at all times. Rules need to be in place about what is acceptable and what is not acceptable behavior and communication. If a team member has a very strong opposition to something that has been said or done, he or she is entitled to express an opinion. He or she is not entitled to make personal attacks or personal comments about anyone else.

You need to be especially wary of this kind of reaction from team members with the Expressive interaction style (discussed in chapter 3). It is much harder to repair rifts virtually than it is in person. So much is impersonal when communicating virtually that it is easy to create a monster out of someone in your mind, just because of one comment. In face-to-face interaction, there is more natural camaraderie, and so people tend to be much more forgiving. Being able to see each other's stress makes it easier to make allowances for someone's abruptness or rudeness. This is not as true on the phone. Grudges are easily started, and they can be borne for years.

Team members need to trust that you will follow through on what you say you will do. If you are unreliable or unsupportive, your team members will not feel comfortable sharing their thoughts and opinions with you. You should be honest about your own thoughts and feelings. If you do not agree with someone, you should tell the person (politely) that you do not agree. If you tell one person one thing and another something different, how will anybody know what is true? You must be consistent in your messaging, and not keep changing your mind or telling people different things. It makes you appear unreliable and untrustworthy. It is also important that you hold team members responsible for their commitments and their actions. If a team member commits to doing something, hold him or her to that commitment.

One of the worst violations of trust for a manager is to ask a team member to take some action the team member is not happy about, and then refuse to back the person up when he or she takes that action. It is inexcusable. Regardless of whether your team is virtual, local, or a bit of both, you must take responsibility for the things you ask team members to do.

Understanding the Dynamics of the Team

The dynamics of the team are created by the unique combination of personalities, interaction styles, learning styles, communication styles, and personal and business cultural backgrounds of the team members. The most influential contributor to the team dynamic is the team manager.

The team manager molds, shapes, directs, and guides the team. As the team members build trust and rapport with each other and start to share experiences and opinions, the personality of the team will emerge. The personality of the team determines its internal dynamics. If one team member leaves or a new team member joins, the team dynamics will change.

> The most influential contributor to the team dynamic is the team manager.

The dynamics are affected by attitudes. If the team is positive and enthusiastic, the dynamics will reflect this. If the team is negative and inflexible, this will be obvious in the way the team members interact with one another and with others outside of the team. You, the manager, are the person who creates the team attitude. It doesn't just happen accidentally. Outside forces can create problems such as unease and uncertainty that will affect the attitude of team members, but a strong virtual manager will protect the team members from as much of this outside influence as possible. The manager is the umbrella that protects the team from all the things coming down from above. If the umbrella is doing its job, the team will hardly be aware that it has been raining for the past week!

If the team is a permanent one whose members have been working together for a long time, the dynamics might be quite complex. For temporary teams whose members have been together for a short time, the dynamics will be more simple.

Creating the Virtual Community

As a team spends more time working and interacting together, the emergence of a virtual community is a natural progression. Most people are part of one or more virtual communities, even if they are not working in a virtual environment. Virtual communities are created from the use of email, instant messaging, phone calls, Websites, and any other types of communication or information sharing that are not face-to-face. Leaving notes for other family members at home is virtual communication, as is sending jokes via email to your parents or siblings.

A successful virtual team community needs to be able to function and thrive without the continual input and supervision of its manager. This does not mean that the team does not need a manager—it certainly does. It means that the team members can interact, make decisions, and deal with problems together, so that not all of the communication needs the involvement of the manager. The virtual community might well include employees who are not assigned to the same team, but who have some common interest in some aspects of the team or a specific project.

Ideally, the virtual team members will have a place where they can interact with other members of the community. Virtual rooms, online bulletin boards, instant messaging, and phone conferencing are all great tools for facilitating community interaction.

A sense of community comes from a sense of belonging. The team belongs together because it is a team, but what makes its members a community is the way they feel about each other—the sense of duty and responsibility they have toward each other. For example, if one team member is involved in an accident, the other team members will be truly concerned about his or her welfare. If the only concern is about who will do that person's work and how the team will meet its deadline next week, there is no community.

It is impossible to create a sense of belonging without being inclusive. It is really horrible to be involved in any kind of work or activity and feel like you are not welcome. Being inclusive means not leaving people out of the activity, the fun, or the joke. If you have ever been around a group of people who started to speak to one another in a language that you do not understand, you will know how it feels to be excluded. If there is only one person who does not understand the conversation, that person will feel very isolated and uncomfortable. The worst thing is when everyone starts laughing, and the single person being excluded from the conversation doesn't know what is funny. That person is probably trying to figure out how to make an escape as fast as possible! This same feeling of isolation and embarrassment is present in any situation where someone feels excluded.

> A successful virtual team community needs to be able to function and thrive without the continual input and supervision of its manager.

If some members of the team have worked together in the past and spend all their time talking about the "old days" and ignoring the newer members of the team, those newer members are going to start to feel left out. If the manager also behaves in an exclusive way, the problem will be exacerbated. You can talk about situations and experiences that others were not involved in, and still be inclusive. If the situation is told as a story, it can be enjoyed by everyone. If it is a funny story, everyone can have a laugh about it, rather than just the people who were there at the time.

One team member who feels isolated from the rest can change the dynamics on the team considerably. Someone who feels left out will gravitate toward others who feel the same way. By doing this, the excluded team members find somewhere to belong. They find friendship and camaraderie with the other "outsiders." Unfortunately, these actions are driven by envy, frustration, and revenge. Before you know it, you have two or more factions on your team plotting against each other. That's not exactly a positive foundation on which to build a highly productive and supportive team!

It is not difficult to feel isolated when working virtually. If you spend a lot of time alone, you will inevitably feel lonely from time to time. Perhaps you will even feel a little envious of those team members who get to travel and interact with each other more than you do. Allowing and even encouraging team members to interact with each other about non-work related things will enhance the sense of community on your team. Shared activities, such as online video games or puzzles, are a great way of bringing the team together without them having to be together. You could run team competitions and bring the team together on a virtual team day to discuss the entries and maybe vote on the winners. Introducing a fun and frivolous element into some of the team interactions will help to solidify the feeling of being part of a virtual community.

Team Member Interaction

The team members will interact in different ways and for different reasons. The most important thing about team interaction is making sure there is some! Actually, make sure there is a lot.

When working virtually, it is so easy to forget you are part of a team. You get into your groove with the work you need to accomplish and, by applying focus and discipline, you can complete the work on time and maybe even a little ahead of schedule. Each team meeting or phone call is a distraction from getting your tasks completed. After a while, it is easy to just stop calling in for meetings and to not answer the phone if you can help it. As time goes by, people invite you to participate in fewer and fewer meetings, and you become almost a non-entity on the team.

If one of your team members has been behaving in this way, what has he accomplished? Perhaps he would say he gets more work done. He might think he is more productive because his work is always completed on time. Is this really true? If he is not participating in the team, then he is not completing all his assigned work. If he has no idea what is going on in his virtual community, how does he know his contributions are valuable? Is he working on the highest priority tasks, or the things that were the highest priority six months ago, when he last called in a for a meeting? If the team can function with hardly any input from this team member, why do you need him? If you hired this person for his knowledge, skills, and experience, what good are those things if the team is not getting any input from him? It is disrespectful to his team mates and to you to refuse to answer phone calls or to attend meetings. Maybe he is "too important" to attend. Is he, then, too important for the job?

If you have a team member who is beginning to skip meetings and not answer the phone, you need to deal with the situation quickly, before he or she becomes isolated from the team. Make sure there is a process for team members to communicate that they are unable to attend a meeting, and that the process includes communicating the reason for non-attendance. It is simple courtesy to let the meeting organizer know if you are unable to attend. If you notice a team member skipping meetings frequently with no apparent reason, speak to that person. Explain that his or her primary role is to be a team member and to play a participative role on the team. If he or she is finding it hard to complete assigned tasks on time due to meetings, phone calls, or other interruptions, work with the team member on prioritizing tasks to use time most efficiently.

> Being a virtual employee means you are working together, apart; it does not mean you are working alone.

If a team member is working on a critical task and needs to be excused from attending meetings for a week or two, that should be your decision as the manager of the team. The non-participation should not be allowed to continue indefinitely. Make sure your team members understand how important the team-member interaction is to the success of the team. Make sure it is part of the job description and that your expectations are clear.

Let all team members know that being part of the team is part of the job. Working virtually is not the same as setting up a sole proprietorship and working for yourself. Being a virtual employee means you are working together, apart; it does not mean you are working alone.

Virtual Communication

Virtual team members communicate via phone, phone conference, email, Internet, virtual workspaces, online chat, and instant messaging. The method of communication is less important than its regularity. One team member might prefer to communicate by phone, but that does not mean nobody should contact that person unless they have time to call. An email or instant message is better than no communication at all. Team members should be encouraged to interact with each other directly, in addition to interacting at virtual team meetings. Try to add a personal note to team meetings. It is important to talk about work and to ensure that you are meeting the objectives of the meeting, but it is also very conducive to team building to allow and encourage some non-work chatter to occur before and after the meeting.

You can add some fun to the meeting by asking participants about their vacations or what they did at the weekend. Try throwing out the question, "Who had the most interesting weekend?" It is sure to get at least a few responses. Even if nobody has anything really exciting to talk about, someone is bound to say something like, "My weekend must have been the most exciting. I mowed the lawn, painted the kitchen, and went to dinner with my in-laws." If nothing else, the question will encourage some humor!

It is great to allow time for team building, but don't make it too contrived. For instance, if you schedule a half-hour meeting each week to "bond," what on earth will you all talk about? Work is the most likely thing that will come up. How about having a team lunch or happy hour instead? Get the team to all call into a conference and chat on the phone while eating or having a glass of wine. Have one rule: No talking about work! Some teams watch movies or TV shows together, virtually. By sharing a desktop, you can all view the same movie at the same time. You can even call into an audio conference, so you can make comments to each other during the show.

One of the least effective team-building exercises we experienced was where the manager went around the room (the virtual room, that is) and asked everyone to say something positive or funny that happened that week. This is not building teamwork and rapport; it is putting people on the spot, trying to control the situation to make it turn out the way you want it to. Invariably, the comments will be about work. Nobody will feel inspired or closer to their team mates as a result of being forced to say something positive—especially if they are not feeling positive. Sometimes a good old moan is a great way to build camaraderie and discover mutual interests!

Instant messaging is another excellent tool for keeping in touch with team members. It is a great communication method for quick messages and for non-work chitchat. Don't discourage your team members from interacting about non-work topics. You don't want team members spending all day chatting and no time working, but you want to encourage some personal interaction. This spontaneous and non-scheduled communication will help you build strong and effective teamwork among your team members.

In-Person Communication

Face-to-face communication between team members whenever possible is great for team building. If the team members can be around one another, they will automatically start chatting casually about this or that.

When the team is together, it is an ideal opportunity to organize a team lunch or a happy hour. Remember the golden rule: No talking about work! If the team members are talking about nothing except work, they might be working together nicely, but they are not building rapport or finding any personal connections to each other. It also means that attending the lunch or happy hour merely means they are adding another hour or two of work to their day. If you have ever been to a team lunch or happy hour and sat bored to tears while everyone droned on and on about when this contract would be signed, or that client would be satisfied, you will know why many people try to avoid attending those kinds of events. It would be much more fun to go home and spend time with your family, and much more productive to be working on that pile of reports sitting on your desk!

Virtual Team Day

The virtual team day is a day that the team spends together virtually, or a day when the team comes together in person. In an ideal world, a virtual team day when the whole team is together in one location would happen once every two or three months. For many virtual teams, this is not possible, so you need to be creative in devising some interesting team activities that do not require all the team members to be in one location. Differences in team members' time zones also need to be taken into account. It might not be possible for the entire team to come together at the same time. In these situations, you might be able to split the team into locations and have the different locations coordinate their times. It is a great idea to have the virtual team day on the same day for all locations. This way, nobody misses out on the fun.

Team days should be fun, team-building days. You might want to organize some special events or training for these days, or you might want to make the whole day a "play day." Some activities that can be shared among team members are easily accessible, like online quizzes, online video games, online chess, and online sports such as fantasy football and fantasy soccer.

Many organizations offer team-building programs and activities that range from outdoor survival programs to Myers Briggs testing, and everything in between. Not as many companies offer virtual team building, however. Some companies offer programs to enhance virtual teamwork, but most require that all team members attend in person. This is ironic, since the goal is to teach you how to build teamwork virtually! The areas of virtual team building and training have a lot of potential, and we anticipate a lot of growth in the next few years.

> Bringing some fun into the mix will make a team-building event more memorable, whether it is held in a classroom or in the Jungle.

If you *are* able to get all your team members together for a day, there are some really exciting opportunities for building teamwork and having fun at the same time. Organizations will work with your team to produce a movie, build a house, assemble bikes for children, or build dog kennels for animal shelters. There is no end of possibilities when thinking of fun ways for the team members to work collaboratively to be successful. Team building that focuses on identifying and understanding personality types or teaching communication and conflict management are also very valuable, and these are great classes for the team members to attend as a group.

Bringing some fun into the mix will make a team-building event more memorable, whether it is held in a classroom or in the jungle. Fond memories of a fun time had by all will have a more positive effect on the team than memories of a really tough day stuck in an uncomfortable situation with coworkers trying to prove that everyone can work together toward a common goal. If your team members enjoy themselves while working toward a goal, they are going to build rapport and respect much more quickly.

Make sure that any activities are appropriate for all members of the team. If you have disabled team members, take any physical or mental limitations into account when deciding what activities are most appropriate. When planning activities that require physical fitness, strength, or a certain body type, make sure that you evaluate and compare the fitness requirements with those of your team members. For example, rock climbing might sound like a really fun way to spend a few hours to some team members, but if a team member is confined to a wheelchair, it is not a good option. Likewise, some team members might not have the level of physical fitness required to tackle an outdoor obstacle course. A virtual team-building activity or event should be something that all of the team members are able to participate in.

Sharing Best Practices

Before you define a process for sharing best practices, make sure you have a clear definition of what *best practice* means, and make sure that everyone on your team also understands it. For example, a best practice is a proven way of doing something "the best possible way," meaning that it is an efficient and effective way of organizing something or doing something. You can also think of it as a "best system" or "best process." A best practice is not necessarily widely or publicly recognized as being the best possible way to do something. A best practice is a way of doing something that you or one of your team members personally believe to be the best, as it pertains to your team processes.

Sharing best practices is a great thing to do whether a team is virtual, blended, or traditional. Many companies and teams forget to do this. They get so caught up in the day-to-day tasks and issues that taking time out to share a great way of doing something never seems to get to the top of the priority list. If you are waiting for this type of communication to just happen naturally, you will be waiting a long time! First, you need to create an environment that is conducive to sharing best practices. Second, you need to create the opportunities to do this.

Sharing best practices for virtual teams is highly recommended. There are not many standard best practices documented for this type of team structure. It is a new way of working, and the virtual workers and managers are figuring out the best way to do a lot of things as they go along. The team members are working individually and not interacting as much as they would in a traditional environment, so the sharing of best practices is even less likely to just "happen" without motivation and some kind of forum.

> Sharing best practices is a great thing to do whether a team is virtual, blended, or traditional.

Best practices are relevant to all types of companies and teams, whether the employees are all performing the same function or their roles are completely different. Teams in which multiple team members perform the same function will likely have more opportunities to define and share best practices than teams where everyone has a different function. Often, best practices come from employees sharing information about the way they did things when they worked at another company or sharing something they read in a book. For example, a virtual employee might have some great suggestions on time management or scheduling meetings. Perhaps someone will suggest that whenever a team member schedules a meeting, he or she creates an agenda so the purpose and objectives of the meeting are clear to both the organizer and the attendees. You might define best practices around hiring and interviewing techniques that all team members agree to adopt. Alternatively, a team member might share a best practice for monitoring and maintaining home networks and computer equipment that will reduce downtime for virtual workers.

When you kick off a best-practices initiative, avoid the round-robin meeting approach to sharing best practices. Going around the room (real or virtual) and asking everyone to share a best practice is not going to result in much quality communication. It might sound ridiculous that anyone would try this approach, but some managers take the "put everyone on the spot" approach to management, and do not seem to realize how ineffective it is. This approach is more likely to hinder teamwork than enhance it!

What is even worse is when the meeting facilitator insists that everyone must contribute. You sit waiting for your turn, feeling agitated and irritated, or perhaps nervous or embarrassed. You hear suggestions from other team members that you think are ludicrous, but realize that they are only saying those things because they don't know what else to say. You then share information about the way you do something. It might not be a good way to do it. Possibly, it is the only way you know how to do it, but it doesn't really work that well. Feeling at a loss for anything really insightful or mind blowing to say, and knowing that you are being judged based on your contribution to the meeting, you make your best practice sound really fantastic, and urge everyone else to adopt this method immediately. Your manager will think you are awesome only because you shared your idea with enthusiasm and energy, not because you contributed anything of any real value.

We have discussed some ideas on what not to do. Let's discuss some ideas that should yield positive and useful results. When designing or implementing a new or improved process, it is very important to define the scope of that process. If the scope is very broad, break it down into sub-processes so that each one is a manageable size.

> A good way to start the process of creating and sharing best practices is to hold a team brainstorming meeting.

A good way to start the process of creating and sharing best practices is to hold a team brainstorming meeting. In addition to an audio conference, a virtual meeting tool should be used for this meeting. This enables the meeting facilitator to share his or her desktop and/or whiteboard space with the meeting attendees. The brainstorming process is an interactive one, so make it as interactive as you can using whatever tools you have available.

The Brainstorming Process

The following is an example brainstorming process that can be used for best practices and process-improvement brainstorming.

If some or all of the participants will be participating remotely, set up an online meeting where you can share your desktop and a whiteboard. This way, the team members can work collaboratively, and everyone can see what is happening with the ideas being captured.

Define the Purpose of the Meeting

The purpose of the meeting is to do the following:

- Identify best practices currently in use.
- Identify areas where best practices are needed.
- Prioritize areas for improvement.
- Define a process for sharing best practices going forward.

Set Rules

The reason for having rules is to ensure that the meeting stays on track and does not deteriorate into a general complaints session. The objective is to identify areas for improvement, not to complain about all the things (or people) that are wrong with the current process. Here are some basic rules:

- You can say anything about anything, as long as it is relevant to the meeting.
- You cannot name people or blame people for problems.
- You cannot defend yourself or others.
- Everyone's opinions are valid.
- Do not interrupt when someone is speaking.
- Nothing discussed in the meeting should be discussed outside of it.

Define Categories or Areas

Team members collectively create a list of broad categories that can be used to define best practices and areas for improvement. This does not have to be a full list—categories can be added later, as necessary. For example, a category list might include the following:

- Time management
- Client liaison
- Contract negotiation
- Scheduling
- Communication
- Escalation procedures
- Change control
- Meetings

The best way to capture these ideas is to create a brainstorming spreadsheet, as shown in Figure 7.1. (A blank copy of the spreadsheet is included in appendix B.)

To save time during the meeting, you might want to define the categories beforehand. That way, you can have your spreadsheet ready to go as soon as you get started. You should share the spreadsheet on your desktop during the meeting.

#	Category	Best Practice Description	Description of Problem	Recommended Action	# Votes	Priority	Approved
1	Meetings	Prepare agendas in advance of meetings and send out minutes afterwards	Noone knows the purpose of the meetings without an agenda. If you miss a meeting you don't know what was decided in the meeting unless there are meeting minutes.	1-Continue using			
2							
3							
4							
5							
6							
7							

Figure 7.1: Brainstorming spreadsheet

Capture Existing Best Practices

You and your team members should discuss processes or best practices currently in use across the organization, within the team, or by individual team members. All team members' comments should be captured by the manager. Define each best practice as one of the following:

- Recommend that the best practice is continued.
- Recommend that the best practice is adopted by everyone on the team.
- Recommend that the best practice is updated/improved to make it more applicable.
- Recommend that the best practice be discontinued, as it is no longer a best practice.

Enter the best practices into the spreadsheet, as shown in Figure 7.1. Use the "Recommended action" column of the spreadsheet to define these four options as:

      1–Continue using
      2–Adopt more widely
      3–Update/Improve
      4–Discontinue Using

Capture Specific Issues or Areas Where Best Practices Are Needed

Team members discuss areas where best practices or new processes are needed. Once again, capture the ideas and comments from all participants and define these as:

- Area where a best practice or process is needed

Enter the best practices into the spreadsheet, as shown in Figure 7.1. Use the "Recommended action" column of the spreadsheet to define this option as:

5–Needs New BP

Sort and Review by Category

When you have completed your list of best practices, sort it by category, and then sort it by action. The items marked as 1s ("continue using") and 4s ("discontinue using") should be very straightforward; you can decide immediately if you wish to approve them.

Depending on how many categories you have and how many items are assigned to each, you can decide to do one of two things now:

1. Assign a category to each team member to summarize the issues, so the team can vote for which categories are the highest priority.

2. Ask the team members to vote on individual items to create a prioritized list.

Present Summaries

Each summary should be presented verbally to the group by the team member who wrote it. The summary should not contain any opinions, comments, or defensive or supportive statements by the presenter. It must present only the facts.

Select Highest Priority Categories or Issues

If there are only two or three problem areas, prioritization of categories or individual issues might not be necessary. It is more likely, however, that there will be numerous opportunities for proposed changes and improvements, and a limited amount of time to implement them, so you will want to choose a subset of the list to focus on immediately. Never try to implement too many improvements or make too many changes in one go. It is too difficult for the team members to remember all the things they need to do differently, which can lead to them slipping back into the old familiar ways very quickly.

The prioritization should be a collaborative effort by the team. An effective way of prioritizing is to give all team members a certain number of votes, and allow them to distribute those votes in any way they please among the categories or individual items (whichever method you chose). For example, if each team member is given 20 votes, he or she might decide to use one vote for 20 things, 20 votes for one thing, or something in between. You can make the voting open or confidential. The best way is to ask each team member to email or IM you with the number of votes for each category or item number.

Tally the votes, add them to the spreadsheet, and prioritize your list. Your spreadsheet should now look something like Figure 7.2.

#	Category	Best Practice Description	Description of Problem	Recommended action	# Votes	Priority	Approved
1	Meetings	Prepare agendas in advance of meetings and send out minutes afterwards.	Noone knows the purpose of the meetings without an agenda. If you miss a meeting you don't know what was decided in the meeting unless there are meeting minutes.	1-Continue using	20	2	Yes
2	Scheduling	Build contingency time into scheduling to allow time for team members to deal with client support issues.	Client support issues take time away from working on scheduled tasks. This is causing problems that results in team members missing deadlines.	5-Needs New BP	10	6	
3	Change control	All changes that will impact scheduled deliverables go through a change control process.	Too many undocumented and unapproved changes occur that impact ability to meet scheduled delivery dates.	3-Update/Improve	15	4	
4	Contract negotiation	Business managers are included in all contract negotiation meetings.	Business managers attend contract meetings to ensure that the legal team understands the implications of contract requirements on costs and timelines. Contracts are now standardized and legal team is very experienced. No longer necessary.	4-Discontinue Using	20	3	Yes
5	Meetings	Everyone turns up on time for meetings. If late, do not announce yourself. Do not ask for anything to be repeated. Read minutes!	Too many people calling in late for meetings. Delays start of meeting and requires repeating parts of the meeting.	2-Adopt more widely	15	5	
6	Communication	Stay logged into Instant messaging whenever at desk. Change status to "away" if not available.	Never sure where anyone is or if they are available to talk.	2-Adopt more widely	25	1	
7							

Figure 7.2: Prioritized list

Discuss the Top Priorities

Choose somewhere between three and 10 priorities to focus on for the next quarter or two. Discuss the top priorities and how and when they will be implemented. You might not be able to take responsibility for all of them yourself, and you probably shouldn't. This is supposed to be a team effort, so try to assign some of the responsibility to other team members. Document action items, agree on timelines and deliverables, and define the process for reporting status on action items and measuring the success of the best practices and process improvements.

Define the Best Practice Process, Going Forward

Discuss the process for creating, sharing, prioritizing, and reporting on best practices going forward. For example, perhaps you should hold a monthly or bimonthly meeting to discuss how the new best practices are going and to discuss any new ones that team members discover.

Communication is the key to good teamwork and to the sharing of best practices. If your team members are sharing ideas and helping each other be more successful on a daily basis, you will have a functional and successful team!

Making It Fun!

How does the virtual manager create an environment that is creative, productive, respectful, and fun? As a good start, try not to take things too seriously! Allowing and encouraging some frivolity and humor in day-to-day life on the team is a great way to make things more fun. Encourage team members to share amusing stories about things that have happened to them, either at work or in their personal lives. Better yet, share amusing stories of your own with your team. Be transparent to your team members by telling a funny story where you are the object of the joke. This is a great way to get the team loosened up a bit. If your team members know that you can take a joke, they will feel more comfortable using humor as a way to express themselves or to lighten the mood in times of stress! Discussing current work problems in a less serious manner and adding a little wry humor or sarcasm can go a long way in helping to ease tension and stress about a situation.

Bouncing off the walls with happiness, and making people feel they must always be positive and enthusiastic when all about them everything is falling apart is not the best way to rally the troops or bring fun into the process. In fact, it can just make people feel under more pressure. If the happiness is too forced or the positive attitude is too phony, it is not going to fly with your team. You will end up with a group of people who are good at smiling through gritted teeth while feeling totally downhearted and demotivated. This kind of environment builds mistrust, as nobody is being truthful about what they think or how they feel. If someone feels really angry or upset by a situation or decision, he or she should feel comfortable sharing that with fellow team members.

Be careful about the use of sarcasm. It can sometimes be misconstrued. It is vitally important that humor or sarcasm is not disrespectful in any way. Jokes about a person's appearance, weight, height, religion, race, sexual orientation, or gender are not appropriate in the workplace. Keep humor clean and respectful.

Playing jokes on team mates can be very amusing. One example that springs to mind is when 10 people called in for a virtual conference call. When connecting to the conference, each caller was asked to state his or her name so it could be announced. On this particular day, everyone announced themselves using the manager's name. It was rather confusing for the manager to hear the participants all logging in using her name. It took her a while to figure out who they really were. Simple jokes like this are great for adding some levity into daily work life. They also promote teamwork, as the team members have to coordinate to pull it off. Teamwork is teamwork, whether it is being used to play a joke on the boss or to solve a serious client issue. The virtual environment can be very impersonal, so anything that gets the team working together and having fun should be encouraged.

> Teamwork is teamwork, whether it is being used to play a joke on the boss or to solve a serious client issue.

If you are in the midst of a serious business problem, maybe even what you would define as a "disaster," it is important not to lose your sense of humor or perspective. Serious problems are generally not fun things to deal with. Allowing some fun and humor to coexist with the tension and seriousness of a stressful situation will not make the problems go away any faster, but it might make it a bit more pleasant getting there! Take any reasonable opportunity that you see to make working on your team more fun. Ask the team members what they consider to be fun. Sharing funny stories, sharing jokes, or just allowing people to be themselves can all be fun.

Celebrations and Rewards

There are so many ways to celebrate success in the traditional work environment. It is harder to celebrate together, apart. However, it is not impossible.

Local teams can celebrate meeting financial goals or completing a project on time by participating in activities together. Competing in sports events like golf, or attending spectator sports like football or soccer matches are wonderful ways to celebrate success. Going out to dinner or organizing a catered party for the team are also nice rewards for team members. The virtual team, however, cannot attend events together, so the manager needs to use other reward methods to celebrate success.

If you have created growth and development plans with all team members, you will know what motivates each person and what types of rewards each likes to get. If you have taken the time to get to know a little more about individual team members, you should have some idea of the hobbies and interests of each person. Use this information to choose appropriate rewards and gifts for celebrating success. For example, if there are team members who like to travel, travel certificates or air miles could be appropriate rewards. For team members who like sporting events, tickets for games would be appreciated. For team members who like to be pampered, spa certificates are a good choice. Restaurant vouchers are also a good idea. If there are team members located close to each other, they might choose to do some activities together. Gift certificates for stores are also good for rewards and incentives. Make sure that the person lives within a reasonable distance of a branch of the store before purchasing a certificate, however. It is no fun having to drive 60 miles to redeem a gift certificate.

Gifts of team merchandise can be good, too. Consider hats, coffee mugs, or t-shirts with the company or team logo on them. Team gifts are also good for establishing some team connections. If your team has its own logo, create merchandise using it. It is much more personal than using a generic company logo. It can be a fun project to create your own team logo, if the scope of the project warrants it. The team members can work together to design a logo, or each team member can submit ideas, and the team can vote for the best one. The creation of the logo can be a fun team-building exercise in itself!

If the budget is available, it is highly desirable to get the whole team together for at least one celebration per project or review cycle. If the team members are going to be in the same location at some point, use that opportunity to plan a team event. For example, all the team members might be attending a kick-off meeting for a project, or they might be attending the same seminar or conference. Take the opportunities as they present themselves. A virtual team might not be able to be brought together at the times you specifically want to celebrate, so celebrate when you can, and enjoy being together!

When you have something to celebrate, you can do it without a lot of pomp and circumstance. You can celebrate in your team meetings by having fun and congratulating one another. You can tell funny stories about how you almost never made it to a successful conclusion. Just being together and getting good news can feel like a great accomplishment. It is always more fun sharing success with others than enjoying it alone.

Remember that you can also reward team members in more simple ways, like sending them an email to say congratulations or thank you for a job well done. You can phone team members or send relatively low-cost gifts like flowers, plants, or brownies as a thank you or just as an incentive not to give up on a difficult problem. A few words of encouragement can go a long way toward making it all seem worthwhile!

Team Processes and Procedures

Team processes and procedures are vital to any team. On a virtual team, though, it is even more important to have well-defined and well-documented processes. Your team members will rely on the processes and procedures to exchange information, report and receive status updates, and escalate problems. Some virtual team processes will be similar to those used on a traditional team, but others will be unique to your virtual environment.

Although we stress that any team will benefit greatly from having fully documented processes and procedures, many traditional companies manage to scrape by with inferred processes that have not been formally documented or distributed. In this situation, someone on the team who is unsure what to do will usually ask the person in the next office or mention it to the team during the pre-meeting time in a meeting room. There are lots of opportunities to ask in passing how one would go about dealing with a situation or requesting some action. This is not an efficient process by any means, but traditional teams can get away with it, at least in the short term.

Using an informal approach to processes on a virtual team would lead not just to inefficient processes, but to non-functioning processes. For the virtual team, everyone needs to be self-sufficient, able to carry out their work independently and efficiently. There must be one place where the team members can go to find the procedure for doing this or that. Otherwise, they will either all be doing things their own way, or they will not be doing them at all. This could easily turn into a virtual manager's nightmare!

The process of documenting processes and procedures is a great way to ensure that you have thought of everything and not forgotten something very important. You can create and document the processes yourself, or you can ask for input from your team members. The most effective way to get the plans in place quickly is for you to document the various processes and procedures, and then review and update them with input from your team.

It is important to evaluate and update the processes as necessary. A process should help the team accomplish things more effectively, more efficiently, and with less confusion and stress. If the processes get in the way of getting things done, they need to be updated or abandoned. Processes should be continually improved. Ideas for how to improve them can come from all sorts of people. Listen to the input, and consider it carefully before dismissing it. It could make a huge difference to your team members. Refining and improving processes is how you create best practices. The best-practices brainstorming process described in chapter 7 is ideal for defining and refining process improvements.

> If the processes get in the way of getting things done, they need to be updated or abandoned.

Communication Process

The communication process or plan will define what should be communicated, who it should be communicated to, and how and when it should be communicated. Sounds easy? Beware; it is not always as straightforward as it first appears. (A full copy of the communication plan is included in appendix B.)

The communication plan should define the process for all formal communications and include some more general guidelines for informal communications. The plan will include all types of communication, for example:

- Meetings
- Conference calls
- Emails
- Letters or mailings
- Phone calls
- Documents
- Website updates

The plan should define the following:

- Stakeholder groups
- Formal communication plan
- Informal communication/escalation plan
- Communication rules

Stakeholder Groups

The first step in defining a communication plan is to define the stakeholder groups. There should be more than one list of stakeholders. If you communicate to everyone about everything, they will soon stop reading or responding to your emails, calls, and meeting requests! Think about the different things you need to communicate and to whom. For example, you might need to send out team updates each week and hold client status meetings each week. You will need to define stakeholder groups to use for each of these communications. A good method is to create a stakeholder groups spreadsheet, such as the one in Figure 8.1. For teams working in a virtual environment, it is helpful to list the location and/or time zone of each team member in the spreadsheet. The time-zone spreadsheet from chapter 4 can be used in conjunction with the communication plan, but listing the locations in this document too will save your team members time having to look up multiple documents to find the information that is needed.

> If you communicate to everyone about everything, they will soon stop reading or responding to your emails, calls, and meeting requests!

Stakeholder Group Name	Description	Members
The Virtual Team	Internal Virtual Team members	*USA (CA)* Melanie Swan, Kevin Li, June Zhang *USA (NY):* George Webley *USA (MA):* Charles Green *INDIA (Bangalore):* Suzi Kumar *Puerto Rico:* David Johnson *UK (London):* Richard Jones, Rebecca Baker
ABC Project	All members of the ABC project team. Internal and external	*USA (CA):* Kevin Li, June Zhang *Puerto Rico:* David Johnson *UK (London):* Richard Jones, Rebecca Baker *USA (TX):* Gregory Pritchard (ABC), Janie Smith (ABC), Donald Trane (XYZ)

Figure 8.1: Stakeholder groups

It is likely that you will have 20 or more different stakeholder groups. Defining the groups and who belongs to them will be very helpful to team members in figuring out who they should be communicating with. Setting up shared email distribution lists for each of the stakeholder groups will make the process even more effective. Try not to choose stakeholder group names that sound very similar, to avoid team members accidentally sending information to the wrong group!

Formal Communication Plan

The formal communication plan should include all scheduled and planned communications. It should be detailed, and include all meetings, status reports, planned email communications, scheduled team chat sessions, and conference calls. For example, if the team members are required to report weekly status, those communications should be included. Team or project status reports prepared by the manager should also be listed. An example of a formal communication plan is shown in Figure 8.2.

Communication	Content	Objective	Owner	Stakeholders	Method	Frequency / Date
Individual Status Reports	Status report includes status on milestones, deliverables, risks, issues, and budget. Includes overall project/task status	Used to prepare the Weekly Team Status Report	All virtual team members	Melanie Swan	Email	Weekly. Due Friday at 1pm (PT)
Weekly Team Status Report	Consolidated list of weekly team member status reports. Report includes status on milestones, deliverables, risks, issues, and budget. Includes overall project/task status	To ensure that team members are aware of what everyone else is working on and aware of any project or task issues or delays.	Melanie Swan	The Virtual Team, VP Product Management, VP Sales,	Email	Weekly. Due Tuesday before noon (PT)
ABC Client Status Meeting	Report status on milestones, deliverables and schedule. Review Risk Management Plan. Raise any budget concerns	To keep client informed and up to date on progress. To ensure any issues are dealt with expeditiously	David Johnson	ABC Project	Web meeting with audio conference dial in	Weekly. Wednesday at 8am (PT)

Figure 8.2: Formal communication plan

As discussed earlier in the book, meetings should always be followed up with written minutes. The distribution of the minutes is a team communication, so it should be included in the communication plan. The distribution list for the minutes might include an additional stakeholder group to the one that attends the meeting. This should be clearly defined.

This communication plan is a great way for team members to ensure that they know what is expected of them and what they can expect from others. It saves a lot of time calling around, trying to find out who is meeting about what and which meetings one should attend to find out about a specific issue or client. It requires some careful thought and planning to create this plan, but once it is created, it should not require too much updating.

> The formal communication plan should include all scheduled and planned communications.

Remember to consider all the communication options when designing your communication processes. Virtual communication needs to be managed carefully to avoid having to continually recommunicate the same information. Web/audio meetings are a great way to appeal to all three learning styles (visual, auditory, and kinesthetic). By including some visuals in your meeting, you are controlling what the participants are looking at, which reduces the chances that they will be reading emails or otherwise not paying attention. The participants have two links to each other, visual and audio, rather than just one with a regular audio conference. This makes the meeting feel a little more personal because you are all looking at the same thing as well as talking about it. The Web tools that are often used for training sessions can be very effective for virtual meetings. They give you the opportunity to share compelling supporting material to really drive the point of your meeting home.

The biggest advantage to creating a formal communication plan is that you are *planning* your team's communication, rather than just letting it all happen on an ad hoc basis. Planning communications will keep them focused, on track, and relevant. If a meeting has no real objective, it will be obvious when you are creating your plan. If you find you are having three separate meetings to talk about the same thing, you can combine them into one. You would never let a project just run itself and expect successful results, so don't be tempted to let the communication on your team just happen willy-nilly and expect it to be successful. The manager is responsible for managing the process, not vice versa!

Informal Communication Plan

The informal communication plan involves planning for the unexpected. It is not possible to anticipate every single problem or issue that might arise during any defined period of time. It is, however, possible to anticipate that there will be problems of some sort, and to categorize those problems or issues according to type or severity. An informal communication plan is not designed to guide the team on every single communication they make. They do not need to consult the plan before communicating with other team members or scheduling a client meeting. The informal plan is designed to deal with communication about issues that are, or have the potential to be, damaging to the company, the client, or the project in some way.

> Web/audio meetings are a great way to appeal to all three learning styles (visual, auditory, and kinesthetic).

The plan includes information on who should be communicated with initially and who is subsequently responsible for communicating to other stakeholders. This kind of information can speed things up a lot when an unexpected problem or delay occurs with a project. If everyone is communicating to everyone else about the issue, it can get very confusing figuring out who knows what and who is taking what action. On a virtual team, you could easily have eight different people working on the same issue and not be aware that anybody else is working on it until those people have all invested a lot of time in trying to resolve the issue. This situation occurs when different managers are calling different people about the same problem, and everyone thinks they "own" the problem. Some people avoid talking to the manager and go directly to the individual who they believe can resolve the problem, as a way to speed things up.

The result of all this confusion is that way too much communication is going on, and too little appropriate action is being taken to resolve the issue. None of the communication is being filtered through a central person or process, so time spent is disproportionate to the size of the problem. In other words, you have created more problems than you are solving. You need to create an environment where the communication is clear, concise, and effective, and the roles and responsibilities are clearly defined. Figure 8.3 shows an example of an informal communication plan.

Issue	Description	Action	Owner (escalate to)	Audience	Method	Timeline
Cannot Meet Scheduled Deliverable	Any technical or non-technical issue that will affect the company's ability to achieve an on-time client deliverable	First escalate to project manager. If project manager cannot resolve the issue within 2 hours, escalate to team manager and communicate status to the internal project team. Project manager communicates with client.	1.David Johnson 2. Melanie Swan	2.Internal project team	Initial email or phone call. If unable to resolve use conference call or in person meeting	Within one day or within 2 hours if less than one week from due date
Security Issue	Critical security issue	Escalate to project manager who will escalate to team manager and security team	David Johnson	Security team	Phone call or in person. No security issues to be discussed in email	Within 2 hours

Figure 8.3: Informal communication plan

It is important to ensure that the information in this plan does not contradict what is contained in the escalation plan, described later in this chapter. The communication plan should reference a contact list that contains current contact information for all team members.

Communication Rules

Communication rules should include those of any organization, company, client, or regulatory body that must be applied to your team's communication. For example, if a company has access to personal client or end-user information, there should be a privacy policy in place to define how that information may be used and who may see it. If the company is government-regulated by, for example, the Securities and Exchange Commission (SEC), the rules specific to that regulation should be documented here.

Your organization might have specific rules. For example, many companies do not allow information concerning security breaches to be discussed via email or mobile phone, as those methods of communication are not secure. Likewise, confidential internal documents might not be authorized for sending outside the corporate network, or perhaps cannot be sent by email at all. The team might have its own rules regarding communication. For instance, the project manager might be the only person authorized to communicate directly with the client.

Often, companies like to have a single point of contact (*SPOC*) to ensure a standard level of service to the client, as well as ensuring that the client is not asking 10 different people to do the same thing. Government contracts include a lot of stipulations that need to be followed. For specific projects, a client might also have special rules. For example, the client might have rules concerning the use of wireless networks. If the client has highly sensitive information and is concerned about the security of wireless networks, the team members might not be allowed to use wireless networks at all while working on the client's project. Alternatively, a high-security project might require that all the team members work inside the same building, to restrict access to the network to those inside the firewall. This would require that the virtual team members work onsite in the same location for the duration of the project.

There are any number of reasons for communication rules, and every single company has some. If you think your company doesn't have any rules at all, think again. Are you allowed to send an email to everyone in the entire company? What would happen if you copied the CEO or president on every single email you sent out? What would the result be if you shared proprietary, internal, technical design documents with your client or vendor? There are always some rules. Many of them are obvious, but some are not so obvious. The communication plan is where you let the team know what those rules are. If they are not aware of the rules, how can they be expected to follow them?

Change-Control Process

Change control is the process used to manage any changes to projects or teams that will affect the successful outcome of a project, job, or contract.

Changes that do not affect final outcomes do not need to be tracked or managed via a change-control process. For example, changes to a project schedule that affect completion of a task, but do not affect the completion date, budget, or quality of the final deliverable do not need to go through change control. If an internal milestone is changed and there is no impact on its project, but there is an impact on another project or contract, then it should go through a change-control process.

Changes fall into many categories, for example:

- ► Resources
- ► Schedule
- ► Technical
- ► Organizational
- ► Business
- ► Scope
- ► New projects
- ► Maintenance
- ► Catastrophic failures or events

Change control is designed to manage the impact of internal and external changes. Change control helps you prioritize tasks and projects, so you can evaluate the potential impact of a change across your team or organization and make appropriate decisions. There will always be some projects or contracts that are more important than others. Just because the issue occurs in one area does not mean that resources could not be moved from elsewhere to resolve that issue. This would affect the final deliverable for the other project or contract in some way.

It is difficult for a virtual manager to keep tabs on everything that is going on unless the remote workers are communicating and following the established team processes and procedures. Without this adherence to the process, you could end up in a big mess very quickly. A week lost here and a few days lost there can soon add up. Within months, your team could be delivering late on everything! The change-control process is what keeps you on track.

Without change control, you are forced into a reactive mode of management. By the time you realize you have a problem, it is too late to do anything about it. The change-control process is designed to proactively manage the effects of change so that you stay in control of events.

> It is difficult for a virtual manager to keep tabs on everything that is going on unless the remote workers are communicating and following the established team processes and procedures.

Resources

Attrition is a fact of life in business. At some point, people will leave the company to pursue other opportunities, to retire, or because they are moving out of the area. People also make internal moves from one team to another. In internal moves, an employee might want to leave the team with the highest priority work for one with lower priority work. That does not necessarily mean the organization should refuse the transfer. If there are no opportunities to change or advance, that employee will start to look for opportunities outside the organization and will possibly become an ex-employee. Having said that, it is important to set realistic expectations for your team members.

Working with each team member to create a career plan is an excellent way for you to understand the career aspirations and timelines of your team members. If you understand the career goals of each team member, you can do a number of things to reduce attrition. You can figure out whether there are sufficient opportunities on your team for every person to grow and advance their careers. If so, define plans to get people where they need to be, so they can advance when they are ready. If the opportunities are not there, you might be able to create them. If you work for a company that has more than one team, you might be able to work with other managers to identify opportunities in their groups for your team members, and vice versa. You should be thinking about where each employee can go next and who can fill the shoes that he or she will vacate. If you have a plan in place, you might still lose an employee unexpectedly, but the chances of not being ready will be smaller.

> Transitioning tasks from one team member to another is much harder when the team members are geographically distant from each another.

On a virtual team, it can be much more challenging to come up with creative and effective ways of managing resource changes. Transitioning tasks from one team member to another is much harder when the team members are geographically distant from each another. They might even be in different time zones. The person being transitioned to might be scheduled for travel during the transition period, so a decision must be made whether to delay the travel or miss the transition. Many virtual teams are composed of individuals with unique skill Sets, so there might not be an obvious choice about who will take on the work an individual has been doing.

Virtual teams are also often bare-bones teams. Today's organizations want to run lean and mean. This leaves no room to maneuver when trying to minimize resource issues. If you have contingency plans drawn up that identify your key resources and who will do what if you lose one of those resources either temporarily or permanently, you should be able to mitigate a lot of the risk. It might be that you can plan to outsource some of the work, or perhaps you can hire in a contractor to help reduce the impact of losing a key team member. The important thing here is to plan ahead and make sure you know what you will do if any of your team members are not available to perform their usual functions.

Hiring a replacement is also more challenging and costly with a virtual team. Candidates and team members who will be involved in the interview process will have to be transported to the interview location. In the traditional work world, it might take a couple of hours of team members' time to conduct an interview. This is very different from taking two whole days to travel to and from the interview location, conduct the interview, and attend the interview debriefing session. If the team members involved in the interview process are assigned to client projects, these costs cannot be passed on to the client. You have to take into account one or two days of time lost to the project for each round of interviews, in addition to the loss from the person who left the team!

When a team member leaves, it can be a great opportunity for another team member to step up and take on a new role. Remember that change might cause some upheaval, but it also creates new opportunities. Don't underestimate the capabilities of your other team members. You might not have someone who can step in and be as good as the person who left, but you might have someone who can grow into the role and who will be a huge asset to your team in the longer term.

Schedule

Various scenarios can result in schedule problems. For example, tasks might have been underestimated; dependencies might not have been identified appropriately so tasks were scheduled in the wrong order; or one task might have been delayed and caused delays to tasks that were dependent on it.

It is rare for a project to run from start through completion with no changes to the original plan. A certain number of changes and delays should have been anticipated during planning, and a contingency buffer added to the schedule to allow for those changes. If a change occurs that cannot be mitigated by using the contingency buffer, and it will affect the end date of the project, that change needs to go through a change-control process.

You have several possible courses of action to address a schedule issue, for example:

- Remove one or more features or functions from the project.
- Reduce the functionality of one or more parts of the project.
- Stagger the final deliverable into separate phases.
- Decrease quality (a known decrease in quality).
- Cut testing or verification tasks (less confidence in the level of quality).
- Buy more hardware, software, or equipment.
- Outsource some of the work.
- Add resources (permanent or contract).
- Increase work hours for existing resources with additional pay.
- Increase work hours for existing resources without additional pay.
- Change the completion date.

These options will all be considered as part of the change-control process. Many of them will require a higher budget. Some will increase risk. Others will work the team into the ground. Often, a combination of these options is the best choice. For instance, you might remove one feature completely, reduce functionality on two other features, add one resource, and delay the completion date by one week. This could be a better option than delaying the release by two months, which would most likely be the default option without a change-control process. As the old saying goes, "There is more than one way to skin a cat." Without change control, you might not even know you have a cat!

Technical

Technical issues can result in changes needing to be made to a project or contract. Technical issues can occur for all sorts of reasons, from many different areas, and with varying degrees of impact. Some examples of technical issues are the following:

- ▶ Network failure
- ▶ Hardware system failure
- ▶ Purchased hardware or software does not perform as expected
- ▶ Integration issues
- ▶ Compatibility issues
- ▶ Lack of technical support
- ▶ Unable to resolve technical issues in timely manner
- ▶ Support for technology discontinued
- ▶ Technical equipment no longer available
- ▶ Change in technical direction based on new market or business information

Anyone who works with technology knows that nothing is ever as straightforward as it should be. Technology that is supposed to be compatible is often incompatible. Sometimes technical issues are not discovered until a lot of time and money has already been invested in solving a particular technical problem. Likewise, sometimes the technical expertise is not available to troubleshoot the type of problems being experienced. Having to hire an expert to find the problem could have a big impact on the budget for the project or contract. If you fly team members onsite to help resolve issues, and the problem is identified as being a client issue, what do you do? Can you charge the client additional fees? Will the client still insist on an on-time delivery of your product, despite the delays? These questions need to be asked prior to flying someone in to look at the problem, to ensure that you and the client agree about who is responsible for covering the costs of these changes to the project plan.

Virtual team members working from home offices have a high probability of running into technical issues from time to time. Without a corporate help desk or systems team to help fix the issues quickly or replace faulty equipment with spares, technical issues can take more time to resolve. Most virtual workers do not have a lot of spare equipment sitting around in case of an emergency.

It can be very challenging troubleshooting and resolving technical issues when the team members are working from separate locations. Coordinating

> Virtual team members working from home offices have a high probability of running into technical issues from time to time.

the effort to resolve, prioritize, and assign resources to problems is a key function of the virtual manager. This is one instance in which the glue is going to be sorely needed to stop everything from falling apart!

To help mitigate the risks from technical issues, it might be prudent for each member to have a certain number of less expensive spare parts and equipment available in the case of failure. As the manager of the team, it would be wise for you to keep a spare laptop available so you can send it overnight to a team member in an emergency and minimize employee downtime. Planning ahead is key to managing issues. You will still need to go through a change-control process if the change has created delays, but at least you can prevent the problems from getting any worse by being ready to take action as quickly as possible. Another suggestion is to have each team member find a local company that leases and repairs equipment, so they are not getting out the Yellow Pages on the day of the disaster, trying to locate someone who can help. If it is going to cost more money diagnosing and fixing the problem than replacing a faulty piece of equipment, you need to be able to make the replacement in a timely manner. To facilitate this, make sure you have a process to fast-track approval for purchasing or leasing replacement equipment.

Organizational

Any major organizational change is going to affect timelines, budgets, quality, and morale. Organizational changes include changes to the structure of the company. Perhaps managers have changed, there have been promotions, or the project managers have been moved around to work on different projects. If a company decides to start outsourcing a number of business functions, the associated changes could disrupt a lot of ongoing work. Transition time working with the outsourcer will be required. Processes will need to be adapted and updated to the new organizational structure. If part of the business is being moved to another country, there will be a lot of changes to integrate the new team members into the existing team. This will take time away from other tasks.

High-impact changes should be managed via change control. In a perfect world, a full impact analysis would have been done at the time the organizational change was decided, so there would not be a need for additional change control to deal with individual issues. Unfortunately, many major organizational issues are kept under wraps until the last possible moment, and the impact analyses are nowhere near detailed enough to identify the extent of the fallout from the changes. These changes will need to be managed by the individual team managers via their own change-control processes.

Business

Market conditions and changes in business direction can create chaos if left unchecked! The change-control process might not be able to stop the changes from happening, but it can control what steps are taken to respond to the changes and minimize the negative impacts.

Sometimes a team might be halfway through a project when the business landscape changes dramatically. All kinds of outside influences can create those changes. Just a few reasons are terrorism, war, oil prices, a stock market crash, pandemics, a new competitor in the market, a major competitor going bankrupt, changes in regulations, changes in the law, or a new technology or service with the potential to make yours obsolete.

Demand and supply for products and services can go through all kinds of transformations over the years. Companies switch their alliances and business partners at different times, so they need to keep changing and evolving their business models. There are many reasons why companies need to change direction quickly. The ability to respond and adapt quickly in an ever-changing world is essential in today's fast-moving global marketspace.

Scope

Changes in scope might reduce or increase it. Mostly, scope changes increase scope. It is common for the increases in scope to be accompanied by a desire to keep the costs and timelines for the project exactly the same!

Scope changes are easy to manage via change control as long as the virtual team is cognizant of the original scope of the work and can quickly recognize and respond to scope creep. Managing the scope of projects as well as managing the scope of team members' responsibilities is a continual process that needs constant attention. The minute it is left unattended, it tends to escalate and very soon gets completely out of control. The result will be that it is not possible to complete projects or tasks successfully (on time, within budget, and with high quality).

It is much more difficult for the manager of the virtual team to spot when scope creep is occurring. Often, it is not identified until it is too late to reverse or control it. With frequent and effective communication with the virtual team members, scope creep should be completely manageable and controllable.

New Projects

New projects come up all the time. Sometimes a new, higher visibility, or higher priority project will affect the team's ability to successfully complete an existing project. In matrix organizations, where team members are shared among groups and projects, it is very common to have a lot of reshuffling of funds and resources on a fairly regular basis. The key to successfully managing these reshuffles is to ensure that all changes go through the change-control and prioritization process.

Many companies are not very skilled at long-term planning. These companies operate in a reactive mode and, as a result, a lot of short-term decisions are made without regard for the long-term goals and objectives of the company. This can result in a lot of confusion. Over time, the managers will find themselves never sure whether any deadlines will be met, no matter how good their up-front planning has been. If you find yourself in situations where a resource who was supposed to be assigned to your project has been assigned to a higher priority project without anyone letting you know, you are working in a reactive environment. You are left with no option but to react to this situation and treat it as an emergency. With better planning and change control, you could have managed the situation proactively and maintained a predictable outcome.

Maintenance

Maintenance issues that create delays, or changes that need to go through change control, are not generally related to regularly scheduled maintenance tasks. Those should be included in the project or contract plan. Delays created by maintenance are usually due to additional, unanticipated work required for previously completed projects or to resolve some unforeseen technical issues. For example, a software project has bugs that were not found or resolved before the project was completed. Resources need to work on fixing the problems, so they are taken away from current projects. As another example, perhaps documentation was not completed correctly for a previous project, or typographical errors in marketing materials have to be fixed. Any issues with past work that need to be completed will take time and resources away from current projects.

Projects that lack good-quality testing and review will result in more work needing to be done after the fact than those projects that are managed more effectively. If quality assurance and review is being carried out by remote team members, ensure that good tracking and monitoring processes are in place to measure how effectively that work is being done, and that it is being done at all!

Catastrophic Failures or Events

The least desirable reason to have to make last-minute plan changes is a catastrophic failure. These failures can occur at a corporate facility, datacenter, onsite at a client location, at a virtual team member's home office, or in your own home office. The cause of a catastrophic event could be unrelated to your business or that of one of your clients. It could be a natural disaster, an act of terrorism, or an accident, such as a plane crash or a freeway collapsing. Any of these events can create havoc with scheduled work.

Catastrophic events such as *denial of service* (*DoS*) attacks on corporate datacenter systems might delay or limit work for some time. If the corporate network has been down for a day and a half, the team's ability to communicate and complete assigned tasks could be severely limited. A virtual team member having a laptop stolen at the airport, containing contracts and client information not backed up to another system, could be considered a catastrophic event for two reasons. First, you have lost data that you need to deliver on a current commitment. Second, you have lost proprietary information that could be damaging to your business if it gets into the wrong hands. Both of these consequences need to be managed simultaneously. In an ideal world, we would all back up our systems daily, but in reality most people do not. Even losing one day's worth of data can be disastrous, not to mention the time it takes getting a new computer, setting it up, and configuring it to be ready to work at full capacity again. This whole process could take a week or two! For virtual team members who travel a lot and take their computers with them, insist on a daily computer backup. As long as the virtual employees have remote access to a corporate backup server via the Internet, daily backups should be an achievable goal.

> For virtual team members who travel a lot and take their computers with them, insist on a daily computer backup.

Change Requests

Creating a change-control process is not that difficult, but it does require proactive attention and management. The first step should be to define who approves changes. The approvers might be the same for the whole organization, or they might be different for each department, team, or project. Changes should be requested using a change-request form. An example of a change request is shown in Figure 8.4.

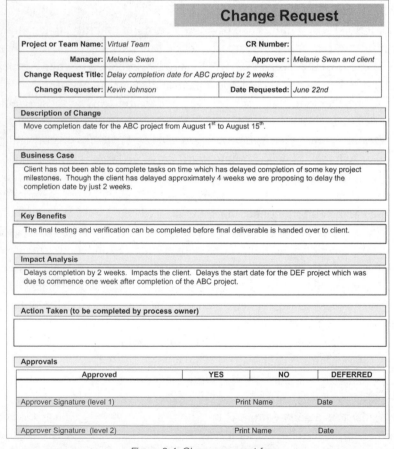

Figure 8.4: Change-request form

The elements of the form should include the submitter and project information in addition to the following:

▸ Detailed description of the change

▸ Business case describing why the change is needed and the importance of making the change

▸ Key benefits describing how the company or client will benefit from the change

▸ Impact analysis clearly identifying all teams, projects, and people affected by the change, as well as information about what will happen if the change is not made

The approvers will evaluate the changes and decide what action should be taken. Some change requests are straightforward and easy to decide whether to approve or deny. Some are trickier and will be deferred, pending additional information to support the request.

To track the status of change requests, you should maintain a change log. This log keeps track of each request with its corresponding request number (so the full request can be looked up, if necessary) and notes the approval status and the date the decision was made. A sample change log is shown in Figure 8.5.

Change Log

CR#	Change Request Title	Project or Team	Requester	Request Date	Status	Manager	Approver(s)	Date Reviewed	Action Taken
100	Delay completion date of ABC project by two weeks, From August 1st to August 15th.	ABC / Virtual Team	Kevin Johnson	June 22nd	Deferred	Melanie Swan	Melanie Swan and Client (ABC)	June 25th	Deferred unitil client has signed release
100	Delay completion date of ABC project by two weeks, From August 1st to August 15th.	ABC / Virtual Team	Kevin Johnson	June 22nd	Approved	Melanie Swan	Melanie Swan and Client (ABC)	July 1st	Client signed release and contract update. Schedule reworked to change completion date.

Figure 8.5: Change log

In the example in Figure 8.5, the change request was submitted to the change control board twice. The first time, the request was deferred; the change could not be made until a contractual amendment was created and signed by the client.

After this step was complete, the request was resubmitted to the change control board and approved.

The change-control process must be easily accessible and usable for remote employees. If your process states that you must attend a weekly meeting in the New York office on Wednesday morning at 9:00 to request your change, remote employees will be unable to submit any change requests. Even if you have an audio conference phone number to call in for the meeting, this is not going to be a feasible time for workers in some other time zones. The process needs to allow requests to be submitted electronically and for the change-control approval process to take place without the personal attendance of the requester. The change log should also be accessible via the virtual team's Website.

> The change-control process must be easily accessible and usable for remote employees.

There should be a special process for submitting Emergency Change Requests (ECRs). ECRs are for changes that need to be expedited. If a change is due to a technical issue or catastrophic failure, action might need to be taken before the ECR can be submitted. The change-control process should allow for this in emergency situations. Otherwise, the process will get in the way of doing the right thing. That is never a good idea!

Defect-Tracking Process (for Technical Projects)

There are many enterprise defect-tracking systems available. Most companies use these tools to track and manage defects (and sometimes also enhancements) across projects and groups. Some of these tools integrate with software and configuration-management tools.

Everyone on the virtual team must have access to the defect-management system, understand how it works, and know the process for using it. Even if some team members are not permitted to enter new defects into the system, they should have visibility into what is being tracked and what is being fixed. Limited access to just run and view reports might be appropriate for some team members; that is fine, just as long as everyone is aware of the process and how to use it.

If defects are being resolved but there is no feedback loop letting the interested parties know the status, then the process is going to be ineffective. Everyone must be using the same process. Keep an eye on the reports to ensure that your team members are not forgetting to keep their assigned defects under control.

The process should include the following information:

- ‣ Definition of a defect
- ‣ Definition of an enhancement
- ‣ Definition of a new feature or project
- ‣ Definition of access levels
  - » Who can submit defects
  - » Who can submit enhancements
  - » Who can submit new features or new projects
- ‣ Description of how to complete
  - » A defect report
  - » An enhancement request
  - » A new feature or project
- ‣ Description of the defect process, including process flow
- ‣ Description of the enhancement or new feature/project process, including process flow
- ‣ How to reopen a resolved or closed defect if it appears not to be fixed
- ‣ How to appeal a decision to defer or close a defect report
- ‣ Process for prioritizing enhancements, new features, and new projects
- ‣ Roles and responsibilities

Make sure team members are not "going around" the defect-tracking system to speed things up. A small change to one part of a system can have a snowball effect and end up creating a major problem if it is not effectively evaluated, estimated, and prioritized. A defect-tracking tool with a Web interface is great for virtual teams. It is much more efficient if you can avoid team members having to install software, and even better if they can access the system without being logged into a corporate network. This results in no excuses for not following the process!

> A defect-tracking tool with a Web interface is great for virtual teams.

Organizational Processes

Organizational processes are any processes created by the organization to manage and control the way things are done within the organization. They can include such things as the following:

- Time tracking
- Requesting time off
- Requesting approval for travel
- Submitting expense reports
- Tuition reimbursement
- Status reporting
- Metrics
- Hiring
- Grievances
- Internal technical processes
- Email or corporate communication processes
- Financial reporting
- Performance management

All companies have internal processes and procedures that must be followed. Virtual team members must be given access to the written process documentation and the appropriate tools, so they are aware of the rules and regulations that exist inside the organization and are able to use the processes effectively. If you are not careful, your remote workers might feel that the company processes do not apply to them because they work outside the corporate office. Alternatively, they might feel that, because they work remotely, they can choose to follow the processes only if it is convenient at the time. It is important to ensure that each member of the virtual team feels like part of the internal team and is committed to playing by the rules. If all the team members want to play by their own individual rules, it will be impossible to manage the team effectively. The more virtual employees you have, the more important it is to have comprehensive, understandable, and usable processes in place for all team members.

> If you are not careful, your remote workers might feel that the company processes do not apply to them because they work outside the corporate office.

You should not have one set of processes for local team members and a separate set of processes for remote workers. If you work on the same team, you are a virtual team, so everyone should be using the virtual team processes.

Client and Vendor Processes

Client and vendor companies will have their own internal processes and procedures. It will not be possible to persuade all the other companies you deal with to follow your guidelines and abide by your rules. Generally, you will need to adapt to each other's processes and come up with compromises that work for all parties involved.

For external projects, the client might require time reporting from each consultant. This will be in addition to the time reporting each team member submits to his or her own organization. Likewise with status reporting. Change-control processes will need to be discussed and documented to ensure that there are no misunderstandings about when and by whom changes can be made. If the client and vendor processes are not integrated into the team's processes, the relationships with these outside companies will become strained, and a lot of miscommunication and misunderstandings will occur.

If you can leverage existing team processes and procedures for managing external processes, this is ideal. The more you can do to reduce the amount of time that your team members spend on reporting the same thing multiple times, in multiple ways, the more productive your team will be, and the more streamlined your processes.

Status Reporting Process

There are different types of status reports. Each contains a different level of detail and is designed for a different audience. For example, the following status reports might be required in your organization:

- Status report from team members to manager
- Status report from manager to team members
- Status report from project manager to client
- Status report to senior executives

Status Report from Team Members to Manager

The weekly status reports that team members submit to you should contain the information you need to effectively manage, monitor, and control the work for which your team is responsible. These reports should also include any information you need to be able to create status reports to send to other groups or companies, or to senior management.

The best way to ensure that you receive the information you need, in the format you need it, is to create a status report template that is customized for your team and for the specific projects or contracts to which your team is assigned. Ideally, a status report will contain high-level information with enough detail to understand the status and the risks. You need to know if the team members are on track with their designated tasks and projects. You also need to know how much time was spent on scheduled versus unscheduled tasks. This information can be used to measure the percentage of time being spent on unanticipated work. If that percentage exceeds the contingency buffer included in your plans, then either the contingency buffer is not sufficient, or the team member has not been effective in prioritizing tasks and balancing workload.

The status report should contain a section to document current issues, as well as an area to document the status and level of risks. Documenting the planned tasks for the following week is a great way of encouraging team members to plan ahead and use good time management to ensure that the highest priority tasks are being accomplished each week. You can use this information to compare the completed work in the following week's status report with what the team member had projected he or she would complete. Seeing this information also gives you the opportunity to evaluate the tasks that the team member has listed, to ensure they are in line with what you consider to be the highest priorities. Managing a virtual team can be challenging to say the least, so the more insight you have into the day-to-day operations of all team members, the more effectively you will be able to manage, coach, and develop them. An example status report is shown in Figure 8.6. A blank copy of the status report is included in appendix B.

Status Report from Manager to Team Members

Use the individual status reports to create a high-level status report to send out to the whole team. The team report does not need to contain as much detail as the individual reports, though you could opt to merge them together and leave the detail intact. Alternatively, you could compile a report categorized by project or by client that includes highlights, major milestones, issues, and risks, and send that out to all the team members.

If the report is too long, nobody will read it. If it lacks substance, nobody will read it either. It is important to find a good balance between the two. The highlights of the status report, or at a minimum the issues and risks in the status report, should be discussed in the weekly (or biweekly) virtual team meeting.

Status Report

Name:	
Manager:	
Date:	
Contact Name:	
Phone / E-mail:	
Reporting Period:	

Are All Tasks:

On or Ahead of Schedule?	Yes		No	
Meeting Requirements?	Yes		No	

Scheduled Tasks

Project/ Client	Task	Hours spent on task	Percentage complete
ABC	Phase one tasks	20	100
ABC	Phase two tasks	8	10
XYZ	Client proposal meetings	8	100

Unscheduled Tasks

Project/ Client	Task	Hours spent on task	Percentage complete
ABC	Meetings regarding ABC issues	4	50

Issues

Project/ Client	Issues	Severity	Time needed to resolve
ABC	Project end date moved from August 1st to 15th. Submitted to change control	High	1 week

Planned Work for Next Period

Project/ Client	Tasks	Hours	% complete expected
ABC	Finalize project end date	2	100
ABC	Complete phase two	30	80
XYZ	First draft of contract	8	100

Risk Assessment

Project/ Client	Risks	Severity	Probability
ABC	Client is behind on scheduled tasks. I have a low level of confidence client will be able to accomplish the tasks in the additional time client has requested	High	High

Recommendations/Comments

Contractual changes due to ABC delay are documented and formal letter sent to client informing that further delays will mean we have to push the project out as we have other project commitments that cannot be delayed any further

Figure 8.6: Status report

Status Report from Project Manager to Client

Client status reports are required when working on external contracts or projects. It is typical to produce weekly reports. These usually come from the project manager assigned to the client for that project.

The format of the status report itself might be designed by the project manager or by the client. Sometimes, the client will require all status reports to be submitted in its format so it can use them to produce high-level reports, just as the virtual team manager does with the team's weekly status reports. The information contained in a client status report will be very similar to that contained in the weekly status report shown in Figure 8.6. It might also contain information pertaining to the overall project hours and costs, so that the budget can be tracked via the same report. Sometimes, the financials are managed separately, as the audience for the implementation status reports is not always privy to the financial aspects of the project. The client might want to keep that information confidential.

Even if the client does not require formal written status reports, it is important that the project manager creates and distributes one. This covers the company in the event that the client denies any knowledge of ongoing issues, status, or budget variances. The reports ensure that everyone is on the same page with the status of tasks as well as expectations for the next period. If the client is responsible for some deliverables, the status report is a great way of tracking those deliverables and ensuring that everyone involved is aware of them. The written reports ensure that the client is not getting one piece of information from one team member and another piece from another, leading to confusion and misunderstandings.

Virtual team members are unlikely be aware of the exact status of everyone else on the team and their tasks at one specific moment in time. The weekly report ensures that everyone has at least one moment during the week when they are all on the same page. Virtual team members need some visibility into what has transpired during that week and the top priorities for the project and the team in the coming week.

Monthly Status Report to Senior Executives

The monthly status report is a "feel good" report. It lets the senior execs know that the budget dollars are being spent appropriately and that progress is being made on projects. These reports are used to monitor budgets and to measure the efficiency of projects, processes, and teams. You, the virtual team manager, will compile these reports based on the reports from individual team members, the project managers' client reports, the change request log, and necessary financial reports. This report is designed to give the 10,000-foot view of the project and highlight only those issues that are appropriate to be communicated to employees at high levels in the company.

It is a good idea to copy your team members on these reports, as long as they do not contain any sensitive financial information that is not appropriate to be shared. Preparing a Web presentation for this report is a great idea if you work remotely from the senior executives to whom you need to present your update.

These reports keep your stakeholders informed and give your team and projects high visibility. In the corporate world, there is no point in doing something well unless all the right people know about it!

Escalation Procedures

Clearly defined escalation procedures are critical to the success of a team or project. There are two reasons why issues need to be escalated. The first is when a critical problem occurs that risks the success of a project or contract. Unless the person who encounters the problem knows what to do and who to contact, the issue could result in a chaotic and uncoordinated response to the issue. The last thing you need in an emergency is to have everyone calling everyone else about it, and seven different people working on the problem in seven different ways. This will lead to inaccurate information being communicated and possibly a full-scale panic.

The second reason for escalating an issue is when a serious problem is being created internally or externally due to the non-responsiveness of an employee, a partner, a vendor, or a client. These types of problems usually need to be escalated to a more senior manager if continual follow-ups have been unsuccessful, and the issue is escalating to the point where it is risking the successful outcome of a project or contract.

When designing an escalation process, you first need to categorize and define the types and criticalities of issues that need escalating. Figure 8.7 shows an example definition of the escalation path.

Escalation Path

Level	Definition	Expected Response	Call Intervals
Priority 1	Critical Issue - critical impact to company or client including security breach	Senior management informed by manager immediately. Security team involved if applicable. Worked on continuously until resolved. Hourly updates for senior executives	Immediate
Priority 2	Major Impact - major impact to our own, a client's, or a partner's, business	Problem is worked on continuously until the problem is resolved	Immediate
Priority 3	Large Impact - significant inconvenience to clients or partners where a workaround might be implemented	Work is expected to continue on a workday basis until a more permanent solution is in place	2 hour maximum
Priority 4	Small to Medium Impact - medium or small inconvenience	Resolution is worked into a planned project list and schedule or it can be deferred until there is time allowed in the project schedule	24 hours maximum

Figure 8.7: Escalation path

An issue might start out as a priority 4 and escalate until it becomes a priority 1. Make sure that the team members understand the difference between a priority 1 and a priority 4. If all issues are escalated to the highest echelons of the company, you will soon find yourself with a lot of explaining to do. If you cry wolf often enough, everyone will stop listening. It is wise to require that all escalation go through you, the team's manager, first. That way, you can evaluate the priority level and ensure that the appropriate escalation process is being followed. Some people think that every problem with their project is a priority 1, because nothing else could possibly be more important. We have all met someone like that at some point. You are probably nodding your head right now as you think of one of these people!

On a virtual team, the members are expected to work independently and be able to make decisions. However, this should not mean working and making decisions in a vacuum. If the team members are involved in what is happening across the team and not just focused on their own small part of the process, you should see some good collaboration and decisions being made about the criticality of issues. Don't count on it, however! You might find that certain team members take issues into

> On a virtual team, the members are expected to work independently and be able to make decisions. However, this should not mean working and making decisions in a vacuum.

their own hands and want to inform senior managers every time something gets prioritized higher than their own project or task.

This is not using the escalation process to resolve critical issues. It is using the political process to try to get one's own way. It shows a lack of maturity and a lack of business professionalism. If you notice this type of behavior in one of your team members, use it as an opportunity to coach the team member as part of his or her overall growth and development plan. The escalation process should never be used to try to reverse a decision made by the change-control board or any other process, or to try to get someone into trouble.

You might need to further break down the escalation path into subcategories to make the process easier to follow. For example, there might be several different "flavors" of critical issues, such as these:

- Internal security issue
- External security issue
- Privacy issue
- Internal catastrophic system failure
- Client catastrophic system failure

This is a just a small example of how you might want to subcategorize each priority level. The nature of the problem might determine such things as who is contacted, the approval process for working on the issue, or how quickly action must be taken. Start with a basic list of four or five priority levels. They can always be expanded and refined later, after you have used the process for a while.

Once you have the escalation path's information fully defined, you need to define the notification procedures. Figure 8.8 is an example of an escalation notification. A full copy of this document is included in appendix B.

Notification					
Sequence	Contact/Name	Work Phone#	Home Phone#	Mobile/Pager #	Title/Description
Priority 1	1. Melanie Swan 2. George Webb 3. Leslie Hewitt	x1234 x4567 x6789	222-222-2222		Virtual Manager COO CIO
Priority 2	1. Melanie Swan 2. George Webb 3. Sammy Walker				
Priority 3	1.Melanie Swan 2. Peter Willow 3. Sammy Walker				
Priority 4	1. Melanie Swan 2. Peter Willow 3. Joan Oliver				

Figure 8.8: Escalation notification

The notification list might have different scenarios for different problems. The process might be that all three people are notified, or that the first person is contacted first. If he or she does not respond within a specified time limit, the next person on the list is contacted, and so on. If the team is global, time zones will need to be taken into account when deciding who should be called first. It might be acceptable to call someone immediately if it is during normal office hours in his or her local time, but not if it is between midnight and 5:00 AM, local time. The more clarity that is added to the escalation document, the more effective the process will be.

The escalation process should also contain a section to document roles and responsibilities and to clearly identify the process owner. The process owner is responsible for ensuring that the escalation process is working effectively and that it is being used appropriately. The process owner is also responsible for scheduling lessons-learned meetings to analyze the causes of issues and make recommendations for process improvements and actions to prevent the same or a similar issue from recurring.

Risk-Management Process

The risk-management process is designed to identify, manage, monitor, and prioritize risks on an ongoing basis. The process needs to be transparent so that everyone on the team has access to an "at a glance" view into the team's overall risk status.

The first step in creating a risk-management process is to define the procedures for identifying, evaluating, prioritizing, and creating action/contingency plans for risks. If the team is working on multiple projects at one time, the most effective way to manage the risks is to create a plan for each individual project and have the assigned project manager manage the individual plan. The virtual team manager should have visibility into all the risks, as the combination of those risks determines the overall risk level for the team.

A risk is something that might happen, and will cause a problem if it does. If it has already happened, it is not a risk. It is a disaster! Well, maybe not a disaster, but it is now an ongoing issue that needs to be managed. Once a risk becomes a reality, it very likely moves into one or more other processes, such as the escalation procedure and the change-control process. At that point, it no longer needs to be tracked as a risk unless it has the potential to intensify and become an even greater problem.

Virtual projects can sometimes carry a higher level of risk than traditional or local projects. The reason for this is the increased communication required to keep the work on track. For outsourced projects, there is always an increase in risk, as the virtual or project manager does not have direct control of the resources working on the project. Any language or cultural differences also need to be taken into account, since they might increase the risk level of the work being undertaken.

Identifying Risks

The identification of a risk can come from many sources. At the start of a project or contract, a list of risks should be compiled based on the information available at that time. If a process or product is being created, there will be risks related to the assumptions made during the planning part of that process. For example, home-renovation projects have a lot of risks. Those projects can easily run over budget and over the original timelines due to issues with availability of materials, inclement weather, delays in getting permits, the client adding or changing features, and so on. Those kinds of risks can be identified up front, as there is high probability that those problems will occur at least once during the project.

> For outsourced projects, there is always an increase in risk, as the virtual or project manager does not have direct control of the resources working on the project.

Any assumptions that are made based on questionable input should also be tracked as risks. For example, when estimating a home-renovation project, the homeowners might state that they will complete part of the work themselves. If the contractor is not confident of the homeowners ability to do this, he or she would list this as an assumption and as a risk, if there is a dependency built into the project plan on the work the homeowners have committed to doing. If there were no dependencies, then the contractor would not need to track this as a risk.

Spend a little time brainstorming with your team members about everything that could possibly go wrong. This will result in a huge list of possibilities. You should remove the highly improbable ones and focus on the things that really might happen.

Evaluating Risks

All risks should be evaluated to determine the following:

- The risk's criticality to the completion of the project
- The probability that the risk will occur

If the risk has low probability or is low risk, it doesn't need to be tracked. If either of those levels increases during the course of the project, the risk should be added to the plan. The remote team members need to monitor the risk log regularly to identify changes in the levels of specific risks.

Prioritizing Risks

Prioritization of risks comes next. The risks should be ranked in order of criticality. The prioritization should be constantly managed and updated. As new risks are added to the list and old risks removed, the rank of the risks will change dramatically. A risk that is a medium priority at the beginning of a project might become a critical priority as the project nears completion. Once again, the remote workers who are working on projects or contracts on a daily basis need to be aware of the current prioritization and know the process for increasing or decreasing the priority level for a specific risk.

Risk Action/Contingency Plan

The risk action/contingency plan is the most exciting part of the risk-management plan. It specifies exactly what action to take if the risk manifests. The plan should include steps to mitigate the risk. It should include an action plan on how to manage the risk, and contingency plans in the event that the action plan is unsuccessful.

More than one alternative option is advisable for critical risks. It is not unusual to see two or three alternative contingency plans identified for one high-priority risk. Why go to all the trouble of defining a plan for something that you are not even sure will happen? It is a good question, and there is a good answer. It is very hard to think straight and make reasonable assumptions and decisions when you are in the middle of a calamity. You might not have time to research alternative options when you are under pressure to resolve a problem

> It is very hard to think straight and make reasonable assumptions and decisions when you are in the middle of a calamity.

quickly. You should put as much effort into the planning as the risk level warrants. If a risk is only likely to lose you two days of productivity, you are not going to spend four weeks planning contingencies for it! On the other hand, if the risk has the potential to completely destroy the project or negate the contract, it is worthwhile putting in some effort to devise an alternative plan.

The Risk Log

Once you have identified, evaluated, and prioritized an initial set of risks, you need a way to manage them. The simplest way is to create a risk log, such as the example in Figure 8.9. A blank risk log is included in appendix B.

#	Description	Originator	Date Identified	Criticality	Probability	Priority	Mitigation Plan	Contingency Plan	Status
22	Contractor budget is cut	Melanie Swan	Jan 1st	High	Medium	1	Work with senior management to get budget approval to extend contractor contracts	1. Remove two features from plan 2. Move completion date out by 3 months	Active

Figure 8.9: Risk log

Create a risk log for each project. Make sure that each of your local and remote project managers gives a risk-management update at the regularly scheduled virtual team meeting. It is great way to get input into mitigation and contingency plans. Other team members might have experienced the same issues and have advice on how to minimize and manage the risk.

A simple way to minimize risk on your team and projects is to always be clear about expectations. If you want something from someone, tell that person exactly what you want and give him or her a specific date and time when you need it. Misunderstandings can create problems and delays, which turn into risks. If you can manage and control understanding and expectations, you will automatically reduce risk.

Documentation Processes

The documentation process will generally consist of three parts. The first part is a documentation plan that specifies what documentation is required and who is responsible for producing it. An example documentation plan is shown in Figure 8.10.

The second part includes documentation templates for each of the documents. These should be stored in a location that is easily accessible to all virtual team members, no matter what their location or travel status.

The third part is a document repository where all created documents are stored. These documents should be accessible to anyone who needs access. Some of the documentation might be confidential and should not be accessible to everyone on the team. Other documents might be approved for general internal distribution only. Others might be for internal and external distribution.

Documentation Plan

Document	Owner	Authorized To Update	Reviewers	Authorized Viewers	Communication Methods Allowed	Approver
Client Contract	Project Manager	Legal Dept. only	Project Manager, Client	Project Manager, Team Manager, Contracts Personnel, Legal Dept., Customer Relationship Manager	Regular mail only (no email)	Legal Dept., Contracts Dept.
Proposal	Project Manager	Project Manager	Project Team	Project Team	Email, Website	Project Manager, Team Manager
Communication Plan	Team Manager	Team Manager	Team	Team	Email, Website	Team Manager

Figure 8.10: Documentation plan

The virtual team members need to follow a consistent documentation process. As the virtual team manager, you are responsible for ensuring that the documentation tasks are scheduled and tracked. A well-organized document repository is essential to a virtual team.

It is often possible to use existing documents as a starting point for new ones, thereby decreasing the time needed to create the documents. If the team members have easy access to all project documents, they will be able to take full advantage of this reuse process. Be sure to let the team members know if document templates are updated, so they know to use a new template rather than starting from an existing document.

Process Management

Everyone knows where to go to find the process documents, but does everyone know exactly what processes exist? It is hard to know. The best way to remedy this is to create a master "team processes" document, with a list of each process, a brief description, and a link to the process document. This way, there is no searching in repositories to see if a process exists and deciding to do it "my own way" when a 10-second search does not culminate in success!

The team process document should be reviewed with each team member. If you have a new employee, you should review the documents and processes in detail with that person within the first few weeks of him or her coming on board.

A fun game to play with the team is "Team Processes Jeopardy." You create a list of Jeopardy-type questions based on the team's processes, procedures, roles and responsibilities, and so on, and hold a contest with prizes for the winners. It can be a lot of fun, although you will need a Web-based tool to create a virtual "buzzer." On conference calls, it might not be possible to do this very effectively. The competitive spirit that lives in most people will drive them to study the documents really hard so they can win the competition! You can also use this strategy for other important documents, like product roadmaps or strategic plans. An alternative to "Jeopardy" is to email to all team members a process-related question at a predefined time each day, or once a week, and see who sends the correct answer first. Reward the winner with a prize.

These strategies are an excellent way to ensure that team members understand and are using the processes. Team meetings are also good checkpoints for making sure processes are followed and understood. You can ask team members if the contract has been signed before approving travel to an onsite kickoff meeting. When an issue is discussed in a meeting, you can ask who the issue has been escalated to and what the results of the escalation were. It is helpful to all team members to discuss how situations and events are

> Processes should be designed to make life easier, make work more effective, decrease time, increase quality, and increase satisfaction.

linked to the process, as it increases familiarity and understanding of the processes.

If you have a policy to continually improve processes, you will be facilitating the understanding and use of the team processes. You can assign each team member a process to own, and ask them to solicit feedback from their teammates on how to improve it or increase its use. You could offer incentives and rewards for process improvements. Make the rewards applicable to how much money the improvement is making or saving the company. If you can make it worthwhile to your team members, they will want to do it!

Sharing best practices starts with good processes. The processes can be shared with other teams or with clients to smooth the progression of working with those other groups. It is a great way to give something of value so that you can receive something of value in return. It is a win-win situation.

Processes should be designed to make life easier, make work more effective, decrease time, increase quality, and increase satisfaction. If a process does not do at least one of these things, it should be reviewed and updated, or dropped altogether. A process that gets in the way of doing a good job is not a good process and should have no place on your team.

CHAPTER
9

Virtual Communication

Humans have been searching for better ways to communicate for thousands of years. A few hundred years ago, journeys that today would be considered a short hop took weeks or months to complete. As a result, people had to devise ways of communicating with others from a distance.

Some early virtual communication methods included fire and smoke, which are reported to have been used in ancient Greece and Israel as communication methods as long ago as 1,000 BC. Pigeons have also been used for thousands of years for carrying messages over long distances. A virtual-communication system that combined optical telegraphs and naval semaphores was very effective for many years in Europe. It was an innovative and efficient system, but a message could only be relayed as far as it could be seen. With the addition of telescopes, a message could be received up to 20 miles away. To send messages longer distances, it was necessary to set up multiple telegraph stations, so a message could be received and passed on continually until the message reached its destination.

Virtual communication has come a long way since the use of bonfires and semaphores. The uses for virtual communication have also changed enormously. No longer is this type of communication used merely to relay urgent messages to others over long distances; it is also used for everyday communication. In fact, virtual communication is often used even when it is not necessary. People instant message or phone each other when they are located next door to each other. People use online chat programs to talk with friends they see everyday. We are so used to these communication methods that we often intentionally substitute them for face-to-face communication. Some level of virtual communication works well for many people. It is convenient, quick, and generally cheap. Using only virtual methods of communication, however, has its challenges.

As mentioned earlier in this book, over 80% of communication is nonverbal. Not only do we communicate with what we say, but also with how we look and sound. A charismatic presenter will find it much more difficult to project his or her charisma in an audio-only presentation. The visual aspects of communication, such as eye contact, facial expressions, gestures, attire, and personal grooming, all contribute to what we perceive about the speaker, and what the speaker is saying. It also contributes to how much we remember about what has been said!

> There is a lot more to communication than arming each team member with a PDA, mobile phone, and email account.

The tactile nature of one-on-one communication also contributes a great deal to setting the tone and establishing rapport between team members. For example, some people are very demonstrative, and will greet each other by shaking hands, slapping on the back, hugging, or kissing on the cheek (or both cheeks, depending on the culture). Some people have a tendency to touch the arm of the person to whom they are speaking, or to nudge the person sitting next to them if something funny or unexpected occurs.

Most of these nonverbal forms of expression are not available to the virtual team. They are certainly not available on a regular basis, so the team has to learn how to function without them. The virtual team also has to learn how to cope with other communication challenges, such as language and cultural differences, and the practical difficulties of communicating with team members in other time zones and on different work schedules.

If you assume that your team members will be able to communicate with no problems as long as you provide adequate tools to enable communication, you are courting disaster. There is a lot more to communication than arming each team member with a PDA, mobile phone, and email account. The virtual manager must overcome the complexities of virtual communication and create an environment in which team members can communicate effectively and successfully. This is no small feat. It requires a significant effort on behalf of the manager and the members of the virtual team.

Communication Complexities

In addition to what we say, there are other elements to communication that are important to the virtual team. The combination of these different elements adds complexity and richness to communication. In the next two sections, we will go into more detail about the importance of the following two elements:

- ► Tone of voice
- ► Body language

We will discuss the importance of these elements in both face to face and virtual communication.

Tone of Voice

Tone of voice can communicate many things. It can indicate what kind of mood you are in, how you feel about a situation, or how you feel about an idea or suggestion that you are responding to. It can also be very deceptive. A loud tone of voice may indicate that you are angry when you may just be a little overexcited about what is being discussed. A quiet tone of voice may imply that you are very calm or are disinterested in what is being discussed when in reality the opposite may be true.

Americans can be very loud, raising their voices if they think they are not being understood or heard. It can be quite intimidating to be in a roomful of people who are all shouting as loudly as they can, interrupting each other, talking over one another, and generally just making a lot of noise. I don't think anyone would describe this as polite, or find this method of communication recommended in a business etiquette book. However, this kind of meeting behavior is prevalent in many companics. Some people seem to think if they shout louder than anyone else, they must be more right than anyone else.

It is just as easy to be understood when speaking in a normal tone of voice and being respectful to those around you. It is especially important to remember this when working on global teams. Other cultures consider it impolite to interrupt or to raise one's voice. Some cultures think it impolite to disagree with someone else in front of other people. People in those cultures would not dream of publicly disagreeing with a colleague!

If you are a remote worker calling into conference call, and a group of people are shouting or talking in raised voices, talking over one another and interrupting each other, it is almost impossible to understand what anyone is saying. If someone is shouting loudly, the remote callers have to turn the volume on their phones down so as not to be deafened. Then when a normal volume speaker starts to speak, they have to turn the volume up again so they can hear what is being said. The remote callers pretty much spend the whole phone conference continually turning the volume up and down and most likely not understanding very much of what is going on.

> Listen carefully to inflections in the voice to give you a clue as to how someone really feels about what is being discussed.

Tone of voice is not just how loudly or softly you speak. Listen carefully to inflections in the voice to give you a clue as to how someone really feels about what is being discussed. Keep things under control in your meetings, and ask people to wait their turn before speaking rather than interrupting others. Request that participants not raise their voices if they feel they are not being understood. You do not want other team members to feel intimidated, afraid, or insulted by impolite behavior. You most certainly do not want people to stop calling in to your meetings because they can never understand what is going on!

Body Language

Why would we talk about body language in a book about virtual management? Well, just because you have virtual team members does not mean that people will stop having body language. It is there, whether you are in the same meeting room together or on the phone and cannot see it. You still smile when you are happy or when someone says something funny or nice. You don't stop smiling just because everyone cannot see you.

Body language is similar to tone of voice, in that it can tell you a lot about how a person is feeling and what they are thinking. It can also be deceptive. You might think that the person sitting opposite you with her arms crossed is being closed and rigid, when she might just be cold!

For face-to-face meetings, try to look relaxed if you want others to feel relaxed. Sit back and unfold your arms. If you want to appear attentive, lean forward slightly toward the person who is speaking, to show that you are paying attention. Eye contact is important to some cultures, but considered rude in others. Do not make people feel uncomfortable by forcing too much eye contact. Body language is different in other countries just as spoken language is.

Nodding the head to signify agreement is common in some countries, but not so common in others. Some people might appear to be shaking their heads "no" or shrugging an "I don't know," when they are actually signifying a definite "yes." Others might be nodding because they knew what you were going to say. They are nodding to themselves that this was inevitable, not necessarily that they agree with what is being said. A grimace or look of resignation accompanying a nod should give you a clue that perhaps the person is not thinking, "Oh yes, boss, how right you are," but rather, "Oh dear, how right I was in thinking that this ridiculous plan was inevitable!"

> Some people might appear to be shaking their heads "no" or shrugging an "I don't know," when they are actually signifying a definite "yes."

What about people who smile or laugh when they are nervous? Or others who roll their eyes or raise their eyebrows? Are you sure they are surprised or disapproving? Possibly, but then again, possibly not.

In virtual meetings, you cannot see anyone (unless you are on a video conferencing call, of course). If you can only hear and not see, you cannot tell if someone looks tired, stressed, happy, sad, cold, or bored. Remember this if you are in a face-to-face meeting and also have remote attendees. If someone is being sarcastic in the meeting room, it might not be obvious to the people on the phone. You need to interject with a comment like, "The people on the phone cannot see that John is smiling. Please don't think that he *really* meant that!" This kind of comment helps the remote callers understand the mood and emotions in the room.

Earlier in the book, we used an analogy about a family who learned sign language because they had a deaf child. Imagine, if you will, that the child is blind instead of deaf. A family with a blind child spends a lot of time describing things to the child. They will talk about how a flower moves in the breeze, the color of rain, or how you cannot see the wind, just feel it.

In a meeting that includes both local and virtual participants, the meeting facilitator needs to be the eyes of the remote callers. If you are facilitating such a meeting, remember to include some commentary about what is happening in the room. Announce when someone enters or leaves the room. Explain to the remote callers when someone gets up to draw on the whiteboard, and try to describe what is being drawn. If someone has said or done something that makes everyone laugh, explain to the remote callers why everyone is laughing. The remote callers are like the blind child who doesn't know that someone just came into the room with a birthday cake for him until everyone starts singing "Happy Birthday."

Which Communication Method to Use in Which Situation?

It is frightening how often one can observe egregious uses of communication tools within the corporate world (and within the non-corporate world, too)! Just because a tool is available and right at your fingertips does not mean that it is an appropriate method of communication.

Etiquette and netiquette are essential at all times. It is rude to force others to listen to your cell phone conversations. If you have to take or make a call when in the company of others, excuse yourself and step outside the room first. If you have to respond to a text message or an email when you are in a meeting or a social situation, apologize and excuse yourself first. Better yet, let the person or people you are with know beforehand that you are expecting an urgent communication and that you will need to respond to it immediately. Then, you can politely excuse yourself later when the communication is received.

When considering the communication method, consider your current situation and whereabouts, as well as the type of information you need to communicate. It is extremely rude to leave your phone turned on in a movie theater, but even ruder to answer it and to engage in a conversation with someone! Don't allow yourself to become one of these people, no matter how important and vital to your company you have become.

> Sometimes it is more effective to schedule a meeting and avoid an email thread that is 100 messages long.

Before communicating, think carefully about what you need to communicate and the potential repercussions of the communication. Sometimes it is more effective to schedule a meeting and avoid an email thread that is 100 messages long. Or it might be more effective to send an email to one person than to discuss the topic in an audio conference with 10 other people. Sensitive information needs to be handled in a sensitive way. Over-communicating to get someone into trouble or make them look bad is unprofessional and unproductive. Using email to admonish someone about performance issues or to relay bad news is never appropriate. A review of appropriate communication methods is shown in Figure 9.1.

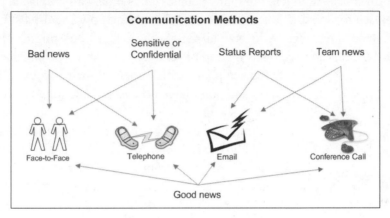

Figure 9.1: Communication methods

Effective Use of Email

Email is overused and abused. Most people would agree with this statement, but do not consider themselves in any way responsible for the current state of email affairs. We all think it is somebody else's fault, and we are the only ones who are using the tool appropriately. The dilemma is that no one seems to know how to fix the overuse and abuse problem. Many consider that the problem might be unsolvable, or that it is not a problem at all. The U.S. Postal Service delivers important mail, it also delivers a lot of junk. The thing is, what is considered junk by some people might be considered useful information by others. For example, you might consider those pages and pages of store coupons in your mailbox each week to be junk; your neighbor, however, might consider them to be one of the best things she receives in her mailbox each week.

And therein lies the key to this issue. We all think we get inundated with too much useless email, but we all have different ideas about what is "useless." This is why none of us is responsible for the problem. We all send useful information; it is others who send the junk! This is one reason that you should have a documented communication plan, as discussed in chapter 8, that defines stakeholder groups. It will help ensure that you are sending communications to people who care about what you have to say and not to those who don't!

Email is an excellent tool. Without it, we would probably not be working in the virtual business world at all. It helps team members keep in touch, and it helps families keep in touch. For many people, it has practically replaced the postal service for sending letters and cards. Pen-pals are now email-pals. Love letters have been replaced by love emails or cutesy "I love you" singing electronic cards. You can use emails instead of sending faxes, and you can use them to replace phone calls, especially when you are in a hurry and don't have time to get into long conversation on the subject.

Email is fast, efficient, and effective. However, it should be used wisely. Antibiotics were an outstanding invention. Used appropriately, they can quickly cure many diseases that used to be fatal. Overuse of antibiotics not only makes them ineffective, it can also exacerbate the initial cause of the illness, the bacteria, by making it stronger and resistant to the drugs. Inappropriate and overuse of email can also exacerbate an initial problem, causing it to escalate out of control. Once it gets out of control, it might be impossible to fix.

> We all think we get inundated with too much useless email, but we all have different ideas about what is "useless."

Email is a great tool to use for non-contentious communications. It is ideal for distributing status reports, informational emails, attached documents, agendas, and meeting minutes. All the information that years ago used to be communicated via interoffice memos can be sent much more easily and quickly via email today.

If content is sensitive in nature, ambiguous, or not suitable for a wide audience, it is wise not to put it into an email. Emails can be easily forwarded to others. If an email is confidential and should not shared, make sure the recipients know that.

You would never send out an email to let family members know that a loved one had died. That type of information would be relayed in person or, at the very least, by telephone. Likewise, you should not send bad news at work via email. If the company is laying off employees, they should not hear about it via email. If a team member needs to be reprimanded for bad behavior or substandard results, don't do it via email. Relaying bad news in person or by phone is much more appropriate. If you think that something you send in email will make a person want to call you immediately to discuss it, then don't send it in email in the first place!

If you have sent an email letting an employee know that he or she will not be receiving a bonus this quarter because of poor performance, how do you think the person will feel upon seeing the email? Will he or she call you to discuss it, or feel too uncomfortable or angry to call? What if the employee receives the email and is not able to get in touch with you for hours or days? How do you think that person will be feeling while waiting to talk to you about it? It is a really awful way to communicate bad news, and it is not going to do anything to help improve the situation.

If a matter is contentious, don't start a huge email chain to discuss it. Schedule a meeting instead. Things can get out of control and very emotional, and it is not possible to contain the emotion or set the tone via email. If you see a topic being discussed in email that is obviously contentious, stop it as soon as possible and schedule a meeting. These types of issues will not get resolved by sending emails. Different people will receive different threads of the email, and everyone will end up confused. Once the tone of the emails starts to get out of control, people might start to forward the messages onto others or blind-copy someone on their responses. The motivation behind this might be because they genuinely think it will help resolve the issue, it might be to get someone into trouble, cover themselves in case of repercussions, or try to make themselves look good. In other words, you don't know who is getting involved in these email threads and who is reading what you have written. Be very careful what you write, as you cannot take anything back in email. People can keep the emails for years, and something you say today might come back to haunt you in the future!

> If you are feeling angry or upset about something, do not write an email.

If you are feeling angry or upset about something, do not write an email. If you are angered or upset by something you just saw in an email, don't be too quick to write a terse response and hit the "Send" button. Think about what you want to communicate before you communicate it. Whatever you do, don't hit the "Reply to All" button unless what you want to say is truly appropriate for everyone to read. If you are upset or angry about something, wait until you have calmed down before taking any action. If you are feeling angry by something you read, the chances are that someone else is feeling the same way. Why not just email the person who wrote the message (without replying to all), informing him or her that you think the issue should be discussed in a meeting/audio conference instead of email? You can either ask that person to schedule the meeting, or you can you schedule the meeting yourself and invite him or her. Containing these issues as early as possible is essential to avoiding complete breakdowns in communication and a lot of angst and animosity on your team.

If you are seeing contentious emails that include outside clients, vendors, or partners on the recipient list, your highest priority should be putting a halt to them as soon as possible. The reputation of your company, as well as the individuals within your company, are at stake. An issue that is allowed to snowball can ruin business and personal relationships for life. One click of the "Send" button can instantly destroy careers.

Most companies have email policies that discuss the uses of email and define what things can and cannot be sent. Information sent outside the company might be restricted or might have a different set of rules than information sent internally. There are often rules about sending confidential documentation via email, discussing any aspects of security, and sending user names or passwords via email.

Email policies generally state that any communication sent or received using the company's email system is the property of the company. This means that none of your communications are private, whether sent inside or outside the company, and whether sent to business associates or to your mom! Even if you delete email, the company keeps a copy of it on the server, often for years. For this reason, we recommend that you do not use your company's email address for sending or receiving personal email and that you are conscientious about what you communicate in email.

If there is a problem in the workplace, it is well within the company's rights to review copies of all the emails and instant messages sent or received by, or between, specific employees. Lots of people lose their jobs after their employer sees the types of communications being sent via email. Suppose it is against the company policy to be sending personal emails or doing a bit of online shopping during work hours. It can mean dismissal if the employer finds that an individual has been sending and receiving a lot of personal email during work hours and has lots of email confirmations for online shopping during work hours. If your employer is paying you, it is your employer's time, not your own. Be careful how you use it.

Used appropriately, however, email can be a time-saving, highly efficient, and effective communication tool.

Effective Use of the Phone

Phones should be used for any communications that are not appropriate for email and cannot be done face-to-face. For the virtual team, the phone is used a lot to replace what on traditional teams would be face-to-face communications. Team meetings, client meetings, and even all-hands organizational meetings are done by phone. Sometimes, the phone is supplemented with other communication methods, such as video conferencing or online presentations.

When communicating via phone, pay attention to what is being said, and be "present" in the meeting at all times. When people call in for audio conferences and you can hear that they are multitasking by the "tap, tap, tap" of their keyboards, it is obvious they are not paying attention.

First, they should mute their phones so everyone else does not have to listen to the noise. More importantly, why are they calling in for a meeting if they cannot be bothered to listen and participate? Perhaps these people do not need to be in the meeting. If a meeting is online or via a phone conference, it should still be a structured meeting with an agenda and minutes. If the meeting has no objective, then cancel it. If it needs an hour of people's time, then it should be worth it to them spending the hour focused on the meeting. If all you are doing is an around-the-(virtual)-room status report, you might as well just send out an email that everyone can read in five minutes, rather than taking an hour each of their time. Effective use of virtual communication methods means using your own and everyone else's time in the most efficient way. Status meetings are necessary. Just make sure you know what status you want to discuss in a meeting before you call it.

> When people call in for audio conferences and you can hear that they are multitasking by the "tap, tap, tap" of their keyboards, it is obvious they are not paying attention.

For the virtual manager, the phone becomes an important link to team members. While a lot of communication can be accomplished via email or instant messaging, some communication is better suited to the phone. For example, one-on-one communication between you and an individual team member should ideally be conducted face-to-face, but as this is not often possible in a virtual environment, the phone is an excellent second choice. As with the team meetings, one-on-one meetings need some structure and objectives. The meeting owner is responsible for this. If you are the manager, you own the one-on-one meeting. Calling a team member and saying, "What shall we talk about?" is not a great way to start. Make sure that as the manager, you know what information you are looking for. You don't necessarily need a written agenda, but you should be able to tell your team member at the beginning of the meeting what you wish to discuss. For example, you might have the following conversation.

"Hello, John. How are you?"

"I am fine. How are you?"

"I am fine, thank you. Today I would like to get a status update from you on projects A, B, and C. I would also like to discuss the Henderson issue that arose earlier this week. I want to talk to you about some organizational changes that might be coming up in the next few weeks, and also to briefly discuss your objectives and growth and development plans to see how you are progressing with those. Is there anything you would like to discuss today?"

"Yes, I also wanted to discuss the organizational changes, as I think there might be some opportunities there for me to meet some of my personal goals."

"OK, that sounds good. We do have a lot to cover, so if we run out of time today, we can schedule some additional time tomorrow. How does your calendar look for the morning?"

This type of conversation sets the goals and objectives of the meeting. The manager is aware the allotted meeting time might not be sufficient and understands that discussions about new opportunities and achieving personal goals usually take more than five or 10 minutes. For this reason, he is letting the team member know ahead of time that he can meet tomorrow to continue the discussion, if necessary. Without this conversation, the meeting is not going to go as well. The team member might be dying to talk about the organizational changes, and if the manager doesn't know that, he might spend most of the time talking about the Henderson issue. The team member then feels like the opportunity slipped away.

Part of the responsibility of the virtual manager is ensuring that communicating virtually does not degrade the quality of the communication unnecessarily. Used appropriately and with the right balance of process and flexibility, the phone can be very effective for one-on-one meetings. It is critical, however, that both parties give 100% of their attention during the meeting. Neither should be reading or responding to emails or putting the other on hold to take other calls. Respect for each other's time is paramount.

When calling a team member for a nonscheduled chat, remember to ask the person if it is a convenient time to talk before you launch into a long diatribe. It could be that the team member is driving on a particularly difficult or dangerous part of the highway and is not able to give you the attention you need in order to have the conversation you have in mind. Alternatively, he or she could be on a conference call on the other line, or in a meeting, and answered your call as a courtesy in case it was urgent. Unless you had a conference call with the team member scheduled, and he or she is anticipating your call, don't expect that person to be instantly available and ready to drop everything to talk to you!

A big problem with telephone conversations is that you cannot see the other person, so it is hard to know how he or she is reacting to what you are saying. If you are talking about a contentious issue or discussing problems with the individual's performance in meeting review objectives, be sure that you are giving the other person time to think. If the line goes quiet, don't be tempted to jump in and keep talking. We all need to think before we respond. If you ask a question and then keep talking, how can you expect an answer? Some people need more time to think than others. Try to listen for changes in the voice or tone that indicate the person is angry, upset, or surprised. Emotions are often evident in the voice, but not as obvious as body language, so paying attention and listening carefully are extremely important. When in doubt, ask. If you think someone is upset but are not sure, ask. Don't ignore it.

> A big problem with telephone conversations is that you cannot see the other person, so it is hard to know how he or she is reacting to what you are saying.

If someone is getting bad news about his or her performance or is being reprimanded for the way he or she handled a situation, it is normal for the person to feel upset, annoyed, or embarrassed. Let the person know it is OK to express what he or she is thinking. This presents an ideal opportunity to use your active listening skills. Active listening is listening to what is being said, and repeating back what you have heard so that the person knows you have understood. It does not mean that you have to agree with the other person. Here is an example:

"David, I received a lot of complaints about the way you handled the Henderson issue. The client complained that you were not responsive to their requests for help. I had other complaints that your communication was abrupt and disrespectful and that you appeared to be more concerned with blaming others than with trying to resolve the issue as quickly as possible."

"The client is on my back the whole time. Nothing I do is ever going to satisfy them. None of this was my fault. The development team did not deliver on time. The sales team gave incorrect information to the client. Legal made changes to the contract that I didn't know about. I am really annoyed that everyone thinks this is all my fault."

"David, what I am hearing you say is that you feel the client is very difficult and is not satisfied with anything you do for them. You are also upset that the development team was late with its delivery. I am also hearing that you believe the client problem is due to sales giving incorrect information, and that the legal department made contractual changes without your knowledge. Is this correct?"

What usually happens next is David either continues ranting, in which case you repeat the active listening until he is finished, or David realizes that he needs to justify or tone down some of his earlier accusations and adds a little more context, perhaps retracts some of what he said or, in some cases, just agrees. Either way, David knows he has been heard. You have not agreed with anything he said; you have merely repeated back to him what he said to you. At this point, David should be listening to you, as he knows he has your attention and wants to hear what you have to say. This is the time to continue with some very clear guidance and expectations:

"David, I know you are upset, but as the virtual project manager for this contract, you are ultimately responsible for any issues that occur with it and for escalating to me if you are unable to resolve problems in a timely manner. This issue could have been managed more effectively and have had more positive results. The legal department sent you a copy of the final contract, which you approved. If you had reviewed the contract thoroughly, you would have known there were some changes made. In future, I would like you to read final contracts thoroughly before approving them. "

You would continue addressing each point David raised, giving specifics about necessary improvements. This type of conversation can be accomplished effectively on the phone, but only if you are focusing all your attention on the conversation. A virtual manager has to have these types of conversations via the phone, so you need to be comfortable communicating in this way. If problems are ignored or allowed to drag on indefinitely because you are avoiding conflict or want to wait until it is possible to meet face-to-face, problems will never get resolved. In our example, David was probably not happy after being reprimanded by his manager. However, the manager explained to David exactly what the problems were, how they could have been solved, and what expectations the manager had of David in managing and escalating issues.

Though the circumstances are not ideal, the manager has given David a growth and development opportunity. David now has a chance to improve his performance, thereby giving him the potential to enhance his career prospects. If the manager ignored this incident, David would never have known what he had done wrong or how he could do it better in future because he would not have understood what his manager expected of him. If David is not given the opportunity to improve his performance, he will continue to make bad decisions, and his career prospects will decline. A manager who allowed that to happen would have clearly failed in his or her responsibilities. If David is given this opportunity to improve and does not take it, then David will have let himself down.

Be sure you are paying total attention in a discussion like this. It should never happen in email or via instant messaging!

Effective Use of Cell Phones

Cell phones are overused and abused almost as much as email, which has led to the current situation in many cities around the world, where cell phone chattering is creating its own type of noise pollution. The constant noise of people having long, drawn out, and often very loud telephone conversations in public places has reached almost epidemic proportions. It is not possible to find much peace and quiet anywhere these days! It used to be that if you were on a long train or bus journey, you could while away the hours reading a book in relative silence. These days you need to plug your ears first, or you will be trying to read while having to listen to three or four phone conversations at the same time.

What happened to nice relaxing dinners in quiet restaurants? You can hardly go five minutes these days without someone's cell phone ringing out an entire Tchaikovsky symphony or the latest rap song. Even worse is that many people take the calls and are not even polite enough to leave the restaurant while they talk. Consequently, everyone in the room is subjected to their loud telephone conversation. Unfortunately, the general public's lack of common courtesy has led to many public and private institutions having to implement strict cell phone policies. It is rather amusing that many establishments now display "no cell phone" signs along with their "no smoking" signs, as shown in Figure 9.2.

Figure 9.2: No cell phones!

Cell phones have a tendency to cut in and out, making it difficult to maintain a consistent connection, especially if the person is on the move. If the person using the cell phone is in a public place, it might not be appropriate for him or her to be participating in a phone conference or even on a one-on-one phone call. First, the caller could be annoying everyone around him or her with a loud conversation. Second, the content of the call might not be suitable for discussion in a public place.

Using a cell phone while driving has been discussed in an earlier chapter. It is not something we advise, for safety reasons as well as for the concentration and focus factor. It is not possible to devote sufficient attention to a phone conference while devoting sufficient attention to driving. One or both are going to suffer.

For remote team members who are traveling, cell phones are great ways to communicate. They are also great for "finding" people when they are not answering their landline phones. This can be abused quite often. You will find that people are being called on their cell phones because they stepped away from their desk for five minutes to visit the restroom or get a cup of coffee. Often, the interruption is for something that the caller could easily have left a message about. Calling someone who just went out to lunch or during the evening because you happen to still be working and want an answer to a non-urgent question right now is being disrespectful of that person's time. Save the cell phone calls for when they are really needed.

Face-to-Face Communication

Virtual managers get very little face-to-face time with their virtual team members. For this reason, it is imperative to use any available face-to-face time to its best advantage.

If you have devastating news that will affect the members of the team, tell them in a face-to-face meeting, if possible. Not only is it easier to gauge their reactions in person, but they also have each other to talk to about the situation. Devastating news would be things like the company laying off employees, the cancellation of a major project or contract that jeopardizes the future of the team or the company, the company moving to a new location (which threatens jobs), or the company changing from or to a virtual company. In these kinds of situations, the manager needs to do some damage control. Having the team members all in the same place will facilitate this.

Team building events are a great way of making good use of precious face-to-face time. Most virtual or blended teams have very few times when they can all be together in person in the same room. Make the most of that time by facilitating team bonding and encouraging the team to have fun. One mistake that a lot of virtual managers make is to get the whole team together in one location for one or two days and to focus the entire time on work.

There is not much exciting about a two-day business trip comprised of team and client meetings, with a working dinner squeezed in.   See example agenda in Figure 9.3.

Offsite Meeting Agenda

Day One: Team Meeting
8.00 - 8.30	Introduction
8.30-10.30	Group Brainstorming
10.30-12.00	Breakout Brainstorming Session #1
12.00-1.00	Lunch and Presentations of Breakout Session #1
1.00-3.00	Breakout Brainstorming Session #2
3.00-4.00	Presentations of Breakout Session #2
4.00	Meeting Adjourned
4.00-6.00	Break
6.00-10.00	Team Dinner and Discussion about Current and Upcoming Projects

Day Two: Client Meetings
8.00-10.00	Client A Meeting
10.00-11.00	Debrief
11.00-3.00	Client B Meeting (Including Lunch)
3.00-3.30	Debrief
3.30	Meeting Adjourned

Figure 9.3: Offsite meeting agenda

With this agenda the team will spend a total of 12 hours together on day one and seven hours on day two. Of the total 19 hours together none of it is allocated to team building or getting to know each other.

With luck, some team members might find a few minutes here and there to speak to one another and work on the team-building and bonding process. It is great to have all-hands business meetings in person, but if those happen exclusively and at the expense of team-building time, the team will not build the strength and rapport it needs to be most effective. Time is precious, and nothing is free. If you want a productive, motivated, close-knit team, you have to invest the time needed to create it.

> There is not much exciting about a two-day business trip comprised of team and client meetings, with a working dinner squeezed in.

Lessons-learned meetings are also best done in face-to-face meetings. It is possible to hold a lessons-learned meeting virtually, but it is not as effective as having the team members in the same room. If the meeting is going to contain some controversial topics, which many do, it will be much easier to get honest and open feedback from participants if they are in the same room. Lessons-learned meetings that really get to the heart of issues tend to get quite emotional. This is not necessarily a bad thing. People tend to get emotional about things they care about. Expressing that emotion in such a setting can be a positive experience for the team, provided the facilitator is managing the meeting so that the emotion doesn't get out of control or become negative.

Meeting face-to-face with the team members is an ideal time to study body language and to start understanding how team members feel about each other and about the things the team is working on. The interaction among the team members creates the dynamic on the team. As the virtual manager, it is imperative that you are in tune with the team dynamic and are able to recognize where problems might exist. This will enable you to continue to work on those issues when the team is once again interacting virtually.

Project Meetings

Project meetings might be strictly internal, or they might include the client, vendors, outsourcers, and members of other teams. Project meetings should be structured and well-managed. The meeting's objective should be to discuss the status and progress of the project. The manager for the project should create a meeting agenda that is sent out to the attendees in advance. The manager should also write up the minutes of the meeting and distribute them to the meeting stakeholder list within a couple of days of the meeting.

Project meetings will mostly be virtual, with some, if not all, team members calling in remotely. Only things that relate directly to the specific project should be discussed in these meetings. Team members must be disciplined in not talking about internal company issues or other projects during a project or client meeting. When the team members are calling in for audio conferences, it is important to be aware of who else is on the call and to ensure that there is no discussion about topics that are not relevant to that project, or that might be damaging in some way.

If a team member wants to stay on the line at the end of the meeting to have a more private discussion with another team member, make sure the team members know to hang up and call each other directly rather than staying on the line. You don't know who else is listening in, and if the topic is not relevant to everyone who was involved in the last meeting, it should not be discussed in what is in effect an "open line."

The meeting facilitator should ensure that the meeting stays on track, that only one person speaks at a time, and that side conversations or detailed conversations are taken offline so the meeting can continue on schedule. Offline topics and subjects can be put in a "parking lot" during the meeting, so they are not forgotten. These topics can then be taken as action items for someone to follow up later, in a separate meeting.

Team Meetings

The virtual team should have regularly scheduled meetings. Ideally, these meetings will be held at least once a week. Most of your meetings will be virtual, or a combination of virtual and local if you are a hybrid team. You should plan a local team meeting if the team members are going to be in the same location for any period of time.

From time to time, it is nice for the team to discuss a few ad hoc topics during the team meeting. These might be related or unrelated to current work. Allowing conversation during the meeting to meander for a while can be beneficial to team building, as long as it doesn't cause the meeting to deviate too far from the agenda.

It is important that you, the manager, are not the one doing all the meandering. A manager should never dominate a team meeting with chitchat about things that only he or she is interested in. For example, having a 20-minute conversation each week about a football game or the state of management in sports these days might not be the best use of your virtual team time. Some team members might find this interesting, but others will be bored out of their minds. They will not want to spend half of the team meeting each week listening to the latest moans and groans about sports from their manager! You need to find some common ground and common interests that you can touch on for five minutes or so. This is more challenging if your team members are located in different countries. For U.S.-based virtual teams, television shows can be good topics. With cable and satellite being so widely available, the same shows are often being watched around the world—sometimes at the same time!

It is usually possible to find some common interest shared by at least 80% of the virtual team. On some teams, it is music, on others it is television, and for others it is cooking, camping, scuba diving, sky diving, baseball, or golf. If you look hard enough, you will find something that will interest most people enough to spend five or 10 minutes talking about it. Once you find a commonality among team members, you need to build on it, using it as more glue to hold the team together. Eventually, you create a "super glue," and hardly anything will be able to tear your team apart. This should be your ultimate goal!

Some weekly team meetings consist of the manager talking, and talking, and then talking some more about all the things that have occurred in the last week. The team members will already know most of the content of these meetings, as they have been in at least one other meeting that week where the same topics were discussed. These are not productive or useful meetings. The team meeting should not be a soapbox for the team manager, whether the topics are work-related or not!

Send out agendas for your meetings to help keep things moving along smoothly and efficiently. Remember to ask if anyone needs to leave the meeting early. That way, you can adjust the agenda to make sure you cover the things you particularly want that person involved in early in the meeting. Generally, when a meeting has no agenda, nobody types up meeting minutes, either. This means that people who can't attend all or part of the meeting not only don't know what they are going to miss beforehand, they never find out what they missed after the fact.

> It is usually possible to find some common interest shared by at least 80% of the virtual team.

The team meeting is a great venue to discuss the highlights of the week and the overall status of the team and related projects. It is not necessary to spend a whole hour talking about every aspect of everyone's status. The team members can all read the status reports they receive from you in email. The team meeting should be used to discuss in more detail any aspects of the report that might have implications for other team members or other projects, and to give the team members an opportunity to ask questions about anything they do not understand.

The team meeting is for the team. This meeting should not just be canceled whenever something else comes up. Keeping a virtual team focused on the same things and working toward common goals requires a lot of good-quality communication among the team members. Make the team meeting a priority, and schedule it at a time that is convenient for as many team members as possible. Sometimes, time zones make it very difficult to schedule one meeting that works for everyone. In this case, the virtual manager might have to schedule multiple meetings with the various team members grouped into complementary time zones.

The team should consider the team meeting the most important one of the week. And, hopefully, the most interesting!

Never use the team meeting to discuss a team member's performance issues, or to reprimand someone for bad results or behavior. Those types of conversations should be personal. They should never be raised as topics for discussions in group meetings. Likewise, do not tolerate any bad-mouthing about other groups, clients, or partners in the team meeting. If the meeting becomes a place to go when you want to complain about things or people, it is going to be very negative. Nobody is going to have a warm and fuzzy feeling about attending it!

Weekly Status Reports

Weekly status reports are essential for virtual teams. How will anyone know what anyone else is doing if it is not being communicated? Weekly status reports should be prepared by each team member for the virtual manager. The virtual manager then prepares and distributes status reports to the various stakeholder groups.

Many companies require time-and-expenses reporting by their employees. Teams working on billable-hours projects must report all hours spent working on client projects. These might be included as part of the weekly status report, or each assigned project manager might have to create a separate report for each project weekly or monthly.

Status reports should contain just the right amount of information for each group of stakeholders. The objective for each status communication should be contained in the communication plan, so the level of granularity required in the reporting should be clearly understood. Communication plan and status reports are covered in detail in chapter 8.

Presentations and Reporting

If you have ever spent a lot of time designing and creating a really amazing PowerPoint presentation, you know that it is great if you can then present it to a room full of people. Unfortunately, the virtual team environment does not often allow this method of delivery. This does not mean that you cannot give visual virtual presentations. It just means that you have to do so virtually. As discussed previously, presentations can be given online very effectively. A Web presentation accompanied by an audio conference can be a very successful way of communicating important or complex information that is not as easily communicated in a hands-off manner.

For global or cross-cultural teams, be particularly aware of using difficult to understand expressions or analogies in online presentations.

Hands-off methods of sharing presentations with team members include Webinars that you can record using slides and audio and make available via the Web. These presentations can then be viewed at-will by team members. You can also use online virtual management Web spaces and tools to share presentations. A more basic method is to send the presentation out to the meeting attendees who can watch the presentation on their own computer screens or using a print out while dialed in for an audio conference. This method means that participants do not have to be online to participate as long as they have access to a phone and have the print out available.

Formal presentations are not necessary for much of the status reporting but might be necessary for some of the less frequent executive reporting or client reporting that is required. Following are some examples of meetings that typically include formal presentations.

- ➤ Project proposal meetings
- ➤ Project kickoff meetings
- ➤ Executive status reports
- ➤ Sales presentations
- ➤ Client presentations
- ➤ Financial and budget reporting
- ➤ Project acceptance meetings
- ➤ Training

Ensure that virtual presentations are understandable and do not contain too much jargon or colloquialisms. Consider your audience when preparing a presentation and ensure that it uses terms generic enough to be easily understood by the intended audience. For global or cross-cultural teams be particularly aware of using difficult to understand expressions or analogies in online presentations.

Communicating Bad News

It is no fun communicating bad news. From time to time, however, it has to be done, and it is the manager's job to do it as effectively as possible. In an ideal world, all bad news would be communicated face-to-face. In the real "virtual" world, this is not always possible. The next best thing to face-to-face is on the phone.

If the news affects the whole team, you can communicate it to everyone in an audio conference. If the news affects some team members more than others because, for example, some of the team members will lose their jobs or have a new manager, those people should be told before the rest of the team. There is nothing worse than receiving devastating news publicly and feeling as though you cannot ask the types of questions you need to ask. Team members are more likely to ask questions when they feel they are in the same situation as their counterparts.

> Never send bad news in email. It is a terrible thing to do.

It would be great if you could speak individually to each team member before talking about bad news in a group setting, but this does not always work well. By the time you are telling the fourth person on your list, persons 1, 2, and 3 have already told the rest of the team, despite you asking them not to talk about it. Most people find it very hard to keep secrets. As much as people dislike hearing bad news, they love to spread the word about it, as long as they are not going to be held accountable for the problem they are communicating. For this reason, it is usually better to make a team announcement and let everyone hear the news at the same time.

Never send bad news in email. It is a terrible thing to do. We have said this before, but it bears repeating because it is very important. Nobody wants to hear bad news in an email. If an unexpected meeting is scheduled, people often wonder if some bad news is coming and can at least brace themselves for it. An email gives the reader no time to prepare. He or she might have received 150 emails that morning, hadn't even read the email yet, and found out the bad news when someone on another team asked for details! Bad-news meetings need to allow the time and opportunity for people to ask questions. Consider the setting before deciding to go ahead and make the announcement.

Here is a real-life example of bad news being communicated in a really bad way: The virtual team members were all in the same location for a couple of days, and the VP of the group planned a team lunch. It had been some time since the team had been together, so everyone was excited about a team event at a nice restaurant overlooking the ocean. The team members arrived at the lunch location in dribs and drabs and were happy chatting about what they had been doing since they had last seen each other. The VP was a bit late arriving, so the team members were in full swing with appetizers and drinks by the time she arrived, accompanied by the team's business director. Just as everyone was settling down to their entrees, the VP said she wanted to make an announcement. She announced that the director was leaving. Two of his direct reports were sitting at the table; neither had any idea that he was leaving.

> People skills, compassion, and common sense should play a major role in deciding where, when, and how to communicate bad news to your team members.

The VP then mentioned some people who were being considered for the director's job, which was also astonishing to the two direct reports sitting very quietly at the table, shocked by the news. It was now being announced publicly who their new manager might be. Most of the people at the table were looking at the two direct reports to gauge their reaction. Understandably, they both just looked stunned and amazed. The rest of the team were confused, not understanding how such an announcement could be made without the direct reports knowing about it beforehand. It was a miserable team lunch for everyone, especially for the two direct reports, who had a million questions to ask but were not prepared to ask them in front of the whole team. This is a guaranteed way to spoil a really nice team outing.

In a well-managed organization, the team members would enjoy their nice lunch, without any unexpected announcements. Later that afternoon or the next morning, the director would speak to his direct reports in person. Then, the VP would call a team meeting to make the announcement to the rest of the team. There would have been good memories of the last time the team was all together for an outing, rather than it being tainted with bad news.

People skills, compassion, and common sense should play a major role in deciding where, when, and how to communicate bad news to your team members. Think about how you would feel if you were in their shoes. Take that into account before rushing in and blurting something out. Not only can you soften the blow of bad news, you also keep the respect of your team. If you treat them with respect and consideration, they will do the same for you.

Virtual Politics

There is not much anyone can do about politics in the workplace, regardless of whether that workplace is virtual or traditional. Pretending politics don't exist will not make them go away. With good-quality management, you can reduce the effect of politics in everyday work life, but you cannot eradicate it altogether.

It is important to understand what politics are, why they exist, and how they manifest themselves in the virtual environment. This knowledge is necessary to help you figure out what political maneuverings are occurring and to anticipate their impact. You might not be able to stop what is happening, but you can at least plan to deal with the after-effects.

It is critical to recognize that we all play a part in company politics, whether we like to admit it or not!

Understanding Company Culture and Politics

Unlike governmental politics, there is nothing democratic about company politics. You don't get to vote on who gets to be the boss or who gets to be the boss's "favorite." You do, however, get to decide if you want to continue working for the company or move to a company with different politics. It is not always as easy to move countries if you decide you do not like the politics of your president or prime minister. You cannot get away from politics in the workplace; you merely trade one set for another.

Company culture is a major contributor to company politics. The type of culture defines the type of politics. Companies with very rigid hierarchies and top-down management tend to have a lot more obvious political maneuvering than those with less hierarchy and more bottom-up decision-making. A culture

> You cannot get away from politics in the workplace; you merely trade one set for another.

that encourages open and honest discussion and feedback without fear of retribution is going to have less visible politics than one that does not. Bear in mind that just because the politics are not immediately obvious, does not mean they do not exist. Manipulative politics can be as detrimental to a company or team as "in your face" politics. That which is more difficult to quantify is more difficult to manage and control. You are more likely to encounter manipulative than "in your face" politics on the virtual team. There are many factors that can maximize or minimize the potential for company or team politics. See Figure 10.1.

Maximizes Politics	Minimizes Politics
Internal competitiveness	Focus on teamwork
Manager competes with team members	Manager grows and develops team members
Manager favors some team members	Manager is fair and unbiased
Animosity among cross-functional teams	Foster respect and teamwork across functional units
Finger pointing and blaming	Focus on solutions rather than apportioning blame
Gossiping and spreading rumors	Team does not participate in spreading rumors
Personal agendas	Focus on team success not individual success
Focus on individual accomplishments	Focus on team accomplishments
Lack of respect for co-workers	High level of respect among team members
Lack of open communication & fear of retribution	Embrace open and honest feedback
High level of conflict	Proactive conflict management and resolution

Figure 10.1: Maximizing or minimizing politics

We all have our own agendas. The members of a virtual team are no exception. For some, the agenda is very selfish—it's all about getting ahead, at any cost. For others, the agenda is focused on doing a great job and getting personal recognition or rewards. Some people just want to do their work everyday, go home, relax, and not get in anybody's face. Politics comes from these personal agendas. The driving force behind people is the driving force behind politics. Whether you are liberal, middle-of-the-road, conservative, or uncommitted, you cannot completely escape politics. Company politics are about getting what you want and influencing others to want the same things, so that you have a better chance of getting things going your way.

Virtual politics are not much different than non-virtual ones, except that it is not as easy to see what is going on "behind the scenes." It is very difficult to keep tabs on who is in cahoots with whom.

Don't get lulled into a false sense of security that, because your team is virtual, politics will not be a part of daily work life. It might take longer for the alliances to form, but they will form.

Some people are more apt to politicking than others. Some personality types thrive on gossip and rumors. They will stop at nothing to spread the word about any little tidbit they get, regardless of how authentic they might think it is. We all know at least one person who fits this category. It could be a coworker, family member, friend, or neighbor. This is the person you go to if you want to know anything about anyone. If that person doesn't know, you can rest assured that nobody else does, either! These people can be fun to know. They tell you lots of juicy gossip and interesting facts that you really shouldn't know about people. However, they also fuel the flames of discontent, exacerbate negative situations, and increase the political unrest within their environment. If this person works on your team, you are going to have a lot of virtual politicking zooming around the various virtual networks!

> Don't get lulled into a false sense of security that because your team is virtual, politics will not be a part of daily work life.

How Your Team Creates Its Own Politics

Small, entrepreneurial companies tend to be less political than large corporations. Smaller companies need good-quality teamwork to be successful. Having said that, smaller companies can be rife with politics if the principals or managers of those companies are highly competitive within the organization. A group of people competing against each other is not going to be a very successful team. Who determines whether a team has internal competitiveness? The manager does!

The manager has the highest level of influence over the team's culture and politics. You might find this hard to believe if you are the manager of a team of 10 or 20 people within an organization that has thousands of employees. It is true that the organization's culture and politics will contribute to the team's culture and politics, but one does not dictate the other unless the manager allows it. The manager can override much of what happens in other parts of the organization by building a strong and supportive team, where the culture inside the team has a stronger influence than the culture outside. This is true whether the culture inside the team is more positive or more negative than the outside culture. The manager's role should be to ensure that the team's culture is always more positive than the organization's culture. This is how you build and maintain a successful and happy team. The happier and more successful the team becomes, the less influence outside negativity or politics will have on it.

The manager should not complain or compete. It doesn't matter if the manager has an idea that is better than someone else's. As the manager, it is not your job to always be right. It is your job to grow and develop your team members, to help them come up with the best ideas. Give them clues to keep them on the right track, rather than telling them they are wrong and explaining what the right way should be. Let your team members take credit for great ideas, even if you helped to develop them.

You demonstrate good teamwork by applauding the results of great team efforts rather than encouraging the team members to continually try to outdo each other. Good teamwork leaves much less room for politics to squeeze their way in. As soon as there is a sign of weakness, the politics will creep in, widening the gaps until the cracks become chasms, and building up molehills until they are the size of mountains.

If the spirit of the team is one of everyone being out for themselves and trying to get noticed, team members will start to feel insecure and self-conscious about their work. This will mutate into feelings of unhappiness, anger against each other, and a desire to do whatever it takes to be the next person who is applauded for doing a great job. When the driving force on a team is the competitiveness among team members, people can get amazingly creative. Unfortunately, this creativity is not channeled into doing great work; it is channeled into getting noticed. This can result in little business benefit from the creative ideas being generated.

Trying to get noticed can manifest itself in many ways. One way is to become one of the boss's favorites. You know how that goes. You tell the manager how great she is, she thinks you are marvelous, and suddenly you can do no wrong! Sometimes people skip a management level and go directly to the manager's boss to form some kind of special bond. The rules for creating and maintaining this bond often include telling on team mates, telling on the manager, repeating things that others have said that puts them in a bad light (especially if it was something about the big boss), spreading rumors, gossiping, and generally making others look bad. At this point, you have a full-scale political problem on your team. Nobody trusts anybody else. Nobody really knows who is saying what to whom. Sometimes, people will lose their jobs over this. People are mysteriously laid off or leave to "pursue other opportunities" or to "spend more time with their families." Once it gets to this point, the outside influences on the team are as strong, if not stronger, than those inside the team.

If a situation is this bad, team members will not be happy. Some will be looking for other jobs. The feeling on the team will be that nothing can be done to make things better because the problem is endemic within the organization. In reality, a lot can be done. As the manager, you might not be able to change what happens outside of your team, but you can shape the culture of your team so that it protects the team members from the negative outside influences. As we have mentioned before in this book, a manager's job is to remove roadblocks that make it hard for team members to complete their tasks, to offer support and guidance, and to provide an umbrella that protects the team from all the debris falling down from above. Inspiring a positive culture and protecting your team from the ravages of internal politics will go a long way toward accomplishing these goals.

As the manager, you still have to deal with the politics outside of your team, but it helps if you are not also dealing with a high level of angst on your own team. Save all your political energy for handling those outside issues and protecting your team members from them as much as possible.

Some very small changes on a team can make a huge difference to how well the team functions :

- ► No complaining about or blaming each other or other teams.
- ► No superstars or superstar behavior.
- ► No reprimanding anyone in front of others.
- ► No rewarding or congratulating individual results in team meetings, unless it is for something unrelated to what the team is working on.
- ► No comparing team members to each other.
- ► No derogatory remarks about team members or stakeholders.
- ► No thinking or assuming you are better than someone else. All jobs are vital to the organization.

Implementing and following these basic rules can have a very positive effect on the team culture and morale. Post a print-out of the rules on your notice board as a constant reminder of the rules. See Figure 10.2.

Rules
No complaining about or blaming each other or other teams.
No superstars or superstar behavior.
No reprimanding anyone in front of others.
No rewarding or congratulating individual results in team meetings, unless it is for something unrelated to what the team is working on.
No comparing team members to each other.
No derogatory remarks about team members or stakeholders.
No thinking or assuming you are better than someone else. All jobs are vital to the organization.

Figure 10.2: Rules

Let's talk in a bit more detail about these rules, and why they are important.

No Complaining About or Blaming Each Other or Other Teams

It is very disrespectful, not to mention unprofessional, to complain or blame people for mistakes or problems. Nobody goes to work planning to do a bad job every day. None of us really understands the challenges and stresses of someone else's job. Even if we do the same job, we experience our lives and work differently. Consequently, one person cannot know with complete certainty how someone else feels or is affected by any situation. On a virtual team, you have even less idea what kind of problems or stresses others are trying to manage as part of their daily work or personal lives. It is imperative that the team members are cognizant of this.

If you are unhappy with a result from another person or team, it is OK to express disappointment, but it is not OK to make disparaging remarks about the team or individual. If you set a bad example by badmouthing others in front of team members, you are setting a negative tone, and the complaining and blaming will become part of your team's culture (and politics). Likewise, turning a blind eye when other team members behave this way is the same as condoning the behavior.

The way to deal with a situation in which you are disappointed by the outcome is to talk to the person or people responsible, explain your position, and see if you can work together to solve the problem. If you encourage your team members to take a positive and proactive approach to solving problems, and lead by example, there will be no need for any backstabbing, badmouthing, or secret allegiances.

No Superstars or Superstar Behavior

When you allow someone to become the team's superstar, you are giving that person preferential treatment. If the person is contributing more to the team than others, it is fair that he or she should be appropriately compensated. Presumably, you are paying the high performing and senior members of your team more than the other members. If this is the case, it is appropriate that the more highly paid team members should be contributing more. It does not also entitle them to preferential treatment.

If you allow superstar behavior, you are encouraging a competitive culture and politics inside the team. Team members will start to resent the superstar, and possibly think he or she is not so "super," after all. Other team members might perceive the superstar as stealing their ideas and doing whatever it takes to maintain the superstar position on the team. If you see the person as a superstar no matter what the person is currently contributing to the team, you are creating a monster. The superstar is now being treated preferentially because of status and not because of merit.

Team members who hear you talk on every conference call about how great so-and-so is will soon get tired of it. Superstardom encourages bad behavior. Over time, this decreases a team's efficiency, productiveness, and collaboration, and thereby its chances of success.

No Reprimanding Anyone in Front of Others

It should go without saying that reprimands must be kept private, but we still see them given publicly. Some managers feel that team members will be motivated by the fear of being embarrassed in front of their team mates to complete tasks on time and with high quality. In reality, this is not true at all. If you embarrass someone in front of his or her peers, that person will feel resentful, angry, and self-conscious. This will not increase productivity or quality. Team members are more likely to try to hide problems or to shift the blame if they fear being made an example of in front of others.

> Some managers feel that team members will be motivated by the fear of being embarrassed in front of their team mates to complete tasks on time and with high quality.

A manager should not allow team members to degrade each other in public, either. If no one is allowed to make mistakes, then there will be little learning, development, or innovation on the team. When we say "in public," we mean in person, in audio or video conferences, online, or in email. Telling someone off in email and copying his or her manager or peers is inexcusable. Never allow yourself to do this, and coach your team members to ensure that they do not do this, either.

No Rewarding or Congratulating Individual Results in Team Meetings

We feel that it is important not to reward or congratulate individuals in team meetings unless it is for something unrelated to what the team is working on. This is one rule that many people might disagree with initially. However, once you give it some thought, you will understand the reasons behind it.

Imagine that you are the manager of a virtual team, and you are running your weekly team meeting. You know that one of your team members has just completed a really successful kickoff meeting with a client for a key project. You tell everyone how great the person is, what a fantastic job he or she did, etc. Meanwhile, the rest of the team members are listening to this and thinking about all the great things they have done in the last year, month, or week. They are wondering why you never mentioned all those great things.

One team member might be wondering why he was not mentioned as the one who stayed up for two nights in a row getting the wrinkles ironed out of the product so it would be perfect for the kickoff meeting (that he was not involved in). Another team member might be thinking about the fact that it was her idea to create this product specifically with this type of client in mind, but her name has never been mentioned in a team meeting in relation to this project. Maybe a more junior team member is upset because he has conducted five successful kickoff meetings in the last month, albeit for smaller clients. He might think that the person being congratulated had an easy time of it, with only one kickoff meeting to conduct this year. Nobody will say anything, but everybody will be feeling a little disappointed that their contributions were not considered important enough to be mentioned in the team meeting.

This situation again can create competitiveness and resentment on a team. Even if you try to name everyone who was involved in a specific success, you will probably miss some people. If you asked, you would find that everyone on team feels that they made some kind of contribution to the overall result. It is like assuming that the only person on a football team who deserves any praise is the person who scores the goals. In reality, the entire team should be credited for a win, not just individual players. Other players, the coach, the manager, and a lot of other behind-the-scenes people contributed to the success.

It is much more appropriate (and safer) to talk about *all* the great things the team has achieved recently, rather than mentioning specific people. The big kickoff meeting was obviously a success for the team. Mention it as a team effort, and thank the person who acted as presenter at the meeting for taking on that role. Mention the other successful kickoff meetings this month and all the people who worked hard to achieve them. Teamwork deserves team praise.

> Individual praise should be given individually. Team praise should be given publicly.

If a team member has accomplished something unrelated to what the team is working on, it is easy for the rest of the team to feel genuine admiration, pride, and/or happiness for that person. For example, perhaps a team member just made it onto the Olympic ski team, finished in the top ten in a marathon, has been awarded a patent for an invention, just got married, or had a baby. These are things that the team can celebrate together with no resentment or competitiveness.

Individual praise should be given individually. Team praise should be given publicly.

No Comparing Team Members to Each Other

Comparing team members is an awful thing to do, whether it is done publicly or privately. Never tell someone, "If only you could be more like Peter," or, "If you try to be more like Jane when you are presenting, you will be more successful."

The only thing comparisons like this accomplish is to make us intensely dislike the person we are being compared to for being so "perfect." Comparisons are bad enough in private meetings, but in a team setting, it is even worse. People do this more than they realize. They say things like, "You did such a great job. If you continue like that, you will be as good as Peter soon." This started out as a nice compliment, but ended up with a comparison to someone who is obviously deemed to be better.

> In the virtual world, we can only perceive what is directly in front of us. We have no peripheral vision.

It is OK to say something like, "You did such a great job. The level of expertise and professionalism you demonstrated is on par with what we see with our senior engineers. It is highly unusual to see this in someone relatively new." This is not a direct comparison to another person, so there is no competition implied in the statement. It is an evaluation of the person's performance against the requirements for a more senior role.

It is very difficult for virtual employees to know where they stand in relation to their peers, from their manager's or the organization's perspective. In the virtual world, we can only perceive what is directly in front of us. We have no peripheral vision. Therefore, it is not possible to intuitively know what others are thinking or planning. Any hint that our manager thinks we are not as good as our peers, and a whole lot of self-confidence is going to disappear very quickly. Be careful with your words. Remember, your remote team members cannot see you, so any humor in your remarks can easily be lost, and your comments taken literally.

No Derogatory Remarks About Team Members or Stakeholders

It is important to make no derogatory remarks about team members or stakeholders. Making derogatory remarks about others is totally unnecessary and unprofessional. You might think that a rude remark, cleverly disguised as a joke, is pretty funny. People laugh, and you think no harm was done. There is always harm done when derogatory remarks are made about others. The person being spoken about might not know what was said, but there is always a chance that someone will tell him or her.

Derogatory remarks decrease the respect that others have for the person being spoken about. They also decrease the respect that the team members have for each other and for you. If you spend a lot of time around someone who is always badmouthing others, it is only a matter of time before you start wondering what is being said about you when you are not there. When you work virtually, a lot goes on that you are not aware of. You receive only the amount of information that others are willing to share with you. If much of what you are hearing is derogatory about other people or teams, you will get a very negative view of the team. It will appear that the only way to get anywhere in the company is to make others look bad. This teaches your team members that politics are the way to succeed in this organization—not a lesson they should be learning from you!

No Thinking or Assuming You Are Better than Someone Else

It is quite common for employees to think they are better than someone else on the team or the organization, and to forget that all jobs are vital to the organization. For example, in many technology organizations, tension exists between the development and quality assurance (QA) teams. Generally, the development team thinks they are more intelligent or valuable than the QA team. The QA people feel that the developers do not respect them (and are often correct in that assumption). Neither team likes the other much. The managers blame each other and each other's teams for problems. Neither tries to work with the other to create a more harmonious environment; rather, the political game is being played. Managers and individual contributors focus too much attention on how their teams can get one-up on each other, rather than focusing on doing a great job.

Make sure there is not a feeling within your team that it is better than another. If that team was not doing its job, who would be doing that work? Would your team want to do it? Would your team have the expertise to do it? If you were continually rude to the person who cleaned your office, how would you feel if you suddenly had to do it yourself? If you had to do your own cleaning for a while, you'd start to miss the cleaner pretty quickly! Bear this in mind the next time you are tempted to make an assumption or a remark about someone being less important or valuable than yourself or your team. Everyone has a role to play, and each role is important.

If you manage a team that is split between two locations or a hybrid team with some local and some remote team members, there is a high risk that assumptions regarding superiority (or inferiority) will be made. The scenario is usually that one part of the team believes itself to be the better part, and believes the other part or parts are inferior. However, they also often believe that the inferior element believes itself to be superior, and so there has to be action taken to show who is the best. The action is invariably negative; it does nothing to increase the quality of teamwork. This type of situation requires proactive management and a lot of emphasis on teamwork and team-building.

If you can avoid negative behaviors, cultivate positive behaviors, and facilitate a supportive and collaborative environment, you will be well on the way to creating and maintaining a strong, successful, and minimally political team.

Identifying Potential Troublemakers

Identifying potential troublemakers is more challenging on a virtual team than on a non-virtual team. You cannot see and hear nearly as much of what goes on virtually as you can locally. Still, there are some clues to help you identify people you need to keep close tabs on. Some of these clues are very obvious, while others are not so obvious. If a team member comes from an environment where negative behavior and politicking were accepted or even encouraged, that person might not perceive his or her own behavior as bad or wrong. If you do not take steps to control potential troublemakers early on, the politics will get out of control very quickly. Before you know it, you will be in the midst of a full-scale political war.

> Identifying potential troublemakers is more challenging on a virtual team than on a non-virtual team.

Here are some very noticeable signs of a troublemaker that you should be able to identify early enough to nip trouble in the bud. These are also shown in Figure 10.3.

- A person who obviously has a hugely inflated ego is going to be troublemaker. This person continually tells everyone how great he or she is, and often puts others down or laughs at them. This person has learned to make himself or herself look good by making others look bad.

- The person who is extremely negative about everything is also potential trouble. This person complains about everything and everyone, is seemingly never satisfied with any decision or outcome, and never shows any signs of being excited or enthusiastic about anything.

- Rumor mongers love to find out the dirt on everyone and spread it around as quickly as possible. The gossip is often negative. Stories are exaggerated and enhanced to make them sound more interesting at the expense of the person who is being gossiped about.

- The attention-seeker wants to be the center of attention as much of the time as possible. He or she will dominate conversations, name-drop, and generally try to impress others.

- Less obvious is the team member who is quiet, tends to keep to himself or herself, and is also rather negative or noncommittal about everything. It could be that this person is quietly working on a personal agenda and doesn't really care much about the team unless it is useful to him or her in some way.

Trait	Description
Inflated Ego	This person continually tells everyone how great he or she is, and often puts others down or laughs at them. This person has learned to make himself or herself look good by making others look bad.
Negative	This person complains about everything and everyone, is seemingly never satisfied with any decision or outcome, and never shows any signs of being excited or enthusiastic about anything.
Rumormonger	These people love to find out the dirt on everyone and spread it around as quickly as possible. The gossip is often negative. Stories are exaggerated and enhanced to make them sound more interesting at the expense of the person who is being gossiped about.
Attention Seeker	This person wants to be the center of attention as much of the time as possible. He or she will dominate conversations, name-drop, and generally try to impress others.
Quiet & Non-Committal	This person tends to keep to himself or herself, and is also rather negative or non-committal about everything. This person quietly works on a personal agenda and doesn't really care much about the team unless it is useful to him or her in some way.

Figure 10.3: Identifying potential troublemakers

Once you have identified a potential troublemaker, ensure that you are working with that person on growth and development plans. Coach that person to develop more positive and beneficial behaviors. If team members come from environments where negative behavior was accepted, you will have to help them relearn how to effectively communicate and teach them how to function as part of a virtual team. There is no room on the virtual team for troublemakers. There are enough challenges operating virtually, even when you have a positive and cooperative team. The last thing you need is to add a lot of negativity and political drama into the mix, creating more challenges to overcome!

Nipping Trouble in the Bud

Suppose you are in a team conference call, and someone makes a derogatory remark about someone from another team. You do not need to reprimand the person in front of the rest of the team, but you should add your own comment to neutralize the remark. Here is an example:

Greg: "There were a lot of problems with the X project last week. The client was working with the product team, who are a bunch of idiots at the best of times, so it took a week for the problem to get solved."

You: "Thank you, Greg, for that update. I would like to clarify what happened with the X project, as I do have more information on that. The product team is a highly skilled group and did a great job of keeping the client happy while the problem was being resolved. The issue with the X project should have been directed to our team immediately, but nobody was available to help with the problem, so the support team engaged the help of the product team. That team was able to make quite a lot of progress with the issue. The client is extremely happy that our company was so responsive to their needs. We assigned someone to work with them within two hours of them reporting it. The problem has now been resolved."

Follow up offline with Greg to talk about the "bunch of idiots at the best of times" remark. Remind Greg that it is important to be respectful of others, and that making another team or person look bad makes everyone look bad. Tell him that it is OK to comment about feeling frustrated that the problem took a long time to resolve, but it is not OK to make derogatory remarks about other teams. Everyone works hard to do their best, and some days the results are better than others.

Another sign of trouble is when two team members who normally get along with each other suddenly do not. This can be a sign that a personal conflict is brewing. These behaviors can become evident during virtual, face-to-face, and even written communication.

How do you recognize a problem early on, if the people involved are intentionally hiding it? For example, you might have team members who behave civilly toward one another in your virtual meetings, but fight likes cats and dogs as soon as you are not involved in the communication. The answer is that it might take you some time to find out about a conflict if the people involved are really good at hiding it from you. You can sometimes pick up inklings of a problem by something that one of them says, or by a comment from someone else. If their behavior is affecting their work, it should be only a matter of time before you start to notice a problem. If two people do not get along, it is usually evident when you get them in the same room for some period of time. It might be that you will not notice there is an issue until you have a face-to-face team event and observe them interacting.

Asking team members for peer reviews of their fellow team members can be a great way to recognize conflict. Ask all team members for verbal feedback on all their fellow team members, rather than asking each person to nominate one or two peers to provide the feedback. This way, you get a view of each person from many different perspectives, rather than just from their friends on the team. It is very likely that you will sense negativity about a person or be told straight out about the problem as soon as you ask. In each one-on-one, make a point to ask each team member if everything is going OK. Also ask if he or she has noticed any issues on the team or between other team members that you should be aware of. As long as your team members are assured of confidentiality and trust you to be discreet, you might find that getting the information you want is as easy as asking for it!

It is important to confront interpersonal problems as soon as you become aware of them. Talk to both team members individually, and ask what the problem is. Come up with a plan to solve it. Monitor the situation. Do not allow the team members to be disrespectful to one another in public or private. If you cannot resolve the situation, and it is creating a problem with other members of the team, be honest with the troubled team members. Tell them that, if the situation cannot be resolved, one or both of them will need to leave the team. Make sure they understand that the rest of the team cannot be made to suffer or take sides because of their bad behavior. They might not like each other, but they must treat each other with respect and dignity. Everyone is entitled to that.

Often, helping two people find commonalities can go a long way toward easing the tension and eventually solving the problem. These things start with a problem between two people, but at some point, others get dragged into it and are pressured to take sides. This is where the politics begin. It will escalate until you have one team divided into two or more factions. Managing a virtual team in which everyone seems to be behaving badly toward at least one other person is a nightmare, so do the right thing: Nip it in the bud!

Troublemakers are not always trying to cause trouble. Sometimes they don't realize their behavior causes problems, or they might not know they are responsible for the big mess resulting from something they did. The onus is on you to help your team members behave well. At the same time, give them the benefit of the doubt as to their intentions. They might not have been as dishonorable as they seemed. If you are positive, motivated, and respectful, it will only be a matter of time before the rest of the team follows your lead!

Managing Conflict

Differences of opinion are common among teammates, family members, friends, or members of any other group. Disagreements do not necessarily need to turn into conflict. A healthy level of disagreement on a team is required to create the best ideas, innovation, and quality. If everyone on the team agrees with everything that anyone else says, it is going to be difficult to cultivate imaginative and creative ideas.

A group of people who respect and support each other, are unafraid to challenge each other's ideas, and are not offended when someone challenges their own ideas have the makings of a great team. Engaging in dialog to justify a new concept or suggestion ensures that the person presenting the concept can defend it and prove its validity. This dialog also allows others to add to, expand, or even change the original concept to make it better. This does not mean that the team members should argue about every little thing. It means that the team thrives in a brainstorming environment, where everybody's input is valued and nobody feels the need to individually protect or own an idea or solution.

Conflict arises for various reasons. For example, when team members do not interact respectfully, or feel that their ideas are not being taken seriously, they will start to feel anger and resentment toward each other. Sometimes, conflict arises due to personality clashes or misunderstandings. There are times when it seems that someone is looking to pick an argument at any cost. Someone on the team who is struggling with difficult situations or stresses in other parts of work or personal life might be susceptible to defensive or offensive behavior that results in conflict. Some conflict is a result of interaction with outside teams,

When stress levels are high, conflicts are more likely to arise.

departments, or companies. Corporate or organizational changes, or sudden changes in policy, can cause confusion and lead to conflict between team members or between the manager and a direct report. When stress levels are high, conflicts are more likely to arise. Figure 11.1 demonstrates the catalysts for conflict in communication.

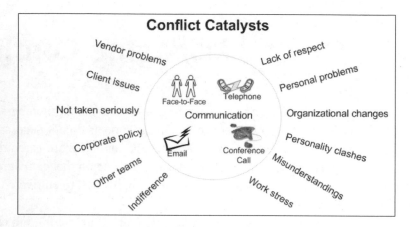

Figure 11.1: Conflict catalysts

A hastily written email can easily spark a conflict, as can a casual, and possibly innocent, remark during a phone conference. Virtual team members often feel indifferent toward one another until they have discovered commonalities and started to bond as a team. These feelings of indifference can sometimes exacerbate disputes and cause conflicts to live for a long time. First impressions are very important. If someone makes a bad impression in the early days on the team, it can linger for years.

If discord is managed effectively, it will never get to the point where it becomes a full-blown conflict. The goal is to contain the irritation so that it never mutates into conflict. This is not the same as conflict avoidance. Avoiding conflict or avoiding confrontation is very unhealthy. If team members and the manager consistently avoid confrontation and pretend that everything is OK when it is not, feelings of anger and resentment will build up and continue to ferment, until the point at which they blow up. Most likely, the blow-up will be completely out of proportion to the original problem. It is like a snowball—the longer you let it keep rolling down the hill, the bigger it will get, and the more damage it will do when it hits something! There is a big difference between avoiding conflict and managing potential conflict situations to diffuse them before they become a problem.

Recognizing a Potential Conflict Situation

To manage conflict, you need to know how to recognize a potential conflict situation. Listening is the most important skill that the manager has. Listen to what is being said, and how it is being said. Pay attention to the interaction among team members, and also pay attention to what is being said by team members to you, the manager. Being aware of subtle changes in the actions and reactions of your team members will aid you in predicting and anticipating potential conflict situations. If you notice any irritation, argumentativeness, unhappiness, lethargy, annoyance, or lack of respectful communication between team members, you know you have a potential conflict situation brewing. Recognizing conflict is not difficult if you pay attention to the early warning signs. See Figure 11.2.

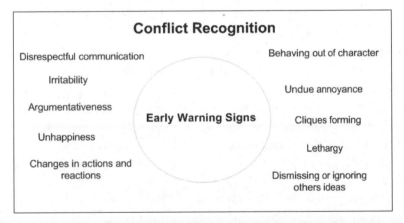

Figure 11.2: Conflict recognition

The conflict might not be related to the specific interaction at which you first recognized there was a problem. It could have been sparked by another event in which you were not involved. If you recognize some signs that a conflict situation might be brewing, don't ignore them. You should not confront somebody publicly, but make a note to follow up with the person offline. Unless you have witnessed extremely egregious behavior, it should not be necessary to follow up immediately after the meeting. It is often better to talk to someone about an issue after the person has had time to calm down and is not feeling as emotional about it. Wait an hour or two, or maybe even a day or two, but do not wait too long. If the situation is escalating, you need to contain it before it gets out of control.

Do not confront a team member in an accusatory way just because you have noticed that he or she is more stressed out than usual. The team member might not be involved in a conflict at all. He or she might be tired or stressed about personal issues, or might just be having a bad day. Be respectful, and give your team members a break occasionally. They cannot be perfect all the time!

If a team member starts to behave out of character, there is a problem of some kind. For example, suppose someone in a team meeting appears to be dismissing a particular team member's comments too quickly, but is listening respectfully to others. This could indicate that a problem is brewing. Sometimes, all it takes is one bad attitude on a team to cause anxiety and stress among all its members. If you notice a common denominator related to a number of different problems, then it is probably safe to assume that the person or situation is creating the problem.

Upsetting the status quo is not the same as creating conflict. The status quo often needs to be challenged. Progress requires change. Often, that change involves some level of risk. Maintaining the status quo might be appropriate in some situations, but not in all situations. Understanding the difference between a respectful challenge of an idea or process and an intentional attempt to create conflict is critical to the virtual manager.

Knowing When and How to Act

Knowing when and how to act might be blatantly obvious, or not the least bit intuitive. As you become more familiar with your team members, it gets easier to spot when there is an issue. It also becomes easier to know how to address it. Generally, most managers wait too long before taking action. Let's face it, dealing with conflict is not a lot of fun. If team members are hostile, they can be difficult to deal with. If the conflict involves you, it is even more difficult to broach the subject and to jump in quickly to resolve it. Do not wait a few days or until after the weekend to see if it is going to "blow over." It is not going to get better or disappear on its own.

If a conflict appears to settle down, but the issues were never dealt with, they are still simmering beneath the surface. As a result, the next time the conflict rears its ugly head, it is going to be even worse than the time before. There will be old resentments mixed in with the new ones, and it will be very difficult to separate the current issues from the historical and emotional ones.

The key is to do something immediately when you suspect there is a problem. If you are mistaken and there is no problem, your team members will not be insulted or upset that you asked questions. They will be heartened that their manager is observant and cares about what is happening on the team. It will increase confidence in your abilities and motivations regarding conflict, and the team members will feel more comfortable approaching you about issues in the future.

Sometimes, you will suspect that there is a problem, but after investigating with your team members (discreetly, we hope), you will be persuaded that there is no problem. It might be that there really isn't a problem, or it might be that the problem was so minor that it has been forgotten already. Alternatively, there might be a real problem, but the team members do not trust you enough yet to be open and honest about the situation. Be patient. You cannot force people to trust you. Keep an eye on the situation, and continue to ask questions when necessary. When the time is right for your team members, they will be honest with you and tell you what you need to know.

Never reprimand anyone for not telling you sooner about a conflict. Never ask why someone denied there was a problem when you asked earlier. You need to thank team members for their input and for their trust in you. Make sure they know how much you appreciate their trust and honesty. Also make sure that you communicate clearly that all conversations will remain confidential. Most importantly, make sure that they do remain confidential. This means keeping positive as well as negative comments confidential. Just because someone says something good about someone else, does not mean it is true. Of course, just because someone says something bad about someone else, does not mean that it

> Just because someone says something good about someone else, does not mean it is true. Of course, just because someone says something bad about someone else, does not mean that it is true, either.

is true, either. The person might intentionally have been untruthful, or might be presenting what he or she perceives to be the truth. Perception is not always the same as reality. Sometimes people tell you things to cover themselves in case there is a problem. People might tell you something to divert attention away from themselves. On occasions, someone will tell you something because he or she is playing political games, and you are being used to help that person get what he or she wants. Be careful that your plans to resolve conflict do not backfire on you! Be aware of people's agendas, perspectives, affiliations, and motivations. These things can all affect how a person reacts and responds to different situations.

If conflict exists between two members of the team, deal with it immediately. If you observe (or hear) disrespectful behavior or hear one or both of the people saying bad things about one another, do not delay. Start by speaking to each team member individually, and be direct in asking what the problem is. Make sure you get an answer. Ask both team members the same questions. If you still cannot get to the bottom of the issue, you might need to speak to both of them at the same time. If you cannot get either party to talk about what the problem is, you can give them an ultimatum, for example:

I cannot make you like each other and I cannot make you enjoy working together. However, I can insist on respectful communication between team members. I require all team members to make a commitment to the team as a whole and to each other. That commitment includes effectively working together and supporting each other to achieve desired results. I will not tolerate team members working against each other or trying to sabotage each other's work. This kind of behavior will result in a divided, unhappy, and unproductive team that will have no chance of success.

I cannot force you to tell me what the problem is, but I know there is a problem. I will insist that you work together to resolve it, either with or without my help. I would like to help resolve the issue, as I am sure that whatever the problem is, it is not insurmountable. However, I need you to be honest with me about what is going on, so I can help. You are both very valuable members of the team. Working together, you are a force to be reckoned with. Working apart or against each other, though, you are counterproductive. You are taking the fun and enjoyment out of the team, not only for yourselves but also for the rest of us. It is imperative that these issues are resolved quickly.

This might resolve the issues, or it might not. You can follow up individually again with both people, and you might find that they become more willing to open up and tell you what the problem is. Often, disputes occur due to one person thinking the other person does not value his or her work or intelligence highly enough, and vice versa. Similar personalities often clash. They see so much of themselves in the other person that it irritates the heck out of them! If you can harness this energy and get the two adversaries working together toward a common goal, you might find that they soon become each other's biggest fans and manage to work together perfectly well.

You might also find that the problems continue, and nothing you do makes them any better. At this point, you need to consider removing one or both of the team members from your team. This is a drastic step, but you cannot risk the entire team due to a conflict between two team members who are unwilling to resolve the problem. It is not fair to the rest of the team, and over time, you will find that the turnover on the team is much higher than it should be. People will try to get away from the negative environment that has been created.

If someone has a beef with you, that is another story altogether! The most important thing, once again, is to deal with the situation quickly. It is usually better to approach the person and ask if you have done something to upset him or her, instead of waiting for the person to call you and start accusing you of all sorts of terrible things in an agitated and emotional state. If someone is honest with you, do not be defensive. Use active listening, and try not to take it personally if you feel you are being accused unjustly. Listen carefully to what is being said to you. Repeat back the highlights to make sure you have understood. Then, ask the person if you may respond. Always ask first, to ensure that the person has had an opportunity to say everything he or she wanted to say, and has run out of steam. Then, explain the situation calmly and unemotionally from your own perspective. If possible, explain why a decision was made or what decision was made. You can apologize that the person is upset, but you do not necessarily need to apologize for your actions, unless you truly feel that you owe an apology.

Never get into a screaming match with anyone or start to throw your own accusations out. No matter how upset you might feel about what is being said, simply listen and respond. Once you understand the problem, ask the other person to tell you what he or she would like to happen next. You do not necessarily have to give what is being asked for, but at least you will know what the person wants and will be able to set appropriate expectations. If you need time to absorb what you have heard and to think about your response, say so. Don't feel that you are on the spot and must respond immediately. You might need time to check some of the facts, or you might just need to time to think and to calm down. Either way, tell your accuser that you need time to think about what he or she has said. Then, make an appointment to call the person back in a few hours or the next day to continue your discussion.

Mediating a Phone Conference

When you have conflict between two virtual team members who are located remotely from each other, you are somewhat limited in your options for getting them talking to each other. Most of the solutions available require building virtual bridges. In the traditional world, you are able to get the two people in the same room together and make them talk about the issues openly and honestly. Alternatively, you might take them both out to lunch, or for a margarita after work, and encourage some lighthearted chatter in addition to some serious discussion about the problems. In the virtual world, you are limited to phone communication, which means no personal contact when trying to resolve the issues. There are advantages and disadvantages to this.

The disadvantages include the following:

- You cannot see facial expressions or read body language to help judge how either party is reacting or thinking.
- If one or both go quiet, you have no idea why.
- It is easy to refuse to participate via phone.
- The meeting participants might not even be listening to each other.

The advantages include the following:

- It is sometimes easier to be honest when you don't have to look someone in the eye.
- Shy people sometimes feel more comfortable talking on the phone than in person.
- The impersonal nature of the phone can make it easier to say things you might feel embarrassed about saying in person.

You need to set the ground rules for the meeting and ask for honesty from both parties. Request that they listen to each other and that they both practice active listening so they both know they have been heard. Ask them not to interrupt each other or to raise their voices. Remind them that, just because someone can shout louder, does not make that person right! Ask them to give each other time to think before responding and not to continue talking while the other person is thinking about his or her response.

You need to be involved as a facilitator and mediator in the discussion. If you leave them to chat between themselves, nothing will get resolved. Stay on the call with them until there is some resolution, even if it takes three hours!

Proactive Conflict Management

Proactive conflict management should become an inherent part of your team. To be successful, conflict management should be put into practice both on an ongoing basis and in special situations. Conflict can be avoided, diffused and resolved quickly by taking a proactive approach to conflict management. See Figure 11.3.

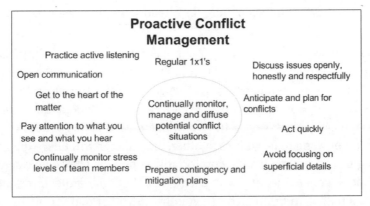

Figure 11.2: Proactive conflict management

Keep an open dialog going with all team members about the current state of affairs. You do this by staying in touch with team members, gauging the stress and anxiety levels on the team, and keeping an eye on the overall issues and situations being dealt with. Ensure that one-on-one discussions get to the heart of the matter, and do not just focus on the superficial details of the current work or project. Listen to what is being said, and read between the lines where necessary. Employ active listening, and encourage team members to speak out honestly and openly about issues and perceptions. If the team members trust you to be supportive and to apply good judgment, they will be more inclined to share their concerns or suggestions with you. If the team members feel confident that you will take appropriate action and treat all team members fairly, conflict is much less likely to occur in the first place.

If you start skipping one-on-ones, or if team members stop calling in for them, you need to deal with the situation quickly. The only way you can proactively manage conflict is if you are having regular one-on-one time with each of your team members. You will not know if someone is behaving out of character if you have not spent enough time interacting with that person to know what is in character!

You should also be anticipating issues and conflicts that might occur as a result of specific actions or situations. If you know that your team members are going to be unhappy about a decision, be prepared to do some damage control before conflict arises as a result of the decision. If you wait until the conflict has already occurred before taking action, the situation might already be out of control.

In circumstances where two team members are constantly at loggerheads, you must proactively manage the situation. Do not allow it to get out of control or to affect other team members. Sometimes managers assign the two combatants to work together on a project, in an attempt to force their cooperation. In reality, this does not usually work well. The two might work together grudgingly, but they will play power games with each other, and neither will enjoy their work while being forced into such an uncomfortable situation. The chances are that they will not be communicating with each other about the project. Instead, they will use the situation to try to prove to you that the other really is incompetent.

On the other hand, if two people are overcoming their difficulties and seem to be forming a more respectful regard for each other, this could be a good time to assign them to work together, but not to work exclusively with each other. It is better to assign them to a project team that includes other team members. This way, they will need to work together, but other team members will also be involved in the decision-making process, so they will not have to make decisions exclusively with each other. It is good to ease the team members into working together if they have experienced a conflict situation rather than throwing them in the deep end!

If you know that a specific person is going to react badly to an upcoming situation, either prepare the person for what is going to happen, or be ready to take action immediately to work with that individual to contain any fallout. Having a plan in place before the problem occurs is always more advantageous than hoping for the best and reacting after the potential problem has become a reality.

The happier the team is, the less likely that serious conflict is going to break out. The better the teamwork, the easier it will be to identify a conflict situation in the early stages. The stronger the connection among the team members, the smoother the road to conflict resolution will be.

It is not possible to avoid all conflict, but it is possible to have plans and ideas in place, ready to deploy if a conflict arises. Quick and decisive action is the most proactive approach a manager can take, even if the problem was not anticipated.

Managing conflict is like managing risk. You identify as much risk as you can up front, and prepare mitigation and contingency plans to try to reduce or avoid it. You also put escalation plans into place for those things that happen regardless of the planning, or that occur unexpectedly. That way, it is possible to take quick and decisive action to reduce the impact of the event or issue.

Imagine what would happen if a manager did not have any contingency or escalation plans. When problems arose, he just ignored them and hoped they would resolve themselves. Maybe a week or more would pass. The problem would continue to get worse, and the manager would continue to avoid dealing with it. Finally, when the problem could be ignored no longer, the manager would step in and try to do something to resolve it. The trouble is, by now so many people have been affected by the problem that is impossible to contain or minimize it. It might take the manager another week or so to decide what to do and, in the meantime, things would continue to get worse and worse. If this happened in most organizations, the manager would likely not have a job for very long.

> Managing conflict is like managing risk. You identify as much risk as you can up front, and prepare mitigation and contingency plans to try to reduce or avoid it.

There is no excuse for not giving the same level of attention to managing conflict as to managing risk and defining escalation procedures. Conflict is risk. The more it can be contained and controlled, the less risk to the team, the project, and the organization.

Change Management

Change management is not the same as change control. Change control is managing changes to a project, contract, or job to ensure that the scope, costs, and timelines are not adversely affected. Change management is working with team members to help them adjust to, and embrace, organizational change.

Organizational change can have a very strong impact on a team. Generally, people do not like change very much. We become comfortable with the familiarity of things, people, and processes, and we are not usually all that happy to change them and learn a new approach to an old problem.

People who have been around the longest are usually the most resistant to change. The old saying "you cannot teach an old dog new tricks" is not always true! You can often teach them new tricks, but they might not be thrilled about having to learn them.

If the team members are feeling insecure about new ways of doing things or about a new organizational structure, there is a much higher probability that conflict will occur. If team members are feeling uncertain or unhappy about the changes, they might become unwilling to work within the new parameters. It is much harder to monitor and control virtual workers' adherence to new processes or business practices than it is for local workers. You need to influence and persuade your team members that the changes are good and that they should embrace them. It is your responsibility to make this happen, using your management skills and the virtual tools at your disposal. The change management checklist shown in Figure 11.4 defines some high level actions you can take to help your team members understand, accept and implement change.

If the team members feel that some employees got a better deal than others out of organizational changes, feelings of jealousy and anger can be created. Team members might feel that they have been unfairly treated, or that the company is taking away from some employees to give to others. Changes that involve adjustments to financial incentives can create a lot of discontent and mistrust on the team. The manager needs to proactively manage this issue. For example, if the board of directors decides to discontinue stock option grants for employees below director level, or to discontinue profit sharing bonuses for employees, in real terms this is like a decrease in pay for most employees. If the employees at director level and above are receiving higher stock option grants than they were before, the perception will be that the company has taken away from the poor to give to the rich.

	Action	Description
1.	Establish the need for change	If team members understand the reason for change they will have a more positive attitude and be more inclined to accept the need for change.
2.	Develop a shared strategy & vision	You and your team members must share the same vision for short and long term results of planned change.
3.	Generate team support and acceptance	Enlist team members participation in defining and planning for the changes. Being involved in the process will give team members "ownership" in implementing and managing the change.
4.	Empower team members to take action	Give team members the knowledge and authority to take action to implement the change and to minimize negative impacts.
5.	Achieve short term improvements	If the change plan includes some short term wins for team members, it will help the team to stay focused on the positive aspects of the change.
6.	Integrate new approach into processes and culture	Update processes and procedures as necessary to reflect the outcomes of the change.
7.	Accomplish long term goals and objectives	Keep team focused and positive about the end result and don't forget to celebrate milestones and deliverables along the way.
8.	Monitor and control change	Monitor the change and ensure that team members are not slipping back into the old, familiar ways of doing or thinking about things.

Figure 11.4: Change management checklist

As the manager, you might also be affected by the organizational changes. It can be very challenging to present negative changes in a positive way to a team, when you are personally feeling unhappy about the changes yourself. If some members of the team lose benefits and others don't, the team members who lose out feel angry at those who didn't. The team members who kept their benefits feel guilty, because they now get more than the others.

These situations can create rivalry between different teams or between members of the same team. When team members are located remotely, the resentment and competitiveness can increase greatly. If team members are not sure what decisions are being made or why, they might feel that other members of their team are out to get what they can for themselves and are sabotaging other team members' chances of success. Tensions are high, and cooperation and goodwill are very fragile at such times. You must put your own feelings aside and focus on keeping team morale as high as possible and minimizing damage.

Major organizational changes can have huge impacts on employees. For example, suppose a new CEO or president is appointed to run the company. These senior executives have a huge influence over the everyday work life of each employee. The decisions made at the top trickle down, and sometimes the result is not even anticipated or acknowledged by those who made the changes.

Executive management changes can change the entire culture of a company in a relatively short time. These changes can create a lot of upheaval. For example, adding more reporting and time-tracking tasks can make employees feel they are being controlled or spied on, and that they are not trusted. Making changes to employee benefits, such as reducing the employer contributions toward health insurance or pension plans, can have a significant impact on employees. Taking away paid time off, increasing work hours, or removing travel incentives can make employees feel very dissatisfied. Sometimes companies try to save money by taking away employee motivation budgets and cutting out things like team events, team gifts, project completion celebrations, or manager-controlled employee incentive programs. All these things mean a lot to employees. They feel cheated if these incentives are taken away. It also makes it very difficult for you to continue to motivate the team members if a lot of incentive opportunities have been taken away.

To cut costs, some companies implement some rather dubious business practices, such as making employees use personal time for business travel and not giving the time back. For example, a company might book employee flights on Sundays so they can start client meetings on Monday morning, book their return flights on Thursday evening, and make them work a full day on Friday. These ways of getting more work time from employees are pretty bad for morale. They make the employees feel cheated by the employer, especially if company policy has just changed. A manager should be able to control some of the outcomes of this. You might, for example, let your team member take Friday off without logging it as a vacation day. If the company rules are unfair, do what you can to make them fairer for your team members. They will appreciate your efforts, feel happier about their jobs, and be less inclined to feel competitive or resentful toward others who are not in the same situation. Virtual teams often incur a lot of travel time, so these types of changes can have a big impact on virtual team members.

The worst changes that a company goes through are mergers, acquisitions, and lay offs. These often go hand-in-hand. These are really big upheavals that lead to a lot of serious changes. The fear of losing one's job can be devastating. It can motivate team members to start looking for a new job right away. This can lead to you losing more team members than planned. If some team members are laid off, the ones who keep their jobs often feel guilty that they were not let go. The ones who kept their jobs are also worried that there might be more cuts, and that they might lose their own jobs in the next round. When companies downsize the workforce, they do not usually decrease the workload by a comparable amount, so the remaining workers are expected to increase their productivity and handle all the work with fewer people. For example, team members who travel 25% to 50% of the time might find they are now expected to travel for 50% to 75% of the time. This might not be acceptable. Remote team members might be expected to start covering a larger geographical area than they did previously. These types of changes can make a huge difference not only to one's work life, but to one's personal life, too.

Outsourcing and offshoring can also decrease the workforce and increase the workload for some employees. The outsourcing might take away some interesting work opportunities for team members, or it might remove the need for international travel. Many consultants enjoy international travel a lot, and think of it as an incentive. If those opportunities are taken away, they might feel that they have lost a large percentage of the "fun" part of their jobs.

From time to time, organizations also change the location and the responsibilities of certain positions within the company. For example, suppose a team comprised of 100% virtual employees works for a hybrid organization. A new CEO joins the company and decides that some of those functions should be carried out at the corporate office. He or she might force those virtual employees to become local employees. Such changes can mean relocating and can also be quite restricting for employees who are used to working virtually. It is not always possible to just up and relocate, especially for team members with families to consider.

Sometimes the opposite happens. A company decides to change its business model to a virtual one, and local employees are asked to work from home. Some team members would never want to work from home. For some people, the face-to-face interaction with others is what motivates them. The thought of working alone every single day is frightening. Not everyone can work well in a virtual environment. Even something as straightforward as the company moving to new offices or rearranging existing office space can be quite stressful for people who do not adapt well to change.

Change can be created by one or more team member opting to leave the company to pursue other career interests. Depending on who is leaving and how many people leave at the same time, the change can be quite traumatic. Sometimes one team member leaving can completely change the team dynamic. Integrating a new team member into a close-knit team can be quite difficult. No matter who the person is, their presence is going to affect the delicate balances among the team members. It might be a positive change in the long run, and it is good to introduce some new blood from time to time, but the initial integration period can be a bit daunting for both the existing team members and the new ones!

If one person leaves the team and others quickly follow, the remaining team members can start to become despondent. A mass exodus is very difficult to deal with, but it must be handled in a positive way. It often follows major organizational changes. You need to focus on the positive aspects of change with your team members. Try to instill some excitement about the opportunities the changes are creating, such as the opportunity to add new skill Sets to the team. Just because the team will be different does not mean that it will not be as good.

Change can be a catalyst for conflict. Therefore, it needs to be managed in the same way as risk and conflict—proactively and quickly.

Removing a Team Member from the Team

Removing a team member from the team can be a very difficult process. Even if the reason for removing the team member is a very good one, the other team members are going to feel insecure about their own positions if they know that a team member was asked to leave. Even though virtual team members have limited face-to-face time, they can often feel more insecure about these types of changes than traditional team members. The isolation from what is happening is a major contributor to this. The team member is unsure whether the circumstances are really what was communicated or if there is more to it. The team member might be concerned that the company is starting to remove its virtual team members. Alternatively, team members might be concerned that because it is harder to prove what you are doing when you work remotely, and it is harder for the company to see your value, maybe their jobs are less secure than local employees who work for the same company.

It is a delicate balancing act, keeping everyone on the team happy while ensuring that everyone is performing well and meeting expectations. It could be that a person needs to be removed from your team because the nature of the work has changed and that person's skill Sets are no longer required. Sometimes a problem occurs when a team member is resistant to learning new skills. The result is, over time, the team member is unable to fulfill his or her role any longer due to the lack of the required skill Sets.

> In an ideal situation, there will be a transition period when the outgoing team member can hand off tasks and responsibilities to other team members.

In an ideal situation, there will be a transition period when the outgoing team member can hand off tasks and responsibilities to other team members. If a team member is removed quickly due to a lay off, or because the company felt that the team member was too negative to be able to handle a smooth transition of tasks, it can be quite a challenge for the manager and the rest of the team to pick up the pieces and figure out what needs to be done. It is very difficult having to go through an ex-team mate's computer to find out the status of tasks and to hand off documents and contracts to other members of the team.

Team members might be reticent about wanting to take on the projects and work of a team member who has been laid off. They might think of that work as stepping into "dead man's shoes." People can be superstitious and think that a project or account is "jinxed" if other team members have been unsuccessful in that role. Sometimes the team members are uncomfortable about taking on the person's work due a sense of loyalty to the ex-team member. Perhaps they were friends, and the remaining person feels that he cannot take on the work of a friend who has lost her job, especially if it is more interesting work than he is working on currently. He would not want his friend to think that he had benefitted as a result of her job loss, or even worse that he had anything to do with the job loss!

If you have been managing a performance problem with an employee that has led to the employee losing his or her job, it can be very difficult relaying that information to the rest of the team. The team might not be aware that the team member had a performance issue, nor that he or she was on a performance plan. This type of information is confidential, so unless the team member had shared this information with other team members, the dismissal might come as a shock. Depending on the country in which the business is located, the dismissal of a team member will be communicated in different ways. In the United States, it is customary to announce that the team member has left to "pursue other opportunities" or "to spend more time with his or her family." It is not often that the company will come out and publicly state that the person was dismissed. The company needs to be careful about what is said about the ex-employee, as they do not want to become the subject of a defamation lawsuit. In many countries, it is illegal to say anything derogatory about an ex-employee.

If an employee is let go due to gross misconduct, the team members will probably know what happened. For example, it is not easy to keep quiet that a team member was caught stealing from the company, insider trading, taking drugs, lying on a job application, or harassing another employee, especially if the employee has been arrested for his or her actions.

> You must tell virtual team members as soon as possible that a team member has been removed from the team.

You must tell virtual team members as soon as possible that a team member has been removed from the team. Forgetting to tell some team members is totally unacceptable. Telling local employees on Monday and waiting until the Friday virtual team meeting to tell the virtual team members is not recommended. Tell everyone at the same time. Otherwise, they might find out from someone else rather than hearing it from you. If you communicate quickly and effectively, you can do damage control at the same time as being the bearer of bad news. Once the rumor mill starts, it can be very difficult to get a positive message across about the change.

Try to communicate the news of a team member leaving in person or via phone whenever possible. Sending an email to notify the team about someone leaving is very impersonal. It does not allow the recipients to ask questions and get an immediate response. If the person leaving has direct reports, or works very closely with one or two other team members, it is polite to let these people know about the change before announcing it the rest of the team. You should ask those team members not to share the information with anyone else until the official announcement has been made. Then, make an announcement as soon as possible to the remainder of the team members. A team meeting is an ideal time to share this type of information.

If a departing team member is working on client projects, assign another team member to those projects as quickly as possible and inform the clients about the change. Never share with a client that a team member has been removed from the team by the company. This will make the client concerned about the quality of that team member's work and might also upset the client if they liked working with that person. Use the generic "pursuing other career opportunities" communication. You do not need to mention that those other opportunities might include unemployment benefits or prison! If the team member is being prosecuted for misconduct, you might have to disclose that to the clients that person was working with. The company's legal department should handle that communication. You should decline to comment, and ask your team members to do the same.

Understanding Your Limitations and When to Ask for Help

As a manager, you are expected to take responsibility for your team and the issues and situations that arise on your team. Your company expects you to be competent and to be able to resolve most issues independently and successfully. There are times, however, when the problems are not solvable by a manager, and you will need to ask for help.

A virtual manager must know when to ask for senior management help. Asking for help does not signify a lack of management skill. It signifies that a situation has arisen needing senior management's involvement or approval. You do not want to give the impression that you are incompetent by asking for help continually, but you also need to be sure that you are not letting a problem intensify for too long before asking for some assistance.

> Whether you are new to virtual management or have been doing it for years, there will be times when you need to ask for help in resolving an issue.

Where is the line between autonomy and collaboration? You need to figure this out for yourself, but there are some guidelines that can help you.

One good piece of advice is to share any major personnel issues with your manager during your one-on-one meetings. You do not need to ask your manager for help, but you should let him or her know that there is a situation and that you are handling it. At this point, you might not even mention the name of any team members involved, but you should give a high-level description of the problem. Your manager, hopefully, will ask if you need any assistance. As long as you are comfortable with the current situation, tell him or her that you believe you have it under control. However, ask if you can come back for some advice if the problem deteriorates. You have not asked for help, but you have given your manager a little teaser about what is going on, so he or she will not be surprised if you need to come later for some assistance if the situation worsens.

You cannot always deal with every situation alone. Whether you are new to virtual management or have been doing it for years, there will be times when you need to ask for help in resolving an issue. Use the resources at your disposal, whether they be your manager, your peers, or your direct reports. Continually learning and growing is what makes a good manager a better one!

CHAPTER

12

Virtual Management of High-Risk and Catastrophic Events

A high-risk or catastrophic event can occur at almost any time. Some events can be anticipated, while others come out of the blue. The key to successfully managing either of these types of events is planning. You might be asking, "How do I plan for an unexpected event?" Good question! If you have high-quality and clearly defined escalation and business-continuity plans in place, you can use those plans to quickly decide on a course of action, no matter how catastrophic or unexpected an event is.

Managing high-risk and catastrophic events on a virtual team requires a lot of close attention to communication. When a team is in the same location, spontaneous meetings can occur where everyone is present and involved, and they all know what is going on. When emergencies occur for a virtual team, people could be in multiple locations. They not only need to be kept informed about status and progress, but they might also need to be involved in managing or solving the problem from a distance. It is very difficult being remote from an emergency situation and not knowing what is happening between updates. The natural instinct is to want to be on the phone constantly, getting a running commentary on everything that is being said and done at the location where the emergency is occurring. If this is allowed to happen, the manager will be unable to effectively manage the emergency situation. The manager must balance his or her time delicately between managing the disaster and managing communication. Ignoring the remote team members and stakeholders is not a good idea. It will exacerbate the problem and give the impression that the manager is incompetent.

What Is a High-Risk or Catastrophic Event?

A high-risk event is one that has the potential to do major damage to the business by its impact on the company, clients, vendors, employees, or the general public, either immediately or at some time in the future. A high-risk event might be one that has already occurred, or one that has not yet occurred but has a high probability of happening. Either way, the risk needs to be managed. Risk management is planning for the expected. It includes mitigation, contingency planning, and containment.

There are four main categories of risks. These categories are shown in the risk table in Figure 12.1.

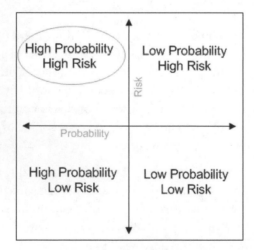

Figure 12.1: Risk table

A high risk event is one that falls into the "high probability, high risk" category shown in the top left quadrant of Figure 12.1.

Catastrophic events are ones that cause immediate and serious damage to the business by its impact on the company, clients, vendors, employees, or the general public. These events might be unavoidable, occurring so suddenly and unexpectedly that there was no time to recognize and manage the risk. Alternatively, they might have been avoidable, had the risk been recognized and managed effectively. Effective risk-management will prevent the second possibility from ever occurring. Catastrophic planning is planning for the unexpected. Catastrophic events will generally fall into one of the two upper quadrants on the risk table shown in Figure 12.1.

Planning for High-Risk Events

Risk management, as discussed in chapter 8, is the process of identifying, evaluating, prioritizing, and creating action and contingency plans for risks. Not all of those risks will fall into the high-risk category. If you have worked with your team to develop a risk-management plan, you will have already identified some high-priority risks for your project or team.

Team members leaving or joining, technology problems that might cause delays in scheduled deliverables, and extended absences by team members are all risks. However, they would not generally be categorized as high risks because they are manageable. Although they might cause temporary problems and delays, they are generally not likely to lead to a catastrophic or disastrous outcome. If the company is not going to go out of business or suffer serious financial damage due to an identified risk, it does not fall into the high-risk category.

High-risk events would seriously affect the company's revenues, cause the company to have to make significant workforce reductions, result in a significant stock price decrease, affect client or end-user confidence in the company and its products or services, result in a lawsuit, or result in the company changing business direction or closing. High-risk events can be defined as events that the CEO or president of the company would want to be informed about immediately.

> High-risk events can be defined as events that the CEO or president of the company would want to be informed about immediately.

It is possible that losing a team member might come into the high-risk category. If the team member was key to the success of the business, losing that person would prevent the company from meeting its financial or business goals. That should be tracked as a high-risk event. The mitigation plan would likely include cross-training or knowledge-transfer to at least one other team member, and ensuring that the key employee has documented his or her work. If there are no suitable candidates for cross-training, it would be in the company's best interests to hire at least one additional employee with the skill Set necessary to cross-train. A company that could go out of business by losing one or two key employees is not in a good position. Managing these key employees could become a problem if they know how valuable they are to the organization.

For a small business, losing one or two key employees could be comparable to losing 25% or more of the workforce, which would definitely be considered a high risk. The options for mitigating that risk might be rather smaller in a company this size than in a large company. But there should still be a plan in place for this situation. Likewise, if you lose a virtual team member located in France, and you do not have another team member who speaks French, you could have a huge problem transitioning that work to another team member. If you have key accounts in France, this would be considered a high risk.

Another high-risk problem is having one client provide a very high percentage of the company's revenues. If anything happens to that client, either intentionally or unintentionally, the company could be risking financial failure. The client might go out of business, or it might decide to take its business to a competitor, or it might push so hard for a better price that the company is unable to make any money from the deal. To mitigate this situation, the company should regularly evaluate the percentage of revenue for each client. If any one client provides over 20% of revenue, it is time to start looking for more clients or diversifying into other areas.

If your company has signed a deal for a very large contract and has hired additional staff to facilitate delivering on that contract, it would be very risky to your business if your client were to cancel its contract. Mitigation would include assigning one or more dedicated resources to manage the client relationship and the project, so that the client is kept happy. Any issues would be escalated immediately to the manager and given high priority. If your virtual team members are managing client relationships such as this one, make sure they are getting adequate training and support, so they can consistently add the value necessary to preserve the client relationship.

Technology risks can also fall into the high-risk category. If the company is relying on a specific piece of technology to make a project or job successful, and that technology does not work or is not available, this could seriously affect the success of the project.

New products can also be high-risk. If a significant investment has been made in a new product, and the company is relying on it for success, this needs to be managed as a high risk. A new product is always risky, and even more so if the company is going to be in financial trouble without it!

Planning for Catastrophic Events

Catastrophic events include those that are caused by both internal and external factors. A catastrophic event might be unanticipated, or it might be the result of a tracked high-risk event that could not be mitigated or contained.

Internal catastrophic events would include such things as the following:

- ➤ Hardware or network failures
- ➤ Large reductions in workforce
- ➤ Losing one or more very large contracts or accounts
- ➤ Loss of multiple team members at one time (perhaps a mass exodus to start a new company or join a competitor)
- ➤ Privacy or security breaches that might become public knowledge
- ➤ Faulty products that have to be recalled, or have caused harm, and for which there has been negative publicity
- ➤ Environmental issues or damage caused by the company or its representatives

External events include such things as the following:

- ➤ Natural disasters
- ➤ Acts of terrorism or war
- ➤ Airplane accidents
- ➤ Client or vendor issues
- ➤ Strikes
- ➤ Lawsuits, arrests, or scandals

Business continuity plans are necessary for all of the external events and many of the internal events. Business continuity plans will cover a lot of scenarios and will often be broken up into separate plans. For example, natural disasters, war, acts of terrorism, or accidents might lead to issues such as these:

- Bombs
- Fire
- Flooding
- Blocked roadways
- Grounded planes
- Closed airports
- Loss of life
- Serious injuries
- Building and infrastructure damage

A sample team business continuity plan template is shown in Figure 12.2.

Team Business Continuity Plan (BCP)

1. *Introduction & Overview*
   - 1.1. Objectives
   - 1.2. Overview Of Company BCP
2. *Emergency Contacts*
   - 2.1. Key Contacts
   - 2.2. Contact Information For Team Members
   - 2.3. Physical Location Of Team Members
   - 2.4. Alternative Work Locations
3. *Roles And Responsibilities*
   - 3.1. Roles And Responsibilities
   - 3.2. Escalation Procedures
   - 3.3. Reporting Requirements
4. *Contingency And Mitigation Plans*
   - 4.1. Location Of Contingency And Mitigation Plans
5. *Disaster Recovery Plan*
   - 5.1. Mission Critical Systems
   - 5.2. Network And Backup
   - 5.3. Other Data And Systems
6. *Communication Plan*
7. *Policies*
   - 7.1. Security
   - 7.2. Regulatory
   - 7.3. Company

Figure 12.2: Team business continuity plan

Due to the geographic diversity of a virtual team, there is a greater chance that someone who works on the team might be involved in a potentially disastrous situation. However, the greater number of team members you have working remotely and the more geographically diverse they are, the less chance that one disaster will affect your entire team. It is more likely to affect only part of the team.

Most large corporations have centralized disaster recovery and business continuity plans in place for large issues that will affect the whole organization. They are looking at the problem from the 10,000-foot view, not analyzing every little detail of the work that might be disrupted.

At the more detailed level for your team, consider putting together your own business continuity plan for any business interruption situation that could affect your team's ability to continue working. For example, if a natural disaster shuts down operations in India, and your team relies on the work that the India office is doing, how long can you operate before some of that office's work needs to be transferred? Your company, looking at how to deal with the disaster on a much larger scale, might have ascertained that it can manage for two weeks with the India site down. For your team, there might be two or three critical functions you could transfer temporarily that will stop you grinding to a halt. Document those in your own plan. Alternatively, if a huge winter storm hits the east coast of the United States, causing power and telephone outages, what should your team members in those areas do? Who should they contact, and how long can those employees be temporarily offline before their functions have to be transferred elsewhere? If you are the only team with virtual team members on the east coast, this might not be part of a company-wide business continuity plan. It would need to be managed in your own team's business continuity plan.

> Due to the geographic diversity of a virtual team, there is a greater chance that someone who works on the team might be involved in a potentially disastrous situation.

Suppose a very high-dollar system or product is sold by your team to a client. Upon installation, the system or product does not work or it fails soon thereafter. There is a high possibility that the client will refuse to accept the deliverable and might cancel the contract. If the contract is large enough, this could be considered a catastrophic event not only for your team, but also for your company.

These types of serious issues need immediate attention and need to be escalated appropriately, so that the necessary people can be involved quickly. Hopefully, with the right people involved, the situation will be resolved satisfactorily for the client without too much of a financial hit for the company. If the virtual team members do not know who to contact in such an emergency, or the people they contact do not understand the urgency of the situation, the crisis could turn into a disaster. If plans are not in place before such a problem occurs, panic and uncertainty will waste precious time, increasing the risk that the situation will escalate out of control.

If your company has a customer-support or technical-support group, make sure that your team understands which clients and contracts are the most critical. This way, if the client calls for assistance, your customer-support team knows who to contact on your team and will do so immediately, rather than logging the call in the system and not taking any immediate action.

How to Recognize and Respond to a Potential Catastrophe

Recognizing a situation that might result in a catastrophe starts with a review of your risk-management plan and your company's disaster recovery and business continuity plan. The combination of the high-level risks from the risk-management plan and the catastrophic event scenarios from your company's business continuity plan should give you a really good sense of the types of things you need to monitor.

Natural Disasters

For many catastrophic events, there are early warning signs. For example, if you know a natural disaster has occurred or is scheduled to occur in a key location for your team or project, you should be monitoring the situation. Start to prepare action plans, and put the appropriate people on alert so that immediate action can be taken should the catastrophic event become a reality.

Project or Product Issues

If the team has a low level of confidence in the suitability or operability of a solution being delivered to a client, and there is a concern that any resulting issues could be disastrous, the team should be on "red alert." It might be prudent to send some key team members onsite or close enough to get there very quickly in the event that a serious problem develops, so that it can be resolved or contained as quickly as possible.

Personnel Issues

If an employee has left the company to join a competitor or to start his or her own business, and is actively recruiting your team members to follow, it is a good time to start working on an action plan. First, make sure the team members who are being solicited are happy in their current positions. Make sure they feel appreciated and valued by you and the organization. Second, identify the team members who you think are most likely to leave. Think about how and to whom you would transition their tasks if that happens. Consider what projects or tasks you could drop from your overall plan if you end up losing 20 to 40% of your team overnight. It will take time to replace those team members, so you need to plan how the team will survive in the meantime.

Bear in mind that, if employees leave to work for a competitor, not only will you lose valuable team members and be short-staffed, but those employees might try to convince your current customers to move their business to the competitor. You need to have a plan in place for doing some damage control with your clients as soon as you are aware there is a potential problem.

Public Transport

Being aware of anticipated public transport strikes or other disruptions to service in countries and principalities where team members or clients are located will allow you to prepare some contingency plans to minimize the impact on your business. Make sure your virtual team members keep you informed about any potential or existing transportation issues due to strikes, inclement weather, or accidents in their region.

Freak Accidents

Some catastrophes cannot be anticipated, such as a plane crash that damages company property, or a freeway collapse that prevents employees from getting to work. These types of disasters need to be handled as they occur, following the guidelines in your company's business continuity plan.

Acts of War or Terrorism

You might have team members located in troubled areas of the world where acts of war or terrorism are a real threat to them on a daily basis. You and the company need to make sure you have plans in place for dealing with an emergency situation, should it arise. You also need to decide at which point you pull your team members out of those areas and relocate them somewhere safer.

Risk Management

In chapter 8, we talked about the development of a risk-management process and the activities that the manager employs to identify as many risks as possible early in the process. As a project, contract, or customer relationship progresses, some risks will become moot, others will increase or decrease in priority, and new ones will be created. You are responsible for ensuring that your risk-management plan is reviewed and updated on a regular basis. A risk log is a living document that can change on a daily or weekly basis.

The high-priority risks that portend disaster must be kept up to date. Something that is a low risk at the beginning of a project might increase in risk level as the project progresses, becoming a potential disaster by the time the project is close to completion. Risk must be evaluated and re-evaluated on a continual basis, in order for it to be effectively monitored and managed. If a risk plan is never updated, all you are doing is tracking the risks that existed at the specific time the list was created. This is not effective risk management.

The things you were concerned about at 12 years old are different from the things you are concerned about at 37 years old, which are different from those you are concerned about at 55 years old. If the things you are concerned about for your project never change, it is like continuing to worry about your 12-year-old concerns when you are 55! This is not very effective or a good use of your time. It suggests that little progress had been made in the meantime.

Scope Management

Failing to manage and control the scope of a project, contract, or team's responsibilities can introduce unnecessary risk factors. If the scope continues to increase, the team will become overwhelmed and unable to successfully meet expectations or deliverables. Setting and managing internal and external expectations is key to keeping the contract or project in scope and on track. You must be prepared to say "no" and to stand your ground if what is being asked of your team is out of scope and not appropriate to be brought into the scope.

If working on a client contract, a new Statement of Work should be prepared for any additions or changes to the original contract. Educate your team members on scope and on client-expectation management. If they start to agree to scope changes with the client, they will find that they are unable to meet deadlines. A client should never be promised anything that is not included in a contract. If promises are made and subsequently not kept, or if keeping the promise affects the completion date, the client will be unhappy, and you might lose future business. It is much better to learn how to say "no" politely, firmly, and effectively. The client will respect you for working to the predefined plan and for being honest and straightforward about what you have been contracted to deliver. If client expectations are managed successfully, the delivery will be on time and will be exactly what the contract stated. This is a great topic for an online team training or coaching session. If you can teach every one of your virtual employees how to effectively manage client expectations, you will have an awesome team and your clients will love working with you!

> Risk must be evaluated and re-evaluated on a continual basis, in order for it to be effectively monitored and managed.

Many virtual teams have problems with client expectations. The remote employees often feel isolated from their teammates, but have close contact with their clients. This leads to the remote worker feeling a stronger allegiance with the client than with the company for which he or she works. To keep the client happy, he or she agrees that it should have the additional things it is asking for, but omits the step of formally discussing and documenting the additional costs and the impact to timelines that these changes will have on the project. When you, as the manager, discover that the client is expecting additional work, you get the wheels in motion to document an amendment to the Statement of Work and ask the client to sign off on the additional costs and timelines. At this point, the virtual worker can blame you for wanting to charge more, aligning even closer with the client. The client is unhappy. The virtual employee has created this problem by managing the client relationship and the client expectations inappropriately. A strong virtual-team connection can help to reduce the possibility of these kinds of problems occurring.

Non-delivery or late delivery on contracts due to expanding scope and ineffective management of expectations can lead to very serious problems. The company might be in breach of contract for the late delivery. It might find itself in breach of contract for delivering something that was not part of the contract, because the additional functionality requires the client to do more work, for which they do not have an approved internal budget. As a result, the client might refuse delivery of the product or service. The client might cancel this contract or future contracts because it is unhappy with the service or product received.

> The remote employees often feel isolated from their teammates, but have close contact with their clients.

Clients that demand the most "extras" are usually those who are most unhappy at the completion of the contract, even if they ended up receiving some of these extras free of charge. They are unhappy because the expectations have not been managed effectively. This makes them feel they are being short-changed in some way, even though they actually got more than they paid for!

If a team member is unable to effectively say "no" to a client, a peer, or another employee, you will be better off without him or her on your team. This person will be consistently over-promising and under-delivering and will never be successful.

How to React to and Manage a Catastrophic Event

The most important thing to remember when there is a catastrophic event is to remain calm and not make any rash decisions. Make sure you have all facts before taking any action. The desire to do something as soon as possible will be intense. Do not let it overwhelm common sense. Most disaster situations take hours, days, or weeks to resolve. Spending half an hour getting all the facts and calmly putting together an action and communication plan will result in a more effective and efficient resolution or containment of the problem.

Managing a crisis when your team members are scattered throughout the country or globe has its own unique challenges. Communication is the key to success. If part of the catastrophe involves communication outages, you need to be creative in figuring out how to manage that effectively, so that all team members are aware of what is happening and what is expected of them. It is recommended to have multiple phone numbers and emergency contact information for each team member, so you have multiple ways of contacting each of your employees in an emergency.

In a crisis, every resource must be used to the company's best advantage. Make sure people are not duplicating effort. Communicate to your remote workers that they are not to work on anything unless you specifically ask them to. Otherwise, you will have a whole team of people with good intentions, all working on the things they think are important instead of the things you have assigned to them. Make sure that everyone who needs to know what is happening is part of the communication plan. Make it clear who is responsible for what. Assign one owner or leader for each major issue, and make sure that all communication is funneled through that person (or team), so that communications are cohesive and accurate, and everyone has the same information.

If you feel yourself getting worked up, wanting to scream your head off, or even worse, run away, sit down, take a few deep breaths, have a cup of tea or coffee (or perhaps something stronger, if the enormity of the problem warrants it), and relax for a few minutes. Get your wits about you and clear your head. When you feel calm and in control, take action. Coach your team members on how to act and react during emergency situations, so when they occur, you have a team of people who are well prepared to deal with the problems in a calm and reasonable manner.

> Managing a crisis when your team members are scattered throughout the country or globe has its own unique challenges.

It is very important during any crisis to remember to eat. Everyone needs food or they will become tired, grumpy, and unable to make good decisions. If the disaster is going to take multiple days to resolve, you should also make sure that everyone gets breaks and gets some sleep. You don't want anyone collapsing from hunger or exhaustion. Make sure that you eat and sleep and that everyone on your team does the same. Take time differences into account when calling on your team members to take action. Whenever possible, have team members work during their daytime hours and take breaks in the evening. If this is not possible, at least make sure that you have your team working in shifts. Otherwise, nobody will get any rest!

The team will take its cues from its manager. If you have a calm disposition and a positive attitude, implying that the problem will be resolved successfully, your team members will feel the same way. If you are all doom and gloom, panicking and complaining every time there is another issue, your team will feel helpless, hopeless, and unable to function effectively. In a time of crisis, you need your team members to be confident and energized, and to believe they are an incredible team that can solve any problem by working together.

Imagine how you would feel if you had a manager who said, "Oh no, we are in really big trouble. We are never going to solve this problem, but we will all be fired if we don't figure out how to fix it. So we are going to stay up all night for as many nights as it takes to find a solution!" You are not going to feel very inspired. On the other hand, if your manager says something like, "We have a serious problem that we need to work together to solve. It is going to be a big challenge, but I have every confidence that each one of you is up to the challenge. You are like an Olympic team that has been in training for four years. Finally, you are getting your chance to show the world how creative, talented, and unbeatable you are! I have no doubt whatsoever that this team will find the best solution to this problem. We need to work together, and we need to consider every idea or suggestion, no matter how crazy it might seem." This kind of pep talk is far more likely to make you and your team feel enthusiastic and excited about embarking on such a challenging task.

Evaluating the Catastrophe

Catastrophic events can be evaluated using a red, yellow, and green status system, as follows:

- Red—The issue is already catastrophic and requires immediate attention of the manager and team members. Red status indicates that senior management must be informed immediately about the problem.

- Yellow—The issue is serious and has the potential to become catastrophic. The issue might be escalating and need containment, or it might have been downgraded from red status and is continuing to be worked to reduce its severity even further.

- Green—The problem has not yet manifested itself (but is imminent), or the issue has been resolved or reduced to the point that it is no longer considered a high risk.

These descriptions are fairly generic, and the definition of status codes might vary from company to company. Many organizations will have their own written guidelines that describe the elements of red, yellow, and green statuses.

Ensure that your evaluation of the event and the resulting status code is consistent with the guidelines set by your organization. Never exaggerate a problem just to get attention. If the issue is a yellow status, and you have a high level of concern that it is going to escalate quickly to red, use your discretion when deciding if you need to contact senior managers. It might be better to present an issue as yellow trending to red, rather than waiting until it is red before informing anyone. Once the status is red, you cannot increase the status to anything higher even if the problem gets worse, so leave yourself some headroom if you think the issue is escalating to a higher level of disaster!

Ensure that your virtual team members have a convenient and accessible method of reporting status updates to you. You will need this information to monitor and update the emergency level of the event.

Minimizing the Damage

As soon as it becomes apparent that a high-risk or catastrophic event has occurred, it is vital to find a way to minimize the damage as soon as possible. During large fires, the fire department will often start "back fires" to head off and control the burn. You might need to use similar tactics to control a catastrophic event and prevent it from doing further damage.

For example, suppose the catastrophic event is that half your team has quit, and there are too many projects and not enough people to work on them. It is wise to cancel or postpone some of the projects as quickly as possible, so that the remaining team members can focus on completing at least some of the projects successfully. If you try to keep your team going at full speed on everything, hoping for a miracle, none of your projects will be completed successfully, and the resulting damage will be much worse. Consider what the most strategic projects or contracts are. Make a commitment to focus on them, and be prepared to sacrifice some of the lower-priority work. If you don't make the decision about what is going to be sacrificed, you will be leaving it to chance, and you risk losing everything.

A catastrophic event has the potential to have a negative effect on your team. Managing and controlling the impact on your team is very important. In the frenzy of putting escalation plans into effect, mobilizing personnel, and communicating with stakeholders, it is easy to forget to check in with your team members to make sure they are feeling OK about what is going on.

Remember to ask your team members for input before you run off and start implementing solutions. They will have ideas on how to contain the problem and minimize the fallout. If you forget to ask, they might think you have it all under control and do not need any additional ideas or suggestions. If you are trying to contact a team member to ask for input or advice on the problem, and he or she is not answering her phone, give that person a reasonable amount of time to respond before moving ahead with a solution you are not sure about. Your team members need to feel that they are not only involved in the process, but vital to the success of the operation. The more valuable the team members feel and the more visibility they have, the more inspired they will be to perform well. If the team members feel confident and positive about their involvement, they will focus on the solution rather than on all the things that could go wrong or how unhappy they are that they have to work on their day off.

> Your team members need to feel that they are not only involved in the process, but vital to the success of the operation.

If possible, postpone or cancel other commitments for yourself and your team members during the emergency. This will allow everyone to focus as much as possible on minimizing, controlling, and resolving the catastrophe without being distracted by other tasks or issues.

Keeping Team Members and Stakeholders Informed

Effective and planned communication is key to managing an emergency situation as effectively and efficiently as possible. If the people working on resolving the problem are being constantly interrupted by different people wanting to know how things are going, they are never going to be able to get anything done.

The escalation procedures should define who is responsible for communication during an emergency. It should be clear that all requests for information should go through one central resource. The first communication that you make to the stakeholders and team members should clearly define roles and responsibilities. It should also specifically state that no requests for status updates should go directly to team members working on the problem, as this distracts those team members and takes time away from working on resolving the problems.

You should have email distribution lists, IM lists, text lists, and pager lists included in your escalation procedures plan, ready for use in an emergency. There will not be time to set these up or type in 40 pager numbers or email addresses at the time an emergency occurs, so it is important to make sure you are well-prepared. Your goal should be to type one message and send it with one click to a predefined list of recipients.

For a red status emergency, here is an example of a communication plan:

- All communication goes through the manager.
- There will be no direct communication with team members, apart from communications between emergency team members.
- The manager will stay in constant communication with emergency team members throughout the emergency situation.
- Unless it is of vital importance, stakeholders should wait for scheduled updates and not call the manager to ask for additional updates.
- Initial phone calls will alert priority personnel and stakeholders.
- Email updates will be sent every two hours, containing details of progress and the current status level.
- Text messages and IMs will be sent every two hours, giving the current status level and whether the criticality level is trending up or down.
- Three meetings/phone conferences will be held daily at 8:00 AM, 12:00 noon, and 5:00 PM local time at the location of the emergency.

The more time the manager and the emergency team can spend on managing, controlling, and resolving the catastrophic event, the more quickly the situation will be resolved. The stakeholders need to be managed so that they are not constantly making phone calls or insisting on meetings with you or your team members outside of the scheduled updates. You need to focus your efforts on managing and controlling events and communicating with team members.

It is important to make the stakeholders feel they are involved in what is happening. Not knowing what is happening is very difficult. If you skip a communication because there is nothing new to report, the phone calls will start to flood in. If nobody is getting any information, they will think the emergency is not being managed well and will quickly lose confidence in your ability to resolve the situation.

Being remote from a problem, whether you are involved in trying resolve it or are simply an interested bystander, is very difficult. The need to constantly know what is happening can become a driving force that causes people to take action that ultimately hampers solving the problem. Coach your team members so they know what is expected of them in an emergency, in regards to taking action and communicating or receiving status updates. The well-oiled machine will function just as well in an emergency situation as in a regular one.

If it is time to send out a status report, and there is nothing new to report, it is not wise to send an email saying, "Nothing new to report." That will not give anyone a warm and fuzzy feeling. The following email is an example of a much more effective communication, designed to give the recipients a sufficient comfort level to prevent those pesky phone calls:

The status of the emergency situation remains RED. The team is continuing to follow the plan set out this morning to resolve the issues. Progress has been made on the steps set out in the plan, but the tasks are time-consuming, and we anticipate it will be a few more hours before we see any significant progress. The situation has been stabilized and is no longer deteriorating. The next update will be sent in two hours.

The email is stating that there is no change in status, but is presented in such a way that the recipients feel like they are being given some new information. You might think it should be obvious to everyone that the team is continuing to work to the plan, but that does not mean you cannot state the obvious. You might also have previously communicated that you do not anticipate any status changes for some time, but giving a little more information and reiterating what has already been said will make the stakeholders feel involved. The communication itself is as important as the action being taken. If you want the stakeholders to have confidence in your abilities to manage a crisis, make sure they know what you are doing. If you don't tell them, they will be none the wiser.

Communication Methods

Various communication methods are available for managing an emergency. Ideally, the best course of action is to use a combination of tools and methods to ensure the best possible coverage.

When there is a breaking news story, it will be reported on the local and national television news, on various radio stations, in the newspapers, and online. There are multiple ways to hear about and stay up to date with the situation. If you need to leave the house, you can safely turn off the television and continue listening to updates on the radio in the car. When you get to work, you can continue monitoring the story using online news Websites. You do not need to change your normal behavior or movements to keep abreast of the latest developments in the news story. The same should be true for the stakeholders who need to stay in touch with the latest status of your team's emergency. Give them the option to get the news via different mediums, and include the granularity that is appropriate for each method.

The communication methods available should include some, if not all, of the following:

- Phone calls—landline and mobile
- Pager
- Text message via pager, phone, or PDA
- Instant messaging via phone, PDA, or computer
- Online chat
- Email
- Conference calls—audio or video
- Onsite meetings (face-to-face communications)

Phone Calls: Landline and Mobile

The initial communications about a catastrophic event will most likely be made by phone. It is important to ensure that these phone calls are kept as short and concise as possible. There could be a lot of phone calls to make, and you might need to move on to formulating an action plan as quickly as possible. Share the high-level details, and let the stakeholder know that you will follow up with a more detailed email report within the next hour.

Write down what you are going to say before making the calls. This way, you will avoid sharing different information with different individuals and leaving out important facts. It is easy to get distracted and off-track when you are being asked lots of questions. If you are calling multiple people, you might remember telling a person something, when in fact you are remembering what you told the last person you were talking to. Just as call centers have scripts that they follow when talking to customers, you should prepare a script for talking to your stakeholders. Here is an example script:

- There is a red-alert problem affecting X functions of our business.
- The problem is contained/continues/is increasing/is decreasing.
- The problem occurred as a result of [explain].
- The problem has caused/is causing the following the damage: [explain].
- The problem is affecting the following systems: [list].
- The problem is affecting the following people (or organizations): [list].
- The problem has/hasn't the potential to intensify [explain].
- The response team has been mobilized. Current status of team is: [explain].
- Damage is being minimized by these immediate actions: [list].
- We will put into place the escalation/business continuity plan: [specify].
- We will complete the detailed action plan by [time/date].
- We anticipate the issue will be contained or resolved by [time/date].
- A detailed report and communication plan will be emailed at [time/date].

Once the initial communication has been completed, the phone is usually not the most effective tool for keeping the stakeholders and team members informed of progress. It is advisable to use the phone for keeping in touch with the emergency team members only. Ask stakeholders not to contact you via phone unless the issue is urgent, as your phone is the emergency "hotline" for the team members to report progress and request assistance.

Pager

Pagers may be used to contact primary stakeholders who were not available via phone on the first attempt. In this situation, pages should be used to request that the person call to speak to you or one of your representatives personally. You will need a feedback loop, so you can ensure that the message was received.

Keep in mind that using pagers for critical messages can be unreliable for various reasons:

- The person might have left the pager at home or in another room, where it cannot be heard.
- The sound might be turned off.
- The pager's batteries might have run down.
- The paging system might be very slow, and the message might be delayed for some time before receipt.

For these reasons, it is advisable to use the page as a last resort if other methods of contacting a primary stakeholder prove unsuccessful.

If a pager is being used to send a message to a non-primary stakeholder, you could simply send a message asking that the recipient check his or her email for a report on a red-status emergency. Using a pager or text-message distribution list is a great way of getting a short message to a lot of people very quickly.

Text Message via Pager, Phone, or PDA

Text messages are great for sending brief, concise updates that give a high-level status and advise recipients to check their email for more details. A text message should ideally be no longer than two or three sentences. Many text systems truncate longer messages, so get the most important information into the first two sentences. Texts are notoriously unreliable, so never use this method of communication for urgent information, unless no other method is available. As with the other communication methods, using a distribution list is a great way of getting a brief message out to a lot of people quickly, and with minimal effort.

A text message should contain high-level information, for example:

- Sentence 1: Cat event status RED.
- Sentence 2: Check email for details.
- Sentence 3: Phone conf at 4pm 1-800-555-5555 code:1234.

If possible, assign the sending of the text updates to an administrative assistant or other team member, to free up your time to continue to monitor and manage the emergency.

Instant Messaging via Phone, PDA, or Computer

Similar to the text messaging, phone, PDA, or computer messages should be kept brief and to the point. Messages received on mobile phones, PDAs, or computers might be redundant if you are also sending text and paged messages. However, there is no harm in adding an additional communication channel if this has the potential to increase the reliability of the communication.

Online Chat

Online chats are not appropriate for initial contact, but might be used for ongoing communication. Perhaps someone on the emergency operations team will maintain a chat session, where he or she can answer questions and keep the lines of communication open. For a high-impact issue, this might give stakeholders an additional feeling of comfort that they are on top of all the details as they emerge. Although the emergency might not get resolved any more quickly, the stakeholders will feel better about what is going on.

For virtual teams, it is very difficult collaborating on an emergency situation, since they cannot sit in the same room to discuss it with other team members! The chat room becomes the virtual meeting place, where team members can pop in and out as their schedules allow. This prevents team members from feeling isolated during the emergency.

Email

Email is an excellent tool for communicating the finer details of the situation and the action plan for managing and resolving it. Set up an email template to be used for all updates. The recipients will become familiar with the format very quickly, and will be able to scroll to the part they are most interested in. Here is an example template for email status updates:

- Subject: [Provide a codename or descriptive name.]
- Current status: [define]
- Status change since last update: [explain]
- Last email update: time/date
- Next email update: time/date
- Next meeting/phone conference: time/date/call-in details
- Emergency team:[List the team members.]
- Roles and responsibilities: [List them here.]

- ‣ Progress overview: general overview
- ‣ Issue 1: description of what has happened since last update
- ‣ Issue 2: description of what has happened since last update
- ‣ Issue 3: description of what has happened since last update
- ‣ Issue 4: description of what has happened since last update
- ‣ Highest priority tasks: description of high-priority tasks for the next reporting period
- ‣ Other info: [This section can be used to communicate shift changes for the emergency team, time and location of food deliveries if onsite meals are being provided, or any other information useful to the team that is not necessarily directly related to the progress on the emergency situation.]
- ‣ Links to more information: [Include links to the action plan, message board or chat room, or any other pertinent information or documentation that will help keep the recipients informed.]

Some of the information will not change between updates, and some will. It is a good idea to change the font color for the information that has changed, so it easy for recipients to see the progress and changes since the last update they read. See Figure 12.3 for an example status-update email.

Current Status:	Red
Status Change Since Last Update:	None
Current Email Update:	June 28th 2pm (PDT)
Next Email Update:	June 28th 6pm (PDT)
Next Meeting/Phone Conference:	June 28th 5pm (PDT) 1-800 555 5555 code:1234
Emergency Team:	Melanie Swan, David Johnson, June Zhang, Peter Barth
Roles And Responsibilities:	Melanie: Coordination and management David: Issue One June: Issue Two Peter: Issue Three
Progress Overview:	Situation is stable but no improvement yet. Anticipate situation will start to improve in approximately 5 - 7 hours
Issue One:	Continuing to work on issue. No significant progress yet
Issue Two:	Continuing to work on issue. No significant progress yet
Issue Three:	Continuing to work on issue. No significant progress yet
Issue Four:	Not assigned yet
Highest Priority Tasks:	Keep system stable to prevent further problems from developing
Other info: [this section can be used to communicate shift changes for the emergency team, time and location of food deliveries if onsite meals are being provided, or any other information useful to the team but not necessarily directly related to the progress on the emergency situation]	Anticipate assigning 2 more resources at 9am (PDT) tomorrow. Peter will take a break 10pm to 3am. June will break 3am - 8am. Melanie will break 4am - 9am.
Links to more information:	Website: https://privatenetwork.emergency.com Chat: https://privatenetwork.emergency.com/chat

Figure 12.3: Catastrophic event status report

Conference Calls: Audio or Video

Conference calls are an excellent communication medium for virtual emergencies. They can be used to keep the emergency taskforce in communication with each other, as well as being a very effective way to give regular status updates to the team and stakeholders.

As with the other communication methods, you must ensure that status update conference calls are scheduled, that the appropriate people are invited, and that everyone has the necessary call-in information. The meeting should have an agenda to ensure that the update is cohesive, informative, and contains key pieces of information. The agenda does not necessarily need to be written or distributed ahead of time. You can put it together as late as a few minutes before the meeting, as long as you share it with the conference attendees at the beginning of the call. This will help keep the meeting on track and ensure that it does not become a long discussion about every small detail of the problem, or about what caused the problem.

Here is an example agenda:

- Purpose of the conference
- Conference rules
- Current status
- High-level overview of progress
- Issue 1 status since last update
- Issue 2 status since last update
- Issue 3 status since last update
- Issue 4 status since last update
- New developments
- Top priorities and objectives for the next few hours
- Team status
- Q&A
- Wrap up: Give the time of the next conference call. Remind attendees of when to expect interim email updates. Request that attendees not contact team members—they need to focus on their tasks. If it is urgent, attendees should contact the manager. If it is not urgent, they should wait until the next update or until the emergency situation is resolved.

You should also prepare conference rules and ensure that they are restated at the beginning of each call, for example:

- The meeting will follow the agenda.
- Please keep all questions until the end. It is very likely that your question will be answered before we get to the Q&A section.
- The meeting will finish at exactly [time]. Please assist me in keeping the meeting on track.
- Anything not relevant to the agenda will be requested to be taken offline.
- Do not ask questions or make comments about why the problem occurred or what we can do to prevent it in the future. This is outside the scope of this meeting and will be the focus of a lessons-learned meeting after the emergency is resolved.
- No blaming anyone or making derogatory remarks. This is a stressful time for everyone, and we all need to stay positive and work together to achieve a successful and speedy resolution to this problem.

The agenda and the rules are extremely important. Without them, the meetings will be chaotic and stressful, and it will be hard to keep within the allotted time limit. The aim of the meetings is to inform stakeholders of the latest developments, increase confidence in the team and its abilities, and decrease stress. The more structure you build around the meetings, the more comfortable the attendees will feel. The more assertive and confident you are, the higher the level of confidence the stakeholders will have in you.

Onsite Meetings

Onsite meetings might be combined with conference calls if some of the team members or stakeholders are remote while others are local. Alternatively, onsite meetings might be held at a corporate or emergency location and not include any remote participants. If some stakeholders or team members are located in distant time zones, it might not make sense to have those people call in for meetings at unsociable hours. If the virtual team is split between locations in opposite time zones, it is possible to switch the emergency control from one location to the other at certain times of day. This way, the team that is off-duty can sleep while the on-duty team continues to work on the problem.

If the virtual team is split between locations in opposite time zones, it is possible to switch the emergency control from one location to the other at certain times of day.

Some catastrophes are highly confidential, and the organization will have strict rules about what and how information is shared. For security issues, some companies do not allow any communication about the problem to be discussed via email, phone conference, mobile phone, or text messages, as these are not considered secure methods of communication. In these highly sensitive situations, all communication is conducted at one onsite location with a select group of people present. Anyone who is remote and needs to be involved travels to the site as soon as possible and is updated upon his or her arrival.

As with the audio and video conference meetings, you should prepare both an agenda and a list of rules to ensure that onsite meetings are effective, efficient, and informative.

Managing the Aftermath

Catastrophic events can be very stressful and can have a domino effect that creates all types of interesting and unusual problems. The virtual team members might feel exhausted, overwhelmed, worried, relieved, upset, ecstatic, or a combination of all these emotions! The challenge for the manager is to figure out how each person is feeling and ensure that he or she is being managed appropriately. If the team members are a mass of conflicting emotions, it is important for the manager to talk to them to figure out what action to take to make them feel more grounded and centered.

First, talk to each team member individually. Thank the person for his or her help in resolving the problem (if appropriate), and ask how he or she is feeling. Next, schedule a team meeting or conference call to discuss how everyone is feeling and what action should be taken to get thing settled down and back to normal as soon as possible.

Before deciding on a course of action and implementing it, make sure you gauge the reaction of your team members to the plan. For example, giving all team members two days off might seem like a great plan to you. After all, they must be tired and stressed. Your team members, however, might feel the need to communicate with each other about what happened, to relieve some of the stress.

Taking two days off will make this difficult. Alternatively, the team members might be feeling stressed because they have neglected a lot of other work during the emergency, and want to get caught up on that before taking a break.

The team members might be very open to being given a couple of days off, but might want to choose for themselves when they take that time. Perhaps they would rather schedule a long weekend at a time when they are able to travel somewhere, or would like to coordinate the days off with those of their spouses or children. It is great to reward your team members for a job well done; just make sure you are giving them what they really want, and not just what you think they want!

If the team members feel like they need time to talk about what happened, give them that time by scheduling a phone conference. This can be especially important for any remote team members who were not involved in resolving the issues. Those team members might be feeling a bit left out. Scheduling some team time to talk about what happened and what needs to happen next gives those team members an opportunity to contribute ideas and to volunteer to help with some of the aftermath tasks. It closes the loop for your team and gives everyone the feeling that they are all involved in the solution.

Lessons Learned and Best Practices

What is the most important thing to do as soon as the emergency is under control? Schedule a lessons-learned meeting! Lessons-learned meetings are vitally important element to managing and controlling catastrophic events. They provide a great opportunity for team members to:

- Vent frustrations
- Discuss issues
- Be heard
- Be catalysts for change
- Present ideas
- Make suggestions
- Perform root-cause analysis
- Be creative and innovative
- Improve processes
- Build teamwork

Lessons-learned meetings are incredibly valuable to the company, the team, and the employees. It is important, however, not to let these meetings degenerate into a general forum for moaning, groaning, and complaining. They need to be focused on two things:

- ▸ Identify issues
- ▸ Find ways, through positive thought processes and teamwork, to improve processes and procedures that will minimize risk and maximize productivity, reliability, predictability, effectiveness, and efficiency

Lesson-learned meetings help the team focus on continually improving process. No matter how serious or devastating the catastrophe, the lessons-learned meeting gives a very positive end to a difficult situation. The team can move on feeling positive about what has been learned and the improvements that will be put in place as a result of those feelings. Ideally, the lessons-learned meeting will be followed by a team celebration to thank everyone for their efforts during and after the emergency.

Virtual Management and Communication Tools

It is important not to confuse tools with processes. This might seem like an obvious statement, but many people make this mistake. Before choosing which tools to use, it is important to define the processes and functions for which the tools will be used.

How many times have you witnessed a manager responding to a process issue by creating a new spreadsheet or report that employees must complete each month, but which doesn't address the cause of the problem at all? How many times have you observed a company rushing out to buy PDAs for a team because they are going to be working virtually, and expecting that everything will run smoothly because they have a spreadsheet and a PDA?

When deciding which virtual tools are required, ensure that the processes, procedures, functions, and methods are clearly defined and documented first. A carpenter will not use a drill to cut a piece of wood in half. It is possible that he or she could drill a series of holes that would result in the piece of wood being halved, but this would not be very efficient or clean. If you choose the tools before you have defined the purpose, or if you opt to use the same tool for every process, you are not going to be able to complete your projects with high quality or in a timely manner.

If the virtual team is composed of employees who work in different locations but work out of local offices and rarely travel, they probably don't need PDAs with integrated email and phones. If the team members call in regularly for conference calls, it would be a better use of funds to purchase conference phones or a video conferencing system for each location. If the team members communicate directly with each other on a regular basis, individual Webcams might help to bring the team closer together and are much cheaper than integrated phones or PDAs. Good virtual-management software that allows the users to share documentation and to communicate in real time or via a message board would also be a great idea for a virtual, static environment.

> No amount of virtual communication tools can replace good process and effective management.

Think about the functions, locations, and mobility requirements for each team member before deciding which applications and tools will be the most appropriate. No amount of virtual communication tools can replace good process and effective management. Your team members will very likely be eager to get their hands on as many cool gadgets and toys as possible, but that does not mean those gadgets will make them more effective or efficient. The tool must fit the purpose. A landline phone enables the user to make phone calls. A mobile phone does the same. If the user never travels and only needs to be contactable while in the office, a mobile phone is not necessary. It allows mobility, but at the expense of quality and security. Consider what is most important: the mobility of the user, or the quality and security of the call?

There are many tools that enhance the virtual team's ability to communicate and work collaboratively. Some of these tools are more elaborate and expensive than others. Some are more reliable than others. Some tools will be necessary for every team member, while others will be needed for specific team members only. Some tools will be essential to the running of the business, while others will be supplemental tools to enhance or improve the functionality of the standard tools.

The more technology you use, the more things can go wrong. Wherever possible, have backup processes or tools that can be used if there is a problem with a specific tool. Too much reliance on one tool can result in unnecessary problems, which could have been completely avoided with some contingency planning.

Collaborative Tools

There are a variety of collaborative tools on the market, with different degrees of functionality and cost. These virtual-management tools allow team members to share virtual workspaces, so that each team member has access to the same information, documents, and tools. The virtual workspaces enable team members to run virtual meetings, share applications, give presentations, and access desktops across the team. They also give you the ability to communicate via a message board or in real time, using audio and/or video communication methods.

Collaboration software is available for different platforms and operating systems. Some have multiplatform support, while others require that all users are on the same platform. Some of the systems require that each user install software, while others require server-side installation only. Many of the tools include a Web client, so users can connect to the system using a standard browser.

There are many combinations of features, accessibility, and cost. The most expensive tools are not necessarily the best ones. Most companies allow you to download free, trial versions of the software. We highly recommend that you do this before you decide to buy. Allow yourself adequate time to use the tools as much as possible during the trial period in exactly the same way you plan to use them once they are in general use. This is the only way to evaluate the suitability of the tools for your specific environment.

We tried out a few different tools, and found that we liked the features of one, the user interface of another, and the cost of still another. It was hard to find a perfect virtual collaboration tool, even when looking at the most highly priced systems. Use the information you gather from evaluating the available tools to find the most appropriate tool (or combination of tools) at a price that fits your budget. Buying a system containing lots of features you will never use is not necessarily the best use of your budget dollars, unless you are also purchasing it because it meets your needs for the user interface, flexibility, and accessibility you require.

> It was hard to find a perfect virtual collaboration tool, even when looking at the most highly priced systems.

We looked at a lot of collaborative tools while writing this book. Some of the tools were complete integrated solutions, but most of them fell into one of the following three categories:

- Online meetings
- Online document management
- Online scheduling

The virtual level of your team and how much collaboration is required will help determine whether a fully integrated tool is the best solution, or if more specialized tools will better meet your needs.

With the integrated solutions, you are getting a lot of tools in one, but you might not be getting the best tools for the job. Many companies are very good at designing and developing one or two excellent features, while the rest of the features are acceptable or, in some cases, barely usable. It would be great if you could find one product to meet all your needs, but if you can't, the best solution might be to implement more than one product and be confident that the tools will meet the needs of your users and your organization.

Make sure you have adequately prioritized the features you need, and that you test the tools before purchasing them to verify that they live up to your expectations. It is not a good idea to base your purchase decision on marketing materials. The tool might advertise itself as being able to do "X," but in reality, using the tool to do "X" might be a lot more time-consuming and clunky than is acceptable.

Integrated Virtual-Management Tools

Windows SharePoint is one of the only truly integrated virtual-management tools we could find. Many of the others that advertised themselves as such had some key functionality missing. The SharePoint tool includes the following features:

- Document library
- Shared calendar
- Online meetings
- Online scheduling/planning
- Discussion forum
- Integrated with Microsoft office programs

The SharePoint site is available via the Web. Users are not required to download and install software to use the system.

Online Meeting Tools

There are plenty of online meeting tools on the market. They vary greatly in price and functionality.

Netmeeting

Netmeeting comes as a standard feature in Microsoft Office. It is best used for small meetings, but it does include some nice features like audio, whiteboard, document sharing, and workspace sharing. The biggest limitation with Netmeeting is that all attendees have to be connected to the same Microsoft Exchange server. This can seriously limit the virtual team's ability to communicate, as it is not always possible for team members to be connected to the same Exchange server. This requirement also means that the tool is not applicable for client or vendor meetings.

Global Crossing

The Global Crossing, Ready Access tools includes communication tools for audio conferencing, video conferencing, and online meetings. The tools are very easy to use. Minimal to no training is required to learn how to set up and run an online meeting. It is has an intuitive and easy-to-use interface for giving presentations and sharing desktops. Global Crossing tools are available via a subscription service. Global Crossing offer support for both Mac and Windows platforms.

Webex

Webex is an online meeting and presentation system. It can be a bit complicated to use, but the company offers online training to help users learn how to use the tools. It is a great way to share information across the Web because it offers both flexibility and rich functionality. Webex offers audio, video, and online meeting services. It is available via subscription, or pay-per-use with charges per-minute, per-user. Webex is cross-platform, supported on Windows, Mac, and Linux.

Microsoft Live Meeting

Microsoft Live Meeting is available via the Web. Users have the option to install the Live Meeting Console on their desktops or to connect using the Web Console, which requires no software installation. This offers the flexibility that virtual team members often need when traveling. They can connect to meetings from any computer. One-time attendees can connect to the meetings without having to go through the task of installing software. If clients or vendors are invited to participate in meetings, they might be unable to install software on their systems that has not been approved by their IT group. Live Meeting is supported on Windows only.

Document-Management Systems

Virtual teams require a centralized document repository to enable them to manage and have access to the same sets of files. It is very difficult to maintain version control if documents are distributed, reviewed, and updated by sending them out in emails to numerous folks. In that situation, you don't know if you have the latest version on your own desktop, and the chances are that you will make updates to older versions of documents. This can add a lot of confusion and additional work for the documentation's author.

Storing documents online is a much more streamlined and efficient process. Many online collaboration tools include some level of document sharing. Not all of them are true document-management systems, but they do facilitate a central place for storing and accessing documents. Some online collaboration tools are primarily document-management systems. We found, however, many of the tools lacked support for document versioning and source control. This means that the virtual team needs to manage version control manually, by leaving change-tracking turned on in the document (which can get messy after numerous updates), or by saving a new copy of the document each time it is updated.

E-room

E-room is primarily a document-management system. It includes version control for documents. E-room also includes some project planning and instant messaging functionality. The project planning is quite limited, but it can be integrated with Microsoft Office programs. It is not easy navigating around E-room. We often found that we could not get back to where we started, and ended up having to log out and back in to get to the page where we wanted to be.

Groove

Groove is primarily a document-management program. It is does not include any version control for documents. You can drag and drop files from your desktop into Groove, but there is limited drag-and-drop functionality between folders inside Groove, which limits the user in file management. The user interface is a bit clunky and not customizable. Users can post messages in Groove, but it is not integrated with email so, unless users login and check for new messages regularly, they will not know a message is waiting. For the price, it is good tool, but you get what you pay for.

Online Scheduling and Time Tracking

There are a lot of online scheduling and time-tracking systems. Many of these tools have an interface similar to Microsoft Project. Some of them are very limited in functionality, lacking even basic functions like adding dependencies to tasks, so you definitely need to try these tools before deciding to purchase.

Microsoft Project Server

Microsoft Project Server allows team members to collaborate on project schedules via the Web. It is ideal for virtual teams. If only one person updates the project plans, however, it is much cheaper to upload a standard Microsoft Project schedule to the team's virtual or document-management system, so team members can view it and the project owner can make the updates and upload the changes.

Quickarrow

Quickarrow combines scheduling, time and expense reporting, and document management. This is a great tool for project time accounting and project expense tracking. It also contains some useful reporting tools. It has a browser-based user interface, which makes it easily accessible for all team members and locations.

PDAs and Smartphones

The PDA market is huge. It seems everyone has their own version of a PDA or smartphone these days. Some offer more integrated solutions than others, and PDAs are available in numerous price ranges. PDAs give users the ability to stay in touch while mobile, but what is gained in convenience is definitely lost in the quality of communications. Even with QWERTY keyboards, you need very nimble fingers to be able to type on a tiny, little keypad. Many PDA users now suffer from what has become known as "BlackBerry thumb." This is a repetitive-strain injury in the thumb from using the BlackBerry device's wheel.

There is also a growing social addiction to PDAs. Most of us are used to seeing people with mobile phones constantly pressed to their ears and a seeming inability to go more than 10 minutes without needing to make or receive a call. The PDA addiction is fast catching up and might even be surpassing the mobile phone addiction. At least sitting twiddling with wheels and typing on miniature keyboards is not as loud and distracting as the phone conversations over dinner or in the movies, but the rudeness factor when using the tool in company is at a comparable level. The media have coined the expression "Crackberry" to describe the current PDA addiction.

Some popular PDAs include the following:

- ► BlackBerry
- ► Palm Treo
- ► T-Mobile Sidekick

BlackBerry

The BlackBerry is a very popular PDA. It is so popular, in fact, that many people now refer to all PDAs as BlackBerrys, just as they refer to all facial tissues as Kleenex! The BlackBerry is available in various models with different combinations of features. The features include a mobile phone, conference calling, an electronic organizer, instant messaging, a Web browser, GPS, and email. The BlackBerry has its limitations, as do most integrated tools. For example, there is a limit on the size of documents that can be viewed, and some attachments cannot be opened because they require special software not yet available on the BlackBerry.

Palm Treo

The Treo is another combination tool that comes in a variety of models. The Treo combines a mobile phone with text and instant messages, email, an organizer, an mp3 player, a camera, and Microsoft Office Mobile programs. Palm has been producing Palm PDAs for many years; as such, it has a loyal customer base. The Palm Treo gets excellent reviews and is consistently rated higher than other PDAs/smartphones.

T-Mobile Sidekick

The Sidekick is also a combination tool. The Sidekick combines a mobile phone with Internet, text messaging, instant messaging, email, an organizer, a camera, and a QWERTY keyboard. It cannot play mp3s, which is disappointing to some users. However, it gets great reviews for its flip-up screen.

IM and SMS

Instant messaging (IM) and text messaging (SMS, for "short messaging service") are helpful tools for the virtual team. Messages can be received via computer, phone, or PDA. This makes IM and SMS great for contacting people, whether they are in the office, on the move, or at unknown whereabouts!

There are a few different IM tools from various companies. Incompatibility between the tools means that many people need to have two or more IM programs installed. Some of the IM companies have Web portals that enable users to send and receive messages without having to install the software on their computers. This functionality is ideal for users who are limited to one type of IM program on a work computer system, or for those who are using someone else's computer.

Some of the more popular instant messaging services include the following:

- ‣ America Online's, AOL Instant Messenger
- ‣ Yahoo's Yahoo! Messenger
- ‣ Microsoft Network's MSN Messenger
- ‣ IBM's Lotus Sametime

Text messages (SMS) are another great way to communicate via cell phone, pager, or PDA. SMS is a very effective communication tool for getting short messages to recipients quickly. Most people keep their mobile phones and PDAs with them in meetings, even if they do not take their laptops. For time-critical messages that cannot wait until the recipient checks his or her email, text messaging is ideal.

Text messaging is used much more extensively in the United Kingdom and Europe than in the United States This is mainly due to the high cost of making calls to mobile phones in those regions, versus the low (or no) cost of sending text messages. In the United States, calls to mobile phones are relatively cheap, and text messages tend to be relatively expensive. Therefore, phone calls are still a more popular communication method than texts in the United States

Video Conferencing

Video conferencing is a great tool, but it doesn't work all that well for more than two locations, unless there is a presenter in one location and the other locations are all calling in just to view the presentation without two-way communication. It would be too difficult for the presenter to try to squeeze five or six video feeds onto one monitor and keep an eye on what all the participants are doing. Generally, this method of communication will work really well for the split team, or for a team with only one or two virtual members.

Video conferencing is great for communicating between two locations, such as when running remote client meetings or project kickoff meetings. Sometimes, it is more viable to run a large meeting from two locations rather than transporting the whole team to a single location. It is often more time- and cost-effective for team members to travel to the closest of two locations and set up a video conference between the locations.

For one-on-one video conferencing, by far the cheapest tool is a Webcam. It is a fraction of the cost of a professional video conferencing system, although the quality is lower. Often, using online meeting tools combined with a phone conference will meet all the needs of the meeting participants.

Most corporate offices have at least one video conference room. It is also possible to rent video conferencing services from companies such as Kinkos.

Phone Conferencing

What would a virtual team be without phone conferencing? So many companies and teams rely on phone conferencing these days that it is hard to imagine how we managed without them! There is hardly a meeting room in any organization in the world without the spaceship-shaped phone conference unit sitting in the middle of the table.

Phone conferencing phones and sound stations are available from companies such as these:

- ➤ Polycom
- ➤ Nortel
- ➤ Lucent
- ➤ AT&T

There are hundreds of companies offering conferencing services, just as there are hundreds of companies offering other telephone services. You can find a service to meet every budget. The appropriate service provider should be chosen based on the frequency of calls and the number of attendees.

Phone conferencing is heavily used by both virtual and non-virtual teams. It is a great tool for communicating with employees, clients, and vendors.

CHAPTER

14

Virtual Leadership

If you ask 100 people what makes a successful leader, you will notice that many of the respondents quote similar qualities and characteristics, including these:

» Competence
» Self-assurance
» Courage
» Commitment
» Passion
» Integrity
» Accountability
» Teaching skills
» Interpersonal skills
» Ability to drive issues to resolution

» Character
» Charisma
» Focus
» Initiative
» Vision
» Team-building ability
» Trustworthy
» Inspired
» Motivated
» Decision-making ability

» Confidence
» Communication skills
» Generosity
» Listening skills
» Attitude
» Ownership/responsibility
» Strategic thinking
» Self-disciplined
» Ethical
» Conflict-management skills

Every leader does not possess every single one of these qualities or characteristics, of course. Each leader will possess his or her own unique combination of them.

It is important not to confuse intelligence or knowledge with leadership. Knowing more about a subject than others or being smarter than others does not necessarily equate to being a good leader. A leader does not need to tell others what to do. A leader inspires, encourages, and enables others to achieve more and to realize their full potential. A leader strives for commitment from others, not compliance. Demanding compliance is dictatorship; inspiring commitment is leadership.

Here are a few quotes about leadership:

Albert Einstein said of leaders, "We should take care not to make the intellect our god; it has, of course, powerful muscles but no personality. It cannot lead; it can only serve."

President Harry Truman said, "My definition of a leader in a free country is a man who can persuade people to do what they don't want to do, or do what they're too lazy to do, and like it."

General George S. Patton said, "Never tell people how to do things. Tell them what to do and they will surprise you with their ingenuity."

There are many different perspectives and opinions about leadership, but most would agree that leading others is not telling them what to do and how to do it, it is telling them what you need and empowering and inspiring them to figure out the best way to do it. A leader should worry about the *what* and let others worry about the *how*.

Leading the Virtual Team

Leading a virtual team requires that you have a very strong presence on the team. Your team members need to feel that you are influencing every aspect of the work they do, even though you are not involved in managing the details. You should definitely not try to micro-manage your team members, however. Your presence should be felt in a positive, non-invasive way.

Leadership on virtual teams does not and cannot work the same way it does on a traditional team. On a traditional team, the manager is the de facto leader. The manager then establishes himself or herself as worthy of the leadership title by demonstrating some number of the traditional leadership qualities, like charisma and accountability. Some managers in traditional organizations are not very good leaders. In many organizations, it seems to be acceptable to be an average leader as long as the basic management skills are present.

In a virtual environment, there is no such thing as a de facto leader. The manager has to become the leader through influence, not through authority or implied right. If the manager is not able to establish himself or herself as an effective leader very early on, the virtual team members will not bond with each other or with the manager, and the team will not be successful. In virtual leadership, knowledge and experience have a greater influence than charisma and ownership.

This is the opposite of how it works in a traditional leadership role. On a virtual team, the ability to articulate and empathize is more important than courage or generosity. If you are unable to establish yourself as the team's leader, the team members will look to other members of the team for the leadership influence they need. You will find that the team members are not following your direction, but are taking it from elsewhere.

> In a virtual environment, there is no such thing as a de facto leader. The manager has to become the leader through influence, not through authority or implied right.

To demonstrate our point, consider this: Successful, traditional leaders are often described as being charismatic. People often describe Tony Blair, the Prime Minister of the United Kingdom, as charismatic. Many believe that his charismatic appeal is what makes him so successful. Does he sound charismatic, though, when you hear him speak? Charismatic is probably not a word you can use to describe how someone sounds. How do you demonstrate charisma via a phone conference or an email? The answer is, you can't. You cannot emulate a quality that is mostly non-verbal using primarily verbal communication. For this reason, virtual leadership requires a different balance of leadership qualities.

Maintaining Professional Integrity

A true leader will practice integrity without compromise. Integrity is being true to yourself and to others. It is practicing what you preach. It is doing what you say you will do. It is taking responsibility for your own decisions or actions, and not blaming others for your mistakes. Having integrity means being honest, following your team's or company's rules, having a good work ethic, being considerate to others, and doing the right thing.

As the leader of a virtual team, your team members will be guided and influenced by you and your actions. To exert the necessary influence over your team to establish yourself as the leader, you need to demonstrate personal integrity, and you need to encourage and value it in others.

A true leader will lead by example, and others will follow. If you are true to yourself, you learn how to see the truth in others. If you have integrity, you have honesty. If you are honest, you never have to worry about keeping your facts straight and remembering what you said yesterday, as you will not forget the truth. Your decisions might not always be popular, but your team will know that your decisions are fair, appropriate, and made for the right reasons. You will encounter fewer conflicts if others can see that you are the person you present yourself to be.

You cannot change the fundamental beliefs of any of your team members, but you can insist that they maintain minimum standards of behavior while they are part of your team. You have a responsibility as a leader to make it very clear to your team members what you expect from them. For example, you should communicate that every team member must be honest. This means they must tell the truth; not lie, mislead, or hold back information that would put a different light on whatever it is they are communicating about or working on. Honesty should be a requirement for team members in interactions and communications with you and other leaders within the organization, as well as with each other and with clients, vendors, and partners. You should communicate clearly the consequences of dishonesty within your organization. In most organizations, dishonesty is grounds for dismissal. Depending on the extent of the dishonesty, it might also be grounds for legal action.

Some organizations create operating values or codes of conduct for their employees that define what is expected of the company and the employees of the company. This is not the same as a charter, which is focused more on the goals of the team, the *what*. The operating values act as the team's values or behavior guide, the *how*. If your organization has existing operating values or a code of conduct, make sure that you know what it is and that you live up to it.

If you do not currently have a code of conduct, consider working with your team members to create one for your team. If your team members have been involved in creating your team's operating values, they will be more inclined to follow them. Here are some examples of operating values:

- Integrity
- Doing the right thing
- Treating others with respect and dignity
- Honesty
- Teamwork
- Commitment

Each value will need a definition that clearly explains what it means. Figure 14.1 shows an example company values document. Ideally, the definitions will be crafted by the team members collaboratively, so they have a strong sense of ownership for the team's values. Creating operating values would be an excellent team-building activity for your next face-to-face meeting.

Integrity
Practice integrity without compromise. Be true to yourself and to others. Practice what you preach. Do what you say you will do. Take responsibility for your own decisions and actions, and do not blame others for your mistakes.

Doing The Right Thing
You know what is right and wrong. If you always do the right thing you will not have to make excuses for why you did the wrong thing. If your manager asks you do something that you know is not the right thing, you have a responsibility to challenge the request, and the right not to do it.

Treating Others With Respect And Dignity
If you are unsure whether something you want to say might be considered rude or disrespectful, don't say it. Our company is comprised of a diverse team of people with different personal values and beliefs. Be respectful of those values and beliefs. Do not do or say anything that others might find insulting, demeaning, or compromising of their personal integrity.

Honesty
If you are honest, you never have to worry about keeping your facts straight and remembering what you said yesterday, as you will not forget the truth. This means you must tell the truth; not lie, mislead, or hold back information that would put a different light on whatever it is you are communicating about or working on. Honesty should be a requirement for all team members in interactions and communications with their manager and other leaders within the organization, as well as with each other and with clients, vendors, and partners.

Teamwork
Without teamwork none of us can be successful. Your work should not be focused on achieving personal recognition but on building and contributing to outstanding teamwork, as that will lead us all to true success.

Commitment
Commitment to yourself, your team, your manager, your clients, your projects, the company and to following the company values is key to the long-term success of all employees.

Figure 14.1 -Company values

Controlling Your Emotions

There are times when things get stressful, and sometimes frustration leads to emotional, angry outbursts. These outbursts might be acceptable at home for members of the household younger than six, but they are not acceptable for adults in the workplace, virtual or not. Emotional outbursts are extremely destructive for anyone in a supervisory role. A manager can destroy years of reputation and good teamwork in minutes by losing control over a work issue.

Sometimes it is impossible not to feel totally frustrated. When you have told the same person the same thing 10 times this week, and they still do not seem to understand, it can be hard to keep your tone calm and your demeanor cool. When you have repeatedly requested that a specific action not be taken, have explained why it should not be taken, and then find out that you were completely ignored and it was taken, it can be hard to stay calm. Now you must clean up the mess that someone else created, and restraining yourself from virtually strangling someone might be quite an effort. Remember, restraint is the appropriate response.

As stated earlier in this book, never take action or communicate your opinions while you are feeling angry about a situation. Give yourself time to calm down, put things into perspective, and think about the most constructive way of responding to the situation. Sometimes, you might need to delay your response for a few hours or even a few days. Do whatever it takes to ensure that you do not lose your cool and react from emotion rather than reason.

There is a great poem, *If*, by Rudyard Kipling, that comes to mind regarding staying calm and keeping your head in a crisis. Here is the first verse:

If you can keep your head when all about you
Are losing theirs and blaming it on you,
If you can trust yourself when all men doubt you
But make allowance for their doubting too,
If you can wait and not be tired by waiting,
Or being lied about, don't deal in lies,
Or being hated, don't give way to hating,
And yet don't look too good, nor talk too wise.

Staying calm and unemotional are the keys to successfully managing conflict and highly emotional situations. When everyone else is stressed out, angry, and frustrated, it takes just one person remaining calm and being the voice of reason to bring everyone else back to resembling normal, healthy human beings! Strive to be that person. Do not allow yourself to the perpetrator of the angst. Be the peacemaker. The mere act of trying to keep the peace will start to calm you down and help you put things into perspective. This does not mean that you should not be firm and assertive. You are not required to agree with everyone, or to let anyone off the hook for actions that led to bad results. You must conduct yourself respectfully and maintain a high level of integrity at all times.

The most widely used communication method on the virtual team is email. When someone riles you, it is not possible to go to his or her office and talk about it. You need to either call or email. Wait until you have calmed down before doing either. Never send angry emails, never send accusatory emails, and never reprimand anyone via email. It is unprofessional and cowardly. The first choice is to speak to someone face-to-face, the second choice is to speak via the phone. There isn't really a third choice, but if all else fails, and the only way to correspond is via email, be very careful how you word what you want to say. Never, ever copy anyone on an email that contains anything that might make the recipient look bad or feel humiliated. It might make you feel better temporarily, but in the long run, it makes you look unprofessional and petty, and the recipient will feel anger and resentment toward you.

> To be an effective leader, you need others to be inspired by you, to admire you, and to emulate your professional behavior.

To be an effective leader, you need others to be inspired by you, to admire you, and to emulate your professional behavior. You do not want others to despise you for humiliating them, and be hoping you mess up really badly so that you get fired! A supportive team will get you a long way in business, but they will only support you if you earn that privilege. If you are concerned about how something you need to communicate might be received, you could bounce it off someone else on the team first, to ensure that you are accurately conveying the message you want to get across without making anyone feel or look bad. A sanity check, input from a voice of reason on your team before you communicate, can save you a lot of back-pedaling and damage control after the fact.

Professionalism at All Costs

Being professional means showing respect for others. If you are unsure whether something you want to say might be considered rude or disrespectful, don't say it. Remember that you are dealing with a diverse team of people who most likely have personal values and beliefs different from yours. Do not take chances on saying or doing things that your team members might find insulting, demeaning, or compromising of their personal integrity.

Be very careful when telling jokes. It is very easy to insult someone if the joke refers to such things as religion, sex, race, sexual orientation, gender, nationality, and so on. You never know in which context someone will take a joke, so

> How you behave at home or with your friends is your business; how you behave in the presence of your work colleagues is everyone's business.

unless it is very generic, it might be better to save it for your friends and not share it with your work colleagues.

Staying down to earth, having personal and professional integrity, respecting others, and being committed to teamwork will not only make you a better manager and a more effective leader, it will give you a huge amount of personal satisfaction. Conduct yourself in the way that you know to be right. How you behave at home or with your friends is your business; how you behave in the presence of your work colleagues is everyone's business.

Prejudice in the Workplace—Intentional and Unintentional

Prejudice takes two forms: intentional and unintentional. Intentional prejudice is premeditated discrimination, intolerance, unfairness, narrow-mindedness, or bigotry. Intentional prejudice is destructive and should never be tolerated in the workplace. It is usually obvious when someone has the intention to discriminate against someone else, but it is not always easy to prove, as people who take those kinds of actions are often careful to cover their tracks.

Unintentional prejudice is when someone says or does something unintentionally that offends another person in some way. It might be that what was said was perceived as being unfair or discriminatory, or that it made someone feel he or she is considered to have a lower worth than his or her peers. Unintentional prejudice can also be detrimental, but the situations that are created by it can often be put right if immediate and decisive action is taken.

No matter what we might wish to think, every single one of us has prejudices. It is normal human behavior. The word prejudice has very negative connotations, but not all prejudice is negative or unacceptable. Most people have a tendency to be prejudiced in favor of their own family members, for example. We think the children in our own family are more intelligent, talented, pretty, handsome, or accomplished than other people's children. It is a prejudice to feel that other children are not up to the same standards as your own. If a mother feels this way about her child, most people would think it perfectly normal. What happens, though, if she is a teacher, and one of the children she teaches is her own child? Does she favor her child over other children, or is she harder on her child than the others to try to prove that she is not favoring her own? It can be a tricky situation. Any prejudice that results from it is most likely unintentional, but it still has the potential to have very negative results.

A similar situation can occur with your team. You might feel that your virtual team is the best one in your entire company. You might think that your team members are more accomplished, intelligent, experienced, smarter, and more fun than those on other teams. You would not be accused of prejudice against another person or team, unless you had to work with them on a project, you proceeded to assign your team members all the interesting and challenging work, and only let the other team members work on the easy, boring stuff. See how easy it is to cross the line between having the best intentions and demonstrating prejudice?

If a person feels unfairly or inappropriately treated by his or her colleagues or manager, it could be that the manager or colleagues are intentionally or unintentionally being prejudiced. Alternatively, it could be that the employee is over sensitive and is being treated fairly and appropriately.

It is appropriate for a high-performing team member to be paid more than a lower-performing team member. It is appropriate for the more qualified and experienced team members to be given more complex assignments than are junior team members.

It is not appropriate for assignments to be made according to the manager's personal favorites, favoring one gender, nationality, or race over another. These are clearly prejudices. Sometimes, the people who are prejudiced do not believe that they are. They think, because they truly believe one gender, race, or nationality is likely to perform better than another, that their decisions are based on facts, not prejudice. This is not unintentional prejudice. The actions were intentional and were based on discrimination and narrow-mindedness.

A lot of discriminatory behavior, opinions, and attitudes are the result of stereotypes. Generalizations are made about people based on gender, race, religion, educational background, accent, nationality, and so on. Decisions based on these generalizations are prejudice. People should be evaluated based on their personal actions, proven abilities, and merit, not on a general idea about what other people from the same place or background might be like. We live in a global environment and work on cross-cultural teams,

> A lot of discriminatory behavior, opinions, and attitudes are the result of stereotypes.

with people located in diverse geographical regions. We cannot afford to judge others based on generalizations and stereotypes.

Be aware of your own motivations, attitudes, and opinions. Do not try to kid yourself that you have no prejudice. Instead, try to understand it, and strive to make decisions about people based on facts and observations, not on prejudice and general assumptions. You do not have to act on unsubstantiated gut feelings. Your first impulse might be to do one thing, but the best decision might be to do something else. This is where you put your personal feelings and biases aside and do the right thing. This is personal integrity. This is what will make you an excellent and accomplished leader.

Inspiring Others

If you are able to take the advice contained in this chapter and lead by walking ahead so that others can follow, rather than by walking behind so you can push others where you want them to go, you will inspire your team.

If your actions speak louder than your words and reflect an impeccable personal integrity, others will aspire to be like you. If you encourage and praise, rather than bully and reprimand, you will make others feel good about themselves. If you give others the authority to make decisions, take responsibility, and be accountable, you are empowering them. Empowerment gives people the tools they need to be successful in business and in life. Each person must choose if and how to use the tools you make available. You cannot direct people to do this. You can only inspire them. The rest, they have to do for themselves.

You cannot inspire others by controlling them, or by forcing them to your will. Their will might be different from yours, and we all have to be true to ourselves. You will inspire others by showing the way, and being living proof that doing the right thing and never compromising personal integrity will make them happy and successful. We each need to decide what happiness and success means to us. We need to find our own way, follow our own dreams, and live by our own codes of conduct.

A true virtual leader will influence and inspire others to reach for greatness, to find the path that is right for them, and to go their own way.

Virtual Skill Set Checklists

Throughout this book, we discuss the specific skill Sets that both the virtual manager and the remote worker need to maximize success. This section consolidates that information into high-level checklists of skills and qualities.

Skill Sets Required for the Virtual Manager

Virtual managers need the following skill Sets:

- General management
- People management
- Communication
- Technical
- Decision making
- Problem solving
- Team building
- Administrative
- Personal

General-Management Skill Set

The general-management skill Set includes the ability to stay in control of the project, contract or team; to keep things on track; and to know the project's current status.

General-Management Skill Set	Description
Scheduling tasks	Ability to plan and schedule tasks, milestones, and deliverables across a geographically diverse team.
Organization	High level of organizational skill. Ability to plan and organize management and team tasks and events.
Time management	Ability to manage time and tasks across time zones. Understand how cultural differences affect an individual's concept of time.
Decision making	Ability to make and communicate decisions clearly and unambiguously. Ability to understand and act on information related to remote problems.
Leadership	Ability to lead by influence rather than authority. Establish and maintain trust with diverse team members across cultures, time zones, and functional units. Accountable for decisions and outcomes for the virtual team.
Prioritization	Prioritize work for self and team members. Ownership for setting, changing, and communicating team and individual priorities for local and remote team members.
Goal setting (manager and team)	Ability to set clear, measurable goals and objectives for self and the team as a whole. Ability to accurately measure and verify results. Ability to effectively communicate results to senior management.
Tracking and reporting progress	Set up processes and procedures for tracking, reporting, and verifying status for virtual team members. Ability to translate individual status reports into the overall progress report. Ability to communicate status to team members and stakeholders using virtual communication methods and tools.
Managing change	Ability to evaluate and manage change across a geographically and culturally diverse team.
Budgets and finance	Work with team members to set, manage, and control budgets, costs, and revenues. Use a virtual reporting system to maintain the appropriate level of control and understanding of the financial status at all times.

People-Management Skill Set

People-management skills are required for virtual managers whether or not they have direct reports. Virtual managers manage by influence rather than authority, which requires a much greater level of people-management and communication skills.

People-Management Skill Set	Description
Active listening	High level of skill in active listening. Ability to listen and mirror back what has been heard. Ability to "hear between the lines" and understand what is not being said as well as what is being said.
Coordinating and scheduling resources	Coordinate and schedule resources. Ability to gain an understanding of remote team members' abilities and interests to facilitate effective resource assignments and scheduling.
Hiring and firing	Excellent phone interview skills. Ability to conduct the initial interview, evaluation, and short-listing of candidates via phone. Understand when someone needs to be removed from the team. Understand how to conduct necessary steps leading up to termination. Understand applicable labor laws in each region or country. Be willing and able to take necessary action to terminate team members remotely or travel to do so in person. Know which course of action is most appropriate.
Pay decisions	Understand what pay decisions are appropriate for a virtual team. Pay decisions are based on individual performance and results, as well as the role on the team and the region in which each team member resides. Cost of living, inflation, and special regional or national circumstances can all play a part in pay decisions for geographically diverse teams.
Goal setting (individual)	Use team and management goals to set trickle-down individual goals for team members. Some goals might depend on geography or nationality.
Setting personal objectives	Ability to communicate with and understand each remote team member. Set appropriate, measurable, and verifiable objectives for each team member. Work with each team member to define personal growth and development wants and needs.
Performance evaluation	Evaluate performance from a distance by accurately measuring and verifying individual accomplishments and results. Ability to successfully communicate performance feedback and ratings verbally.

People-Management Skill Set	Description
Meeting facilitation	Virtual meetings require a high level of skill in facilitation and an acute awareness of what is occurring during the meetings. Ensure that only one person speaks at a time and that everyone gets to speak. Maintain awareness of who is paying attention and who is distracted. Strong note-taking ability, so meetings can be followed up with minutes to review and reiterate details and important points.
Conflict resolution	High level of skill in conflict management and excellent verbal communication (speaking and listening) skills, since virtual conflict is harder to recognize and resolve than conflict between local workers.
Coaching and development	High level of skill and comfort giving online, phone, and email coaching and development. Includes online training and presentation skills.

Communication Skill Set

Effective and well-managed communication is essential for successful virtual management. A plethora of tools are available for conducting many different types of communication, but the tools alone cannot facilitate effective communication. To be successful, the virtual manager needs high levels of verbal and written communication skills, in addition to a high level of competency using virtual-management tools.

Communication Skill Set	Description
Email	Excellent written communication skills. Ability to write clear, concise, and unambiguous emails. Understanding of and adherence to netiquette and etiquette rules to avoid creating or accelerating conflict or confusion.
Phone	High comfort level using the phone for communication. Ability to listen attentively and hear changes in tone and mood of others over the phone. Clear speaking voice.
Instant messaging	Ability to write short, concise messages without appearing to be abrupt. Understanding of when IM is appropriate and when email or phone would be a better option.

Communication Skill Set	Description
Meeting facilitation	Ability to set up and control online and audio meetings. Keep meetings on track using an agenda, and keep meeting attendees involved and participating in the meeting.
Written agendas and minutes	High level of skill preparing agendas and other meeting materials. Skilled note-taking is required, as well as good time-management and prioritization skills to ensure minutes are typed up and distributed in a timely manner.
One-on-ones	Comfortable conducting one-on-one meetings via the phone. Ability to give and receive both positive and negative feedback in a constructive manner. Ability to coach and develop via phone. Skilled note-taking is essential to keep a record of what was discussed and agreed to in one-on-one meetings.
Status reporting	Ability to collate, create, and communicate status reports for diverse stakeholder groups, spanning multiple levels within the organization. Skilled at creating and presenting reports and presentations virtually.
Communicating change	Ability to communicate controversial or sensitive information in a positive and constructive manner via audio or video conference.
Catastrophic event status reporting	Ability to manage catastrophic events from a distance. Skilled at managing team members remotely during high-stress, high-visibility events. Ability to keep team members calm and focused, to enable accurate and timely status reporting.
Documentation management	Ability to design, implement, and manage an effective document-management process for virtual team.
Presentations	Comfortable and skilled in all areas of virtual presentations, including online, audio, and video.

Technical Skill Set

Virtual managers require more than a basic level of technical knowledge and ability, to set up and maintain the equipment and tools required to run a home office.

Technical Skill Set	Description
Setting up a computer	Ability to set up, install, and maintain own computer system with little or no assistance.
Computer management and troubleshooting	Knowledge and understanding of computer administration and troubleshooting. Ability to manage a variety of computer-related tasks, including changing administrative and security settings, performing backups, configuring a firewall, and running routine maintenance tasks.
Connecting a printer	Ability to install and set up printer, and troubleshoot printing problems.
Setting up a network	Ability to set up, install, and configure a home computer networking system. Understanding of Ethernet and wireless networks, network security, and firewalls. Ability to troubleshoot connectivity problems.
Installing and configuring software	Ability to install and configure software and to troubleshoot problems.
Setting up email accounts	Comfortable with setting up and configuring email accounts.
Connecting to a VPN	Ability to install and configure computer to connect to a VPN (Virtual Private Network). Ability to troubleshoot basic connectivity problems.
Creating spreadsheets and presentations	Experience creating spreadsheets, presentations, and training sessions for sharing online, via audio or video. Knowledge and understanding of the tools for creating presentations.
Writing and proofreading emails and documents	High level of writing and proofreading skills. Knowledge of computer tools used to assist with spelling, grammar, and readability.
Document management	Ability to set up and maintain an online document-management system.
Setting up and configuring a mobile phone or PDA	Ability to set up and configure a mobile phone or PDA using manuals or online help.

Technical Skill Set	Description
Setting up and configuring Internet service (cable, DSL, or dial-up)	Ability to set up, configure, and troubleshoot problems with Internet connectivity.
Troubleshooting connectivity or technical issues	Ability to troubleshoot connectivity issues and identify where in the system problems are occurring.

Decision-Making Skill Set

Communicating decisions must be done unambiguously and assertively. Otherwise, the recipients of the communication will be unclear about what to do with the information and how to act upon it.

Decision-Making Skill Set	Description
Making decisions	Ability to take ownership and make decisions with authority and conviction.
Communicating decisions	Ability to clearly communicate decisions and reasons for decisions to virtual team members. Ability to ensure that decisions are accepted and adopted by all team members.
Reviewing and updating tasks or processes affected by decision	Ability to review and update processes, procedures, tasks, priorities, and assignments to align with new decisions.

Problem-Solving Skill Set

Problems arise in many different areas, including technical, political, administrative, and managerial. No matter what type of problem, where it occurs, or who it affects, the virtual manager is responsible for ensuring it gets resolved appropriately and in a timely manner.

Problem-Solving Skill Set	Description
Detecting problems	Ability to recognize that a problem exists whether or not it is reported to the manager. Ability to recognize issues occurring remotely, or local issues negatively affecting remote team members.
Evaluating problems	Ability to evaluate the extent and criticality of a problem and to assess its impact on the team or project. Excellent virtual coordination and fact-finding skills to expeditiously complete the evaluation.
Identifying root cause	Ability to drill down into the details and identify the root cause of the problem. Ability to engage remote team members to assist with identifying the cause of the problem.
Resolving problems	Ability to define appropriate steps to resolve a problem and to roll out any required process or task changes to remote team members.

Team-Building Skill Set

Creating a team from a group of geographically diverse team members requires an understanding of interaction styles; a desire to build rapport, respect, and trust among team members; and the people skills required to achieve this virtually.

Team-Building Skill Set	Description
Understanding interaction and communication styles	At least a basic understanding of interaction styles. Virtual team members are bereft of the non-verbal 80% of communication that traditional teams enjoy. How team members interact determines how they will bond with each other.
Discovering commonalities	Ability to work with team members both individually and as a team to help them discover commonalities among themselves.
Building rapport	Ability to encourage and facilitate the building of rapport among team members regardless of any geographical, cultural, or time-zone differences
Creating the virtual water cooler	Ability to create a culture of openness and sociability on the team, to facilitate team members keeping in touch on a daily basis. The virtual manager needs to set examples of collaboration for work- and non-work related topics.
Building virtual bridges	Ability to build bridges between team members, especially those with opposing interaction styles, where there is a high probability of conflict.
Having fun	Ability to influence team members to have fun with each other and to enjoy virtual meetings with team members. More fun equals more participation and attention to the content of meetings.
Conducting virtual team-building events	Ability to come up with creative and practical ideas for participative and effective team events that span geography, culture, language, and time zones.

Administrative Skill Set

As a virtual manager, you need to manage most, if not all, of the day-to-day administrative tasks for yourself and possibly for your remote team members.

Administrative Skill Set	Description
Typing correspondence	Ability to type, spell, and use appropriate grammar in communications.
Scheduling meetings	Ability to schedule meetings using online tools. Ability to coordinate with others to make calendar adjustments where necessary. Understanding of time zones.
Preparing and submitting expense claims	Ability to track, manage, and approve expenses for self and virtual team members.
Reading and responding to emails	Excellent time-management skills to ensure that emails are read and responded to in a timely manner. Team members expect a manager to be responsive and informed.
Taking meeting minutes, and typing and distributing them to meeting attendees	Excellent note-taking skills, to ensure that communications are complete and accurate. Excellent time-management skills to ensure that notes are distributed in a timely manner.
Filing	Ability to keep track of documentation, whether paper or electronic.
Ordering/replenishing stationery supplies	Ability to keep track of stationery and order supplies before running out.
Handling mail	Ability to efficiently read and respond to mail. Ability to set up and manage courier accounts, if necessary.
Making travel arrangements	Ability to make travel arrangements and review and approve travel for virtual team members. Good budgeting skills to keep costs within budget and ensure that clients are charged for travel costs when appropriate.
Typing and distributing status reports	Ownership for virtual status-reporting process. Good time management and organizational skills to manage virtual status reporting.

Personal Qualities

Some people are very well-suited to working on a virtual team. Generally, these people possess certain personal qualities that are highly desirable in virtual managers.

Personal Quality	Description
Independent	Enjoys working independently in an isolated environment with little face-to-face interaction with others.
Communicative	Comfortable communicating using different communication methods, including email and phone. Enjoys communication and interaction with others.
Proactive	Has a proactive approach to communication and tasks. Plans ahead. Is not reactive. Provides information proactively rather than waiting to be asked.
Self-motivated	Does not require others' input to stay motivated. Can push and motivate self to stay focused, energized, and on track.
Articulate	Articulate and clear speaker. Able to clearly communicate the point of a message and to explain details in language that can be understood by all team members.
Enthusiastic	Is positive and enthusiastic. Team members will avoid speaking to a manager who is negative or lacks enthusiasm for the team or the work.
Honest	Is honest with self and with manager. Does not hold information back, and provides honest answers and feedback when requested. Does not intentionally lie or mislead.

Required Skill Sets for the Remote Team Member

Members of a virtual team need the same basic skill Sets (general management, people management, etc.) as their managers.

General-Management Skill Set

Many aspects of the general-management skill Sets apply to individual remote workers as well as to the manager of a virtual team. Remote workers need the ability to stay in control of their tasks, keep things on track, and to report current statuses.

General-Management Skill Set	Description
Organization	Intermediate to high level of organizational skill. Ability to plan and organize tasks, meetings, and documentation.
Time management	Ability to manage time and tasks so that work is completed on time. Take time zones into account when planning time.
Decision making	Ability to make and communicate decisions appropriate to position.
Prioritization	Ability to prioritize tasks to ensure highest priority tasks are completed first.
Goal setting	Ability to set clear, measurable goals and objectives for self. Ability to accurately measure, verify, and communicate results to manager.
Tracking and reporting progress	Ability to follow processes and procedures for tracking and reporting status. Ability to communicate status clearly, concisely, and on schedule.
Budgets and finance	Ability to manage costs and keep them within budget. Ability to read and understand financial reports. Ability to manage and report costs for client projects.

People-Management Skill Set

People-management skills are required for all virtual team members. Remote workers need the ability to influence others, understand and respect differing viewpoints, and communicate in a positive and collaborative manner.

People-Management Skill Set	Description
Active listening	High level of skill in active listening. Ability to listen and mirror back what has been heard. Ability to "hear between the lines" and to understand what is not being said as well as what is being said.
Coordination and scheduling	Ability to coordinate and schedule own tasks and work with other team members and clients to schedule joint tasks.
Meeting facilitation	Ability to set up and run virtual meetings with team members and clients. Ability to keep meetings on track and avoid unnecessary digressions. Understanding of meeting etiquette.
Conflict resolution	Knowledge and experience of conflict management. Ability to discuss controversial topics in a respectful and positive manner to avoid creating a conflict situation.

Communication Skill Set

Effective and well-managed communication is essential for each member of a virtual team. A plethora of tools are available for many different types of communication, but the tools alone cannot facilitate effective communication. To be successful, the remote team member needs high levels of verbal and written communication skills, in addition to a high level of competency using virtual communication tools.

Communication Skill Set	Description
Email	Excellent written communication skills. Ability to write clear, concise, and unambiguous emails. Understanding of and adherence to netiquette and etiquette rules to avoid creating or accelerating conflict or confusion.
Phone	High comfort level using the phone for communication. Ability to listen attentively and respond appropriately. Clear speaking voice.

Communication Skill Set	Description
Instant messaging	Ability to write short, concise messages without appearing to be abrupt. Understanding of when IM is appropriate and when email or phone would be a better option.
Meeting facilitation	Ability to set up and control online and audio meetings. Keep meetings on track using an agenda, and keep meeting attendees involved and participating in the meeting.
Written agendas and minutes	Skilled at preparing agendas and other meeting materials. Ability to take notes and capture key points. Attention to detail to ensure notes are typed up and distributed in a timely manner.
One-on-ones	Comfortable participating in one-on-one meetings with manager via phone. Ability to receive both positive and negative feedback in a constructive manner.
Status reporting	Ability to create and communicate status reports for manager and clients. Ability to present status verbally, via email, and via formal presentations.
Communicating change	Ability to communicate controversial or sensitive information in a positive and constructive manner to manager, teammates, and clients.
Catastrophic event status reporting	Ability to participate in resolving catastrophic events while working remotely from the rest of the team. Ability to stay calm and focused in a crisis and to communicate coherently using the virtual tools available.
Documentation management	Ability to follow processes and procedures for setting up and managing documentation for own use and for sharing with virtual team members.
Presentations	Comfortable and skilled in all areas of virtual presentations, including online, audio, and video.

Technical Skill Set

Virtual workers require much more than a basic level of technical knowledge and ability, to set up and maintain the equipment and tools required to operate from a home office.

Technical Skill Set	Description
Setting up a computer	Ability to set up, install, and maintain own computer system with little or no assistance.
Computer management and troubleshooting	Knowledge and understanding of computer administration and troubleshooting. Ability to manage a variety of computer-related tasks, including changing administrative and security settings, performing backups, configuring a firewall, and running routine maintenance tasks.
Connecting a printer	Ability to install and set up printer, and troubleshoot printing problems.
Setting up a network	Ability to set up, install, and configure a home computer networking system. Understanding of Ethernet and wireless networks, network security, and firewalls. Ability to troubleshoot connectivity problems.
Installing and configuring software	Ability to install and configure software and to troubleshoot problems.
Setting up email accounts	Comfortable with setting up and configuring email accounts.
Connecting to a VPN	Ability to install and configure computer to connect to a VPN (Virtual Private Network). Ability to troubleshoot basic connectivity problems.
Creating spreadsheets and presentations	Experience creating spreadsheets, presentations, and training sessions for sharing online, via audio or video. Knowledge and understanding of the tools for creating presentations.
Writing and proofreading emails and documents	High level of writing and proofreading skills. Knowledge of computer tools used to assist with spelling, grammar, and readability.
Document management	Ability to set up and maintain an online document-management system.
Setting up and configuring a mobile phone or PDA	Ability to set up and configure a mobile phone or PDA using manuals or online help.
Setting up and configuring Internet service (cable, DSL, or dial-up)	Ability to set up, configure, and troubleshoot problems with Internet connectivity.
Troubleshooting connectivity or technical issues	Ability to troubleshoot connectivity issues and identify where in the system a problem is occurring.

Decision-Making Skill Set

Communicating decisions must be done clearly and unambiguously. Understanding who is responsible for making which decisions is essential for remote workers.

Decision-Making Skill Set	Description
Making and communicating decisions	Ability to make and communicate decisions appropriate to team member's position and level of responsibility.
Reviewing and updating tasks or processes affected by decisions	Ability to review and update processes, procedures, tasks, priorities, and assignments to align with new decisions.

Problem-Solving Skill Set

Problems arise in many different areas, including technical, political, administrative, and managerial. No matter what type of problem, where it occurs, or who it affects, the remote worker is responsible for participating in the resolution of the problem or escalating to the appropriate person.

Problem-Solving Skill Set	Description
Detecting problems	Ability to recognize that a problem exists and to take appropriate action.
Evaluating problems	Ability to evaluate the extent and criticality of a problem, and to assess its impact on the team or project.
Identifying root cause	Ability to drill down into the details and identify the root cause of a problem. Ability to engage other remote team members as necessary to assist with identifying the cause of the problem.
Resolving problems	Ability to define appropriate steps to resolve a problem and to communicate information clearly and unambiguously to virtual manager, team members, and clients.

Team-Orientation Skill Set

To be effective, virtual teams need to be comprised of team-oriented members. Team members need to be able to work independently, but not to make decisions or take action independently of the rest of the team. Successful virtual teams do not work apart, they work together, apart.

Team-Orientation Skill Set	Description
Team player	Ability to form working relationships across cultures, geography, and time zones. Enjoys interaction with team members. Communicates and interacts well virtually.
Understanding impact of actions on other team members	Ability to see the consequences of decisions and actions on other team members, clients, and projects. Focused on team rather than self.
Building rapport	Able to build rapport with manager, clients, and other team members, while working remotely from them. Understands the need for rapport among virtual team members.

Administrative Skill Set

A remote worker needs to manage most, if not all, of his or her day-to-day administrative tasks.

Administrative Skill Set	Description
Typing correspondence	Ability to type, spell, and use appropriate grammar in communications.
Scheduling meetings	Ability to schedule meetings using online tools. Ability to coordinate with others to make calendar adjustments where necessary. Understanding of time zones.
Preparing and submitting expense claims	Ability to track, prepare, categorize, and submit expenses in timely manner.
Reading and responding to emails	Ability to keep up with emails and respond in a timely manner.
Taking meeting minutes, typing and distributing them to meeting attendees	High-quality note-taking skills to ensure that communications are complete and accurate. Time-management skills to ensure that notes are distributed in a timely manner.
Filing	Ability to keep track of documentation, whether paper or electronic.
Ordering/replenishing stationery supplies	Ability to keep track of stationery and order supplies before running out.
Handling mail	Ability to efficiently read and respond to mail. Ability to set up and manage courier accounts, if necessary.
Making travel arrangements	Ability to get approval for travel and make travel arrangements. Good budgeting skills to keep travel costs within budget and ensure that clients are charged for travel costs when appropriate.
Typing and distributing status reports	Ability to prepare and submit status report to the manager using a predefined process.

Personal Qualities

Some people are very well-suited to working on a virtual team. Generally, these people possess certain personal qualities that are highly desirable for working in a virtual environment.

Personal Quality	Description
Independent	Enjoys working independently in an isolated environment with little face-to-face interaction with others.
Communicative	Comfortable communicating using different communication methods, including email and phone. Enjoys virtual communication and interaction with others.
Proactive	Has a proactive approach to communication and tasks. Plans ahead. Is not reactive. Provides information without waiting to be asked.
Self-motivated	Does not require others' input to stay motivated. Can push and motivate self to stay focused, energized, and on track.
Articulate	Articulate and clear speaker. Able to clearly communicate the point of a message and to explain details in language that can be understood by all team members.
Enthusiastic	Is positive and enthusiastic. Encourages and appreciates enthusiasm in others.
Honest	Is honest with self and with manager. Does not hold information back, and provides honest answers and feedback when requested. Does not intentionally lie or mislead.

Reports and Documentation

Throughout the book, there are example reports and documentation that can be used to manage the processes and procedures for a virtual team. This appendix contains the blank templates for those documents. Table B.1 displays the chapter number where the process or procedure for each document is described in detail. It also includes the document type (Microsoft Word or Excel) to make it easier for you to recreate these documents yourself. These documents are also available for download from the MC Press Website at *http://www.mcpressonline.com/mc/Forums/Reviews/5078*

	Table B.1: Sample Documentation			
Chapter	Document Name	Document Type	Pages	ID
3	Staffing plan	MS Word	3	Figures B1.1-B1.3
3	Job description	MS Word	1	Figure B.2
3	Interview evaluation form	MS Word	1	Figure B.3
4	Team time-zone spreadsheet	MS Excel	1	Figure B.4
5	Statement of Work (SOW)	MS Word	1	Figure B.5
6	Task-management list	MS Excel	1	Figure B.6
6	Forced-pair comparisons grid	MS Excel	1	Figure B.7
7	Brainstorming spreadsheet	MS Excel	1	Figure B.8
8	Communication plan	MS Word	1	Figure B.9
8	Status report	MS Word	1	Figure B.10
8	Escalation procedures	MS Word	1	Figure B.11
8	Risk log	MS Excel	1	Figure B.12
8	Documentation plan	MS Word	1	Figure B.13
8	Roles and responsibilities chart	MS Excel	1	Figure B.14
12	Catastrophic event status report	MS Word	1	Figure B.15

Staffing Plan - [Team Name]

General Information

This staffing plan identifies the staffing needs and skillsets for the [team/project name]. This document was created by [creator's name] on [date].

The team or project is scheduled to be created on [date] and disbanded on [date] (if applicable).

Staffing Process

1. Staffing plan is created by the team manager.
2. Plan is approved by Department Vice President and CEO.
3. Requisitions opened and posted internally and externally by human resources.
4. Internal resumes sent directly to hiring manager.
5. External Resumes
   a. Screened by human resources before sending to hiring manager.
   b. Hiring manager requests human resources to do pre-screening phone interviews.
6. Hiring manager conducts initial phone interview .
7. Short listed candidates bought to corporate office for round of face-to-face interviews.
8. For successful candidates - verbal offer made.
9. Offer documentation prepared and sent overnight.
10. Signed offer letter received.
11. Human resources begin new hire process.

Goals, Objectives and Timelines

The manager of the team is [manager's name]. The following objectives and timelines have been identified:

- Staffing plan completed by [date].
- Plan submitted and approved by [date].
- Hiring requisitions opened by [date].
- Positions posted internally [date].
- Positions posted externally [date].
- Initial phone interview completed by [date].
- Onsite interviews completed by [date].
- First offer made by [date].
- All positions filled by [date].

Figure B.1.1: Staffing plan (page 1)

Staffing Profile

Dates required	Title (personnel category)	Job level	Terms	Rate
Immediate - perm	Manager/Director	Senior	Full time virtual employee	$150k

Skill sets and Requirements

Resource Title	Job Description	Source	Job level	Skills	Resource Name
Manager/Director	Virtual manager working from home office. Responsible for managing virtual team responsible for development and implementation of projects.	Internal	Senior	10+ years management experience. 5+ years working in a consulting organization.	John Smith

Figure B.1.2: Staffing plan (page 2)

Organization Chart

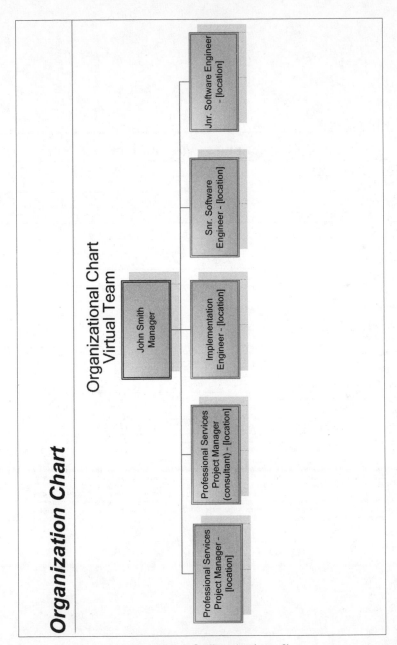

Organizational Chart
Virtual Team

- John Smith
  Manager
  - Professional Services
    Project Manager –
    [location]
  - Professional Services
    Project Manager
    (consultant) – [location]
  - Implementation
    Engineer – [location]
  - Snr. Software
    Engineer – [location]
  - Jnr. Software Engineer
    – [location]

Figure B.1.3: Staffing plan (page 3)

Job Description - Virtual Team

Requisition Number :	
Job Title :	
Job Level :	
Functional Discipline :	
Job Type :	
Job Category :	
Dept. Group :	
Travel % :	
Travel Type:	
Languages:	
Country :	
State/Province :	
Work Location:	
Office Location :	
Functional Job Description :	
Job Description, Duties and Responsibilities :	
Experience/Qualifications :	

Figure B.2: Job description

Interview Evaluation Form

Candidate's Name	
Position Applied For	
Interviewer's Name & Title	
Interview Date	

Evaluation: 1 is highest 5 is lowest. Circle appropriate number.

Has knowledge and skillsets required for the specific position
Evaluation: 1   2   3   4   5

Description and comments:

Has domain knowledge and experience required
Evaluation: 1   2   3   4   5

Description and comments:

Possesses technical knowledge and experience required
Evaluation: 1   2   3   4   5

Description and comments:

Ability to work and think independently
Evaluation: 1   2   3   4   5

Description and comments:

Resourcefulness
Evaluation: 1   2   3   4   5

Description and comments:

Level of team orientation (teamwork)
Evaluation: 1   2   3   4   5

Description and comments:

Personality and attitude and the affect candidate would have on the team
Evaluation: 1   2   3   4   5

Description and comments:

Summary (overall impression and recommendation to hire)
Evaluation: 1   2   3   4   5

Description and comments:

Figure B.3: Interview evaluation form

Name	City	Country	Region	Time Difference	Start No Earlier Than (PT)	End No Later Than (PT)	Notes
Bruce	Auckland	Australia	AP	+18hrs	2pm		Mon-Thurs

Figure B.4: Team time-zone spreadsheet

Statement of Work

1. Introduction
    1.1.   Objectives
2. Project Scope
    2.1.   In Scope
    2.2.   Out Of Scope
3. Period Of Contract
4. Specific Tasks
5. Schedule Of Deliverables
6. Completion Criteria
7. Fees And Payments
    7.1.   Fees
    7.2.   Payment Not To Exceed
    7.3.   Payment Terms
8. Roles And Responsibilities
    8.1.   Vendor (Outsource) Company Responsibilities
    8.2.   Client Responsibilities
    8.3.   Conflict Of Interest
    8.4.   Key Contacts
    8.5.   Reporting Requirements
9. Assumptions And Constraints
10. Staffing
    10.1.   Staffing Plan
    10.2.   Physical Location
    10.3.   Workers Citizenship
    10.4.   Security Clearance
11. General Provisions
    11.1.   Change Process
    11.2.   Cancellation/Termination Terms
    11.3.   Renewal Terms
    11.4.   Disputes
    11.5.   Delays
    11.6.   Legal Compliance
    11.7.   Intellectual Property Rights
    11.8.   Security
    11.9.   Inspection And Acceptance

Figure B.5: Statement of Work

Category	Priority	Task Name	Frequency	Start Date	Duration (hrs)	Due Date
Reports	1	Weekly Work Results Report	daily	daily	0.5	each Friday 4pm

Figure B.6: Task-management list

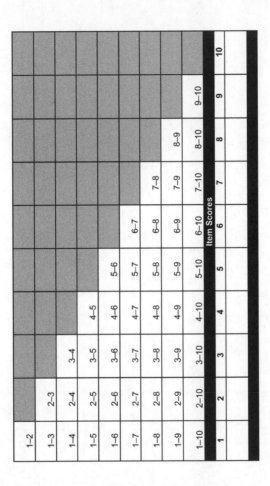

Figure B.7: Forced-pair comparisons

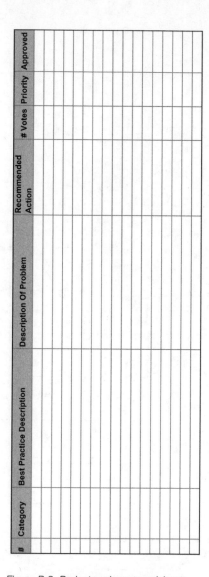

Figure B.8: Brainstorming spreadsheet

Communication Plan

1. Introduction

2. Stakeholder Groups

Stakeholder Group Name	Description	Members

3. Formal Communication Plan

Communication	Content	Objective	Owner	Stakeholder	Method	Frequency / Date

4. Informal Communication Plan

Issue	Description	Action	Owner (escalate to)	Audience	Method	Timeline

5. Communication Rules

    5.1.   Organizational

    5.2.   Company

    5.3.   Team

    5.4.   Client

    5.5.   Regulatory

Figure B.9: Communication plan

Status Report

Name:	
Manager:	
Date:	
Contact Name:	
Phone / E-mail:	
Reporting Period:	

Are All Tasks:				
On or Ahead of Schedule?	Yes		No	
Meeting Requirements?	Yes		No	

Scheduled Tasks

Project/ Client	Task	Hours spent on task	Percentage complete

Unscheduled Tasks

Project/ Client	Task	Hours spent on task	Percentage complete

Issues

Project/ Client	Issues	Severity	Time needed to resolve

Planned Work for Next Period

Project/ Client	Tasks	Hours	% Complete expected

Risk Assessment

Project/ Client	Risks	Severity	Probability

Recommendations/Comments

**Status reports need to be turned into the Project Manager every Monday before noon (PT)

Figure B.10: Status report

Escalation Procedures

1. Introduction

1.1. General Information

2. Escalation Path

Level	Definition	Expected Response	Call Intervals
Priority 1	Critical Issue - Critical impact on company or client including security breach	Senior management informed by manager immediately. Security team involved if applicable. Worked on continuously until resolved. Hourly updates with senior executives	Immediate
Priority 2	Major Impact - Impact to our own, a client's or a partner's, Business	Problem is worked on continuously until the problem is resolved.	Immediate
Priority 3	Large Impact - Significant inconvenience to clients or partners where a workaround might be implemented	Work is expected to continue on a workday basis until a more permanent solution is in place.	2 hour maximum
Priority 4	Small to Medium Impact - Medium or small inconvenience	Resolution is worked into a planned project list and schedule or it can be deferred until there is time allowed in the project schedule.	24 hours maximum

3. Notification

Sequence	Contact/Name	Work Phone#	Home Phone#	Mobile/Pager #	Title/Description
Priority 1	1. 2. 3.				
Priority 2	1. 2. 3.				
Priority 3	1. 2. 3.				
Priority 4	1. 2. 3.				

4. Roles and Responsibilities

4.1. Process Owner

Figure B.11: Escalation procedures

Risk Log

No	Description	Originator	Date Identified	Criticality	Probability	Priority	Mitigation Plan	Contingency Plan	Status
22	Contractor budget is cut	Melanie Swan	Jan 1st	High	Medium	1	Work with senior mgmt to get budget approval to extend contractor contracts	1. Remove two features from plan 2. Move completion date out by 3 months	Active

Figure B.12: Risk log

Documentation Plan

1 Introduction

1.1 General Information

2 Documentation Plan

Document	Owner	Authorized to update	Reviewers	Authorized viewers	Communication Methods allowed	Approver
Client Contract	Project Manager	Legal only	Project Manager, Client	Project Manager, Team Manager, Contracts Personnel, Legal Dept., Customer Relationship Manager	Regular mail only (no email)	Legal Dept., Contracts Dept.

Figure B.13: Documentation plan

Roles and Responsibilities

Name	Title	Primary Role	Backup Role	Projects	Document / Webpage Owner	Report Owner	Go To Person For
David Johnson	Snr Project Manager	Project Manager	Backup for Melanie Swan, Team Manager & June Zhang Implementation Manager	ABC, JMT Corp,	ABC, JMT and team calendar	Weekly status, weekly client status, monthly budget report	Project Management, ABC, BRM Technology,

Figure B.14: Roles and responsibilities

Catastrophic Event Status Report

1. *Overview*

1.1. Description of Event

Current Status:	
Status Change Since Last Update	
Current Email Update:	
Next Email Update:	
Next Meeting/Phone Conference	
Emergency Team:	
Roles And Responsibilities:	
Progress Overview:	
Issue One:	
Issue Two:	
Issue Three:	
Issue Four:	
Highest Priority Tasks:	
Other Info:	[this section can be used to communicate shift changes for the emergency team, time and location of food deliveries if onsite meals are being provided, or any other information useful to the team but not necessarily directly related to the progress on the emergency situation]
Links To More Information:	

Figure B.15: Catastrophic event status report

Case Study

Company Background

ABC is a Web publishing company founded approximately seven years ago. The three founders of the company are former employees of XYZ, Inc. XYZ ceased trading seven years ago and laid off all its employees, including the three founders of ABC. The three XYZ employees decided to form a partnership, start their own Web publishing company, and hire some of their coworkers from XYZ to work for them at the new company.

The Business Decision

The challenge for ABC was that the people they wanted to hire were located all over the United States. Even the three business partners were located in different states. It was not feasible for everyone to move to the same location, and none of the business partners were interested in relocating or exclusively hiring local people to work for them. The obvious solution to this problem was to become a virtual company. The three partners agreed that this was the right decision, and ABC, the virtual Web publishing company, was born.

The Virtual Solution

ABC started with eight employees: the three business partners plus five additional employees. That number has now grown to 15 employees, including the partners.

Apart from a bookkeeper who works in the same location as one of the partners and administrative assistants who work in the same locations as the other partners, all the employees are geographically dispersed. The company has employees in Maine, Tennessee, Ohio, New York, Colorado, Illinois, and Arizona. All employees work from home offices, apart from the bookkeeper and the administrative assistants, who work out of the home offices of the partners.

In addition to the virtual employees, ABC also works virtually with two outsource companies. One of the outsourcers is domestic, located in Chicago. The other is located overseas in Bangalore, India. ABC also contracts with outside companies for payroll and tax services.

The Virtual Team's Operations

The virtual team consists of the three partners and 12 employees. The employees' roles break down into the following categories:

- General and vendor management
- Editorial management
- Content providers/writers
- Website/graphic design
- Marketing
- IT professionals
- Ad sales
- Bookkeeping
- Administrative support

Some team members fill more than one role on the team, and split their time between the functions. The team members coordinate efforts, but generally do not work collaboratively on specific tasks or projects due to the diverse nature of their roles on the team. Most of the business functions are very self-contained, and employees are expected to work independently.

To effectively manage the business and the individual team members, the partners and employees need to pay close attention to two key areas:

- Communication
- Personnel management

Communication

Communication is the keystone to success for a virtual company. ABC could not survive without regular, good-quality communication among its team members. ABC uses various virtual-communication methods and tools.

Virtual-Management Tools

For overall virtual management, ABC uses the Groove virtual-management software program. This tool allows the users to interact on a daily basis. They share files, calendars, and online discussion areas. The centralized document-management system enables the team to work together effectively and efficiently without being affected by geography or time zones. As a Web publisher, the ability to share documentation is critical to ABC's business.

Virtual-Communication Tools

Instant messaging and email are both used on a daily basis for communication among team members. The team members have become so comfortable using these virtual-communication tools that they often use them when making a phone call would be much more effective.

The phone is used for formal and informal communication between team members and between ABC and its vendors. One-on-one meetings between managers and individual contributors are conducted via phone.

The phone is also used in conjunction with audio conferencing software for virtual meetings. Online meeting tools are used for team presentations. The team also uses Webcams for their one-on-one communications between team members, in an attempt to add some nonverbal elements to its communications.

Virtual Meetings

ABC has a virtual team meeting every Monday morning. The first 10 minutes of the meeting are reserved for some "virtual water cooler" discussion time. Having 10 minutes of informal chat at the start of the meeting lightens the mood and creates a feeling of commonality and teamwork among the team members. The water-cooler discussion generally consists of conversation about what team members did on the weekend, vacation plans and stories, and interesting or amusing anecdotes. The remaining 50 minutes of the meeting time are spent on general discussion about each person's assignments, so everyone knows what everyone else is working on. This is also an opportunity for the partners to let the team members know about new business deals or decisions. The objective of the meeting is to maintain synergy among the virtual team members by ensuring that everyone has a common, high-level understanding of the current statuses and issues in all areas of the business.

In addition to the weekly team meeting, ABC has several meetings that focus on specific areas of the business. For example, there are weekly editorial, IT, and marketing meetings, attended by a subset of the virtual team. ABC managers also participate in monthly meeting with the outsource vendors.

Face-to-Face Meetings

The virtual team members rarely meet face-to-face, apart from planned team events. The team holds an annual strategic-planning meeting, where all employees travel to the same location for a few days of meetings. The business partners organize a lot of team-building and social events to occur during this time. They also make sure there is plenty of time for the team members to relax and unwind together in comfortable surroundings. The partners have learned that, if there are too many planned activities in addition to the strategic planning sessions, the team members get burned out very quickly. This is not conducive to team bonding. The partners usually rent a large house that can accommodate all the employees for these meetings. This way, the surroundings are more personal and comfortable than they would be in a hotel. It also gives the team members the flexibility to schedule their work and relaxation time to suit themselves and not to have to stick too rigidly to a predefined plan. The employees can cook together and hang out with each other for a few days in a quiet location, which enhances the team-building experience.

The ABC team attends two conferences each year. Every team member flies to the conference location two days before the start of the conference. The team meets for dinner the first evening, and then spends the whole of the next day together doing a fun activity. The focus of this team day is on fun and team-building, and no talk about business matters is allowed. During the course of the conference, the partners have a breakfast, lunch, or dinner meeting with each of the team members individually. This gives each team member some quality one-on-one time with the three managers. It is a great opportunity to discuss issues or ideas, or to generally chat about how things are going. The team members meet informally for dinner in the evenings, but attendance is not required.

Being at a conference all day can get very tiring, and some of the team members need some downtime at the end of the day!

There are occasional face-to-face meetings with both outsource vendors. Meetings with the domestic outsourcer generally take place onsite at the outsourcer's premises. Meetings with the Indian outsourcer take place once or twice a year in the United States. None of the ABC employees have visited the outsourcer in India.

Written Communication

ABC team members communicate via email on a daily basis, for both formal and informal communications. Online discussion areas within Groove are also used by team members to share information. Instant messaging is the preferred informal communication tool for team members.

The ABC team members submit weekly written status reports and weekly time and expense reports. These reports are used by management to verify that hours logged correspond to status reports. The reports are also used for payroll purposes.

Personnel Management

Personnel management at ABC involves two main areas: recruitment and performance management.

Recruitment

When ABC was founded, the partners hired people they knew. As the company has grown, they have had to use conventional recruiting methods to find new employees.

Virtual recruitment can be very challenging. ABC looks for employees who are self-starters, highly motivated, competent, experienced, honest, and trustworthy. ABC does not hire any junior people, as it does not have the means to effectively train or mentor them. In addition to the skills needed to perform the specific role being filled, all virtual employees need to possess the necessary IT skills to set up and maintain their home office environments. The employees need good computer and networking skills, together with a knowledge of office equipment such as printers and routers. Prospective employees also need excellent troubleshooting and problem-solving skills. Applicants who lack the ability to quickly resolve technical issues with home office equipment are not good candidates for the virtual team.

The biggest challenge in hiring is recognizing whether a candidate possesses the necessary skills and qualities to be successful on a virtual team during the initial phone interview. It can be costly paying travel and lodging expenses for candidates to attend face-to-face interviews, so the partners need to have a high confidence that they have found the right candidate before arranging the first meeting.

Performance Management

ABC's employee performance is managed using a quarterly review process. This recently changed from an annual process. Each employee is reviewed on business and personal performance objectives, which are defined by the company's partners. Each employee also provides a written self-review to the manager.

The company recently incorporated peer reviews into the process. ABC does not have formal growth and development or career-planning processes, as the company has so few employees. These areas of performance are managed informally and incorporated into the review process where appropriate.

Outsourced Operations

ABC manages two major outsourcing relationships, one internationally and one domestically. The company also contracts out its payroll and tax accounting work. When the company first started, it also contracted out bookkeeping and some administrative work, but that work has since been bought in-house and is performed by ABC employees.

Primary communication methods used are email, fax, and phone. There are also regular conference-call meetings with outsourcers in the United States and India.

Offshore Outsourcing in India

ABC outsources Web layout work to a vendor in India. The relationship requires little ongoing management from the ABC team. There is minimal interaction needed between the employees of the two companies. The work has clearly defined requirements, which are consistent across different jobs. The outsourcer uses standard templates and methods for producing the work. There are very rarely any problems with the work. The 12-hour time difference and the language differences can create some difficulties with communication. ABC has to wait until the following day to get responses to enquiries, and sometimes the language issues create misunderstandings.

The owner off the offshore company visits ABC in the United States annually, which helps to maintain a strong working relationship between the two companies.

Inshore Outsourcing in Chicago

ABC outsources its promotional and marketing work to a vendor in Chicago. This outsource relationship requires a lot more management than the one in India. Sometimes, ABC needs something done a certain way, while the outsourcer wants to do it a different way. This type of situation usually culminates in one of ABC's employees having to visit the vendor in person to resolve the issue. ABC has invested time training the outsource employees, and must continually work with them whenever changes are required to the process. This relationship has been a significant time investment, but it would take a lot more time and be more costly to bring those functions in-house.

As ABC has grown over the past five years, it has needed to make occasional changes to its business processes. As a result of these changes, ABC's first vendor could no longer support its needs. ABC had to find a new outsourcer, which proved to be very time-consuming and costly. The new vendor is able to support ABC's needs, but only with a lot of hands-on management. As soon as ABC tries to become hands-off, things start to go wrong.

Contracted-Out Work

ABC contracts out payroll and tax accounting services to companies in the United States Neither of these relationships requires much management. The companies offer standard services. ABC sends the necessary paperwork and forms, and the payroll and tax-accounting companies do the rest.

Benefits

There are many important benefits to being a virtual company. The lower cost of doing business makes this type of business model very attractive. The company does not have to buy or lease business premises. It has no facilities, utilities, or infrastructure costs. It hires only the employees it needs, as it does not require additional support staff.

For ABC's founders, the ability to hire the best people no matter where they are located is the main reason they decided to form a virtual company in the first place. It is still a compelling reason to stay virtual.

If an ABC employee decides to move to a new city, state, or country, that employee does not have to leave his or her job. The ability to be mobile and stay employed is a huge benefit to the partners and the employees. In fact, one of the firm's employees splits his time between two locations, spending six months in each. This biannual change of scenery does not prevent the employee from continuing to work as usual.

The staff at ABC loves to work at home. The employees see it as one of the most valuable benefits to working at ABC. They love the freedom and flexibility they have in planning and executing their assignments. There is no rush-hour traffic to deal with, and all the time involved in work is productive. No spending two or three hours a day driving through rush-hour traffic!

Challenges

The biggest challenge to being virtual for ABC is the fact that they are virtual. The nature of the virtual environment, with its lack of personal interaction, can lead to conflicts and grudges over relatively minor things. It is harder for the managers to recognize a conflict between team members when they cannot see them, and it takes more time and effort to resolve the issues. The lack of face-to-face interaction can also lead the managers to lose touch with what is going on day by day for each of the employees. It takes a lot of effort to keep the lines of communication open and working.

ABC's partners have found that their employees are a bit too comfortable using virtual tools, to the extent that they forget they can communicate by talking to each other. The reluctance to pick up a phone to talk about something can sometimes lead to frustration, misunderstandings, and delays in getting things done.

ABC has learned that to be successful, a virtual company needs employees who are independent and self-directed. However, employees who possess these qualities often want to go off on their own, do things their own way, and are resistant to taking direction from others. The very things that make them excellent virtual team members can also make them less-than-perfect virtual team members.

When hiring employees you do not know personally, there is a risk that you will never really get to know the person. The person you believe the employee to be is the persona that he or she demonstrates virtually. You can easily be misled. You are trusting your employees with your business, and your livelihood. You do not know what they are doing with your proprietary information; you have to trust that they are protecting it.

Lessons Learned

ABC has had some employee issues. The problems started when they first began hiring people they didn't know. One employee started to behave a bit erratically. He became very moody and started to make a lot of excuses about why he was not getting his work done. One day he disappeared. Nobody could contact him, and nobody knew where he had gone. It turned out that he had been arrested and was in prison on drugs charges. ABC learned from this experience to run credit and background checks on all employees before hiring them. The employee had been arrested before; he had a lot of bad debts and some past employment issues. All of these would have been uncovered by running the necessary background checks. ABC also always checks references for new hires and verifies employment by talking directly to the HR departments of the employers listed on the resume. It is possible for a prospective employee to give false information and a friend's phone number as a reference. Being diligent in checking the information provided can save a lot of problems later on.

ABC has learned that, if at all possible, managers should spend at least a week in the same location as a new hire as early as possible in his or her employment. This is an excellent way to get to know the employee a little better, build some rapport, and establish trust. ABC often combines the week with training or new-hire orientation to make good use of the time.

Honesty is extremely important in any employment situation, but it is hard to evaluate when working virtually. ABC tries to evaluate someone's honesty as early as possible. In addition, it puts some checks and balances in place to monitor and verify such things as working hours and task status. This removes some of the guesswork in trying to figure out if an employee is telling the truth about his or her work time, availability, results, or commitment. Staying in regular contact with employees via phone and Web conference is also key. It is almost impossible to sense if there is a problem when communicating via email or instant messaging. The phone contact takes more time, but it is time well spent.

Outsourcing is another area where ABC has learned a few lessons. Never assume that an outsourcer can work effectively without a lot of input from you. Though one of ABC's outsource vendors works very independently, the other does not. It is important to choose the right outsourcer the first time. Once you have made the commitment, changing vendors can be very painful and expensive. There are a lot of costs associated with changing outsourcers. You have to pay setup fees again, and those are usually not refundable from the company you stopped working with. You might also have to go through a training process, and it will take time for the new vendor to become familiar with your projects. When choosing a vendor, ABC learned that liking the vendor is not enough. You must also consider the long-term direction for your company and ascertain whether the vendor will be able grow and change with you.

One of the hardest things about outsourcing is that you have a lot less control over the process than you would if you were doing the work in-house. Make wise decisions about what part of your business to outsource. If it is something you need to control, do not outsource it.

ABC also learned a valuable lesson about performance management. It started out using an annual review and goal-setting process. As time has gone on, ABC's managers have learned that a year is too long in a virtual environment, although it might work for traditional companies. Just over a year ago, ABC moved to a quarterly review cycle, which is working much better. There is no danger that the employees will "forget" their goals and objectives when they know they have to report on them every three months. ABC has also started to solicit verbal peer input from every employee, in addition to the self-review process. This process change helps the partners understand how well the employees know and interact with each other. It also helps to identify any issues or conflicts between employees.

Most importantly, ABC's managers and employees have learned that, despite the challenges, a virtual organization is a great place to work!

Index

A

abilities of individual team members, 87
accidents, catastrophic events management and, 317
active listening skills, 33–34, 56
adaptation stage of cultural adjustment, 135
administrative skillset
    for remote worker, 51, 376
    for virtual manager, 45–46, 368
agenda for meeting, **264**, 267
airline lounges as work locations, 71–72
airplanes as work locations, 70
airports (and other transit stations) as work
    location, 71–73
Amiable members, 89, 90, 91
Analytical members, 89, 90–91
auditory learners, 93–94
availability of virtual manager, 52–53

B

bad news, delivering correctly, 270–272
best practices sharing, 200–206
BlackBerry, 344
blame assignment, politics and, 278–279
brainstorming for best practices, 202–206, **204**,
    206, **390**
brainstorming spreadsheet, **204**, **206**, **390**
business centers as work locations, 71
business continuity plans, 313–314, **314**
business cycle, economics, team processes and
    procedures and, 225
business operating values and, 352–353, **353**

C

career development. *See* coaching, career
    development skills
cars as work location, 72–73
case study in virtual management, 399–408
catastrophic events management, 309–336. *See*
    also politics; risk management
    aftermath of, management of, 334–335
    business continuity plans in, 313–314, **314**
    categories of risk in, 310–311, **310**
    change-control process and, 227
    communications vital in, 324–334
    conference calls in, 332–333
    controlling emotions in, 321–322
    damage control in, 323–324
    delivering bad news and, 270–272
    disaster recovery plans in, 315
    email in, 330–331
    escalation procedures in, 237–240
    freak accidents as, 317
    instant messaging in, 330
    internal vs. external events in, 313–314
    key persons and, 317
    lessons-learned meeting and, 335–336
    natural disasters as, 316
    nipping trouble in the bud to prevent, 286–288
    online chat in, 330
    onsite meetings and, 333–334
    pagers in, 328–329
    personnel issues as, 317
    phone calls in, 327–328

catastrophic events management, *continued*
  planning for, 311–313, 313–316
  project or product issues as, 316–317
  public transport failures as, 317
  reacting to, 320–322
  recognizing high-risk and, 310–311, 316–318
  red, yellow, green level evaluation of, 322–323
  risk management and, 318–320
  scope management and, 318–320
  status report for, 331, **331**, **397**
  text messaging in, 329
  war or terrorism as, 318
celebrations and rewards, 208–209
cell phones. *See also* communications; telephone
  catastrophic events management and, 327–328
  community center access to, 66–67
  cyber café and coffee houses and, 67
  driving while using, 72–73
  effective uses of, 262–263
  hotel rooms and, 67–68
  library access to, 65–66
challenges of outsourcing, 151–153
challenges of virtual management, 21–23, 406–407
change log, 229–230, **229**
change management, 300–304, **301**
change request, 228–230, **228**
change-control process, 218–230
  business cycle, economics and, 225
  catastrophic failures or events and, 227. *See also* catastrophic events management
  categories of change and, 219
  change logs used in, 229–230, **229**
  change requests used in, 228–230, **228**
  impact of change and, 218–219
  maintenance and, 226–227
  new projects and, 226
  organizational upheavals and, 224–225
  proactive vs. reactive response to change via, 219
  resource allocations and, 220–221
  scheduling and, 221–222
  scope and, 225–226
  technical issues, technical support and, 222–224
chat rooms, catastrophic events management and, 330
citizenship requirements for contracts, 166–167
client and vendor processes, 233
  status report from project manager to client in, 236
client onsite work locations, 68–69

coaching, personal/career development skills, 34–35, 55, 56, 100–102, 104–105
coffee houses as work locations, 67
collaborative tools, 339–343
common interests, 190–191
communication, 13–14, **14**, 22–23, 29–30, 36–38, 212–218, 247–272, 401–403
  active listening skills and, 33–34, 56
  auditory learners and, 93–94
  bad news in, correct techniques for, 270–272
  case study in, 401–403
  catastrophic events management and, 324–334
  cell phones in, 262–263
  choosing appropriate tools for, 337–338
  clarity and completeness of, 40–43, **42**, **43**
  clarity of speech in, when dealing with non-native speakers, 125–127
  collaborative tools for, 339–343
  complexities of, 249–252
  conference call meetings and, 13
  cultural differences and, 113, 116, 130–133, 136–138, 153–154
  document-management systems and, 342–343
  documentation and note taking in, 38, 243–244, **244**
  email in, 253–257
  English as second language (ESL) speakers and, 122–124
  face-to-face, 263–265
  formal plan for, 214–215, **214**
  gestures and body language in, 128–129, 248, 250–252
  global team management and, 113
  in-person, 198
  informal plan for, 216–217, **217**
  instant messaging and, 14, 345–346
  integrated virtual management tools for, 340–341
  language barriers and, 38, 113, 122–124, 153–154
  learning styles of members and, 92–94
  listening skills for, when dealing with non-native speakers, 127–128
  meetings and, 401–402
  nonverbal, 36–37, 248
  notification list, for escalation procedures, 239–240
  online meeting tools for, 341–342
  online scheduling and time tracking tools for, 343
  PDAs for, 337–338, 344–345
  phone conferencing in, 347

physical or kinesthetic learners and, 94
preferences for, of individual team members, 95
presentations as, 269–270
process documentation for, 212–218
project meetings as, 265–266
question asking style in, when dealing with non-native speakers, 129–130
remote worker and, skills at, 48–49
reports as, 269–270
rules for, 24, 217–218
selecting best method for, 252–253, **253**
SharePoint tool in, 340–341
smartphones for, 344
stakeholder groups in, 213–214, **213**
status reporting process and, 233–237, 268
team meetings as, 266–268
telephone in, 257–262
text messaging in, 345–346
time management and, 172
time zone differences and, 119–122
tone of voice in, 249–252
tools for, 337–347, 401
translation and translators for, 124–125
video conferencing and, 346
virtual manager and, 22–23, 29–30, 36–38, 362–363
virtual teamwork and, 197–198
virtual types of, history and development of, 247–248
visual learners and, 93
written, 403
communication plans, 214–215, **214**, 216–217, **217**, 391
community building, 193–195
community centers as work locations, 66–67
company culture, politics and, 273–275. *See also* cultural differences
comparing team members, problems with, 281–282
complaints, politics and, 278–279
computers and equipment. *See also* technical skillset
remote worker and, 49
technical issues, technical support and, 222–224
virtual manager and, 38–39
conference call meeting, 13, 27, 257. *See also* meetings; telephone
catastrophic events management and, 332–333
language barriers and, 126–127

phone conferencing in, 347
time zone differences and, 119–122, 153
video conferencing and, 346
conflict management, 289–308. *See also* team building; virtual teamwork
asking for help with, 307–308
catalysts of, 289–291, **290**
change management and, 300–304, **301**
controlling emotions in, 295–296
encouraging cooperation in, 294–295
knowing when and how to act in, 292–296
limitations to, 307–308
outsourcing and, 167–168
phone conference mediation in, 296–287
proactive management of situations in, 297–300, **297**
quick action in, 290–296
recognizing potential situations for, 291–292, **291**
removing a team member from the team in, 304–307
reprimanding others in, 293–294
conflict stage of cultural adjustment, 134
contingency plans, 242–243
corporate office as work location, 73
costs of outsourcing, 140, 142
creating the virtual team. *See* team building
crisis management. *See* catastrophic events management
cultural adjustment, stages of, 133–135
adaptation stage of, 135
conflict stage of, 134
honeymoon stage in, 133
integration stage of, 134–135
cultural differences, 113, 116, 130–133, 136–138, 153–154
culture, company, 273–275
cyber café and coffee houses as work locations, 67

D

damage control, 323–324
daylight savings time. *See* time zone differences
decision making skills
for remote worker, 50, 374
for virtual manager, 40–43, 365
defect-tracking process (technical projects), 230–231
derogatory remarks, 282–283
disaster recovery plans, 315

dispute resolution. *See* conflict resolution
document-management systems, 342–343
documentation and note taking, 38
    document-management systems and, 342–343
    documentation plan, for **244**, **395**
    documentation process, 243–244, **244**
    forms for, 379–397, **380**
domestic inshoring. *See* farmsourcing/farmshoring
Driver members, 89, 90, 91
driving and cell phone use, 72–73
dynamics of the team, 85–86, 193. *See also* virtual
    teamwork
    change management and, 300–304, **301**

E

E-room, 342–343
economic factors
    change-control process and, 225
    outsourcing and, 146–147
email, 24. *See also* communication
    catastrophic events management and, 330–331
    effective uses of, 253–257
emotional control, 353–355
    catastrophic events management and, 321–322
    conflict management and, 295–296
employee benefits
    case study in, 405–406
    globalization and, 118–119
English as second language (ESL) speakers,
    122–124
enthusiasm, 56–57
escalation notification form, 239, **239**
escalation path, 237–238, **238**
escalation procedures, 237–240, **394**. *See also*
    catastrophic events management
    categorizing events for, 239
    escalation notification form for, 239, **239**
    escalation path defined for, 237–238, **238**
    notification list for, 239–240
    prioritizing events for, 237–238
ethics. *See* business operating values
events
    celebrations and rewards as, 208–209
    humor and, 207–208
    virtual team days and, 199–200
Expressive members, 89, 90, 91–92
extendability of processes, outsourcing and, 142

F

face-to-face communication, 263–265. *See also*
    one-on-one meetings
farmsourcing/farmshoring, 140, 149–151, 405. *See*
    also outsourcing
feedback, 103
firing practices, 304–307
flexibility and outsourcing, 142
forced-pair comparison in prioritizing tasks,
    185–188, **185**, **187**, **389**

G

general management skills
    for remote worker, 46–47, 370
    for virtual manager, 28–30, 360
gestures and body language, 128–129, 248,
    250–252. *See also* cultural differences
Global Crossing, 341
global team management, 113–138. *See also*
    cultural differences; globalization; language
    barriers; outsourcing; virtual teamwork
    communication issues and, 113
    cultural adjustment, stages of, 133–135
    cultural differences and, 113, 116, 130–133,
        136–138, 153–154
    English as second language (ESL) speakers and,
        122–124
    globalization and, 114–130
    language barriers and, 113, 122–124, 153–154
    paid days off, holiday leave, and, 118, 137–138
    team building and, 135–138
    time zone differences and, 119–122
    training programs and, 116
globalization, 2–3, 114–130. *See also* outsourcing
    cost savings of, 115, 116–117
    cultural differences and, 116, 130–133,
        136–138, 153
    decision to go global in, 114–115
    employee benefits and, 118–119
    English as second language (ESL) speakers and,
        122–124
    indirect costs of, 115
    language barriers and, 122–124, 153–154
    legal issues of, 117–118, 168
    paid days off, holiday leave, and, 118, 137–138
    preparing for, 115–119
    satellite offices for, 116
    time zone differences and, 119–122

training programs and, 116
virtual management and, 2–3
goal and objectives setting, 54–55, 98–99
Groove, 343

H

hiring plan, team building and, 74
holidays, 118, 137–138
home office, 64–65
  technical issues, technical support and, 38–39, 49, 222–224
honesty, virtual manager and, 55–56
honeymoon stage of cultural adjustment, 133
hotel rooms as work location, 67–68
hoteling offices, 69–70
humor, virtual teamwork and, 207–208
hybrid virtual managers, 20–21, 25–27, **26**

I

If (Rudyard Kipling poem), 354
in-person communication, 198
inshoring. *See* farmsourcing/farmshoring
inspection, outsourcing and, 168
inspiring others through good leadership, 357
instant messaging, 14, 345–346
  catastrophic events management and, 330
integration stage of cultural adjustment, 134–135
integrity, 351–353
intellectual property rights, outsourcing and, 168
interaction styles, 89–95
  Amiable members in, 89, 90, 91
  Analytical members in, 89, 90–91
  Driver members in, 89, 90, 91
  Expressive members in, 89, 90, 91–92
Internet access. *See also* wireless (WiFi) access
  airline lounges and, 71–72
  airports (and other transit stations) and, 71–73
  buses, trains, airplanes and, 70
  business centers and, 71
  client onsite work locations and, 68–69
  community centers and, 66–67
  cyber café and coffee houses and, 67
  hotel rooms and, 67–68
  kiosks for, 71
  libraries and, 65–66
  shared or hoteling offices and, 69–70
Internet kiosks, 71
interview evaluation form, 80–84, **85, 385**

interviewing team candidates, and interview evaluation form, 80–84, **85**

J

job descriptions, 75, 78, **79, 384**

K

key persons, loss of, catastrophic events management and, 317
kinesthetic learners, 94
kiosks, Internet, 71
Kipling, Rudyard, 354

L

language barriers, 38, 113, 122–124. *See also* communication; gestures and body language
layoffs, 304–307
leadership skills, 29, 95, 349–358
  business operating values and, 352–353, **353**
  controlling emotions and, 353–355
  inspiring others through, 357
  prejudice and stereotypes vs., 356–358
  professional integrity and, 351–353
  professionalism as highest quality of, 355–356
  qualities of a leader and, 349–350
  situational, 95
  virtual team and, special challenges of, 350–351
learning styles of virtual team members, 92–94
  auditory, 93–94
  physical or kinesthetic, 94
  virtual training sessions and, 105–108
  visual, 93
legal issues, 117–118, 168
  globalization and, 117–118, 168
  outsourcing and, 168
lessons-learned meeting, 335–336
libraries as work locations, 65–66
Live Meeting, Microsoft, 342
local office as work location, 73

M

maintenance, change-control process and, 226–227
manager. *See* virtual manager
managing the virtual team. *See* team building; virtual management
meetings, 52–53, 265–268, 401–402. *See also* conference call meetings

meetings, *continued*
   agendas for, 263–264, **264**, 267
   bad news delivered in, 270–272
   catastrophic events management and, 333–334
   effective use of, 265–268
   face-to-face, 263–265, 402–403
   lessons-learned, 335–336
   online meeting tools for, 341–342
   prioritizing, 176–177
   project type, effective use of, 265–266
   team type, effective use of, 266–268
   time management and, 181–182
Microsoft Live Meeting, 342
Microsoft Project Saver, 343

N

natural disasters, catastrophic events management
   and, 316
Netmeeting, 341
nipping trouble in the bud, 286–288
nonverbal communication, 36–37, 248
notification list, escalation procedures and, 239–240

O

offshoring, 145–149, 404–405. *See also*
   farmshoring; globalization; outsourcing
   costs of, 147
   economic factors in, 146–147
   full offshore outsourcings option in, 146–148
   offshore office option in, 148–149
   progress and performance tracking in, 146
   quality control and, 148
   staff assignment responsibilities and, 147–148
   training programs and, 147
one-on-one meetings, 15–103, 270–272. *See also*
   meetings
online chat, in catastrophic events management, 330
online meeting tools, 341–342
online scheduling and time tracking tools, 343
onsite meetings, catastrophic events management
   and, 333–334
organizational processes, 232–233
organizational upheavals
   change management and, 309–304, **301**
   change-control process and, 224–225
outsourced teams, 10–11, **10**
outsourcing, 1–2, 139–168
   case study in, 404–405

challenges of, 151–153
change management and, 303–304
citizenship requirements and, 166–167
cost savings of, 140, 145
costs of, 140–141, 142, 147
cultural differences and, 153–154
decision to, vital considerations in, 140–145
dispute resolution and, 167–168
economic factors in, 146–147
existing employees and, impact on, 151–152
expanding business and, 144
extendability of processes in, 142
failure of, reasons for, 152
farmsourcing/farmshoring as, 140, 149–151
flexibility and, 142
history of, 139
independence of outsourcer in, 141–142
inshoring. *See* farmsourcing/farmshoring
inspection and acceptance issues in, 168
intellectual property rights and, 168
language barriers and, 153–154
legal issues and, 168
local or regional (within U.S.), 139–140, 149–151.
   See also farmsourcing/farmshoring
management for, 141, 153–157
offshoring as, 145–149
ongoing business functions for, 156–157
product development and, 154–157
progress and performance tracking in, 146
project-specific, 154–156
pros and cons of, 144–145
quality control and, 141, 148
risk assessment for, 141
scalability of processes in, 142
scheduling (timeliness) and, 141
security clearance requirements in, 167, 168
service sector and, 144, 155–156, 157
setup time, effort, costs in, 142–143
sharing knowledge with outsources in, 143
specification and process control in, 142
staff assignment responsibilities and, 147–148
Statement of Work for, 158–168, **159**. *See also*
   Statement of Work
time zone differences and, 143, 153
training programs and, 147
vendor relationships in, 157–158
virtual management and, 1–2, 10–11, **10**

P

pagers, catastrophic events management and, 328–329

paid holidays, globalization and, 118, 137–138

Palm Treo, 345

Payment Not to Exceed clause, in Statement of Work (outsourcing contract), 163

Payment Terms clause, in Statement of Work (outsourcing contract), 163

PDAs, 337–338, 344–345. *See also* communication; instant messaging; text messaging

people management skills
    change management and, 300–304, **301**
    for remote worker, 47–48, 371
    for virtual manager, 32–35, 361–362

personal qualities required by remote worker, 377

personal qualities required by virtual manager, 369

personal time management, 173–181

personal/career development skills, 34–35, 100–102, 104–105

personalities within the team, 86–87

personnel issues, in catastrophic events management, 317

personnel management. *See* team building

phone. *See* telephone

physical or kinesthetic learners, 94

politics in the virtual office, 273–288
    company culture and, 273–275
    comparing team members and, 281–282
    complaints and blame in, 278–279
    creation of, within a team, 275–283
    derogatory remarks and, 282–283
    identifying potential troublemakers and, 284–286, **285**
    manager's behavior as tone-setter for, 276–283
    maximizing vs. minimizing behaviors in, 274, **274**
    nipping trouble in the bud to prevent, 286–288
    reprimands and, 279–280
    rewards and congratulations in, 280–281
    rules of behavior vs. 277–278, **278**
    superiority assumptions and, 283–284
    superstar behaviors and, 279

prejudice and stereotypes, 356–358

presentations, 269–270

prioritizing meetings, 176–177

prioritizing tasks, 173, 176–178, **178**, 185–188

problem solving skills
    for remote workers, 50, 374
    for virtual manager, 43–44, 57, 366

process control, outsourcing and, 142

process management, 245–246

processes and procedures. *See* team processes and procedures

product development and outsourcing and, 154–157

professional integrity, 351–353

professionalism, 355–356

progress and performance tracking, 23–25, 30–31, 99–100, 404
    feedback and, 103
    outsourcing and, 146
    reprimands and, 279–280
    rewards and congratulations in, 280–281
    status reporting process and, 233–237, **235**

project or product issues
    catastrophic events management and, 316–317
    change-control process and, 226
    outsourcing and, 154–156

Project Saver, Microsoft, 343

project teams, virtual, 25

public transport failures, catastrophic events management and, 317

Q

quality control
    defect-tracking process (technical projects) in, 230–231
    outsourcing and, 141, 148
    team processes and procedures and for, 230–231

question asking style, when dealing with non-native speakers, 129–130

Quickarrow, 343

R

Ready Access, 341

recruiting team members, 403–404

red, yellow, green level evaluation of catastrophe, 322–323

remote workers, 46–51
    administrative skills for, 51, 376
    communication and, 48–49, 371–372
    decision making skills for, 50, 374
    general management skills for, 46–47, 370
    knowing your team members as, 57–58

remote workers, *continued*
  meetings with, 52–53
  one-on-one meetings with, 103
  people skills for, 47–48, 371
  personal qualities required of, 377
  problem solving skills for, 50, 374
  reallocation of, 220–221
  removing, 304–307
  skillsets required by, 46–51, 370–377
  team orientation/team playing in, 50, 375
  technical knowledge skills and, 49, 372–373
  time management and, 170–183
removing a team member from the team, 304–307
reporting, 269–270, 379–397, **380**. *See also* status
  reporting process
reprimands, 279–280, 293–294
resource allocation, in change-control process,
  220–221
rewards and congratulations, 280–281
risk action/contingency plans, 242–243
risk log, 243, **243**, **393**
risk management, 240–243, 318–320. *See also*
  catastrophic events management
  categories of risk in, 310–311, **310**
  evaluating risk for, 242
  identifying risk for, 241–243
  outsourcing and, 141
  planning for high-risk events in, 311–313
  prioritizing risk for, 242
  risk action/contingency plans for, 242–243
  risk log for, 243, **243**
  scope management and, 318–320
roles and responsibility, 53–54, 88–89, **88**, **396**

S
satellite team members, 8–9, 116
scalability of processes, outsourcing and, 142
scheduling
  change-control process and, 221–222
  online scheduling and time tracking tools for, 343
  outsourcing and, 141
  time management and, 178–179
scope management, 318–320
  change-control process and, 225–226
security clearance requirements, outsourcing, 167,
  168
service sector outsourcing, 144, 155–157
setup time, effort, costs, outsourcing and, 142–143
shared or hoteling offices, 69–70

SharePoint tool, 340–341
short messaging service (SMS). *See* text messaging
Sidekick, T-Mobile, 345
situational leadership, 95
skillsets for remote workers/managers, 28–46, 75,
  77, 359–377
smartphones, 344
SMS. *See* text messaging
specification and process control, outsourcing and,
  142
split virtual teams, 7–8, **8**, 96–97
spontaneity and the virtual manager, 27
staff assignment responsibilities, outsourcing and,
  147–148
staffing plan, 75, **76**, **381–383**
staffing profiles, 75, **77**
stakeholder groups, communication and, 213–214,
  213
standards setting, 15, 52–54
Statement of Work (outsourcing contract),
  158–168, **159**, **387**
  Assumptions and Constraints section in, 165
  change process provisions in, 167
  client responsibilities in, 164
  completion criteria listed in, 162
  conflict of interest and, 164
  delay management details in, 168
  dispute resolution provisions in, 167–168
  fees and payments listed in, 162–163
  fixed costs in, 162
  General Provisions section in, 167–168
  inspection and acceptance issues in, 168
  intellectual property rights and, 168
  introduction for, 160
  key contacts section in, 165
  legal compliance clause in, 168
  objectives section for, 160
  Payment Not to Exceed clause in, 163
  Payment Terms clause in, 163
  period of contract for, 161
  physical location outlined in, 166
  project scope for, 160–161
  renewal term details in, 167
  reporting requirements section in, 165
  Roles and responsibilities documented in, 164
  schedule of deliverables in, 161–162
  security clearance requirements in, 167
  security issues and, 168
  specific tasks listed in, 161

staffing section in, 166
time and materials costs in, 162–163
vendor company responsibilities in, 164
worker citizenship requirements and, 166–167
status reports and reporting process, 24–25,
233–237, **235**, 268, **392**
catastrophic events management and, 331, **331**
monthly status report to senior executives in, 236
status report from manager to team members in,
234–235
status report from project manager to client in, 236
status report from team members to manager in,
234
superiority assumptions, office politics and, 283–284
superstar behaviors, office politics and, 279

T

T-Mobile Sidekick, 345
task management
estimating time for, 180
forced-pair comparison in prioritizing tasks in,
185–188, **185**, **187**, **389**
prioritizing or ranking tasks in, 173, 176–178,
178, 185–188
progress and status reporting in, 181
scheduling tasks in, 178–179
to-do lists for, 175–176, **175**
tracking and completing tasks in, 180–181
updating and reprioritizing in, 179–180
task management list, **388**
team building, 61–111. *See also* global team
management; politics in the virtual office
abilities of individual members in, 87
Amiable members in, 89, 90, 91
Analytical members in, 89, 90–91
auditory learners and, 93–94
case study in, 403–404
choosing members in, 73–89
communication preferences of team members
and, 95
Driver members in, 89, 90, 91
Expressive members in, 89, 90, 91–92
feedback and, 103
global team management and, 135–138
goal and objective setting in, 98–99
hiring plan for, 74
interaction styles of members and, 89–95
internal vs. external hires in, 78–80

interviewing candidates for, and interview
evaluation form, 80–84, **85**
job descriptions and, 75, 78, **79**
learning styles of members and, 92–94
one-on-one meetings with members and, 103
personalities in, 86–87
prejudice and stereotypes vs., 356–358
recruitment for, 403–404
remote worker and, 375
roles and responsibility setting for, 53–54,
88–89, **88**
skillset requirements for, 61–62, 74–75, **77**
split local/remote teams and, 96–97
staffing plan in, 75, **76**
staffing profiles in, 75, **77**
team dynamics and, 85–86, 193. *See also*
change management
time management and, 172–173
troublemakers and, 284–286, **285**
virtual manager and, 44–45, 53, 367
virtual training sessions and, 105–108
visual learners and, 93
work locations and, 62–73
team dynamics, 85–86, 193
change management and, 300–304, **301**
team events, 14–15
team member interactions, virtual teamwork and,
195–206
team orientation/team playing, remote worker and,
50
team processes and procedures, 211–246
change-control process in, 218–230
client and vendor processes, 233
communication process as, 212–218
defect-tracking process (technical projects) in,
230–231
documentation process in, 243–244, **244**
educating team members about, 245–246
escalation procedures in, 237–240
importance of documenting, 211–212
organizational processes in, 232–233
process management and, 245–246
risk management process in, 240–243
status reporting process and, 233–237
teamwork. *See* virtual teamwork
technical issues, technical support, 222–224
for remote worker, 49, 372–373
for virtual manager, 38–39, 364–365

telephone. *See also* cell phones; communication; conference call meetings
  catastrophic events management and, 327–328
  conflict management and, mediation and, 296–297
  effective uses of, 257–262
  phone conferencing in, 347
terrorism, catastrophic events management and, 318
text messaging, 345–346
  catastrophic events management and, 329
time management, 169–188
  collaborative tasks and, 171
  communication and, 172
  estimating time requirements for, 180
  importance of, 169–170
  meetings and, 181–182
  meetings and, prioritizing, 176–177
  online scheduling and time tracking tools for, 343
  personal, 173–181
  speeding up time-consuming tasks in, 183–184
  task management in, 174
    estimating time for, 180
    forced-pair comparison in prioritizing tasks in, 185–188, **185**, **187**
    prioritizing or ranking tasks in, 173, 176–178, **178**, 185–188
    progress and status reporting in, 181
    scheduling, 178–179
    to-do lists for, 174–176, **175**
    tracking and completing tasks in, 180–181
    updating and reprioritizing in, 179–180
  teams and, 172–173
  tools for, 183
  virtual (remote) workers and, 170–183
  virtual manager and, 31–32, 33, 170–183
time zone differences
  global team management and, 119–122
  outsourcing and, 143, 153
time-zone spreadsheet, **120**, **386**
to-do lists, in time management, 175–176, **175**
tone of voice, communication and, 249–252
traditional organization structure, 3–5, **5**
traditional vs. virtual management, 3–11
  satellite team members and, 8–9, 116
  some remote team members in, 6–7
  split teams in, 7–8, **8**, 96–97
  traditional manager and, 18–20, **19**
  traditional organization structure and, 3–5, **5**

virtual organization structure and, 6
training. *See* virtual training sessions
trains as work locations, 70
translation and translators, 124–125
Treo, Palm, 345
troublemakers, identifying, 284–286, **285**
trust, virtual teamwork and, 191–192

V

vendor relationships, outsourcing and, 157–158
video conferencing, 346. *See also* conference call meetings
virtual management, xxi–xxii, 1–16. *See also* global team management; virtual manager
  challenges of, 21–23, 406–407
  communication and, 13–14, **14**
  conference call meetings and, 13
  document-management systems and, 342–343
  global teams, 2–3. *See also* global team management
  instant messaging and, 14
  mixed teams in, 6–7
  need for, xxi–xxii, 1–3
  one-on-one meetings with members and, 15, 103
  online meeting tools for, 341–342
  outsourced teams and, 1–2, 10–11, **10**, 153–157. *See also* global team management
  pure virtual teams in, 10
  reasons for, 1–3
  satellite team members and, 8–9, 116
  SharePoint tool in, 340–341
  split local/remote teams in, 7–8, **8**, 96–97
  standards setting for, 15, 52–54
  team events and, 14–15
  team interaction and, 11–16
  tools for, 340–341, 401
  traditional management vs., 3–11
virtual manager, 17–59, **21**. *See also* team building; virtual management
  active listening skills and, 33–34, 56
  administrative skills of, 45–46, 368
  availability of, 52–53
  challenges facing, 21–23, 406–407
  coaching, personal/career development skills and, 34–35, 55, 56, 100–102, 104–105
  communication and, 22–23, 29–30, 36–38, 362–363
  decision making skills for, 40–43, 365
  employee needs and, 51–59

enthusiasm in, 56–57
general management skills for, 28–30, 360
goal and objectives setting by, 54–55, 98–99
honesty and, 55–56
hybrid, 20–21, 25–27, **26**
knowing your team members as, 57–58
leadership and, 29, 349–358
meetings with virtual members and, 52–53
people management skills and, 32–35, 361–362
personal qualities required by, 369
problem solving skills of, 43–44, 57, 366
progress and performance tracking by, 23–25,
    30–31, 99–100
project teams and, 25
roles and responsibility setting by, 53–54,
    88–89, **88**
skillsets required by, 28–46
spontaneity and, 27
status reporting and, 24–25
team building skills of, 44–45, 53, 367
technical knowledge skills for, 38–39, 364–365
time management and, 31–32, 33
traditional management vs., 18–20, **19**
virtual managers
    cultural differences and, 153–154, 153
    global teams and. *See* global team management,
        113
    language barriers and, 153–154, 153
    leadership and, 95
    outsourcing and, 153–157, 153
    prejudice and stereotypes vs., 356–358, 356
    professionalism as highest quality of, 355–356,
        355
    situational leadership and, 95
    skillsets for, 359–377, 359
    time management and, 170–183, 170
    time zone differences and, 153
virtual organizations, 6
virtual politics. *See* politics, 273
virtual private networks (VPNs), 9
virtual teams, 6–8. *See also* global team
    management; virtual management
    abilities of individual members in, 87
    best practices sharing and, 200–206
    brainstorming for best practices and, 202–206,
        204, **206**
    celebrations and rewards for, 208–209
    common interests in, 190–191
    communication and, 197–198

communication preferences of team members
    and, 95
community building for, 193–195
dynamics of, 85–86, 193. *See also* change
    management
humor and, 207–208
in-person communication and, 198
interaction among members of, 11–16, 89–95
knowing your team members as, 57–58
learning styles of members and, 92–94
outsourced teams and, 10–11, **10**
personality mix in, 86–87
prejudice and stereotypes vs., 356–358
recruiting, 403–404
removing members from, 304–307
roles and responsibility setting for, 53–54,
        88–89, **88**
satellite team members and, 8–9, 116
split local/remote, 7–8, **8**, 96–97
team member interactions and, 195–206
team processes and procedures and, learning
    about, 245–246
troublemakers and, 284–286, **285**
trust and, 191–192
variations on, 6–8
virtual team days for, 199–200
virtual training sessions and, 105–108
work locations for, 62–73
virtual team days, 199–200
virtual teamwork, 180–209, 286. *See also* politics
    in the virtual office; team building
    best practices sharing and, 200–206
    brainstorming for best practices and, 202–206,
        204, **206**
    celebrations and rewards for, 208–209
    characteristics of success in, 189
    commonalities as basis for, 190–191
    communication and, 197–198
    community building for, 193–195
    dynamics of team and, 193
    humor and, 207–208
    in-person communication and, 198
    nipping trouble in the bud to prevent, 286–288
    prejudice and stereotypes vs., 356–358
    remote worker and, 375
    team member interactions and, 195–206
    troublemakers and, 284–286, **285**
    trust and, 191–192
    virtual team days and, 199–200

virtual training sessions, 105–108
   globalization and, 116
   outsourcing and, 147
   prerecorded, 111
   Webinars and, 110
visual learners, 93

W

war, catastrophic events management and, 318
Webex, 341
Webinars, 110
wireless (WiFi) access, 72
   airline lounges and, 71–72
   airports (and other transit stations) and, 71–73
   buses, trains, airplanes and, 70
   business centers and, 71
   community centers and, 66–67
   cyber café and coffee houses and, 67
   hotel rooms and, 67–68
   libraries and, 65–66

shared or hoteling offices and, 69–70
work locations for virtual members, 62–73
   advantages and disadvantages of, 63
   airline lounges as, 71–72
   airports (and other transit stations) as, 71–73
   buses, trains, airplanes as, 70
   business centers as, 71
   cars as, 72–73
   client onsite locations for, 68–69
   community centers as, 66–67
   cyber café and coffee houses as, 67
   general management skills for, 28–30
   home office as, 64–65
   hotel rooms as, 67–68
   libraries as, 65–66
   local or corporate office as, 73
      policies for, 62
      selecting appropriate, 63–64
   shared or hoteling offices as, 69–70
   wireless access for, 72
written communication, 403